D0793267

ALSO BY RICHARD D. SMITH

Bluegrass: An Informal Guide
Images of America: Princeton

CAN'T YOU

THE LIFE OF

HEAR

BILL MONROE,

ME

FATHER OF BLUEGRASS

CALLIN'

RICHARD D. SMITH

LITTLE, BROWN AND COMPANY

BOSTON NEW YORK LONDON

This book is respectfully dedicated to
Rosetta Monroe Kiper,
a grand lady I am proud to call friend.

Copyright © 2000 by Richard D. Smith

First Edition

Library of Congress Cataloging-in-Publication Data
Smith, Richard D.
Can't you hear me callin': the life of Bill Monroe, father of bluegrass /
by Richard D. Smith. — 1st ed.
p.   cm.
Discography: p.
Includes bibliographical references and index.
ISBN 0-316-80381-2 (hc)
1. Monroe, Bill, 1911–   2. Bluegrass musicians — United States — Biography.   I. Title.
ML420.M5595 S65 2000
781.642'092 — dc21
[B]
99-054372

10   9   8   7   6   5   4   3   2   1

Text Designed by Chris Welch

Q-FF

Printed in the United States of America

Talking to him was like talking to poetry. Just a few words or a line, if you listened closely to them, those words could mean so much. Just a simple statement could have such depth. Just like his music.

People ask me what it was like talking with Bill Monroe. It was like speaking to a poem that spoke back. — *Kim Koskela*

Bill Monroe is one of the ultimate "feel" players. If he played it, it's because he felt it. — *Sam Bush*

People say you've never met anyone like Bill Monroe. They're right. — *Mike Seeger*

✭ CONTENTS ✭

★ INTRODUCTION ★

On the night of October 2, 1954, two future legends of American popular music faced each other backstage at the Grand Ole Opry in Nashville, Tennessee. One — a skinny, nervous kid from Memphis named Elvis Presley — was offering apologies to the other — a taciturn and physically powerful Kentuckian named Bill Monroe.

At the time, Presley was an up-and-coming singer making a guest appearance on the popular country music stage show and radio broadcast. But Monroe was a star and one of Presley's idols, a fifteen-year Opry veteran backed by a hot band called the Blue Grass Boys. Elvis might have had gyrating hips, but he had firmly planted feet: one in black rhythm and blues, one in white country (or "hillbilly") music. And Bill Monroe was Elvis Presley's favorite hillbilly singer.

On July 6, while recording their first single for Sun Records, Elvis and his sidemen had transformed Monroe's sentimental waltz "Blue Moon of Kentucky" into a rousing 2/4-time rocker that was a near parody of the original. To Presley's immense relief the composer was gracious about the liberties taken with his song.

"If it helps your career," Monroe said, "I'm for it one hundred percent."

When each man left the Ryman Auditorium that evening, much was ahead of him. Presley would of course be elevated to the status of a nearly mythical cultural icon. But Monroe's life would continue to be extraordinarily eventful and his influence even more multifaceted than Presley's. Indeed, Bill Monroe would become the most broadly talented and broadly influential figure in the history of American popular music.

This assessment is supported by the facts of Monroe's career. Certainly, Elvis Presley, Louis Armstrong, and Hank Williams had greater specific impacts as, respectively, a rock star, a jazz instrumentalist, and a country singer-songwriter. But Monroe's varied influence as a singer, instrumentalist, composer, and bandleader was felt in early commercial country music, rockabilly and later rock, the folk music revival, contemporary country, and, of course, bluegrass. In addition to scores of famed musical disciples, Bill Monroe was admired by artists as prominent (and diverse) as Bob Dylan and Frank Sinatra.

Born in 1911, this youngest child of a large Kentucky farming family grew up in an essentially nineteenth-century world. He was surrounded by ancient folkways that had survived among settlers of the southern hills. He benefited in childhood from the economic exploitation of resource-rich Kentucky, and the interplays of white and black cultures. Then he was thrust into the twentieth century as part of the great southern exodus to northern industry, coming to know the role of country music as a cultural anchor for rural people transported to the cities.

By the time he met Presley, he had been a member of one of the most successful country duet acts of all time, the Monroe Brothers. He had formed his own band (named in honor of his home state) and won a spot on the Opry. He was present when the radio and record businesses parented the mass media age and country music evolved from grassroots novelty into multibillion-dollar entertainment industry.

His chief claim to fame has been as the creator of a highly personal and instantly recognizable style of acoustic country music. It flowered from the grafting of multiple musical roots and branches — square dance fiddle tunes and modal ballads rooted in British Isles traditions, African-American blues, southern Protestant church harmonies, Tin Pan Alley pop elements, and the sheer creativity of Monroe and scores of his innovative sidemen.

This music was eventually termed "bluegrass" in honor of Monroe's band the Blue Grass Boys. It featured high lead vocal lines and close harmonies backed by fiddle, mandolin, banjo, guitar, and upright bass played in surging, anticipating rhythms within a jazz-influenced improvisational format. So potent was this combination that bluegrass began to take on an identity beyond that of Bill Monroe's personal band sound. (The term itself has been used erroneously as a generic name for centuries-old mountain music.) Later, Monroe would be rightly lauded as "the Father of Bluegrass" and the only person to create — not just dominate but wholly create — a distinctive musical genre.

"If you really watch it close, look at all of it, it makes a powerful music," he said with pride and honesty. "I have never heard any music I thought would beat it, myself."

Monroe distanced himself from many country artists who had preceded him. He eschewed the old hayseed-with-a-jug image and dressed band members in sober ties and dress shirts, polished boots, and neatly pressed slacks. Bluegrass was traditional-style music made professional.

Through the decades, a stint in the Blue Grass Boys became the equivalent of an advanced degree program (or a boot camp) for aspiring entertainers. (Former sideman Doug Green recalls that all the time he played with Bill, he felt like he was "walking on air — and walking on eggs." Numerous Monroe protégés formed their own groups performing in his style. The most famous were Lester Flatt and Earl Scruggs, respectively the guitarist–lead vocalist and the banjo picker who were core members of the classic Blue Grass Boys lineup of the late 1940s. They left to form the tremendously successful partnership of Flatt and Scruggs & the Foggy Mountain Boys, gaining crossover fame in the 1960s by contributing music to the soundtracks of the *Beverly Hillbillies* television show and the movie *Bonnie and Clyde*. Monroe brooded for years over what he considered creative theft of his sound until hindsight showed that he had been honored by imitation.

Ironically, Elvis Presley caused bluegrass many hungry years when rock took audiences away from acoustic country music. The double irony is that Presley was not the only rockabilly to admire Bill Monroe's singing and the energy and sheer attitude of his music: Buddy Holly, Carl Perkins, and Johnny Cash were all huge Monroe fans, as was rhythm and blues great Chuck Berry. Pop stars Levon Helm of The Band, Chris Hillman of the Byrds, and Jerry Garcia of the Grateful Dead were also directly influenced by Monroe.

Bill Monroe's innovations and influence on country music and rock 'n' roll would be enough to assure him a place in the American music pantheon. But more was to come in the 1960s, thanks to his discovery by the folk revival. A mutual interest in Monroe's music was a prime motivation behind one of the most remarkable examples of cooperative exchange between rural southerners and urban northerners in American history. This productive and even joyful meeting of disparate North/South cultures — right at the height of national divisions over the civil rights movement and the Vietnam war — literally set the stage in the 1970s for the triumph of the bluegrass festival movement, which coalesced around Monroe as its central figure. (There are now some five hundred bluegrass festivals held each year worldwide.)

As country music met the rock 'n' roll challenge by electronically amplifying instruments, even adding string sections on records and generally slicking up its image, bluegrass was widely perceived in the industry as a rough-hewn hick cousin, a quaint diversion but ultimately an unsophisticated embarrassment. But in the 1980s bluegrass was championed by Nashville's New Traditionalists. Ricky Skaggs, Marty Stuart, Keith Whitley, Vince Gill, Emmylou Harris, and other young country stars lauded Monroe as an influence and revered him. In the 1990s, bluegrass found additional favor within the Alternative Country movement and on FM radio within the emerging Americana format of acoustic music, further disseminations of the Monroe influence.

But how much of bluegrass did Monroe really invent? Was he the true father of bluegrass or just one of its many parents? There is intense debate over the relative contributions of Monroe and his sidemen, notably the great Earl Scruggs. The Scruggscentric view is that bluegrass as we know it today is defined by the bright percolating sound of syncopated three-finger banjo picking, and Monroe's music did not have this sound until Scruggs was hired as a Blue Grass Boy. The Monroecentric view is that lonesome themes, bluesy vocal and instrumental ornamentations, and surging, anticipating rhythms are the true hallmarks of bluegrass and were present in Monroe's band sound right from the beginning.

Arguments about the origins of bluegrass are particularly intense because — as "traditional" as bluegrass is in comparison to the rest of American popular music — it has a starting point within living memory (unlike opera or symphonic music), and its origins can arguably be credited to one man (unlike jazz or rock 'n' roll). The who-invented-bluegrass debate bespeaks the vitality of this American art form. Of course, it will be considered in depth here.

Also examined in depth will be one of the most notorious yet least understood episodes in country music history — the Bill Monroe vs. Flatt and Scruggs feud. The long-running antipathy between Monroe and his former employees has become the stuff of Nashville legend. Like most legends, it has a basis in historical fact but has been embellished and distorted. The account given in these pages will not only set the record straight but reveal the very different professional and personal attitudes that led to the estrangement. (The circumstances surrounding the breakup of Bill's influential duet act with his brother Charlie have been similarly distorted over the years by untruths and inaccurate assumptions. The dissolution of the Monroe Brothers will similarly be covered here.)

Sadly, such debates and yarns tend to obscure what is of ultimate importance — the eclectic genius of Bill Monroe.

He was a peerless vocalist whose keening, bluesy high tenor transfixed listeners. He was an electrifying and widely imitated instrumentalist who reinvented the mandolin's role as a solo and rhythm instrument. He was a band leader who possessed an impeccable ear for talent and was a brilliant synthesizer of influences. He was a composer of heart-quickening instrumentals and heart-piercing love songs. (Indeed, some of his greatest "true songs," as he termed them, predate the compositions of Hank Williams Sr., making Bill Monroe the pioneer of autobiographical country music and a progenitor of the modern singer-songwriter movement.)

When Bill Monroe died on September 9, 1996, just four days shy of his eighty-fifth birthday, he received lengthy obituaries in the *New York*

Times, Wall Street Journal, Newsweek, and even *Rolling Stone.* A winner of the National Medal of the Arts and a Grammy for lifetime achievement, and member of both the Country Music Hall of Fame and Rock and Roll Hall of Fame, he is justifiably ranked with Duke Ellington, Louis Armstrong, Charles Ives, and Hank Williams as a true giant of American music.

The prospect for the biographer is therefore daunting: Bill Monroe is a subject who must be chronicled and evaluated not simply as a major figure in country music and the specific genre of bluegrass, but within the contexts of rock 'n' roll, folk, and even contemporary hybrid acoustic musics. But to force Bill Monroe to serve a particular academic argument or to deconstruct his music would do an unacceptable disservice to this great American's life and art. And Monroe's life was so colorful that his story is intrinsically interesting on its own merits.

Making the biographer's task is even more challenging is the fact that Bill Monroe was one of the most contradictory and enigmatic performers who ever lived.

He could be evasive or blunt, dour or witty, tightfisted or generous, dismissive or nurturing, obtuse or perceptive, cruel or kind. Bill Monroe stories abound; some are very amusing, others are heartrending.

It is telling that Monroe did not grant his first in-depth interview until 1962, when he was nearly fifty-one years old and had been a professional musician for more than a quarter of a century. Friends and associates speak of his intimidating persona; how the fire and emotion of his singing and playing contrasted dramatically with his offstage dignity and reserve; his emotional and physical unassailability and way of keeping the world at arm's length; his penchant for holding a grudge. Monroe was also one of those rare individuals who truly changed over a lifetime: There was not one Bill Monroe but several, his personalities distinct in childhood, young manhood, adulthood, and old age. As he strove in his final years to reconnect with his fellow humans, Monroe could be communicative, even merry, and that came as a surprising contrast not typical of the man.

When Monroe acted or spoke, his actions or words were deceptively simple. But on almost every occasion, deep prethought yielded subtle, extraordinarily significant gestures or utterances. In this, his expressions were very much like bluegrass music itself: simple, yet with a cunning sophistication. And in the main, he preferred to let his music represent him. His fierce desire to be the top man in all he undertook — and the lingering effects of an emotionally starved childhood — yielded an art that was as flinty and as tender, as exuberant and as harrowed as his own feelings and experiences.

Monroe's "lonesomeness" was more than simple loneliness or the garden-variety depression common to creative personalities. It constituted a true Weltanschauung based in his sense of separation from the people and things to which, paradoxically, he felt his closest connections. There are profound reasons why the music of Bill Monroe has been called "the high, lonesome sound." Monroe's sense of isolation and his romantic yearning to touch the hearts of others made his art universal, resonating as powerfully with subway straphangers and college students as it had with the farm families and transplanted southerners working in factories who constituted his first audience. From his farmboy youth to his last days as a revered icon, Monroe's lonesomeness was both a creative wellspring and a torment. It remains the key to understanding him.

Much of Monroe's story will be told from the perspective of people who knew him. This is altogether fitting. As noted, Monroe was for decades a distant figure who rarely volunteered statements about his creative process or, for that matter, statements of any kind. In addition, Monroe's story is very much the story of the musicians, friends, and lovers whose lives were changed by his. The immense Monroe persona attracted people like a mammoth star whose gravity holds planets and comets in orbit, and even shapes the fabric of surrounding space and time.

But many of the thoughts and feelings of this enigmatic man can be accurately reported. If there is a tendency by some contemporary biographers to turn their books into sociopolitical tracts, there is a tendency among others to "novelize" their subjects, creating thoughts or dialogue in order to flesh out characters and events. That has not been necessary in the case of Bill Monroe. If a statement or feeling is attributed to Monroe or any other figure in this book, it is because that person once expressed such a sentiment directly or a reliable source has reported it. No dialogues, thoughts, or situations in this book have been invented.

Despite the mixture of shyness and suspicion that caused Monroe to be so private through much of his life, there are rich sources of information about him. Particularly valuable have been the writings of Ralph Rinzler, the folklorist who revived Monroe's career and helped bring the taciturn musician out of his shell. Extraordinary unpublished taped interviews are on deposit at the Smithsonian Institution's Division of Folklife and Cultural Programs, where Rinzler spent the latter part of his career. (This material appears to have been intended for an unrealized Monroe biography.) As Monroe opened up, he became more accessible to newspaper and magazine writers who recorded his pronouncements; many of the resulting articles have been highly useful. Equally valuable is the internal evidence about Monroe's life — especially his childhood experiences and his adult love affairs — found in his autobiographical "true songs."

Band members and other professional associates have been tremendously helpful in chronicling Monroe's life and times. So have relatives and former neighbors in his hometown of Rosine, Kentucky, many of whom have never been previously interviewed. (The reader is urged to peruse the Acknowledgments section for the names and contributions of these wonderful people.) The author has been deeply involved with bluegrass as a sometime-musician since 1963 and a writer since 1971, so he — like so many others — retains keen memories of Bill Monroe. It is not just that Monroe died relatively recently: So awe-inspiring was this man, so carefully did he choose his words, and so directly did he deliver them, that his utterances are retained in memory as vividly as if they had been spoken last week. Prominent banjo player Tony Trischka has a theory that anything Monroe ever said to you, you remember. Tony is quite right.

But the greatest untapped sources of information about Bill Monroe have been the women in his life. Unlike the stereotyped carousing, hotel room–smashing, self-destructive pop star, Monroe did not smoke, drink, or use drugs. But he did love women. Many of them. Conversations with several who knew Monroe intimately and loved him dearly have provided valuable new information or confirmed prior speculations. Divorce filings and other public documents — rich biographical sources surprisingly ignored in histories of bluegrass prior to the writing of this book — have been extremely useful in providing data about places, dates, people, and events.

The examination of Bill Monroe's private life may prove controversial. How could that be? After all, the substance abuse of Elvis Presley and Johnny Cash, the heavy drinking of Hank Williams, George Jones, and even Ernest Tubb, and the criminal records of Lefty Frizzell and Merle Haggard are all well known. If anything, Monroe's womanizing was far less blameworthy than the behavior of many other pillars of country music. Why, then, might it be a touchy subject?

Monroe's love for the ladies is well known within country music circles. But the appellation "Father of Bluegrass" bespeaks not just a siring but a nearly godlike role. It is understandable that some Monroe devotees will wish Bill to be mighty, noble, and perfect, not vulnerable, occasionally petty or selfish, and all too human. The truth is that as a musical deity Monroe was less of a Jehovah and more of a Zeus.

During Monroe's lifetime, writers studiously avoided the subject of his almost compulsive skirt chasing. This was partly due to a bluegrass and country music culture in which journalism is quite genteel and sexual peccadilloes are simply not written about. Most writers wished to retain Monroe's goodwill: They likely had nothing to fear physically from Bill (although he was almost superhumanly strong and no stranger to fighting), but there was high anxiety over his quick displeasure and the cold, silent fury that invariably led to years of ostracism. Monroe's private affairs were considered off-limits when he lived; as a result, the stories behind his most beautiful and passionate love songs were rarely revealed. And the women who were such a part of his life, with whom he shared thoughts and stories that he would not confide to men, were — without exception — never interviewed prior to the undertaking of this project.

Monroe's business affairs, like his love affairs, could be either rewarding or chaotic. An examination of them is vital to providing a true understanding of his life and times, especially his poignant final years. As the reader will discern, this examination has been made with sympathy and an understanding heart. Monroe's romances were not so much conquests as contacts, his way of touching a world that he ever feared would pull away and leave him alone. And his attitudes toward money and investment say much about his heritage, his stubbornness, and the priority he ultimately placed on music and family.

In particular, the research and writing of this biography have provided a sorely needed opportunity to elevate the women in Bill Monroe's life. The cliché about a great woman being behind every great man has multiple truth in Monroe's case. There were several strong and energetic women in his life. It was from his mother's side of the family and not his father's that the Monroe children drew a creative wellspring. Malissa Ann Vandiver Monroe was a singer, dancer, and multi-instrumentalist who passed along her love of music and a lively spirit to her offspring. Bill's first wife, Carolyn Minnie Brown Monroe, was present when his career blossomed and demonstrated a nearly lifelong loyalty to his professional endeavors. And Bessie Lee Mauldin, Bill's longtime companion, was not only the muse who inspired his greatest and most passionate love songs but a vital participant in his life and times. Bessie Lee's significant influence makes especially shameful the neglect she has suffered in previous histories of bluegrass, a situation that will at last be remedied in these pages. Intimate details will be revealed about the lives of these and other women, but in the process the untold stories of their roles in the career of this American musical giant will finally be recorded.

In the end, Bill Monroe probably would have wanted the complete tale to be told. Although he could be fiercely protective of his privacy, he valued honesty above almost anything. When asked about famous sidemen, he typically would not comment at first about their prowess as a singer, fiddler, or banjo picker, but about their veracity. "He was an honest man," or "He never lied to me," Monroe would say before discussing their musicianship.

And when Bill Monroe finally granted his first in-depth interview to folklorist Ralph Rinzler, such was his candor that the considerate Rinzler asked, "Is there anything you've said that you would not want to see in print?"

Monroe replied simply, "It's all true."

The same can be said of this book.

CAN'T YOU HEAR ME CALLIN'

CHAPTER 1

BLUE MOON OF KENTUCKY RISING

(THE BEGINNINGS TO 1929)

> The soul is a newly skinned hide, bloody and gross.
> Work on it with manual discipline,
> and the bitter tanning acid of grief,
> and you'll become lovely, and *very* strong.
>   — *Jelaluddin Rumi*

A wagon road led south from the railroad depot in Rosine, Kentucky. It ran through a hollow, then turned west through the woods of Ohio County. It climbed and topped an elongated geological feature known locally as Jerusalem Ridge, proceeding parallel to the railway tracks below. Then it descended by curves into the little community of Horton and continued on to the larger town of Beaver Dam.

The road bore traffic and commerce. Along it were carried corn and tobacco from the region's gently sloping fields, coal from its rolling hills, and — in particular — hardwood timber from its old-growth forests. And this road carried pain to a little boy living on a large farm on the ridge, midway between Rosine and Horton.

The child, the youngest of the eight children of James Buchanan Monroe and Malissa Vandiver Monroe, was born with a left eye that turned inward. The medical term for the condition is esotropia.[1] In this time and place, the brutal slang expression was "hug-eyed."

His overall vision was very poor. In compensation, his auditory sense developed keenly. He learned to recognize from miles away the hoof-beats of horses and mules and the roll of wooden wheels.[2] Experience taught that passersby were coming who would laugh and joke about this cross-eyed boy if they saw him. So he would run and hide in the barn until they passed.[3]

As the youngest of a large family, he was often left alone by his busy parents and impatient siblings. He grew thoughtful, his feelings sensitive, his emotions powerful but unexpressed, yearning for human contact but too proud to admit pain.

He once looked back on his childhood and said:

For many years, I had nobody to play with or nobody to work under. You just had to kindly grow up. Just like a little dog outside, tryin' to make his own way, trying to make out the best way he can.[4]

Thus began the life of William Smith Monroe.

By the time Bill Monroe had become a living legend and his style of American country-folk music was termed "bluegrass," in honor of his band the Blue Grass Boys, all this was known. And other stories became well established.

Bill, it was said, was a direct descendant of President James Monroe; he grew up in the mountains; he rose from hardscrabble poverty in a back-ward, backwoods culture; bluegrass music sprang from ancient Scots-Irish culture transplanted to the Appalachians, where it blossomed as a traditional folk art.

Compelling as these other tales were, none were true. Bill Monroe was a plainspoken and typically honest man. These misconceptions did not arise from him, yet he did little to correct them. As it turns out, the truth is even more compelling than the myths now interwoven through the history of this larger-than-life character.

*   *   *

Some sources on Scottish clan names state that "Monroe" means "Man of Roe," a river in Northern Ireland near which many Scots settled; hence the claims of Scots-Irish ancestry for Bill. But Clan Monroe has its roots firmly in the Scottish Highlands, specifically in Easter Ross, north of Moray Firth and the Great Glen.[5] The name, first recorded around the twelfth century, may be from the Norman-influenced "Mon Rosse" ("hillmen of Ross"). It is almost always spelled "Munro" in Scotland, and it was pronounced exactly that way by Bill's family, right into the twentieth century — MUN-ro, with emphasis on the first syllable.

The Monroes had a warrior heritage. President Monroe's first ancestor in America is believed to have been a Royalist Highlander who fought Cromwell's Puritans in 1648; Sir Robert Munro was the first colonel of the famed Black Watch, leading them in 1745 against Bonnie Prince Charlie's rebellion. John Monroe, patriarch of the Ohio County Monroes, was a soldier of the Virginia Line during the Revolutionary War and one of many veterans rewarded for his service with land grants in the Commonwealth of Kentucky.

John Monroe was born November 10, 1749, in Westmoreland County, Virginia, where James Monroe also resided. (It is quite possible that they were distant cousins, making Bill Monroe at least a collateral descendant of the fifth American president.) John moved to Kentucky in January 1801, bringing his family with him. By April 1832, he had made a permanent home in Ohio County, where he died in 1837.

His descendants settled down to prosperous lives as landowners. John had three children, including a son, Andrew B. Monroe. The 1850 Ohio County census found Andrew to be a fifty-five-year-old, Virginia-born farmer with property valued at $2,700. Andrew and his wife Alysie had eight children. Their eldest son, John J., had eight children by his first wife, Lydia Charlotte Stevens. John and Lydia's eldest, James Buchanan, born October 28, 1857, was known as "J.B." or "Buck."

No wonder J.B.'s son Bill Monroe would grow up feeling deeply connected to the past, revering things that, as he put it, "go a way on back in time." Bill's father would have remembered the Civil War, and his great-great-grandfather actually fought in the American Revolution.

Ohio County lies in western Kentucky, far from the Appalachian Mountains with which bluegrass music is now associated. It is even quite distinct from the famed "bluegrass" region of central Kentucky, which helped give the music its name. Nevertheless, the Monroes could hardly have found a better place to call home. The region was lovely, fertile and rich in the natural resources needed by a vigorously expanding America. As far back as 1840, the first edition of Lewis Collins's *History of Kentucky* noted that Ohio County produced "excellent crops of corn, tobacco, potatoes, clover and other grasses," adding that "timber is heavy and of a superior quality . . . and the coal is inexhaustible."

And soon a town conceived as a major metropolis was founded just down the wagon road from the Monroe farms.

Shrewdly calculating the region's potential, Henry D. McHenry, a banker, businessman, and Kentucky state legislator, used his influence in 1870 to get the Elizabethtown & Paducah Railroad (later the Illinois Central) to establish an east-west main line through a settlement known as Pigeon Roost. McHenry and some business partners then bought up land in the area and formally incorporated a town there in 1873. McHenry named it "Rosine" after the pen name of his wife, poet Jenny Taylor McHenry.

Rosine was laid out on a grid pattern, with streets sixty feet in width to allow for the heavy commercial traffic the investors expected. Front Street, the town's main commercial district, ran along the north side of the railroad tracks facing the passenger depot and freight yard. From here, the train carried passengers and goods east to Louisville, where connections were made to the rest of America, or west to Beaver Dam. With the railway to bring in people and transport out timber, coal, and crops, McHenry believed, Rosine would be the next Pittsburgh or Chicago.

Although Rosine never became a city, for nearly half a century it was a boom town. There were nine stores along Front Street, plus a barbershop and doctors' offices. There was a flour and gristmill, a creamery, and warehouses for drying tobacco and sumac, a shingle mill and a barrel stave mill. Rosine's downtown even had paved streets, made with local sandstone and maintained by inmates from the jail. It had hotels, bars, and poolrooms. (McHenry knew full well that a wet town in an otherwise dry region would have considerable advantages.) The Earp family of western lore had roots in Ohio County, and just as Wyatt, Virgil, and Morgan worked as both lawmen and purveyors of base pleasures, so did their Rosine cousins: Walter C. Earp was sworn in as a town judge in 1907 and Russell Earp owned a local pool hall.

And like most American communities of the late nineteenth and early twentieth centuries, Rosine loved its baseball. Just west of town was a baseball park, home to the Rosine Red Legs.

In fact, Rosine played a vital role in the national pastime: Until well into the 1970s, the hardwoods used by the Hillerich & Bradsby Company for their world-famous "Louisville Slugger" bats came from here. Many a major league home run has been hit off Rosine wood.

Such was bustling Rosine in the days when the Monroes would come to town on Saturday afternoons to trade or on Sunday mornings to attend the Methodist church (later celebrated by Bill in song as "The Little Community Church"). It was hardly the backwoods community of folk and old-time music mythology.[6]

And the Monroes were anything but backward hillbillies. They were proud, hardworking, honest, and law-abiding. They were a bit aloof, shy actually. (Neighbors recall that they would often stand off by themselves after church.) They were considered quite wealthy by local standards, and they were highly educated for the times.

A profile of J.B.'s brother John H. Monroe in an 1885 history of Kentucky recorded that at age twenty-one, Jack had "traveled for pleasure for one year, visiting many important and interesting points in the South and West. . . . Mr. Monroe has had fair advantages in education, and his mind is well stored with the learning of books, as well as with that of practical life."[7] Where a fifth-grade education was considered quite sufficient, Bill's father J.B. had finished the eighth grade. He read *The Shorthorn in America*,[8] the publication of the American Shorthorn Breeders' Association. He was skilled in basic arithmetic.[9] He recorded every penny of income and expenditure in a series of notebooks and ledgers.

Ambitious young men, J.B. and Jack soon made a career move from the timber and stave-cutting business they had been running: In 1883, with brother Andrew and two backers, they formed the firm of

J. B. Monroe & Co. and opened a general store in Horton, selling clothing, shoes, canned goods, and household items.

The enterprise failed quickly.[10] The Monroes became overextended and were sued by suppliers because of overdue accounts. They tried valiantly to keep up payments but were forced to liquidate their holdings and sell other assets to satisfy their debts. It would not be the last time that a Monroe would venture into a major business commitment and, despite bright expectations, watch it inexorably become a money hole. This sad aspect of family history was destined to repeat itself.

J.B. returned to the soil. At first he was a tenant farmer,[11] but soon he prospered enough to purchase land on a long wooded hill almost halfway between Rosine and Horton. In a time when most hills and hollows were given place names, Buck's farm was situated on Pigeon Ridge.[12] But adjacent to Pigeon Ridge was a larger geological feature, and the Monroes preferred to identify their home with that more nobly named comb — Jerusalem Ridge.

J.B. began assembling property there as early as September 30, 1903, when he purchased 320 acres from brother Jack and his wife, who remained neighboring landholders.[13] Over the next decade, he acquired adjoining land until his central holdings were about 655 acres.[14]

Buck's farm was not especially cash-generating, but it was busy, successful, and above all diversified.[15] Timber, coal, tobacco, corn, and molasses were sold, hay was grown, livestock pastured.

Buck's land contained large coal reserves, and he had a little mine complete with tracks and handcar. His surviving ledgers record brisk sales to companies, individuals, the Rosine school, and the nearby Horse Branch church (rendered as "kirk," the old Scottish term, in J.B.'s account books).

But for Buck Monroe and many other landowners, the important cash crop was timber, much of it valuable old-growth hardwood from their heavily forested lands. J.B. sold trees for "telefon" poles and "tall timber," long, straight wood commanding high prices.[16] He sold tons of cross ties to the railroad. The Kentucky Wagon Manufacturing Company of Louisville was also a customer.

Even if the twentieth century had begun, the Monroes were living in a nineteenth-century world.

*   *   *

J.B. soon took a bride. And it was through her that music came into the Monroe family.

The object of his affections was Malissa A. Vandiver of neighboring Butler County. Born July 12, 1870, she was the youngest of ten children of Joseph M. Vandiver, a farmer born in Tennessee, and his wife, Manerva J. Farris, born in Kentucky.

Malissa's parents had foreign roots, and these roots were close to the surface.[17] Vandivers from the Netherlands had settled in New York, New Jersey, and Delaware in the 1600s, then migrated west. Joseph's nickname, in fact, was "Dutch." Malissa's maternal grandmother was of recent Irish descent and spoke in a brogue.

Malissa's family initially settled in Banock near the Ohio County border (although by the time of her marriage they had moved to Horton).[18] Manerva passed away in 1897. Joseph died in 1905, nine days after being hit by a train near White Run, five miles east of Rosine. His estate sued the Illinois Central Railroad for $2,000. It settled out of court for $100.

Most of the Vandivers were musically gifted, playing instruments and singing. Malissa's next oldest sibling was her brother Pendleton M. Vandiver, a.k.a. Pen. Born in 1869, Pen was a sometime farmworker, sometime trader, and oft-time fiddler whose infectious rhythm shuffle with the bow caused him to be in great demand at local square dances. And "Uncle Pen" was destined to become the great early musical influence on one of his nephews.

How J.B. and Malissa met is now forgotten, but it was probably at a dance, the major social nexus for young people in those days. Malissa loved to do the Kentucky backstep, J.B. could buck-and-wing dance, and both certainly danced "quadrilles" (square dances).[19]

The Monroes were by now an old family in that part of Kentucky, relatively prosperous and well educated. The Vandivers were recent arrivals, farmworkers, not landowners. Some, including Malissa and Pen, were illiterate.[20] The elder Monroes disapproved at first of Buck's marriage, feeling that a Vandiver was socially beneath him.[21]

Buck was undeterred. He was entranced. Malissa was tall and attractive, with blue eyes, red hair, and freckles. She grew white roses and wore them in her hair from the first buds of spring to the last flowers of fall.

She was high-spirited. She loved to dance and loved to horserace against friends.[22]

And she sang old ballads in a high, clear voice, and played fiddle, accordion, and harmonica, and probably other instruments as well during her free moments.[23] Like all farm women, these free moments were precious few: Malissa raised chickens and turkeys for the home table and sold the eggs and meat in town. She canned the summer's produce. She cooked for the household and for hired hands, who, in keeping with the custom of the day, were given their midday meals where they worked. She did unending chores.

When Buck and Malissa were courting, the journey between Ohio and Butler counties took so long by bridge or ferry across the Green River that Buck couldn't wait. He would simply swim straight across the flow to visit his beloved.[24]

J.B. and Malissa were married on August 2, 1892. He was thirty-four, she was twenty-two. It would be the first and last marriage for both.

A large family followed: Harry C. (born in 1893); Speed V., his surname from the Vandiver family (1894); John J., named after his grandfather (1896); Maude Bell (1898); Birch, named after one of Buck's brothers (1901); Charles Pendleton, his middle name of course honoring Malissa's brother (1903); and Bertha, who later married a German railroad engineer named Bernard Kurth (1908).[25]

The Vandivers were as gregarious as the Monroes were reserved, and a mix of these contrasting personality traits were inherited by the children. Although the daughters were somewhat diminutive, the sons were robust young men, some tall or wiry like the Dutch Vandivers, some big and solid like the Scottish Monroes. The youngsters were taught to stand up straight and not slouch. "Get them shoulders back" was a frequent parental admonition in the Monroe household.[26] The boys were remarkable for their strong, balanced postures, even when standing in casual conversation.

J.B. became a significant local employer, paying good wages, as much as a dollar a day, with as many as ten people working for him full or part time. One longtime employee was Hubert Stringfield. Hubert had a hobby that was later of special interest to one of Buck's children — he played the mandolin.[27]

By the autumn of 1911, J.B. Monroe had a home farm of more than 360 acres plus four additional lots in the town of Rosine.[28] He owned three horses, five mules, various head of cattle, a breeding bull, hogs, and two prize foxhounds, plus various plows, wagons and mowers. He estimated the value of his land and movables at $2661.00.

Soon Buck Monroe would have another addition to his homestead. Earlier that year, Malissa had again found herself pregnant.

This last child was surely an accident, unplanned at a time when there was not much in the way of family planning. Malissa was forty-one years old, J.B. nearly fifty-four; their previous child, Bertha, had been born three years earlier, and Charlie five years before her. Who would have expected Malissa to conceive an eighth time?

Perhaps the family's attitude to this final arrival was unintentionally expressed by Buck, who quipped after its birth, "Malissa, I wouldn't take a thousand dollars for all of the children, but I wouldn't give a dime for another one!"[29]

A neighbor came to visit Malissa late in her pregnancy on a miserably hot and humid day.[30] Her ankles were swollen and she was sitting outside her house, vigorously picking away on an instrument, trying to distract herself. The child within her, very soon to be born, must have felt the vibrations.

September 13, 1911, was an uncharacteristically quiet day at the Monroe farm.[31] J.B. sold 31 pounds of coal for $1.44, and he paid brothers Riley and Mose Hunt $1 each for a full day's work hauling railroad cross ties. ("Haled ties," Buck wrote in one of his ever-present ledger books.)

Perhaps little had gotten done because J.B. was otherwise occupied. On this day, his and Malissa's eighth child was born, a boy. He was named in honor of two of J.B.'s brothers: William Smith Monroe.

Bill had been born on a Friday the 13th. In later years, he would turn this inauspicious date into a good omen, jauntily declaring that he was "lucky from Kentucky."[32] In fact, Bill was unlucky at the very start, thanks to his poor vision and the inwardly crossed eye that soon made him a target for teasing.

His eyes were more than a cosmetic problem.[33] If not corrected by age six or seven by operating on the eye and straightening it, esotropia inevitably leads to amblyopia, in which the central neural connections of the eye to the brain fail to develop. After age eight, although the eye can still be physically straightened, the atrophied nerve pathways will cause lifelong vision dimness, blurring, even pattern confusion. A child's ability to see and interact with people, succeed at school, play and enjoy sports are all disrupted. As best as can be determined, Bill Monroe's eye was not straightened until he was well into his teens.

Strangers were not the only ones to tease him about his eyes. At times, his siblings did too. His mother would shush the others if she caught them at it.[34] But Willie, as he was called in the family, came in for some maternal disciplining as well. He adored his father and became frustrated when his dad wouldn't take him along during a busy day's work. If he complained, Malissa quickly put an end to it. Bill tried to understand.[35]

The Monroe children attended school in Horton, slightly closer to their home than Rosine. They walked to school, of course. Their mother knew right to the second when they should be walking back in the afternoon.

Sometimes the children played on the handcar in J.B.'s coal mine.[36] Once they overloaded it with playmates, sending it off its tracks and rolling down into the woods. Charlie was nominated to confess to J.B. Buck was a tough disciplinarian but he also knew when a whupping was not necessary. ("He could look at you harder than any man you ever seen in your life," Charlie recalled years later.) On this occasion, Buck simply hauled the cart back into the mine, reset it on the tracks, and made the kids promise never to pull that stunt again.

And where was Bill during these fine youthful misadventures? He was left out. In large farming families, older siblings were expected to raise the youngest. But the older Monroe children often couldn't be bothered with little Willie. They didn't hate him, but he was a social liability, a cross-eyed embarrassment. They treated him more like a stepchild than a full family member, often ignoring him, even when he followed them devotedly.[37]

Left to himself, Bill wandered the woods and fields of the sprawling property, thinking: Lonesome is walking around by yourself, wondering where your brothers are.[38]

Because of his eyes and his lowly status, Bill's social development was stunted. He became guarded and thoughtful. He grew desperately to need love and affirmation. And his auditory senses grew keen: Many of his childhood memories remained not in the form of visual images but the recollections of sounds. The child would truly become the father to the man.

The circumstances of Bill's birth had other implications. Current research into family birth order strongly suggests that the youngest children of large families, in an effort to find a niche for themselves, tend to become innovators, even rebels.[39] As adults, they not only free themselves from old rules and stereotypes, they create entirely new paradigms. If so, the youngest child of J.B. and Malissa Monroe was going to be a textbook example.

One night when Bill was about four, a neighbor woman came to the Monroe home. Bill had no way of knowing she was a midwife, the same one who had delivered him. There was a 30-by-12-foot corn crib near the house, and the children still living there — Birch, Charlie, Bertha, and Bill — were sent out to sleep in it. The adults didn't want them around for what was about to happen: the wife of one of Bill's oldest brothers had come home to have a baby.

The birth of this niece was one of the most painful milestones in Bill's childhood, as he admitted years later to some close friends:

> The next morning, my father came and told us kids a new baby had been born. That was the first I ever heard of a new baby coming around, me being the youngest. So they bought us into the house so we could see the new baby.
>
> Back in those days, a kid was babied and petted more than they are today. So when she came into the picture, you know, that kind of

shoved me out. My mother would hold her, and I'd have to stand down beside her and wish I was in her lap. So from that time on, [Mother] acted like that. It made it a sad life, a lonesome life.[40]

Not surprisingly, the little boy who lost his mother's lap would exhibit a lifelong pattern of competitiveness and jealousies.

Malissa and J.B. were not neglectful parents. They were simply middle-aged people in a labor-intensive world who were nearly overwhelmed with work. Bill idolized his father. In the mornings he would stand next to him at the table (the family was so large there was no room for him to sit), eating his breakfast out of a little blue and white bowl.[41] He followed his dad around, watching what Buck did.[42] Bill learned silently, just by watching.

Little Willie was so acutely shy that during visits to town he would hide behind his dad like a little squirrel scurrying around a tree trunk.[43] When Buck received change from a purchase, he sometimes gave Bill a nickel or a dime. For the rest of his days, Bill cherished the memory of receiving those shiny coins and the paternal affection they represented.[44]

As a child, Bill literally had few conversations with anyone. (Bertha, closest to him in age, was the only sibling who really spent time playing with him.)[45] Much later he began to wonder if — because he had been so withdrawn and looked so odd with his crossed eye — people around Rosine thought he was retarded.[46]

Bill's father never gave him a whupping.[47] But as an adult, Bill confided to a few people that he had suffered some physical abuse. One of his oldest brothers (whose name is now lost to history) would drink, get surly, and hit him.[48] There is no indication that alcoholism was a problem in the family (indeed, Uncle Jack Monroe was a temperance man and most of Buck's children grew up to be teetotalers).[49] But there was some drinking among the Monroes. Buck's ledger books record occasional purchases of whiskey,[50] and he would occasionally have a pick-me-up dram of bourbon at the start of a hard day. When Bill became old enough to work, Buck shared this daily ritual with him.[51] Bill realized that he liked the taste of bourbon too much, and he remembered the whiskey-fueled abuse he had suffered; so he stopped drinking hard liquor and never touched it again. For the rest of his life, he only imbibed a small glass of wine with dinner and this only on rare occasions.[52]

For all the hardworking Monroes, including shy, lonely Willie, music was a diversion and a comfort. Malissa often placed her fiddle and bow carefully on a bed, and when she had a moment's rest would play a number like "Old Joe Clark." (Malissa once played fiddle for an entire evening's square dance when the regular fiddler took sick and couldn't attend.) Or she would pick up her little accordion and play "Heel and Toe Polka." Or sing an old ballad from the English Isles, like "The Butcher Boy." Malissa's music permeated the very atmosphere of the Monroe home. To Bill, the small boy with terribly limited vision, these sounds were among the most beautiful sensations to penetrate his consciousness.

And there was Malissa's brother Pen.[53]

Pendleton Vandiver was tall and slender like his sister. In his older years, he was nearly bald but had a striking white handlebar mustache. With his bib overalls and a broadbrimmed black hat set back on his head, if anyone ever looked like a real country old-timer, it was Uncle Pen.

In 1901, at age thirty-two, Pen had married Anna Belle Johnson, age fifteen. Both were living in Sulphur Springs, Kentucky, at the time. Pen was farming, but may also have worked as an entertainer at the health spas in that town. The couple had two children but soon separated. The daughter, Leona, went with Anna Belle, who remarried. The son, Cecil Clarence (named in part for Pen's longtime friend Clarence Remus Wilson), went with Pen, who moved back to Rosine where he was an occasional employee of his brother-in-law Buck Monroe.[54]

The sight of Pen riding up on his mule at sundown sent excitement through his nieces and nephews. He often brought them sticks of hard candy. And he brought an even greater treat — his music. He would stay to supper and fiddle such wonderful tunes: "Soldier's Joy," "Boston Boy," "Going Across the Ocean," "Methodist Preacher," "Pretty Betty Martin," "Going Up Caney" (which might have been inspired by the Caney River east of Rosine). Bill adored "Jenny Lynn" and thought it was the best one Pen played, the one he would rather hear than anything else.[55] The youngsters begged for tune after tune until J.B. firmly packed them off to bed.

*   *   *

The fiddle — no different from a violin — was the instrument of choice throughout much of the South for listening and to accompany dancing. Uncle Pen kept a rattlesnake tail in his violin, a common practice among old-time fiddlers, said variously to improve the tone, prevent mice from attacking the instrument, or collect the dust that settled inside.[56] Pen was a solid musician. Like many old-time–style rural fiddlers, his noting and intonation were only adequate,[57] but he possessed a superb sense of timing and bowing that made him a popular dance fiddler around Rosine.[58]

As Bill became involved in music, he would not specifically ask Uncle Pen how to play numbers. He learned the way he learned farm chores from his father, by close attention and private practice.[59] Pen showed him other things,[60] how to make rabbit snares and how to dance the Kentucky backstep. He gave Bill quiet but firm advice if he did something wrong. If Pen didn't say anything, Bill knew he was doing pretty well right. Bill's future style of instructing his musical sidemen was being formed.

There was other music around, other sounds to enthrall and delight the boy. Uncle Pen's friend Clarence Wilson played five-string banjo in a basic two-finger picking style. Uncle Birch Monroe played a cello with a bow, proving a bass line for the fiddler and banjo during parlor music sessions. The very first live music Bill heard was the three men playing the old frolic tune "Soldier's Joy."

There were local ensembles like the Foster String Band and Faught's Entertainers[61] that played "breakdowns" (fast square dance tunes), waltzes, even a little Hawaiian music. Mechanical music was moving into the hills by now. The Monroes' nineteenth-century-style world had admitted no electricity, not even, it seems, a battery-powered radio. But J.B. purchased a windup Victrola.[62]

Most of the children learned to play instruments. Speed became a fine if reticent fiddler. Bertha could play the guitar a little and loved to sing the old hymns. But it was Birch and Charlie who started practicing in earnest.

Birch was the oldest of the children still living at home. At age thirteen, he laid claim to the use of his mother's fiddle. Charlie purchased his first guitar a few years later, when he was about eleven. It was an old thing and had only one string on it, but he bought it on credit, promising to pay three dollars.

"Well, Charlie, how in the world are you going to pay for it?" Malissa asked.[63]

If that weren't bad enough, Charlie had a further problem: "Mama, I've got to have five more strings."

Another parent might have sent Charlie straight back to return the instrument. Instead Malissa said, "Well, if you're going to have five more strings, we're going to have to pick up a few chickens and take them to town." Malissa selected some frying chickens, sold them, and with the proceeds bought Charlie his strings. Charlie strung up the guitar and then sat up all night, beating on it, unable to make chords, unable even to tune it, but too excited to leave it alone.

When Bill was older, he helped the sons of a family that worked on the Monroe land to take horses to water at a creek on the property. He loved racing the horses — like mother, like son in this case — and on one occasion Bill was thrown, partially dislocating his hip.[64] He tried to hide his limp, but his parents summoned a doctor who popped Bill's leg back into its socket. Bill was already showing the traits that would characterize him as a man: his willingness to break the rules, his fierce competitiveness, his stoicism.

That stoicism almost killed him. When Bill was about ten, he developed abdominal pains. He did not complain or show discomfort — until he collapsed in agony. Neighbors helped carry the boy on a makeshift stretcher to the Horton station, where he was transported by train to the hospital in Owensboro. It was discovered that his appendix was about to rupture. If an emergency operation had not been performed, Bill would have died.[65]

One day, around 1918, the train stopped in Rosine and some men — once young, but now older in many ways — got off.[66] In the distance, Bill could hear them singing an old hymn: "By and by when the morning comes, when all the Saints of God shall gather home. . . ."

It was his brother Speed and some other boys from Rosine who had survived the carnage of the Great War. The snow was deep, but no deeper than the mud of France had been.

Malissa insisted on going out to meet them. This despite the fact that she was very ill. In fact, Bill's mother was dying.

There are conflicting reports as to the cause of Malissa's death.[67] Family tradition varies, holding that she had a brain tumor or spinal meningitis. Her death certificate lists antero myelitis, a degenerative disease of the spinal cord.

Most of the Monroe children had been born in an old log house that later burned down.[68] Bertha and Bill were born in another home on the property. Now, a new farmhouse was constructed, begun around 1919 and completed in 1920,[69] a final gift of love from J.B. to Malissa. It was thoughtfully designed, a modest but rather elegant one-story structure with Victorian elements laid out in a T-pattern. Front and back porches with small gingerbread appointments on their columns ran the length of the bedroom wing. Although not spacious, the house was cheery. Surprisingly long windows opened nearly floor to ceiling. Their size certainly was the cause of Bill recalling vividly in his song "I'm on My Way to the Old Home" the lights in the window that had shone there long ago. To a child with poor eyesight, these illuminated windows would have shone like lighthouse beacons.

Malissa's condition worsened. She was in ghastly pain. It was hard on everyone. Speed would sometimes flee to the farthest reaches of the property and clamp his hands over his ears, trying to escape the agony of hearing her screams.[70] Somehow, walking seemed to have eased the pain. One of Bill's last memories of his mother was that she walked and walked and walked, supported by his father and one of his older brothers.[71]

On the afternoon of October 31, 1921, Malissa Vandiver Monroe died. She was laid out in the living room. What happened next was one of the most painfully perplexing experiences of Bill's life. Malissa was carried out of the house to be buried in Rosine. No one had bothered to explain to ten-year-old Willie what was happening. Having only the vaguest idea of what death was, he was not sure why his mother was being taken away.[72]

Malissa's cries were gone but so too was her lovely music, the mountain ballads, the lilting fiddle, the jaunty accordion. Bill's overwhelming association with the loss of his mother was the shattering silence of the house. Later, in his song "Memories of Mother and Dad," he would write of her death and a home "silent and so sad."

His mother, sister Bertha, and other women had been kind to him. His father had been a good man but busy, distant, and his brothers had teased or ignored him, even bullied him. Bill had learned: Women were to be found and clung to. But with men you had to be strong, unyielding, a competitor and a victor.

He soon learned something else. On the first Christmas morning after his mother's death, Bill got up and found no gift awaiting him. His father had been too distracted to buy him a present and his siblings too disinterested. Little Willie found out the hard way that there is no Santa Claus.[73]

Bill began going out into the fields, far away from the house. Speed had gone there to escape his mother's dying wails; Bill was probably escaping the silence. He specifically went to sing old numbers like "Old Joe Clark." There was true freedom in this, because Bill thought that he could sing loud there, and no one would hear and then make fun of him if they didn't like it.[74]

But others did hear him. As he walked away from the house he was walking closer to other properties. His voice drifted over to other farms. The neighbors were attracted to the high, clear quality of his voice.

As a boy, Bill had heard men walking the nearby railroad tracks and "hollering," a special kind of keening falsetto cry that carries more efficiently than simple shouting. Similar to Swiss yodeling (which also started as a means of communication and became a musical form), hollering was a favored mode of communication among southern farmhands and track workers. Bill tried it. When he saw animals at the edge of the forest, he would try to sing loudly yet gently, forcefully but compellingly, in a way that attracted their attention but didn't frighten them off.[75] A powerful vocal style was being developed that would captivate listeners far beyond the fields and forests of Jerusalem Ridge.

Charlie was younger than Birch, but with his outgoing personality he had become de facto leader of a little musical trio that began to form around the Monroe household. Its third and rather unlikely member was Bill.

Bill wanted to play music, too, but his brothers were not about to share the fiddle or the guitar. So he picked up a mandolin in the family collection. Like so many momentous choices made in the course of great lives, it was initially just a matter of necessity disguised as convenience.

Hubert Stringfield, the farmhand, was the first mandolin player Bill had ever seen or heard. He had a well-developed tremolo and a little repertoire of tunes. Stringfield gave the boy his first pointers on the instrument. From the beginning, he impressed on Bill the importance of forcing himself to use the often uncooperative little finger of the left hand in reaching for high notes and playing descending and ascending scales.[76]

Bill's first instrument was a little Neapolitan-style mandolin that was lying around the house.[77] With its rounded, lutelike back and construction of alternating strips of light and dark wood, it looked like a notorious insect that infested tubers; so the slang name for it among rural musicians was "potato bug mandolin" to differentiate it from the flat-backed instruments that had guitar-style construction (one of which Bill would soon acquire).

Bill gained some ability on the mandolin. Birch and Charlie grudgingly allowed him to play with them but with the stipulation that he only use four single strings instead of the full complement of eight strings in four pairs.

His brothers didn't want him to make too much noise.[78]

Contrary to popular belief, the performers who emerged from the southern hills to become the pioneers of country music and bluegrass were not from an exclusively aural folk tradition. Formal musical education, albeit rudimentary, was available each summer in towns like Rosine in the form of "singing schools."

A local person or traveling teacher would give choir lessons to classes of adults and older youngsters. Students were taught "shape notes," a system invented around 1800 in New England,[79] in which notes on the musical staff were also assigned specific shapes (eg., round, square, triangular), thus giving additional visual cues to intervals. Students learned the notes of their parts first — singing do, re, mi, etc. — before they learned the words to a song. They were also taught the basic principles of music: keys, measures, rhythms, timing, rests.

Gospel songs with responsive sections in which lead, tenor, baritone, or bass voices each stood out momentarily were especially prized — songs like "A Beautiful Life,"[80] "He Will Set Your Fields on Fire," and "What Would You Give in Exchange for Your Soul." These would become familiar to wide new audiences thanks to the Monroes and other hill country musicians. At the end of the course, the class would join with others from nearby towns at a centrally located "singing convention" to show off their new skills. This was true country "singing all day and dinner on the ground" — nonstop musical presentations and picnic lunches.

Bill attended one singing school.[81] He also sang in the youth choir of the Rosine Methodist church for about half a year when he was twelve or thirteen, and at first thought he might like to be bass singer because the harmony line was simple.[82] But his eyesight was a major obstacle to his musical education. He could read adequately during slower-paced elementary school sessions, but couldn't decipher the notes and staffs drawn on the blackboard quickly enough to keep up during singing school. He tried to get his brothers to tutor him. They were unable or unwilling to do so.

Bill never went back to singing school after that one cycle. He quietly resolved to learn his music by ear, the way his mother and Uncle Pen had done.

Bill's formal education ended with the fifth grade. He began working for pay when he was about eleven. Although old enough to labor, he was still too young to accompany his brothers into town on Saturday night, his father decreed. So J.B. would take him out to run the foxhounds.[83]

Foxes were a scourge to farm families, who depended on having chickens but couldn't afford expensive fenced enclosures. Thus developed a specialized form of southern foxhunting, and it was not the mounted sport of a red-coated, monied gentry. After dark, hunters would build a big fire near the woods. The hunting horn would be blown to excite the dogs (and again at the end of the evening to bring them back). Once the hounds were loosed, the hunters would stay by the fire and listen as the pack found a scent and pursued their quarry through the night.

Sometimes the dogs succeeded only in chasing off a fox, not catching one. But the kill was secondary to the hunt. As the hounds gave voice in the woods, all joking and joshing would cease. Connoisseurs of foxhunting not only characterized dogs by their mouths — bell-mouths, turkey-mouths, chop-mouths, and half-chops — they could recognize each animal by its distinctive barks and yelps. Thus they tracked the progress of the hunt, which dogs were in the lead, which ones were falling back.

The packs of dogs were exactly like bands of musicians. Put them together and they made a wonderful sound; and even without seeing them, you could tell which ones were soloing, which were in support, which were working their hardest, and which were slacking off.

Bill also helped raise birds for one of Buck's hobbies, cockfighting. Bill loved animals, but this bloody ancient sport held a certain fascination for him. His grittily competitive nature responded to a smaller and younger bird that could defeat a bigger one through spirit and determination.[84]

Violence in Ohio County was not confined to foxhunts or cockfights. Rosine was a pleasant community, but not a paradise. It had churches and tight-knit farming families, but there was also drinking and the need of some men to be stronger and tougher than the next man, the "bully of the town." These troublemakers would just as soon fight you as look at you.

Charlie Monroe found out about that.[85] He loved to tease people and, despite his strength and size (he grew to be nearly 6 foot 2), Charlie had a high-pitched, almost giggly laugh. Although Charlie never intended it, both the teasing and the laugh could wear thin in a hurry. That is why, Rosine old-timers believe, when Charlie was in his late teens or early twenties, an exchange turned ugly and another Rosine man slashed him across the left cheek with a straight razor.

Carrying a terrible scar, Charlie would turn the left side of his face away from the camera for the rest of his life whenever he posed for a photograph. One day, this scar would prominently mark the lore and myth surrounding the Monroe brothers.

By age fourteen, Bill was working for his father hauling heavy wagon-loads of cross ties down to the Rosine train depot.[86] It was challenging. He had to heft the heavy chunks of wood into the wagon, then use the horses and brakes to maneuver the dangerously weighty loads safely down the winding road into town.

As people around Horton and Rosine watched so young a lad doing so big a job, Bill began to take pride in his growing strength and skill. He made a silent show of his labor. It was an early experience in public performance.

After work, Bill was becoming more and more of a student of music in his own private, self-taught way. Soon another master appeared to help him.

He was a short, somewhat chubby fellow who usually wore a big black hat. He was quiet but personable when spoken to. He was African-American, a local laborer and a truly exceptional musician. Indeed, the consensus of those who heard him is that Arnold Shultz was one of the greatest blues guitarists who ever lived.[87]

Shultz was born in February 1886 in Ohio County near Cromwell. He worked near McHenry as a coal miner and later as a coal loader around Rosine and Horton. He could lead a gypsylike existence. One day in late autumn he might play a tune on a relative's porch, then without a word walk down the road, then sit and play another tune. His relations would hear Shultz and his music fade away into the distance. He apparently made it to the Mississippi, worked his way south on riverboats as a deck hand, then wintered in New Orleans where he absorbed that city's musical influences.

In addition to his compelling blues picking, his transitions between chords were silky smooth. He also knew how to play in the sliding "bottleneck" style, like most country blues guitarists using a pocketknife to make the notes. The strap holding his guitar was not leather, just an old woven grass rope.

Sadly, Shultz was never recorded. Neither the academicians collecting folk music in the field nor the producers scouring the country for salable "race" artists in the 1920s ever found him. If they had, Arnold Shultz would today share the pantheon of African-American country blues greats with Mississippi John Hurt, Son House, and even Robert Johnson. Those who heard Shultz — blacks and whites alike — assert that they never heard his equal before or after. Even without recording, Arnold Shultz's legacy was profound. Merle Travis, the influential fingerpicking guitarist, and Ike Everly, father of the Everly Brothers of 1950s pop music fame, were among those who learned from disciples of Shultz.

Shultz also played some fiddle, and in the early 1920s performed in the Ohio County–based hillbilly and Dixieland ensemble of Forrest "Boots" Faught. The band was all white except for Arnold. Occasionally someone would complain, "Hey, you've got a colored fiddler. We don't want that."

"The reason I've got the man is because he's a good musician," Faught would reply.[88] Shultz stayed on the bandstand.

Arnold fiddled for square dances around Rosine and Horton, where older residents recall him playing with Charlie and Birch Monroe and other white musicians.[89] All this was in the South and nearly a decade before the Benny Goodman Trio with black pianist Teddy Wilson was hailed as the first racially mixed jazz combo to perform in public. Bill Monroe's earliest paid music work was thanks to Shultz, who asked Bill to "second him" on guitar when he fiddled for square dances.[90] Bill was thrilled by the invitation — and proud of his stamina when the sun came up and they would still be playing. With his growing sense of life as a competitive event, Bill was awed by how Arnold won a music contest by following up his blues numbers with a beautiful waltz.[91] Years later, he recalled the man and his art with gratitude and affection:

> I tried to keep in mind a little of it. . . . I wanted some blues in my music too, you see. . . . I believe if there's ever an old gentleman that passed away and is resting in peace, it was Arnold Shultz — I really believe that.[92]

Around this time, Birch, Charlie, and Bill began playing for parlor parties and dances around Rosine as a trio. (This helps explain later statements by Bill — and a slogan painted on his mandolin case — that his music had been going "since 1927.")[93] But soon the lure of big-paying factory jobs took Charlie and Birch north. Uncle Pen scoffed at it all: "Mark my words, Charlie, you'll soon be back on Jerusalem Ridge, drinkin' lonesome water!"[94]

In Detroit, Charlie and Birch found piecework at the Briggs Motor Company, which made parts under contract to Ford.[95] They brought their instruments and made extra money playing at house parties and dances for fellow southern expatriates. These were mellow affairs, no drinking or fighting; just sandwiches, coffee, Cokes, and fun. Birch played old-time tunes for dancing, and Charlie was beginning to sing numbers like the popular tearjerker "May I Sleep in Your Barn Tonight, Mister?"

And now Birch and Charlie were going by a specific name when they performed — the Monroe Brothers.[96]

Laid off at Christmas, they returned home to Rosine. Charlie, flush with his earnings, had a special present for his dad — a $100 bill. As it turned out, the money exactly covered an account J.B. had in Beaver Dam.

The family knew just what train they would be arriving on, so Bill went down to the station especially to meet his brothers. The train pulled in and, yes, there they were. Bill went up to greet them.

It was just like old times, in the very worst way. Birch and Charlie ignored their kid brother. They walked home the whole way without ever speaking to him.[97]

James Buchanan Monroe succumbed to pneumonia on January 14, 1928, at age seventy.[98] His coffin was carried into town on a horse-drawn wagon. Malissa and J.B. now rested side by side in the little lonesome Rosine cemetery. On her headstone was carved, "Gone But Not Forgotten." On his, "We Will Meet Again."

It is unclear who inherited the farm. (No wills were registered for J.B. or Malissa, and probably none was ever drawn up.) One of the older sons presumably kept working the land, which stayed in the Monroe family for the next four decades. But the days of the J. B. Monroe farm as a major operation employing dozens of local men were over.

Bill's home life became unstable. His sisters Maude and Bertha took care of the household for a time but soon, with brother John, headed north to join Birch and Charlie in the Chicago area.

At age sixteen, Bill's maturity had been thrust upon him. He received a horse from his father's holdings[99] and began farming in the warm months for his uncle Jack Monroe. In the cold weather he worked for his uncle Andrew Monroe, hauling timber for railroad ties and mine supports on a ten-mile round trip from Andrew's land to the Rosine depot.[100]

Bill lived briefly with his namesake, Uncle William, then with Jack, whose second wife, Elda Mary, was a loving mother hen of a woman. At

Jack's house near the Rosine depot, Bill at last found some security. But one day he returned to find even that haven denied him, shut out by a quarantine after an outbreak of measles.

Then someone provided stability in Bill's vertiginously uncertain world. Uncle Pen invited Bill to "batch it"[101] in his humble cabin, high on Tuttle Hill overlooking the town center.[102]

Pen had gotten this place in 1922 after having lived for some time at the home of his longtime friend Clarence Wilson. One evening Pen's mule showed up at the Wilsons', riderless.[103] A search was made, and Pen was found on the ground, his fiddle beside him. His hip was broken. The mule was young, a recent trade acquisition, and it had been spooked by a passing train. The break never healed properly. For the rest of his life, Pen was forced to go around on crutches.

After his accident, Pen had made his living through trading.[104] He was reputed to leave his cabin on a Monday morning with goods of small value. After a week's traveling and trading up, he would return leading a cow.

Bill kept his workhorses in a barn behind his uncle Jack's house near the Rosine depot.[105] Late at the end of a day, in the evening, just about sundown, as Bill put the animals away for the night, he would become aware of a sound ringing out from the nearby hill overlooking the town — Pen sitting outside his cabin, playing his fiddle. To Bill it was an almost human vocalization. He would one day immortalize these sensory impressions in song.

Uncle Pen did all the cooking. The grub was plain but filling, rich in proteins, carbohydrates, and calories, just the thing to fuel hard physical labor.[106] For breakfast, they would have hoecakes topped with sorghum molasses, an all-purpose sweet syrup as truly of the South as maple syrup is of New England. Dinner and supper were often black-eyed peas with fatback (bacon) and cornbread with sorghum. Occasionally, they would have a comparatively extravagant breakfast: fried potatoes and eggs. (Malissa had specialized in fried potatoes, too; forever after they were Bill's favorite dish.) They had no stove; all the cooking was done over the fire.

It was a barebones existence. Yet Bill gratefully communed with every morsel of Pen's magnanimity, as he later reflected:

A man that old, and crippled, that would cook for you and see that you had a bed and a place to stay and something for breakfast and dinner and supper, and you know it come hard for him to get . . .[107]

Pen continued to be in demand for square dances. He took Bill along as his backup musician. They rode their mules to neighboring homes where a large room or a barn floor had been cleared for the party. Sometimes they would make a couple of dollars, sometimes five. Like Shultz, Pen insisted on sharing the money equally with Bill.

Pen gave Bill more: a repertoire of tunes that sank into Bill's aurally trained memory and a sense of rhythm that seeped into his bones. Sometimes Bill played guitar behind his uncle, sometimes the mandolin.[108]

As his playing developed during these long dance sessions, Bill began, in his mind, to move his feet and dance. He would move his right hand in time with the imagined movement. It was the same for the rapid shuffle of a breakdown or the lilting time lifts of a waltz. While playing music, Bill was dancing in his mind.[109]

Music not only gave Bill enjoyment and some cash money. For probably the first time in his life, people he loved were valuing him in return. To Uncle Pen and Arnold Shultz, Bill was a fine young man, a promising musician, a sober, reliable partner, and they were happy to have him.

But for the young Bill Monroe, it was a revelation and a turning point. Thanks to music, he felt he was someone. Thanks to music, he was connecting with people who truly cared.

And there were other connections to be made. Playing at dances probably facilitated his first romance.

Bill had thought that if he was lucky, his life would be this way:[110] I'll stay in Kentucky, keep farming, find a girlfriend, fall in love, get married, have a family. But even finding a girlfriend? Bill was painfully shy. He was afraid that if he said even one wrong word a girl would never talk to him again.

He didn't have his first date or first kiss until he was eighteen years old.[111] It was a late start. But Bill was about to make up for lost time.

CHAPTER 2

THE BIG CITY, THE BIG COUNTRY

(1929 TO 1938)

Great events make me quiet and calm; it is only trifles that irritate my nerves. — *Queen Victoria*

C harlie Monroe had clout at Sinclair Oil. Literally.

By 1929, he and Birch had gone back up north and were now living in Whiting, a community in Indiana that is essentially an extension of greater Chicago. In Whiting, Charlie found work at the Sinclair Oil refinery. The big man from the Kentucky hills would not have been averse to shouldering his way to the front of the crowds seeking relatively high-paying refinery jobs. And at Sinclair, aggressiveness is sometimes what it took.[1]

Wilbur Davison, a native of Grayson County, Kentucky, who worked at Sinclair and knew the Monroe brothers personally, recalls that the crowds of job seekers outside the refinery were often so great that the police would have hard work keeping the intersection of Indianapolis Boulevard and Marks Road open so that streetcars could get through.

That summer, Bill gave in to Birch's and Charlie's urgings and joined them, John, Maude, and Bertha in this strange new world. He was not the only country boy doing so.

Many members of farm families were moving to cities to find employment, and no wonder. By 1930, an average farmer's income was a mere 30 percent of that of an average urban worker.[2] The Monroes followed a classic pattern for southerners in which a "branch family" established itself far away, sending back home to the "stem family" information about employment, housing, and quality of life, then acting as a support system for kin who moved from the stem to the branch.[3]

And so Bill ventured forth. He took the train from Rosine to Louisville and thence made connections to Chicago. The eighteen-year-old former corn grower and timber hauler from Ohio County, Kentucky, disembarked in the Windy City and was afraid. He had absolutely no idea what to expect.[4]

He could have expected one thing: His brothers' attitudes toward him were unchanged, a mixture of maddening condescension and true loving concern. Charlie was arranging a job for Bill at the 1,100-man Sinclair facility. But Charlie was worried: His kid brother had been operated on for appendicitis, after all, so maybe he wouldn't pass the company physical. Never mind that the operation had been some eight years in the past. Never mind that Bill had proved himself an indefatigable laborer back home. Charlie's lack of faith in Bill coexisted with a genuine protectiveness. He determined to use his influence to make sure Bill got a job.

Charlie was a star on the company baseball team, a valuable all-around man. So after clubbing a dramatic game-winning home run, he told Max Tucker, the team manager and also his boss, "Max, I've got a brother here, eighteen years old. Now, he's not well. Now, if we can't get him through that gate out there, I'm going to have to leave Sinclair's ball team and company."[5]

Tucker quickly agreed to help. Both he and Charlie met Bill at the gate the next morning and personally accompanied him to the plant's infirmary. The doctor passed Bill through, probably on his own merits. The youngest Monroe was assigned to work in the steam house.

There, Bill was one of about ten men who unloaded empty barrels from freight trains that came in on a siding, then steam-cleaned them for reuse. Bill was a slender but strong 165 pounds then, a six-footer, and there was already something noteworthy about this quiet young man. "Bill stood out in the crowd," Wilbur Davison recalls.[6] He became able to clean three dozen drums every fifteen minutes. He quickly learned the trick of tilting the drums up on one edge and roll-spinning them across the pavement to the adjacent barrel house where they would be refilled with packing greases and heavy lubricants. (Here Charlie worked, one of about fifteen men.) Roll-spinning the barrels was quite an art;[7] foremen from other parts of the plant would often stop by just to watch it done.

After he became a music star, Bill spoke with pride of his prowess in unloading barrels, cleaning them, and flinging them on their way. But his work did not involve barrel washing alone. He later confessed something to a close woman friend, something he did not tell reporters and scholars: He was also a lowly janitor for that part of the refinery, sweeping out the building and doing the most menial labor.[8]

Of course, the appendicitis had not been Bill's only physical problem. There was the matter of his eyes. His vision did not seem to be an issue during his hiring by Sinclair, and Wilbur Davison recalls that Bill's eyes appeared normal when he was working at the refinery. It seems likely, therefore, that Bill had been operated on to correct his condition prior to his hiring at Sinclair.

Eye doctors in Kentucky would not be capable of performing such a delicate procedure in those days, and the nearest specialists would have been in Chicago.[9] Bill intimated that the operation was performed in Chicago, but — ever sensitive on the subject — never spoke much about the major turning point in his life when his eye was realigned. Exactly when he had the operation and who paid for it are today unknown. Bill's parents probably could not afford the operation. It has been rumored that Charlie paid for the operation, and that story is likely true. Charlie made good money at the Briggs Motor Company and later at Sinclair, and there is no question that beneath his often patronizing treatment of Bill, he genuinely loved his kid brother.

Around 1930, the little Monroe enclave moved to East Chicago, Indiana, with Charlie and Bill continuing to work for Sinclair. They earned about $30 a week each, very good money in the days when a farmhand might make only $6 a week and the cost of a city boardinghouse room was just $15 a month. They rode streetcars back and forth to work. After supper, they often went to square dances in Hammond held in a club or an old storefront.

Transplanted southerners held on to their culture in the big northern cities. It was not, perhaps, a conscious act; they just lived life as best they could in a place where streetcars ran instead of wagons and where new brickhard tenements towered instead of boughy pines and venerable oaks.

Square dances and parlor parties were central to the social life of these expatriates. Birch, Charlie, and Bill played for such soirees just as they had played back home. Recordings of rural music also gave southerners pleasure and kept them connected to their roots. RCA Victor and other record companies recognized this when they developed white "hillbilly" records in parallel with the successful "race" records that had appealed to blacks. Charlie owned a Victrola, and the Monroes listened to such lively string bands as Gid Tanner & the Skillet Lickers and Charlie Poole & the North Carolina Ramblers, the mountain ballad–derived material of the Carter Family, and, of course, the hits of former railroad worker Jimmie Rodgers, "the Singing Brakeman," country music's first superstar. The Monroes loved this music, and it began influencing their own.

Radio also discovered the fans of rural music in this era. The signals of powerful stations reached deep into the hills, but living closest to the transmitters were tens of thousands of transposed country people. Chicago's own WLS was a pioneer,[*] first broadcasting its *Barn Dance* program with the station's powerful 50,000-watt signal in 1924, later syndicating it across America as the *National Barn Dance*.

If Arnold Shultz and other people of color in Ohio County introduced Bill to African-American music, here his education continued and he received his first serious exposure to jazz. The evidence for this comes from Bill's own music: "Milneburg Joys" had become a Chicago jazz standard thanks to Jelly Roll Morton, the New Orleans Rhythm Kings, and others. Bill heard a version being played by the Hoosier Hot Shots string band over WLS, which he later recorded as a mandolin instrumental under the title "Milenberg Joy."[11]

*   *   *

One day, Charlie had a run-in with a big Turkish coworker. The man cursed him. At quitting time, Charlie didn't even change out of his work clothes. He made straight for the time clock house to make sure he'd catch the Turk before he went home. They met just outside the plant and glared at each other. The standoff only fueled Charlie's fury. He suddenly exploded, decking his antagonist with one piledriver blow and knocking out several teeth.

The fight had taken place outside the plant, but Sinclair was very strict in such cases. The next day both men were fired. The same aggressiveness that probably helped Charlie land his position and made him the star of the company baseball team had now put him out of work.

Birch was still unemployed, so every day to salvage their dignity, he and Charlie would arise and put on their best Sunday clothes, then would sit outside their building and converse with great self-importance, often arguing.[11] Every two weeks, they accompanied Bill to the paymaster's office. Bill would draw his money, keep some for a haircut and trolley fare, and turn the rest over to the family to pay the bills. Little Willie was now supporting himself and five of his siblings — a majority of the children of J. B. and Malissa Monroe.

The situation was not lost on the one who had been frequently ignored by the others in childhood. Bill felt conflicted about it, but believed it would be wrong not to help his kin.[12] Such was Monroe family loyalty. It would not be the last time that in financial matters, Bill put family members ahead of himself.

Charlie and Birch did not languish among the unemployed forever. Charlie eventually found work at Standard Oil and Birch also found refinery work around this time.

The Monroes earned money and vacation time enough to allow a trip back home. In Rosine, Bill was stunned to learn that Uncle Pen was dead.

Pen had fallen ill with the respiratory problems that plagued so many of the Monroes and Vandivers.[13] He had developed bronchitis and double pneumonia, and his condition suddenly took a critical turn. A doctor was summoned from the town of Beaver Dam. Speed Monroe rode back to Beaver Dam with the doctor, then hurriedly returned the nine miles on foot to bring his uncle a supply of medicine. But it was no use. Pendleton Vandiver died the next day, June 22, 1932, at age sixty-three.

Some eighteen years later, Bill would write one of his most famous and beloved compositions, a tribute to Pendleton Vandiver titled "Uncle Pen." The lyrics recalled the square dances they had played together, the tunes that Pen performed — "Soldier's Joy," "Boston Boy," and Bill's favorite, "Jenny Lynn" — and the precious memory of Pen's fiddle talking and singing at sundown from the hill above Rosine. Bill also wrote that he would never forget the day of his beloved uncle's passing. This last expression would be a rare instance where wishful thinking got the better of historical accuracy in one of Monroe's autobiographical "true songs."

In fact, Bill had no memory of that mournful day. When Pen died no one made any attempt to contact the Monroes living up north, apparently thinking it would be too difficult to reach them. The burial was held without them.

It was the ultimate example of Bill's being left out of events at home. He came to feel that the worst part of his life was that he didn't get to go to Uncle Pen's funeral.[14]

Bill had no way of knowing that he had lost another musical mentor. Arnold Shultz had died in Morgantown, Butler County, Kentucky, on April 14, 1931.[15] He was only forty-five years old. The cause of death was a mitral lesion, a disease of the heart valves. He was buried in a colored cemetery in Morgantown. Headstones were an impossible luxury for the poor in the depths of the depression, and the exact resting place of Arnold Shultz is today unknown.

The Monroes labored on at the refineries and factories. Soon, they got their big break in show business. But not through their picking or singing. It was because they loved to dance.

One night at a square dance in Hammond, there was a four-couple set that consisted of the Monroes, their girlfriends, and a friend named Larry Moore and his wife. The big, well-coordinated Monroes were excellent dancers who enjoyed showing off. They attracted attention; not just from other dancers but from Tom Owens, a caller and producer of country music programs. He approached them.

"How would you boys like to dance on the stage for a living?" Owens asked.[16]

Owens wanted the Monroes for an exhibition square dance team to perform on the *WLS Barn Dance* and also travel with a country music show sponsored by the station. They jumped at the offer. They had also sung and played a bit at the party, and Owens held out the possibility that they might be able to play on WLS. But he cautioned: "I'll tell you before you go, they got an awful lot of talent."

The Monroes had an awful lot of talent, too. Over the next three months, they were able to get time off from work for short tours with a package show playing theaters in nearby Illinois, Indiana, and Wisconsin. They shared the bill with the likes of Red Foley, the Maple City Four, and the Hoosier Hotshots, and were with the WLS exhibition square dance team that performed at the 1933 Chicago World's Fair.[17]

The breaks kept coming. They were soon on radio station WWAE in Hammond, playing music with a friend, fiddler Bill King.[18] The Monroe Brothers trio then landed a fifteen-minute show five days a week on WJKS in Gary, Indiana, earning $11 a man each week. In all likelihood, Bill probably just played backup mandolin on these radio shows; he was still very much Birch and Charlie's little brother, not a featured soloist. But he was on the air, and in his free time he was experimenting with his mandolin style.

The Monroes got booked as a singing/dancing act at the Palace Theater in Chicago's downtown Loop. This was the big time! The theater's producer had a novel idea for the Monroes' exit: They were to be danced offstage by another group while they played "She'll Be Coming 'Round the Mountain When She Comes."

"Just go over to the other side of the stage," the producer said before the show.[19] "The other dancers are over there." The Monroes went around backstage as instructed — and ran right into two dozen burlesque performers. Unexpectedly surrounded by a bevy of near-naked women, the young country boys were excited and, as Charlie later admitted, "scared smack to death."

They performed "I Dreamed I Searched Heaven for You" and other sentimental numbers. Then upon hearing "She'll Be Coming 'Round the Mountain When She Comes," the girls would come out in their pasties and feathers to dance them offstage. This went on four times a day.

The Monroes were on their way to becoming musical professionals. But what really got their careers moving were laxatives.

The boys probably didn't take such products themselves. But millions of their country cousins did. Constipation seems like a quaint joke now, but in these days of meat- and starch-heavy diets, with fresh fruits and vegetables a summertime luxury, irregularity was a serious health problem. Patent medicines were sold literally by the trainload to farmers and other rural laborers who couldn't afford the luxury of sick days. Laxative manufacturers realized that radio was a highly cost-effective advertising tool, with hillbilly music programs especially good places to buy air time. The Crazy Water Crystals Company of Birmingham, Alabama ("Crazy Water Crystals Bring a Noted Health Resort to Your Home") and arch-rival Texas Crystals pioneered sponsorship of country music. The crystals were similar to Epsom salts. Produced cheaply and sold at a dollar a box, they were huge money makers.

While performing at WJKS in Gary, the Monroes came to the attention of Texas Crystals. The company purchased an after-midnight time slot to try them out. Company representatives liked what they heard and asked Charlie, the group's lead singer and front man, to perform on a Texas Crystals radio show on KFNF in Shenandoah, Iowa. Charlie didn't want to play as a solo, but Birch opted to keep his refinery job and continue to support Maude and Bertha. (John had gone home to Kentucky.)[20] So Bill got the nod.

Charlie and Bill were due to receive two-week paid vacations from Standard and Sinclair. It was the perfect time to give professional music a try, with the paid fortnight a safety net in case things didn't work out. They boarded the Big Four train from East Chicago to Omaha, Nebraska, then traveled, probably by bus, the remaining fifty miles southeast to Shenandoah.

Bill knew they were taking a huge risk.[21] Radio stations didn't pay a lot. It was up to musicians to establish on-air popularity, then parlay it into concert appearances where the real money was.

Things did work out. Bill and Charlie spent three months in Shenandoah as part of the roster of KFNF "Grab Bag Entertainers."[22] They
earned $25 a week each, less than factory employment, but they were
having much more fun. They quit their day jobs and became full-time
musicians. For the rest of his life, Bill Monroe had no other profession.

The Monroes did not pioneer the country brother duet. In fact, they
were entering a field crowded with polished siblings accompanying
themselves on guitars or, like the Monroes, with the enjoyable combination of guitar and mandolin: Bill and Earl Bolick ("The Blue Sky Boys,"
perhaps the most pleasant-voiced of the brother duets), Alton and Rabon
Delmore, Wiley and Zeke Morris, and others. But the Monroe Brothers
quickly created a sensation. If they had meant to imbue their music with
their competitive, broadshouldered attitudes — as well as their rich
romanticism — they succeeded splendidly.

Their tempos could be positively blazing. Charlie had a tendency to
speed up in midsong excitement, but otherwise he was a formidable guitarist. Playing with a thumb pick and index finger pick in a supercharged
version of the old "parlor style" of guitar playing, Charlie possessed a battery of lower string runs and upper string work that provided bass lines as
well as rhythm fill strumming. His style was both support and counterpoint for Bill's bursting and innovative mandolin arpeggios.

Bill was playing mandolin to match his brother's singing and meet the
demands of a two-man band in which a continuous stream of notes was
necessary. Popular string bands contained the mandolin but never really
featured the instrument, so Bill was now on the creative frontiers of the
mandolin's possibilities. Already he was melding the speed, rhythms, and
scalings of fiddle playing with accidental notes and half-tone ornamentations taken from blues guitar.[23] It was not just that Bill could play faster
than any other mandolin player around: He played complex, engaging
lines, even on slow gospel numbers or songs of nostalgia. Bill's impact on
other mandolinists was profound: There simply had never been anyone like
him. The youngest of the Monroe children was finding his creative niche.

Despite their start as a trio with Birch, the Monroe Brothers were not
anxious to add a fiddle or a bass. Bill in particular felt that a third instrument would ruin their tight sound, not enhance it.[24] Neither did they

need a third singer: Their duet was high-pitched, strong and with an edge to it, yet it was clear and with a true purity, equally suited to frolic numbers or songs dripping with sentimentality. Charlie loved to sing high, his voice cutting through like a knife. Bill had to learn how to shift into falsetto just to save his throat. Soon he was doing it effortlessly. Sometimes Charlie would sing notes that were more tenor than original melody, forcing Bill to sing a high baritone–style line. Sometimes Charlie would unexpectedly jump up and double Bill's notes, forcing him to quickly find an even higher harmony part. This aggravated Bill, but it proved superb training for his tenor.[25]

The Monroes' repertoire was growing. They performed "Ain't Gonna Study War No More," an African-American-influenced spiritual; "You're Going to Miss Me When I'm Gone," learned from the Carter Family; and "No Place to Pillow My Head," an orphan's lament made famous by the popular duet act Karl and Harty. The Monroes were getting their material from records and songbooks. Neither of them was writing their own songs. Neither knew how. Not yet.

Bill was still very much the junior Monroe, but he was also becoming very much a man, a big, well-built fellow with blue eyes, wavy hair, and a confident air about him. No longer the hug-eyed boy too shy to kiss a girl, he discovered that women were attracted to him and he began to take advantage of it. Bill was never an aggressive Don Juan, however. His approach was strong but gentle. He would typically approach a young woman, politely engage her in small talk, then sidle up to her and ask, "Would you like to take a walk after the show?"[26]

And there in Shenandoah, Iowa, he met someone very special.

Carolyn Minnie Brown was born May 15, 1913, in Marshalltown, Iowa.[27] Bill met Carolyn while the Monroe Brothers were playing on the KFNF *Barn Dance* show.[28] She was a dark-haired woman with a winning smile.[29] If she was somewhat plain, it was in an attractive way. She was a natural woman, not gaudy, the kind who wouldn't wear lots of makeup.[30] She was not high-strung, but she did have a temper if riled. One day, Bill would find out about that.

Carolyn's father was of Native American extraction, a Blackfoot Indian. He was a minister.[31] Bill had a practice in those days of giving preachers a twenty-dollar bill as a donation.[32] It was an extraordinarily generous act, but one he was genuinely happy to make. Although Carolyn may have attended the *Barn Dance* program as an audience member, it is possible that Bill first met her through her father.

But soon the two were parted. After three months in Shenandoah, the Monroes were transferred to a Texas Crystals show at a larger station, WAAW in Omaha. They worked there for about six months and were raised to the princely sum of $45 per week.

In Omaha the Monroes began working with the now-legendary announcer Byron Parker. Billing himself as "The Old Hired Hand," the twenty-five-year-old Parker evinced such a pleasing and totally sincere manner that, his admirers insisted, he could have sold tap water or used matches if he'd wanted to.[33] Parker was an incredible asset to the Monroes at this stage of their careers,[34] singing occasional bass during their gospel numbers, using his charm as a radio show host to sell Bill and Charlie to a growing audience, and even arranging bookings for them.

The life of a country musician meant radio for exposure and concerts for money. Only cities or the largest towns had actual theaters, so the usual venues for these shows were schools and courthouses. Centrally located for easy access from the surrounding countryside, classrooms and courtrooms were also designed for presentations to be made to fair-sized audiences. Schoolhouses became known among entertainers as "the coal oil circuit" because few had electricity: Coal oil lamps usually provided the only illumination for evening concerts. Microphones were a rarity, but they were generally unnecessary in these days of intimate settings and performers used to playing their instruments loudly and projecting their voices.

To earn their 70 or 75 percent of the receipts from ticket sales, the Monroes gave audiences 100 percent of their abilities. They expected fair payment in return.

On one occasion, Bill and Charlie were playing at a schoolhouse as a benefit for a local church.[35] It was a hot day. A crowd of young men had climbed up on a woodpile and perched themselves in the open windows, of course not paying a penny of admission. Bill and Charlie noticed this. They looked at each other. Then they went outside.

The Monroes presented a two-part argument against freeloading. Bill yanked one man down from the window ledge and flung him past Charlie. Charlie hit him in the face as he flew by and let him fall. Bill then yanked another man out of the window. Past Charlie, wham, fall. Thus did the Monroes clean windows.

The sheriff was called. The interlopers had now regrouped, and the situation was tense. Charlie offered a compromise: Let the young men pay whatever money they had, even if only a nickel, and they'd be allowed in. The sheriff supported the idea, and the concert continued without further incident. Bill must have taken a quiet pride in all this: The puny cross-eyed kid had become a strong young man, his brother's true and valued partner.

The Monroes were now making money and they were spending it. They were not extravagant, but they enjoyed the perks of their upward mobility into a lifestyle that their parents had not known. They bought spiffy outfits and drove sporty new coupes. Big, handsome, cocky, dressed to the nines, the Monroes could stroll down a street and (in the words of one contemporary) "part a crowd like a hot knife through butter."[36]

Their high profiles made them a target in the rough and tumble of depression-era rural America. One night, the Monroes were jumped after a show by a group of men looking to give the well-dressed brothers a humiliating and even savage beating. Seriously outnumbered and with no help around, Charlie and Bill stood back to back. They fought their attackers off. The Monroes were not bullies and, teetotalers both, never engaged in the drunken carousing that spawned brawls. They didn't go looking for trouble, but they were too big, strong, and tough when it found them.

"See this man?" Bill would later say, pointing to himself. "He's never been knocked down."[37]

"Well, sir, back in those days we both were just so hot-headed and mean as snakes," Charlie recalled.[38] "We didn't think anybody could whip us! Pretty much a handful!"

But the Monroes knew when discretion was the better part of valor. While in Omaha, Bill, Charlie, and Byron Parker purchased very big

John B. Stetson hats, then walked resplendently down the street, unabashedly admiring themselves in mirrors and store windows. They went into a swanky restaurant, sat down at a table, and kept their hats on. That was a major social faux pas.

The next thing they knew, they were approached by a huge fellow with street fight–sliced ears and hands as big as country hams.

"I'm sure you boys want to take your hats off," the man said.[39]

Even the Monroes were children next to this fearsome character. Three new Stetsons were quickly removed.

They stayed in Omaha about six months.[40] Texas Crystals then sponsored the Monroes and Byron Parker on WIS in Columbia, South Carolina. After three months there, they were transferred to WBT, a powerful 50,000-watt station in Charlotte, North Carolina.[41]

The move east was proving to be the most eventful of Bill Monroe's young life. He and Charlie were tasting true success. They were out of the Midwest and back in the South, where their music found a true resonance. The Carolinas embraced them, then and for the rest of their careers.

And by the time they settled in Charlotte, it had been nearly nine months since the Monroe Brothers had worked in Shenandoah. Now — probably just before their relocation to Charlotte — someone showed up whom Bill had known during his brief stay in Iowa.

It was Carolyn Minnie Brown.

And she was very pregnant.[42]

Melissa Kathleen Monroe, Carolyn and Bill's child, was born September 17, 1936, in Charlotte, North Carolina. Bill and Carolyn were wed a month later on October 18, 1936, in Spartanburg, South Carolina.

Friends who were privy to the story were given to understand that Carolyn's father had shamed Bill into doing the right thing by his daughter.[43] Whether Mr. Brown accomplished this simply by turning the pregnant young woman out of his house or whether he personally accompanied Carolyn to the Carolinas in pursuit of Bill is now unclear.

Charlie had already wed, on March 16, 1936, to Elizabeth Harreld.[44] The Monroe Brothers now had wives to support and, in Bill's case, a child. Soon they received the worst possible news — they had lost their sponsor. Texas Crystals was experiencing tough competition from its rival cathartic, Crazy Water Crystals, and as a cost-cutting measure had suddenly decided to stop sponsoring old-time string band music. The Monroe Brothers and four other acts were dumped in one day.

The Monroes weren't left hanging for long. Crazy Water Crystals immediately hired the sensational duo to play on its own WBT program, *The Crazy Crystals Barn Dance.*

The Monroes subjected themselves to a grueling if profitable daily schedule. They performed on an early morning radio show in Charlotte, North Carolina, drove nearly one hundred miles to play a noon program on WFNC in Greenville, South Carolina, then played evening concerts at schools and courthouses. Although all this traveling was in the days before the modern interstate highways system, conditions were nowhere near as primitive as they had been just a decade before. States and the federal government had invested heavily in all-weather roads during the depression, partly as employment programs, partly to spur the development of intra- and interstate commerce.[45] The Monroe Brothers were part of the first generation of professional entertainers to benefit from the proliferation of paved roads.

Charlie and Bill were at WFNC in Greenville one day for a program when a telegram arrived for them. Anyone going to the trouble and expense of tracking them down and sending a telegram must be imparting very bad news indeed, another sponsorship cancellation or the death of a loved one.

They opened the message with trepidation and read: WE MUST HAVE THE MONROE BROTHERS ON RECORD STOP WE WON'T TAKE NO FOR AN ANSWER STOP ANSWER REQUESTED.[46]

It was signed by someone named Eli Oberstein of the RCA Victor Recording Company.

Charlie and Bill ignored the offer.

They weren't playing hard to get. Their priorities simply lay elsewhere, in radio and live performances. The cash money they earned every time they filled a courthouse or schoolroom, this they understood. Despite their love of the disks of Jimmie Rodgers and The Skillet Lickers, they did not understand the record business.

But Eli Oberstein did understand the record business. Word of the Monroe Brothers' excellence and popularity had reached his ears, and he was determined to get them for Victor's Bluebird label, which carried "hillbilly" and "string band" artists. When he wrote that he wasn't about to take no for an answer, he meant every nickel per word it cost him.

The next day the Monroes were back at WFNC getting ready for a noon broadcast. Just before air time they were summoned to the phone. Charlie took the call. It was Eli Oberstein.

"Now you don't think we're going to go back to New York without you on record, do you?" Oberstein asked.[47]

"I don't know how you'll get us on if we don't go on," Charlie retorted.

Far from being put off, Oberstein proceeded to talk, as Charlie later recalled, "straighter than I've ever been talked to." The New Yorker's rapid-fire spiel overwhelmed the big Kentuckian. Oberstein got the Monroes to agree to meet him in person. When they did, he told them quite truthfully that as modern professional musicians they absolutely needed to be on records. He offered them complete artistic control over the selection and arrangement of their material. Charlie and Bill signed with Victor.

On February 17, 1936, the Monroe Brothers arrived at RCA Victor's Charlotte recording studio for their first recording session.[48] The "studio" was actually a temporary setup in the back of the second-floor warehouse level of the Southern Radio Corporation, the regional distributor that handled Victor Records. The Arthur Smith Trio was more than midway through its session, having just finished recording "Chittlin' Cooking Time in Cheatam County" and "Fiddler's Blues."[49] Oberstein made Smith's group sit out so the Monroes could record and then rush off to their next commitment. In all, Charlie and Bill recorded ten songs at that first session. They were so polished that almost all the songs were recorded in one take, and Oberstein accepted every one for release.

As rough and ready as the Monroes were, as fiery as their music was, as driving as were some of the classics they committed to disk — "My Long Journey Home," "Nine Pound Hammer Is Too Heavy," "New River Train" — their biggest-selling record was a gospel number recorded that day, "What Would You Give in Exchange for Your Soul," for which they subsequently recorded three sequel versions.

Its chorus featured a stirring answer-back arrangement: Charlie sang "What would you give . . ." — as if he had personally taken the listeners by the shoulders, sat them down, and delivered the words looking right in their eyes — and Bill would respond ". . . in exchange?!" in a heroic tenor, turning the line from a question into a declaration, a plea, and a warning to follow the righteous path. "What Would You Give in Exchange for Your Soul" had been a favorite showcase for singing school choirs back in Kentucky; today, its power to challenge devout and unbeliever alike remains undiminished.

In the spring of 1937, Byron Parker left to star on his own radio program at WIS in Columbia, South Carolina. The split was apparently quite amicable. The Monroes were certainly sorry to see Byron go, but probably thought little about it. They were doing quite well now, also working at WFBC in Greenville. By July 1937, they had a local fifteen-minute radio spot at 7 A.M. at WRTF, Raleigh, North Carolina,[50] and were also playing over WFBC in Greenville, South Carolina, where they were sponsored by Syberland Tires.[51]

What no one realized was that the loss of Byron Parker would prove an absolute disaster, the beginning of the end for the Monroe Brothers act.

Byron had been mutually respected by Charlie and Bill. He had done the emcee work on radio and even handled their bookings. Now the proud, increasingly successful brothers would be forced to work closely without the pleasant buffer of the Old Hired Hand.

And younger brother Bill had finally grown up. Work, a child, and a wife had seen to that. He had his own ideas about music, about its rhythms and timings and how to sing harmony. Still, he was in no hurry to sing lead or solos.[52] Duets were so popular that there seemed no reason to put a solo on their records or shows. So for a while, all went fairly well.

Raleigh, North Carolina, became their next base of operations. With Parker's departure, Charlie's wife Betty had become the act's unofficial manager, collecting the money and helping Charlie send out booking letters and other business correspondence. Her role was unofficial because Bill chafed at the idea of anyone managing him. But Charlie felt, quite rightly, that the Monroes were becoming victims of their own success. Their shows often attracted twice the number of people the schools and courtrooms would hold.

"Bill, we either need a manager, or else we need to separate and get a band apiece," Charlie said.[53] "We'll make more money."

This raised the hackles on the increasingly assertive Bill. "Well, no man will ever manage me!" he declared. The management issue began to be a source of real tension between them.

Carolyn was not particularly involved with Bill's professional activities at this time. She was traveling with the act but, unlike Betty, not contributing to its fortunes. This too began to be a source of tension between the brothers.[54] The Monroes were living in separate house trailers with their wives, and the physical separation doubtless allowed suspicions and misunderstandings to germinate into larger hostilities. Bill was getting irritated by Charlie's paternalism. By 1938, some fans of the Monroe Brothers noticed that they were beginning to arrive at shows separately and not speaking to each other, ignoring each other to the point where they almost seemed facing in different directions onstage.[55]

The end was coming, and Charlie knew it. He tried to keep the duo together for the good of Bill and himself; unfortunately, his tactics were not especially tactful. Charlie admonished Bill that if they separated "I'll never find a tenor singer like you, and you'll never find a lead singer like me."[56] Charlie surely meant that as a genuine compliment; Bill surely took it as just another overbearing lecture from his big brother.

Charlie laid plans for the inevitable. He spoke to Tommy Scott, a Georgia-born performer, and advised him that the act would soon be breaking up. Charlie's visions were ambitious if ambiguous. "I think I'm going to the Wheeling Jamboree or the National Barn Dance," he told Scott.[57] They agreed to work together when the time came.

When that time finally came, a rumor began circulating on the musicians' grapevine that the brothers had split because Charlie had been fooling around with Carolyn, and when Bill caught them together he pulled a knife and slashed his brother. The altercation supposedly occurred when the Monroes were playing over WFBC in Greenville, South Carolina, the year before they arrived in Raleigh.[58] It is a colorful and titillating tale, and it is also untrue.

The proud and contentious Monroes would never have stayed together for nearly a year after such a devastating confrontation. As noted earlier, the knife scar on Charlie's face had been sustained years before in a fight with a Rosine resident. The rumor may have been fueled by confusion over an incident involving another Crazy Water Crystals group in which an argument over song selection escalated until one band member pulled a knife on another.[59] The Monroes apparently witnessed this altercation but had nothing to do with it.

It is significant that although both Bill and Charlie could be quick with their fists, neither was a knife fighter. Brawlers who use bladed weapons typically carry them and use them on other occasions; neither Bill nor Charlie ever packed anything bigger than a pocket knife and neither was known to fight with them.

In addition, Charlie Monroe was, in complete contrast to his kid brother, a one-woman man. He loved to sit a woman on his knee and flirt and tease, but his heart and body belonged to his wife. There is absolutely no evidence that he lusted after Carolyn nor she after him. In an interview published in 1973, Charlie shared his feelings on the subject of marital fidelity.

> I'll tell you something, and I'm going to tell you this, this is facts. Back when I was going with the girls, I only wanted one girl. And after I got married, I just needed one woman. That's all I need. And I believe — I firmly believe — that all the people should feel the same way.[60]

Both brothers adamantly denied that they had had a serious fight.[61] Their own accounts of the breakup, given separately to various writers, are quite consistent. Although there had been interpersonal tensions, both agreed that the immediate issue was their professional careers. Bill came to see that his resistance to a manager was ill-advised, as he told author Jim Rooney:

> If we'd have had a manager, you know, no telling how far we could have gone. But so many times brothers can't get along good, you know. One want to be the boss and the other one's mad because he does and so it was just better that we split up.[62]

The crisis came in early 1938. As good as business was in North Carolina, Charlie wanted to move on to Tennessee right away, although the Monroe Brothers still had at least a month of show dates in the Carolinas. Bill protested at the idea of disappointing all those fans.[63]

Charlie went down to Bill's house trailer.

"Bill, now we're not doing any good like this," he said.[64] "We are arguing and we're not seeing the business alike."

Then Charlie presented an ultimatum: "I'm going to go out back to my trailer. I've already got it jacked up. If you're not there in ten minutes, I'm going to let it down on my car, and I'm going to pull her out of here."

"You wouldn't leave me!" Bill shot back. "You'd starve to death, you know you would!"

"Bill," Charlie replied, "I imagine that's a pretty good feeling, but neither one of us is going to starve to death. But we're better together. If you've got one grain you'll admit that."

Charlie went back to his car and trailer. Whether he was consciously aware of it or not, at some level he must have known that he was playing on Bill's great weakness, his fear of being deserted.

But great as that fear was, Bill's pride and determination were now much stronger. If the quickest way to get Bill's attention was to threaten to leave him, a sure way to get him to dig in his heels was to offer him an ultimatum, no matter how softly the commands were spoken.

Charlie waited. Bill stayed where he was.

Charlie pulled out.

Once again, Bill was left alone.

But not quite alone. This time, he had his willpower, his talent, and a woman who believed in him. Both Bill and Carolyn were about to rise to the new challenges.

$\star$ CHAPTER 3 $\star$

HIS OWN MAN

(1938 TO 1945)

Travel would not be too cold, knowing your warmth at my
side. . . . — Ovid, *The Loves*

C harlie was all confidence after the breakup. He was going to
have a much easier time of it.

"Bill won't find a lead singer like me,"[1] he told Tommy Scott when
they met in Bluefield, West Virginia, to discuss working together. "I can
always find another man to sing tenor to me."

And Charlie indeed found an excellent replacement in the person of
John Ray "Curly" Seckler. With Seckler and Scott, he formed Charlie
Monroe's Boys, the precursor to a larger band, Charlie Monroe & the
Kentucky Pardners.

Charlie had a real advantage over Bill. In contrast to his quiet, shy
brother, he was outgoing with personality plus, a big man whom you'd
be happy to have on your side in a fight, but also genuinely likable, an
affable fellow, the kind you'd be proud to have as a guest at Sunday

dinner. Audiences adored Charlie, and he soon found a base at WBIG in Greensboro, North Carolina.

However, he was unable to retain his old sponsors. Neither Crazy Water Crystals nor Syberland Tires wanted to continue with Charlie or Bill alone, fearing that the Monroe boys apart could never be as good as they had been together. So Charlie decided to sponsor himself and turned to a tried-and-true route: patent medicine. During his medicine show days, Tommy Scott had obtained the formula to an herbal tonic and laxative.[2] Charlie now bottled it under the trade name "Manoree." He sold tons of the stuff.

Meanwhile, Bill had moved with Carolyn and Melissa to Little Rock, Arkansas. Bill seems to have had no connections there, but Arkansas was probably as far away as he could get from Charlie and still be within the Middle South. There, he undertook a radical experiment with his music — he organized a band.

It was called the Kentuckians. Little is known and less remembered about Bill's first attempt at heading a group. There is even scant information on its lineup, but it seems to have included Handy Jamison on fiddle and a cousin of Jamison on guitar. (One source gives Willie Egbert "Cousin Wilbur" Wesbrooks as the bass player, but Wesbrooks did not work with Monroe until later.)[3] The Kentuckians performed for three or four months, getting a spot on KARK radio but never recording.

When Little Rock played out, Bill disbanded the outfit and traveled for a month through Mississippi, essentially on an extended vacation.[4] Bill and his family eventually went to Birmingham, Alabama, where he checked into the music and radio scenes there. Things proved unpromising, so they moved on to Atlanta, Georgia.

There was good reason to be there. Atlanta was a shining sun of early country music.[5] Within its orbit was Fiddlin' John Carson, whose surprise big-selling 1923 recording of "Little Old Log Cabin in the Lane" had made him the first true star of the nascent country music recording industry; Gid Tanner & His Skillet Lickers, the flamboyant and trend-setting string band; and Clayton McMichen, a jazz- and pop-influenced fiddler who left the Skillet Lickers to become Tanner's greatest rival. Atlanta was also the site of the Old Fiddler's Convention, then the nation's most prestigious fiddle contest, founded in 1913 but with precursor events as early as 1899. And it was home to WSB, which became in 1922 the first radio station to broadcast country music.[6]

By the time Bill reached Atlanta, he had made a major decision: He would give up trying to lead a band and go back to what had brought him success — a vocal duet with mandolin and guitar accompaniment.

He advertised in the *Atlanta Constitution* for musicians who could play the guitar and sing old-time songs. The ad came to the attention of Cleo Davis, a guitar player and singer from Cullman, Georgia, then living in Atlanta with a cousin and driving an ice truck for a dollar a day. Cleo was cajoled and finally bullied into auditioning. When Davis protested that he didn't even own a guitar, his cousin bought one at a pawnshop for $2.40. Cleo relented, put on his Sunday suit, and took a streetcar across town, accompanied by his cousin so he wouldn't chicken out.

The ad gave no name, only an address that proved to be a lot next to a service station. There sat a small house trailer. The sound of singing and picking came from inside. Some men came out, and the occupant was heard to say he'd call once he'd made a decision. Davis and his cousin entered to find a man, his wife, and their baby.

Introductions were made, but the nervous Cleo missed the man's name. There was a pause.

"Well," the man asked, "who plays the guitar?"[7]

"I do, sir," said Cleo. He had hidden it behind his back, but now took it out.

"Well, what can you play?"

Cleo had decided to perform two sides of a record by his favorite duet, an act he had never seen in person or even in a photograph — the Monroe Brothers.

"Oh, maybe a verse or two of 'This World Is Not My Home' and 'What Would You Give in Exchange for Your Soul,'" Davis replied.

This was acceptable to the stranger. They tried to tune up, but the man owned a fine Gibson mandolin and Cleo's guitar was too cheaply made to take standard pitch. The stranger obligingly tuned down his instrument.

The two only got through about a verse and a chorus of "What Would You Give in Exchange for Your Soul" when Davis realized he had heard this voice before. This was one of the Monroe Brothers.

Thunderstruck, he stammered and stopped, claiming he had forgotten the words. The mandolin player diplomatically accepted the explanation. They tried "This World Is Not My Home." Davis got through two verses before stage fright strangled him again. But it didn't matter.

"Carolyn, what do you think?" Bill asked his wife.

"He sounds more like Charlie," said Carolyn, "than any man I ever heard who wasn't Charlie Monroe."[8]

A grin spread over Bill's face. They tried the song again, and their blend sounded even better.

"I think I found what I've been looking for," he said. Davis was told to return the next morning.

Bill Monroe and Cleo Davis set about becoming an act. They first went downtown to the music stores and found a fine new large-bodied guitar that Bill played and approved. (In these days before good sound systems, a guitar with volume was as vital as a singer with lung power.) Davis saw the price tag and nearly ran from the store in fright. It cost $37.50. There was no way he could afford it. No problem. Monroe paid cash, and they carried it away.

The next stop was a clothing store. "Fix him from the floor up," Monroe told the salesman. The transformation was completed with the purchase of a wide-brimmed John B. Stetson hat. Davis looked at himself in the mirror, pulled the Stetson down over one eye, and thought: James Cagney and George Raft have nothing on me. Monroe liked the effect so much that he purchased an identical outfit for himself.

Monroe's generosity went beyond the expensive guitar and threads. He proved to be a patient, supportive teacher. Cleo was modest, talented, and hardworking. And he was shy, even shier than Bill himself. Here was someone Bill could nurture, someone to whom the youngest Monroe could play protective elder sibling. Bill had found a surrogate younger brother in Cleo Davis.

Davis was aware of this dynamic in their relationship, as he later told writer Wayne Erbsen:

> Back in those days, Bill was more like my older brother than my employer. I looked at him like a big brother, though he wasn't that much older than me. But he'd been around a lot more than I ever had.

They began rehearsing at Davis's place after Cleo got off work, for an hour, sometimes two and a half hours at a stretch. Bill was a strong guitarist himself; just as he had learned work skills by silently watching his father, he had quietly absorbed every detail of Charlie's playing. He taught Davis all of Charlie's booming, syncopated runs.

This continued until Christmas 1938. After the holidays, Monroe and Davis auditioned for the popular *Crossroads Follies* show on WSB in Atlanta.

They were turned down.

The show's manager was only interested in bands and suggested that if Bill picked up a couple more musicians there might be a place for him on the *Follies*. Monroe made a few well-chosen suggestions about what the manager could do and took his painstakingly rehearsed duet across town to WGST. The managers of that station greatly enjoyed the act, but their duet niche was being filled by the popular Blue Sky Boys, Bill and Earl Bolick.

Angered by this second failure to get back on radio — and therefore all the more determined to succeed — Bill asked Cleo if he could take a few days off work. Soon Davis found himself packed with the Monroe family into Bill's 1938 Hudson Terraplane, the trailer in tow. Davis asked where they were going. "Asheville, North Carolina," Bill replied. To the untraveled Davis, it might as well have been Europe.

They stopped first in Greenville, South Carolina. At WFBC, it was a repeat of the WGST disappointment, with the Delmore Brothers the reigning duet. At least Monroe and Davis were being shut out by high-level competition. And it was not that the Bolicks and the Delmores were necessarily better; they were just there first.

They finally reached Asheville — and success. They were hired at WWNC to take over *Mountain Music Time*. WWNC was a small operation and the program was only fifteen minutes, at 1:30 in the afternoon. Hardly the midday meal prime time at a big station. But it was a start.

The announcer distinctly referred to them as Bill Monroe and Cleo Davis, but mail started coming in addressed to "the Monroe Brothers," proof that they had captured the old magic. He and Davis expanded their repertoire to include material associated with the Delmores and the

Callahan Brothers, but they kept developing their own sound, working up a breathtaking blue yodel duet as a theme to take them on and off the air.

Bill was not going to clone the Monroe Brothers or other duets. Maybe because of his initial creative impulses with the Kentuckians, maybe because of the realities of laboring in a field already lush with outstanding duets, he decided to try again at being a bandleader.

Davis asked what they were going to call the new group.

"Bill Monroe and His Blue Grass Boys," his employer replied.[9]

Davis was puzzled. Blue grass? Monroe explained that it would facilitate quick identification of his home state. "I'm from Kentucky, you know, where the bluegrass grows, and it's got a good ring to it," he said. "I like that." The matter was settled, the new band named.

In Asheville, Monroe renewed the search for sidemen, turning not to the print ads that had brought Davis but the most powerful and specific advertising medium he had at his command — his own radio show. He announced on the air that he was looking for musicians. They started showing up, and Bill and Cleo started auditioning them.

Art Wooten, a fiddler from the nearby town of Marion, was the first to be hired. Monroe already had in mind the kind of fiddle sounds he wanted, and began working with Wooten, playing the parts he wanted on his mandolin, coaching him verbally on the bowing. If Cleo Davis proved to be the first of a very long roster of Blue Grass Boys, Art Wooten was the first of a host of fiddlers to be schooled by Bill Monroe.

Monroe began to develop a total entertainment package for his live shows. There was, of course, the music. The Blue Grass Boys would open with a fast fiddle instrumental like "Fire on the Mountain" or "Katy Hill," then keep the energy level high with a fast duet like "Roll in My Sweet Baby's Arms" or "Foggy Mountain Top." There were blues numbers and yodel duets. Gospel music was not neglected: "What Would You Give in Exchange for Your Soul" always got a huge audience response, not only as a stirring song but one of the Monroe Brothers' greatest hits.

And there was more: Wooten played a strange contraption with a guitar and a banjo built into it, designed so Art could strum and chord these instruments with his feet while playing the fiddle. Adding a harmonica in a holder around his neck, he performed novelty numbers as a one-man band.

Monroe continued to power up the act. He hired Tommy Millard of Canton, North Carolina, to play jug (thus providing the band with some rhythm bass notes) and do comedy. Millard was such a wickedly effective blackface rube comedian that only the stoic Monroe could play straight man in the wacky skits the band developed.

Bill was now starting to sing solos. One of his first was the sentimental "I'm Thinking Tonight of My Blue Eyes." Only freshly out of Charlie's shadow and probably unsure how he would go over, Bill hedged his bets: He used the song as the basis of a comedy routine. Millard would come out in blackface, begin to weep, then lean on his shoulder and dissolve in tearful spasms while the audience went into paroxysms of laughter.

Bill took other roles in the comedy routines. He and Davis got into drag to portray sisters; Cleo would fuss with jealousy over Bill's hot date with Art Wooten until Tommy Millard came on stage and bopped Davis alongside the head with a rolled-up newspaper.

Bill was emerging as his own man. He was in total creative control, he was happy, he was singing solos. Even his hidden childlike playfulness was emerging into public view.

And he continued to be a truly supportive bandleader. One night, Davis forgot a verse to a song. Monroe quickly played an extra mandolin break, but Davis panicked. Bill grinned and waited patiently, and Davis suddenly just made something up, stringing some words together. The band then went offstage to prepare for the comedy skit.

The audience had not noticed anything amiss, but Davis was convinced that he had humiliated himself. "Bill, I don't think I can go out there and face those people again," he said.[10]

Monroe did not laugh or mock, nor order Davis to take the stage. He regarded his frightened sideman calmly.

"You have to go back out there," he said. "Not for me but for yourself. If you let this stop you, you'll never be able to go back out again. You have to prove to yourself that you can do it. You can do the job. You just got scared, and it won't happen again."

Cleo Davis finished the show without a hitch. He stepped off the stage that night a confident veteran.

While Bill was nurturing his musicians, Carolyn was nurturing her husband's career. Gone was her detached attitude from the tense days of the Monroe Brothers caravan. She was no longer the pregnant girlfriend who had shamed Bill into marrying her. Nor was she subjected to the smoldering tensions between Bill and Charlie. All that was over and done. The couple was enjoying a fresh start.

Carolyn was now fully Bill's wife and partner.[11] Her supportiveness, which had budded during Davis's audition, now blossomed. She took care of the mail that began coming in for Bill at the radio station. She assumed an active role in booking the band, traveling around to the schoolhouses that served as theaters, making arrangements, putting up handbills to advertise the shows.

Bill Monroe & His Blue Grass Boys had less work than the Monroe Brothers had enjoyed, they were performing at small schoolhouses holding seventy people at most, and now there were two extra musicians to be paid. Even if they played two shows, with ticket prices 15 or 25 cents depending on age, they might take in only $25 or $30 a night. The band members got $15 a week when they were working, nothing when they weren't (although Bill, committed to having his sidemen looking sharp, always paid for haircuts and laundry).

Things were reaching a crisis. How Charlie would guffaw if his kid brother fell on his face! But after the group had been at WWNC about three months, word came that the Delmore Brothers had left WFBC in Greenville, South Carolina. Remembering the genuine interest that had greeted him there, Bill contacted the station. This time, success. The band was hired immediately.

Relocating to Greenville, Bill took another major step toward establishing his sound. Millard left the show and was replaced by Amos Garren. Amos sang and did comedy, but best of all he played standup bass. The Blue Grass Boys now had a solid bedrock for Davis's fertile rhythm guitar, the strong shoots of Wooten's fiddle, and the bark of Monroe's mandolin.

Money was still tight, and home was still the trailer. It was parked, as it had been in Atlanta, next to a service station. The owner took an interest in Bill and offered an old grease house as a rehearsal space. The band cleaned it up and brought in seats. Then they started assembling and lubricating new material.

None of it was original but it was customized for this sleek string band of fiddle, mandolin, guitar, and bass backing sharp leads, soaring duets, and finely tuned quartets. The band continued to emphasize high-octane instrumentals and vocals, but its repertoire gained variety and depth. They rehearsed trios and gospel quartets. Bill and Cleo worked up "No Letter in the Mail," a Carlisle Brothers number. Although in waltz time, Davis slowed it down even further and the song took on a bluesy, almost despairing edge, a harbinger of the trademark Monroe "high lonesome" sound, which would come to fruition a decade later.

His confidence growing, Bill began to learn more solos. Davis suggested a vocal he had heard his mother sing when he was a boy, "Footprints in the Snow." This tale of love discovered on a winter's night would become one of his most popular vehicles.

An even greater classic was rebuilt, tuned up, and readied for the road in the old grease house. Monroe decided to arrange some Jimmie Rodgers favorites to suit his coalescing style. His tenor range had developed as a matter of survival with Charlie; now the intensely competitive young man was ready to show the world how a "blue yodeler" number should really be yodeled. He selected two of the Rodgers "blue yodels" songs, including "Blue Yodel Number 8." Better known as "Mule Skinner Blues," it was the engaging braggadocio of a mule team driver who can whip the recalcitrant beasts into cooperation and cracks his way through life in the same style. The higher-than-usual keys Bill selected put an extra edge on these numbers, like a knife honed to a razor's edge. But unlike a thin-honed knife, the slicing blade of Monroe's voice was in no danger of bending flat. A nonsmoker and nondrinker with a powerful chest, Monroe was a sheer ax of a singer.

Rodgers had performed "Mule Skinner Blues" in his trademark style: slow, almost drawling vocals; odd-tempoed guitar rhythms; thoroughly influenced by the country blues. Monroe sped up "Mule Skinner" and gave it a more regular rhythm. But he did something more. At this stage, Monroe typically played guitar when he sang leads, trading off the mandolin to Davis. Monroe kicked off "Mule Skinner" with a very funky staccato run, then immediately went into a powerful rhythm strum. The band leaped in, pulled along by the crack of Bill's symbolic whip over the mule team.

Bill's rhythm was special. It was a surging timing that anticipated the main beat. Not in a way that sped up the song but in a way that totally enlivened it. It was like the blues or jazz technique of laying slightly behind the main beat to create dramatic impact, except in reverse: Bill Monroe subtly jumped the timing to create energy. Monroe fully recognized the significance of his innovation, later declaring that "'Mule Skinner Blues' set the timing for bluegrass music."[12]

Also in his music were "the Negro blues," as he called them, yet only a spicing. Too much of their influence, Bill felt, would overpower its other flavorful elements. Much of the Monroe "lonesome" sound actually came from Methodist, Baptist, and Holiness church singing[13] and Bill's own emotions. "It ain't only the colored folks has the blues; there's many a white man that's had 'em," Monroe later said. "I've had 'em many, many times."[14]

Above all, there was the fire and speed and sheer drive of Bill's music. Other southern string bands had spunk aplenty, but compared to the Blue Grass Boys they were just dragging along. Monroe's music also got a major boost from the higher keys in which he pitched many vocals. His decision to sing, for example, in keys like B-flat and B — instead of the G or A favored by most country vocalists of the day — had originally been an expedient to better suit his range: It had the unexpected benefit of putting the keening — and compelling — high element into Monroe's high, lonesome sound.[15]

Bill Monroe & His Blue Grass Boys made Greenville their home base for about six months. In a short time, Bill had gone from junior partner to Charlie to being a leader of fortitude, patience, and courage. Now he was about to prove himself to be a true risk taker.

For their part, Charlie Monroe & the Kentucky Pardners were doing quite well. Their music had less of a hard edge than that of the Blue Grass Boys or even the Monroe Brothers, more flowing in its timings, its song material more sentimental. Charlie's garrulous personality and convivial show drew big crowds and won him a spot on the popular WWVA *Jamboree* in Wheeling, West Virginia, another successful rival to WSM's

Opry and WLS's *Barn Dance.* Although WWVA's signal was much less powerful than that of WSM or WLS — 1,000 versus 50,000 watts — it reached near-South and midwestern states densely populated with country music fans.

But Charlie had plans. Big plans. Early in October, his confident, happy smile on his face, he gave his band the news.

"Well," he said, "we've got a chance to go down and try out for the Opry."[16]

Carried on WSM, Nashville's powerful 50,000-watt station, *The Grand Ole Opry* was eclipsing the *WLS Barn Dance* as the nation's premier country music program. WSM, 650 AM, was owned and operated by the National Life and Accident Insurance Company, headquartered in Nashville, Tennessee. Its call letters came from National Life's motto: "We Shield Millions."

The station had been the brainchild of Edwin Craig, a National Life vice president and a radio nut as obsessed with new communications technology as any modern computer geek. As son of the company's president, twenty-nine-year-old Edwin was able to convince the board of directors to build a radio station, emphasizing its potential for advertising National Life's policy services. WSM went on the air October 5, 1925. At one time, it had the tallest radio tower in the United States. Eventually granted "clear channel" status, with exclusive use of its frequency within a 750-mile radius of Nashville, WSM was heard at even greater distances, throughout the South and Midwest, and, during good atmospheric conditions, to an estimated thirty-eight states and parts of Canada.

As in all early radio, there was virtually no use of recorded music. Entertainment on WSM was live. And there were no country or "hillbilly" artists on the station at first. In keeping with the high tone of Nashville ("The Athens of the South") and National Life's dignified corporate image, WSM presented classical and semiclassical soloists, refined harmony groups, and instrumental ensembles.

The hayseeds were sown at WSM when Indiana-born George D. Hay was hired as program director. A former newspaper man, Hay had attended a backwoods hoedown in Mammoth Spring, Arkansas, and gotten hooked on authentic, foot-tapping mountain fiddling. In 1924, he became chief announcer for the *WLS Barn Dance.* With his enthusiasm for the music, his persona as "the Solemn Old Judge" (at the ripe old age of twenty-nine) plus his gimmick of blowing a steamboat whistle to open and close the show, Hay had been a natural for the show.

On the evening of Saturday, November 28, 1925, contest-winning octogenarian fiddler Jimmy Thompson performed on WSM accompanied by his niece Eva Thompson Jones on piano. They evoked such a favorable response that they became a regular Saturday night feature. This was essentially the birth of what would become The Grand Ole Opry.[17]

Throughout the heartland, the old tunes were heard with joy. Cards, letters, telegrams, and phone calls poured in, pleading for more. By December 26, a regular two-hour program of old-time music was being broadcast live each Saturday night from the WSM studios. Joining the growing cast of regulars was David Harrison "Uncle Dave" Macon, a.k.a. "The Dixie Dewdrop," a former freight line operator and rollicking banjo picker who, at age fifty-two, became the show's first real star.

Initially known as the WSM Barn Dance, the broadcast attracted a live audience that filled the WSM studios beyond capacity. And one night a comment was made that would echo through American popular music history. The Barn Dance was following the nationally broadcast Music Appreciation Hour, featuring the New York Symphony orchestra and carried via a feed from the NBC radio network. Introducing the Barn Dance that fateful evening, George D. Hay ad-libbed, "For the past hour we have been listening to music taken largely from Grand Opera. From now on, we will present the Grand Ole Opry."[18]

The name stuck, and the show grew. Hay now concentrated on his hit program, and Harry Stone replaced him as station manager. By 1930, the Opry had thirty regular cast members and audiences so large that WSM built a special 500-seat studio theater, which quickly proved too small as the program became as much a live event as a radio broadcast. The Opry was forced to move twice. In 1939, it landed at the then-new War Memorial Auditorium. A 25-cent admission was charged for the first time in an unsuccessful attempt to reduce the throngs.

Soon the Opry had its first modern star — Roy Acuff, who debuted in 1937 and joined as a regular member in 1938. Acuff was the first great country "heart" singer. He oozed sincerity. His version of "Wabash Cannonball" quickly became a country anthem, and while performing emotion-filled numbers like "Wreck on the Highway" and "Great Speckled Bird" the tears would literally stream down his face.

So in planning to go to the WSM Grand Ole Opry, Charlie Monroe was making a brilliant career move. The trip to Nashville, he told the Kentucky Pardners, would be taken in about two weeks.[19]

But unbeknownst to Charlie — unbeknownst to anyone — his younger brother had exactly the same plans.

"What do you think about us going on The Grand Ole Opry?" Bill asked Cleo Davis one day.[20]

"Do you think we're good enough?" Cleo gaped.

Bill laughed. "We're as good as the best over there, and right now, we're better than most of the rest."

Bill had been paying very close attention to what was going on at WSM. It would be this way for the rest of his life: The laconic Monroe, driving along, listening in deceptively casual silence to the radio, seeming to just enjoy the music. But in fact he was making mental notes, assessing the strengths and weaknesses of other performers, of stars and sidemen alike, weighing what he heard — and remembering.

"Tell the other boys to get their toothbrushes ready," Bill said. "We're going to Nashville."

Bill Monroe crossed the Cumberland River into downtown Nashville like George Washington crossing the Delaware and marching on Trenton, New Jersey, steely determined yet at a moment of crisis, desperately needing a victory. Bill and the group went to the WSM offices and studios, located then on the top floor of the five-story National Life and Accident Insurance Company building at Seventh and Union streets. Getting off the elevator, they encountered David Stone, a WSM executive, and George D. Hay.

Right away, problems. Stone and Hay were headed out to get coffee, and anyway Monday was not audition day, Wednesday was. But they were persuaded to hear Monroe's band after lunch.

That afternoon, Hay and Stone ushered the ensemble into a studio. They turned on the microphones — the Blue Grass Boys were no good to WSM if they couldn't work in front of a mike — then sat back in the control room and waited.

Filled with nervous energy and as ready as they would ever be, the Blue Grass Boys tore into the audition. They started with "Foggy Mountain Top," a familiar, upbeat Carter Family number done by Monroe and Davis as a crackling duet. Bill trotted out his arrangement of "Mule Skinner Blues," and finally Wooten was featured on "Fire on the Mountain." The audition had encompassed a favorite old standard with an athletic duet, an innovative solo, and finally a foot-tapping fiddle number.

Hay was impressed. He thought: This is a big, good-looking fellow, and he's just given us a sample of folk music as she should be sung and played. He's exactly what the show needs.[21] Hay asked if the band could open the Opry that Saturday night, first spot.

"Yes, sir," Monroe replied.

"Well," said Hay, "you're here, and if you ever leave, you'll have to fire yourself."[22]

Hay came to genuinely like Monroe, although Bill could be a standoffish person. In his 1945 book *A Story of the Grand Ole Opry*, Hay ended his entry on Bill with these words and much between the lines: "Bill Monroe is a good citizen and the longer one knows him the better one likes him."[23]

Now the Blue Grass Boys had some heavy traveling to do. They returned to Greenville, South Carolina, picked up Carolyn, Melissa, and the trailer, then blazed back to Nashville, a journey of at least four hundred miles each way. They arrived well in time for their first Opry appearance on October 28, 1939.

Monroe's overall timing was excellent. Not only was *Opry* becoming America's most successful country music radio show, it was beginning to be heard nationwide. On October 14, a half-hour segment had been carried for the first time on the NBC "Red" network, a system of twenty-six stations. And the show's cast was starting to change. The original members had been local hobbyists, old-time fiddlers and banjo pickers. Now a new breed was arriving from greater distances, performers like Acuff and Monroe, modern full-time professionals — and vocalists.

*   *   *

The Solemn Old Judge announced Bill Monroe & His Blue Grass Boys' first Opry appearance, and the band tore into "Foggy Mountain Top." The audience loved it. The music had originality and sheer energy. Then Bill took the guitar and sang "Mule Skinner Blues." It was Bill's first vocal solo on the Opry show and the true debut of his innovative arrangement of the Jimmie Rodgers classic. (Prior performances had been in little school-houses, after all, not live over a 50,000-watt radio broadcast.) They got an encore, an *Opry* first.[24]

The Blue Grass Boys left the stage with the live audience cheering, the home listeners excited, and other Opry performers suitably impressed. They had traveled a long, long road from the Greenville grease house to the stage of the War Memorial Auditorium.

Up in Wheeling, West Virginia, Charlie Monroe & the Kentucky Pardners had finished the first of their two segments on the Jamboree. In the dressing room, they tuned in to WSM and heard the Solemn Old Judge announce the new band.

Thunderstruck — knowing that his kid brother had beaten him to the Opry by a mere fortnight and that George Hay would never hire both Monroes for the show — Charlie jumped up and left the room.[25]

Later, after regaining his composure, he breezily dismissed this development. "He won't last," he told Tommy Scott.[26] "Wait 'til people down there find out how difficult he is to get along with."

In fact, it was Charlie who didn't last at WWVA, leaving the station after an argument with the program director.[27] Inwardly, Charlie was frustrated. He refused to let matters rest there, as sideman Curly Seckler recalls:

I'm not saying anything against either of them, Bill or Charlie. But one was jealous of the other one. Of course, WWVA in Wheeling was only a 1,000-watt station. Bill was down at WSM which was 50,000 watts. Charlie said he wasn't going to be outdone, so he was going to go to WHAS in Louisville, a 50,000-watt station, to be up with him. You know, I don't get that. He was making pretty good money at Wheeling. In Louisville, no sponsor, no nothing. But he didn't want to be outdone. It's something for brothers to have been that way, but that's the way they was.[28]

Bill had won a big round in the Monroe brothers' unspoken competition, and his Blue Grass Boys began a string of *Opry* firsts: In addition to their historic encore, they became the first band to perform gospel quartets, again raising the vocal standards on a show that had started as a fiddlers' frolic.

Another first was not musical, but in its own way just as significant: Monroe's musicians were the first to play as part of the Opry stage show wearing ties and white shirts. They still wore Stetsons, but Bill had gone back to the natty jodhpur riding pants and high-top riding boots that the Monroe Brothers had featured at the end of their career. This gentleman planter's uniform would be retained for the next three or four years.

Early Opry performers had arrived at the WSM studios respectfully dressed as if going to church. But as the show attracted a live audience and publicity photos were published, Hay had encouraged them to wear hillbilly outfits to communicate the show's rural orientation. But this, Monroe believed, created stereotypes calculated to attract urban sophisticates engaged in a musical slumming expedition.[29] (Monroe even hated the self-deprecating term "hillbilly music" and took immense satisfaction when it was supplanted by "folk" and then "country" to describe rural southern sounds.)

Corny country comedy with funny costumes had a place in Bill's early shows. (Until the early 1960s, a succession of Monroe sidemen portrayed "Sparkplug," a rube dressed in a loud shirt, baggy pants, and skewed baseball cap.)[30] But in the main, the Blue Grass Boys were sharply attired and all business on stage. Real country people had pride and dignity, and they dressed as well as their economic situations would allow. A houndstooth jacket and an upright bearing were the hallmarks of a gentleman in western Kentucky. Monroe's formalization of attitudes and clothing for his band was actually more faithful to real country life than the antics of ragged pseudo-mountaineers.

As fiery as Bill's Opry debut had been, he did not shoot to stardom immediately. In the spring of 1940, he was touring with the tent show of comedian-showman Silas Green ("I'm Silas Green from New Orleans!") at the bottom of the bill, beneath Uncle Dave Macon and fancy fiddler Curly Fox.[31] By the end of the year, Bill's band had completely changed, but if anything, it was even stronger: On fiddle was now the able Tommy Magness; the great bass-playing comedian Egbert "Cousin Wilbur" Wesbrooks had joined the lineup; and Clyde Moody had replaced Cleo Davis, the original Blue Grass Boy, who had got his own radio show in Lakeland, Florida.[32]

Davis just missed the Blue Grass Boys' first recording session on October 7, 1940. Bill had signed again with Victor Records, and the session was held in the Kimball Hotel in Atlanta. (Nashville was not yet a recording center.) Monroe opened the proceedings with his Opry debut hit "Mule Skinner Blues," but the day's final selection was the true harbinger of things to come: the instrumental "Tennessee Blues." It was Bill's first original composition,[33] and it was a winner.

Bill was now truly his own man. His persona and his music were coalescing in tandem.[34]

First and foremost, he was a striking figure. A six-footer, his solid body, balanced posture, and confident manner made him seem much bigger. He would rarely lean against anything or put his hands in his pockets. He would stand on his two feet and let his arms hang comfortably at his sides.

He was unhurried but had a ferocious work ethic. His strength was very real, truly that of a Highlander of yore. Once around this time, for a lark, he invited his band to get on him: One sat on his shoulders, one climbed on his back, and he held the other two in his right and left arms, easily supporting them all.[35]

Bill's physical strength and balance had a mental counterpart. It was difficult, even impossible, to pull him off balance physically or psychologically. It was usually Bill who subtly led others around. He measured his words carefully and rarely responded without thinking, although when he spoke his sentences sometimes came out rapidly. Things he said to people made such an impression that years later they could recall his utterances as vividly as if they had been made that morning.

Outwardly, he seemed inaccessible and impervious. He was proud. But inwardly, his feelings could be hurt easily. When he was angry, he rarely lashed out. He would instead turn cold and stop speaking to the person who had offended him. The length of his feuds was matched by the constancy of his loyalties, especially to family members.

He had rawhide-tough willpower. Intertwined with that willpower, and reinforcing it, was a gristly stubbornness. He was supremely competitive, especially with other men. This extended to his art, and he believed that spirited competition within the otherwise friendly teamwork of the band peaked the music to its greatest heights. (In a significant choice of words, Monroe would often praise a lead vocalist not as being a good man to sing with but as possessing "a good voice to sing against.") Musically, physically, romantically, he would never allow himself to be bested without putting up a fight, and he seldom lost. Yet he did not fight physically unless attacked or provoked. (One provocation was rowdiness at his shows; if a heckler turned up, Monroe was known to put down his mandolin, go into the audience, throw the loudmouth out, then return to the stage — often before the song was finished.)

He did not boast of his strength or his talent or his romantic conquests. He rarely cursed and hated to hear others use such language. In particular, he would not tolerate foul speech when a lady was present. He was impulsive in love, perhaps even compulsive, but he never forced himself on a woman. He would accept no for an answer.

He had clear blue eyes and tended to stare down his nose at people or seem to look right past them. Although he could truly be aloof, this behavior was often caused by poor vision. (He hated to wear his eyeglasses in public.) He appeared very reserved (like the Monroes) but had a lively sense of humor (like the Vandivers). When something struck him funny, he would laugh merrily. He treasured the celebration of Christmas.

He had escaped the farming life, yet he truly was a man of the soil. He loved what he called "Mother Nature." One of the few modern technologies that he seemed to really embrace was the telephone.

He loved Tennessee walking horses and foxhunting. He was a Democrat. He savored fried potatoes and fried chicken and baked beans. Donuts and peanut butter were a favorite snack. He had the eccentric habit of wetting himself down in the shower, turning the water off, stepping out of the tub, lathering himself up with soap, then stepping back into the tub, turning on the water again, and completing his shower.

He took scant interest in business matters, but he hated the idea of anyone making money off him and was suspicious of those who came to him with business deals. He was usually a good judge of character, and once he accepted a person he trusted that person implicitly. When he didn't have money, he was stingy. When he did, he was touchingly generous. He never used money to buy friends or impress people. The thick wad of cash once given a poor vendor so Monroe could buy the man's undernourished cart horse and provide it a new home on his farm; the quarters he gave children (a memory of the coins given him by his father); the appearance fees often returned at benefit concerts — all these gifts of money had deliberate thought and feeling behind them.

He was a man of action. But he was very, very thoughtful.

His married life appeared stable. He and Carolyn seemed happy together, and on March 15, 1941, their second child was born, James William Monroe.[36] (Bill had named his daughter and son after his parents, but no Freudian subtext should be read into this. It was common practice in the Monroe family to thus honor relatives and forebears.)

Almost exactly a year after the first Blue Grass Boys session, on October 2, 1941, the band was back at Victor's studios in the Kimball Hotel in Atlanta to cut another eight sides for the label. The lead singer-guitarist slot was proving to be a springboard that launched careers: Pete Pyle had replaced Clyde Moody, who had gone out on his own (although Moody would return for another hitch with the Blue Grass Boys the following year).

Art Wooten, back on fiddle, was featured on a very hot instrumental with vocal bridge — "Orange Blossom Special" — written in 1938 as a rousing tribute to the Miami-to-Chicago streamliner by Florida-based fiddler Ervin Rouse of the Rouse Brothers. The number had been brought into the band repertoire by Wooten and Cleo Davis,[37] and the Blue Grass Boys' 1941 version helped establish it as country music's most popular fiddle showcase.

The session ended with the instrumental "Back Up and Push," with Wooten and Monroe trading breaks, anticipating the jazzlike soloist-friendly format that would distinguish bluegrass, Wooten stating and brilliantly restating the melody, Monroe providing fiery variations.

What was happening behind the fiddle was just as significant. In this period, when Bill wasn't soloing he strummed his mandolin in a shuffling rhythm inspired by Uncle Pen's bowing or played counterpoint lines. But from time to time on "Back Up and Push" he added a strong, straight downstroke on the second and fourth beats. It was an early example of the "rhythm chop," the backbeat emphasis that added yet another dimension to the mandolin. Monroe had been using the instrument like a fiddle, guitar, or even a banjo. Now he was starting to use it percussively, like a snare drum.

Despite their musical discipline, these Blue Grass Boys would josh like a jug band, even bantering on records just as they'd do onstage. And because many a true word is said in jest, the joking that accompanied the Jimmie Rodgers/George Vaughn number "Blue Yodel No. 7" had a deep meaning indeed.

Monroe sang the verse celebrating the singer's love for Mississippi and Tennessee, throwing in a quick aside "Give me Kentucky, boy!" in tribute to his native state. Then he finished with the standard punch line that the women in Texas "done got the best of me."

"North Carolina women get him," gibed a band member, probably bassist Wesbrooks.

There can be no doubt as to the reference. A North Carolina woman had indeed got him. And as much as Bill genuinely cared for the mother of his children, if longevity of a relationship is any measure, this other woman was the great love of his life.

Her name was Bessie Lee Mauldin. She was born December 28, 1920, in the town of Norwood in Stanley County.[38] She was the third of four daughters of Samuel Lee Mauldin and Lilly Thompson Mauldin. Lee Mauldin was a mechanical genius, "a fixer" who could repair just about anything he could get a tool around. He held an important position as a machinist and operator at Norwood Manufacturing (later Collings & Akeman Co.), a large textile mill and the major local employer. The Mauldin family lived next door, in a two-story house.

Mr. Mauldin could pick the five-string banjo, a popular instrument in North Carolina. Bessie did not immediately learn to play an instrument herself but had a sweet voice. As a child, her family had to beg her to dance, but once she got started they had to beg her to stop. When she was older, she enjoyed going to square dances at the Norwood Hotel.

She was a very good cook. She was mischievous. She always seemed to know how to get her sisters in trouble while cleverly escaping a spanking herself. When Bessie went too far, one sister would lock her in the outhouse, knowing that Bessie was claustrophobic. Bessie would scream and holler and the sister would get a whupping but it all was worth it. The sisters had a lively childhood and loved each other very much.

Bessie grew into a very attractive if rather hefty blond woman, a flashy dresser, strong, spirited, and quite earthy — just Bill's type. It is believed that they met at a show in Albemarle, North Carolina, not far from her home.[39] But the act that night, it seems, was not the Blue Grass Boys. It was the Monroe Brothers.

Persons close to Bill had the impression that he had met Bessie not long after meeting Carolyn.[40] And in a 1975 legal filing, Bessie claimed that "on or about September, 1941 . . . at the age of 17" she was "lured" by Bill "from her home and family in Norwood, North Carolina."[41] The lurid use of "lured" aside, the statement is inaccurate: Bessie would have been twenty-one or twenty-two at that time. However, it is likely that she meant (and her attorney misunderstood) that she originally met Bill at age seventeen, probably in 1938, then moved to Nashville in 1941.

Bessie later claimed she and her parents were unaware for some time that Bill was married.[42] As doubtful as that seems, it is likely that Bill eventually told her the circumstances of his marrying Carolyn to explain why he was not free.

In September 1941, Bill brought Bessie to Nashville and installed her in a hotel.[43] She became his road girlfriend. The pattern was the same for years:[44] The Blue Grass Boys would start to leave town; Bill would stop at a pay phone and make a call; Bessie would then meet them at a designated pickup spot to join him for the trip. Meanwhile, Carolyn was keeping their house and Bill's books, keeping family and business together.[45] The arrangement worked for a long time, because Bill was spending a lot of time on the road.[46] But Carolyn knew full well what was going on.[47]

Bessie's move to Nashville occurred just prior to the October 2 recording session. Given that she was now traveling with Bill outside Nashville, it is possible, even likely, that Bessie was sitting in the studio in Atlanta when "Blue Yodel No. 7" with its impromptu gibe about North Carolina women was recorded. Whatever the case, the fact that Bill and the band felt free enough to joke about Bill's affair — on a record that would be heard nationally — is sad evidence of how little concern they gave Carolyn's feelings in the matter.

Nashville's city fathers were becoming rather unhappy with WSM's hit show. The War Memorial Building had been intended for long-term use as a concert hall and theater; now it was receiving serious wear from thousands of Grand Ole Opry fans visiting it each week. In 1943, a new venue was found that would be the Opry's temple during its golden era — the Ryman Auditorium.

In 1891, Tom Ryman, a riverboat captain and shipping company president, experienced salvation and caused the brick-built Union Gospel Tabernacle to rise on a hill overlooking Nashville's commercial and saloon districts.[48] The building eventually became an all-purpose auditorium renamed in his honor. With the construction of a great balcony to accommodate an 1897 convention of Civil War veterans (henceforth known as the "Confederate balcony"), the Ryman attained a capacity of more than 3,000 seats. Its oaken pews were uncomfortable and the lack of air conditioning made the jam-packed place almost unbearable in summer. But the semicircular seating arrangement focused attention on the stage and gave audience members a feeling of shared intimacy. Best of all, the Ryman had superb acoustics. It had been a successful concert venue. (Enrico Caruso, John Philip Sousa, and Jeanette MacDonald had all appeared there.)[49] Now it proved ideal for the Opry's presentation of country music.

Opry rules were very strict at this time: Cast members were expected to appear on the show every Saturday evening. (Although this precluded Saturday night show dates for the cast members, at the time it didn't matter much: Most of the fans would be at home tuning into the Opry anyway.) From Sunday through Saturday morning the performers were at liberty. Some veteran cast members, essentially talented amateurs, were content to stay at home. Bill Monroe was one of the new Opry professionals, and he reveled in what he called "heavy traffic."

He toured almost constantly during the 1940s,[50] working as much as six or seven days a week and doing as many as four shows a day. The Blue Grass Boys were now regulars on the 10 P.M. Opry segment sponsored by

Wall-Rite, a paint manufacturer. After performing, they would usually head right out on the road for an all-night and all-next-day drive to the first of the week's gigs. The band drove in a 1941 Chevrolet airport stretch limo with four seats. It handled well and went fast. Bill often took the wheel himself in those days, a swift but cautious driver.[51] Despite the extra seats, the musicians and their luggage were crammed inside, with the bass fiddle and other instruments in a special rack strapped to the roof.

Bill was a demanding but fair boss. He continued to look after his side-men as if they were his younger siblings, except he treated them with far more caring attention than he had received as a child. A band member who came down with a cold would be put to bed to rest before the next show. Monroe would bring medicine and regularly check on him.[52]

In 1942, Monroe began touring with the tent show of Jamup and Honey, the popular Opry blackface comedy duo. After a year of this, he decided to start his own tent show.[53] He initially worked with Billy Whalley of Miami, Florida, who provided the canvas while Monroe filled it with entertainment. It proved so successful that Monroe invested in his own equipment and for the next three or four years ran the entire show himself. It was another manifestation of a lifelong pattern: Just as Bill had resisted Charlie's idea of hiring a manager for the Monroe Brothers, he was often unhappy with middlemen, agents, and others profiting from him, even if their percentages were reasonable and, in the long run, they made money for him.

At its peak, Bill Monroe's tent show was a marvelous enterprise, not simply a band under canvas but a circuslike total entertainment experience. The advance person was first in town, getting the necessary permits, renting a field or lot, putting up posters and window cards, and taking out newspaper ads. About sixty-five dollars would cover it all, and to Monroe it was money well spent. "After you got a lot permit for the show, there was nothing anybody could do to give you any trouble," he said.[54] "It was like owning your own house, until you left the next day."

The crew soon arrived to set up the tent and concession stand, lights, sound system, and generator. In addition to the stretch limo, the show had five separate trucks to haul the tent, the tent poles, the seats and bleachers (nearly a thousand seats in all), an electric generator, and a rolling kitchen. Of course, the procession drove through each new town to promote the show.

But the pre-concert ballyhoo didn't stop there. For several seasons, the show featured a semiprofessional ball team.

"We've got a team that's real good," one of the Blue Grass Boys would declare.[55] "Do you have a team around here?"

In this era, many American small towns did. A game was quickly organized at the local field. Despite having one weak eye, Monroe played. He was hell on bats, breaking many as he smashed into pitches.[56]

It was excellent promo. Country music fans liked baseball, and baseball fans liked country music. With a large crowd now gathered, after the last pitch the Blue Grass Boys would make a pitch of their own, quickly setting up a microphone at home plate and playing a short set to preview what ticket buyers would enjoy at the evening's show.

(Monroe remained a devoted baseball fan. During the prosperous years of the 1940s, he ran two clubs:[57] the Blue Grass Boys Ball Club, which consisted of band members and ringer athletes and traveled on the road, and the Blue Grass All Stars, based in Nashville. Student baseballers from Vanderbilt University in Nashville who yearned to keep playing over the summer break would start coming to Bill's shows in the spring, asking to be hired for his teams.)

Admission to the show was sixty cents for adults, thirty cents for children. The band gave an hour-and-a-half performance. The concession stand would sell Cokes, peanuts, popcorn, and Grand Ole Opry souvenir song and picture books. Monroe sold his own popular songbook, which featured a cover picture of him and King Wilkie, his Tennessee walking horse.

Monroe learned early on that as the boss, he had to be tough enough to outwork or even outfight the top roustabout, otherwise the crew would dawdle.[58] He was tough enough.

The tour pulled in for one show badly behind schedule. Faced with the need for a quick setup, the show hired extra manpower in town. One local was driving tent stakes with a member of the tour, a big fellow in work clothes.

"Show sure is late getting here,"[59] the townie said, alternating sledgehammer strikes with the stranger.

"Yessir," the other man replied, powering his own hammer down.

"I wonder if Bill Monroe's gonna get here."

"Don't you worry," snapped the show worker. "He'll be here."

One can only imagine the man's astonishment when he took his seat that night, looked up at the stage, and realized that he had been driving stakes with Bill Monroe himself.

The bass fiddle would already be lying on the stage. Suddenly, the band would run out and the bass player would stomp on the instrument's metal stand pin. The bass would spring up into his hands and the band would tear into the first notes while the audience cheered. There would be fifteen or twenty minutes of music with the Blue Grass Boys, then a fifteen-minute interlude of comedy. Then the group would return with gospel quartets followed by more hot instrumentals. On some tours, Bill would ride up on King Wilkie and have the horse perform some tricks.[60]

There was always comedy on these shows, and much of it was still being done by white comedians in blackface. Monroe cheerfully employed such acts and occasionally used racially tinged humor in private conversation. (One of his favorite gibes at musicians who had grown beards or long hair was that they "used to look like a white boy.")[61] But Monroe was not a racist, as witness his relationship with DeFord Bailey.[62]

Bailey was a phenomenal harmonica player who had come to the Opry in 1925. For years, he was among the Opry's most popular stars, famed for his renditions of "The Pan American" (in which he imitated a rushing train) and "The Fox Chase" (in which he reproduced a hunting horn and baying hounds). Monroe hired Bailey as an attraction, and what followed speaks volumes about Bill's attitudes toward African-Americans in that day and age.

Having Bailey on tour might have caused dissent in the band: Who was going to sit next to this black man in the close confines of the limo for hours on end? But there was no problem, because Bill instructed DeFord to sit with him in the backseat. Meals and accommodations would have been problematic in the South in that era, but Monroe brought food out to Bailey (who loved "that old ham sandwich," an expensive treat at thirty-five cents when most other sandwiches cost a quarter).

After the shows, Monroe and other band members would have to find a hotel or rooming house that would accept a black man. Sometimes they were forced to walk around at three in the morning in the most unsavory neighborhoods until their quest was successful. In the dark, dressed in their riding pants and Stetsons, the Blue Grass Boys might have been mistaken for state troopers, but it was certainly the size and determined air of Bill Monroe that prevented any assaults.

Bailey was highly vulnerable in those strange towns, a diminutive man carrying large amounts of cash. So Monroe would make sure that DeFord had locked himself securely in his room. He wouldn't open the door until Monroe personally returned in the daylight to bring him out.

This went on day after day, mile after mile, night after night, whenever they toured, Bill Monroe functioning as traveling companion, caterer, and bodyguard to DeFord Bailey.

One of Bill's most popular comedians, in black- or whiteface, was discovered not on stage but on the diamond. David Akeman was playing on WLAP near Winchester, Kentucky, when Monroe hired him as a player for his barnstorming tent show baseball team.[63] Akeman was a good pitcher and a reliable hitter, and Monroe apparently wasn't even aware at first that he was a performer who played the banjo.

David Akeman had been born in Jackson County, Kentucky. Several greats of the old-time banjo came from there, including Buell Kaze, Lily May Ledford, and Marion Underwood. Akeman's father, a corn and tobacco farmer, also played the instrument. David was a natural entertainer who grew into a tall, skinny young man and adopted the comedy stage persona of "Stringbean."

Stringbean joined Bill full time in July 1942, first as a comedian, but soon as a banjo picker. Bill had enjoyed hearing the banjo in childhood: Uncle Pen's friends Cletis Smith and Clarence Wilson had played the instrument.[64] The Blue Grass Boys was now a fivesome.

The five-string banjo is the only widely played instrument to have been developed primarily in the United States.[65] It descended from three-string West African gourd instruments brought to America during the slave trade. It was known by various names including the "merrywang."

(How far might it have gotten if a stage full of minstrels announced they were going to play with their merrywangs in public?) But it was best known as the "bajar," "banjar," and finally, the "banjo."

As the banjo fully evolved in the nineteenth century, it gained four main strings and a high-tuned fifth string that ran about three-quarters of the length of the instrument's neck. This was primarily used as a drone string and characterized the five-string "regular banjo" favored by rural musicians. The five-string was usually played by strumming the main strings with the fingernails and sounding the fifth string with the thumb (a technique known as "clawhammer," from the shape the hand took, or "frailing"); alternatively, the strings were picked with the thumb and one or two fingers. (Tenor and plectrum banjos used in jazz and Dixieland had four strings and were strummed with a flat pick.)

The gourd had long since been replaced by a wood and metal drum with thin calfskin stretched across it and increasingly sophisticated systems of tone rings and resonators to improve sound quality and volume. Its bright sound and manageable dynamic range made it a great favorite for early recorded music. By the 1940s, though, the five-string banjo had largely become a prop for country comedians, having been displaced as a solo instrument by the fiddle. So for now Bill was only using, as he put it, "the touch of the banjo."[66] Soon, though, he was going to help make the five-string a star.

In 1942, a man arrived who would begin to truly define a distinctive bluegrass style of fiddling — a native of Tennessee named Howdy Forrester.

Howard Wilson Forrester was a nineteen-year-old playing in a San Antonio club on December 7, 1941, when word came of the Japanese attack on Pearl Harbor. Knowing that America would go immediately to war, Howard went to Nashville, where he had some family. But he was not drafted at once, and in early 1942, "Big Howdy" landed a job with Bill Monroe.

Tommy Magness and Art Wooten had been pioneers in the adaption of old-time fiddling to the demands of a new music where vocalization played an equal role with instrumental work. Now Forrester developed additional strategies for playing song melodies. His most common approach was to state the melody close to the way it was sung, but when the end of a line was reached — at the point where the singer would typically be holding a note or taking a breath to start a new line — he'd add a brief scale or arpeggio. This improvised string of notes would lead to the next major melody note.

Due to early wartime restrictions on recording, Howdy never got on disk with Monroe. But the *Opry* broadcasts were widely heard and Howdy Forrester became a highly influential fiddler.

Howdy's draft notice came in early 1943. Monroe promised Forrester his job back when he returned.[67] And as it turned out, Howdy's wife, Goldie Sue Wilene Russell Forrester, was an excellent musician who played piano, guitar, and violin. It is not clear they ever played at the same time in the Blue Grass Boys, but by the time Howdy joined the navy, Wilene — rechristened "Sally Ann" by Monroe — had joined the group, the first of only two women to do so officially. Surprisingly, she also played accordion. A reed instrument was a departure for Bill, but he thought of his mother's accordion playing and said yes.[68] Her vamping chords enlivened the band's already strutting rhythm, and she was an equally engaging vocalist.[69]

Mrs. Forrester also kept the band's books during tours. She'd frequently find herself carrying thousands of dollars in cash, as her son Robert Forrester reports:

> She would have two or three days of receipts built up. According to Mom, Bill didn't want to be bothered with business. He trusted Momma implicitly, and left it to her. He didn't look after business the way a Roy Acuff did. He was in the music business, but his emphasis was on the music.[70]

Of course, when Carolyn appeared there would be a lot of frantic business behind the scenes.

> As Mom told me, at the time Bill married Carolyn, he could have married Bessie. Carolyn's father was a preacher and Momma thought that perhaps Bill feared a preacher's wrath if he didn't marry her.

Bessie would be out on a show, and Carolyn would come around, and [Mom] would have to hide Bessie out. Bessie and Carolyn were at odds over Bill, but he also had other women on the side.

Bill was a very romantic person, but Momma also said that in all the years she worked with him, he never made an advance toward her. She said the same about all the guys in the band. They were always gentlemen and treated her with the utmost respect. They never used foul language around her. She said, "Bill always treated me just like I was his sister or a member of his family. He was always a perfect gentleman."[71]

Of the many paradoxes of the man who was Bill Monroe, this is perhaps the most intriguing. He seemed incapable of fidelity to Carolyn, to Bessie, to any woman. He chased skirts so incessantly that colleagues joked that Bill Monroe had just two things on his mind — and one of them was music. Yet Bill observed definite boundaries. He firmly believed that married women should be off-limits. His code of honor extended to his musicians' girlfriends, in stark contrast to many bandleaders who considered their sidemen's women fair game. Bill Monroe's gallant and respectful treatment of women already spoken for was a lifelong pattern.

On March 4, 1943, Bill and Carolyn paid $11,000 cash for a 44-acre farm on Dickerson Road.[72] There they lived, according to George D. Hay, in "a very comfortable American home, the kind one reads about but seldom sees."[73] Sometime that year, Bill made another investment, modest in capital and profound in return.

It was in October 1943, as best as can be determined,[74] that Bill was in Florida and, while wandering around after breakfast, happened to pass a barbershop and look in the window.

There, for sale, was a used mandolin. Monroe was looking for a second instrument, perhaps one to use for nonstandard tunings. He went in and played it.

The mandolin was a Gibson F-5 Master model, serial number 73987. A label glued inside the body, visible by peering through the lower sound hole, certified that this instrument had been tested and approved on July 9, 1923, by someone with the rather prosaic name of Lloyd Loar.[75]

Bill purchased it, case included, for about $150.[76] It was to become the most famous single instrument in country music history.

In the late nineteenth century, long after the mandolin had evolved in Europe from the lute, it enjoyed a new popularity in America.[77] Mandolin and guitar combinations became the perfect complement for courting couples or merry campus music making. Mandolin orchestras became popular. Foremost in the reinvention of the mandolin was Orville Gibson of Michigan, who, by 1898, had totally redesigned the instrument. Instead of a round-backed, Neapolitan-style instrument, Gibson's was larger and flat-backed, constructed more like a guitar for extra volume. Its body was highlighted by a hollow curled scroll that gave it some added acoustical properties as well as an Italianate appearance.

By 1921, as the Jazz Age dawned, the mandolin had been supplanted in popularity by the tenor banjo and the ukulele. The Gibson Guitar and Mandolin Company decided to boost mandolin sales by improving the instrument. A series of crucial refinements were made, most notably carving and tuning the tops in the manner of violins to improve tone and increase volume. The Gibson F-5 mandolins even had violin-style f-shaped sound holes.

Lloyd Loar was a concert master hired by Gibson in 1919, first as a demonstrator but later as an acoustic engineer. He worked with the engineering department on the development of the 5-series or "Master Model" instruments, including the L-5 guitar (which quickly became favored by jazz guitarists) and the F-5 mandolin.

During the four years Loar was supervising engineer at Gibson, 1921 through 1924, he approved and signed about 170 of the F-5 mandolins. (These instruments are now commonly referred to as "Lloyd Loars.") They were notable for their fine woods, beautiful craftsmanship, superior tone, brilliant balance of sound throughout their ranges, and increased volume. In the hands of a skilled player, they could project notes clearly to the back of large concert halls. (When Bill worked with Charlie and during the first years of the Blue Grass Boys, he played a Gibson F-7, a good but much less expensive instrument.)

In the 1920s, brand-new Gibson F-5s retailed for $250 plus $25 for a hardshell, plush-lined case. The peg head of each was topped with the company's name inlaid in flowing mother-of-pearl script: not simply Gibson, but "The Gibson." But the F-5 was a commercial failure when first introduced. Musical tastes had changed dramatically. "It was like inventing the ultimate buggy whip after the invention of the automobile," says Nashville-based instrument expert George Gruhn. "Nobody cared."

It took a new use for the Gibson mandolin to reemerge. It was a long way from a classical musician performing a Vivaldi mandolin concerto to a country performer like Bill Monroe picking a hot breakdown on the stage of the Grand Ole Opry. But the Gibson mandolins were ideally suited for their new niche. In these days of rudimentary sound systems, a Lloyd Loar Gibson F-5 could be counted on to cut through an ensemble of fiddle, banjo, guitar, bass, and even accordion, and be heard.

This is a marvelous irony in American music history: None of the instruments that came to be used so effectively by bluegrass musicians — the fiddles built on the design of Stradivarius violins, the Gibson Master Model F-5 mandolins, the large-bodied Martin D-28 "dreadnought" guitars, the Gibson Mastertone RB-series banjos, the "three-quarter" bass fiddles — were ever designed to be played by country or folk performers. All were developed for classical or professional artists in orchestral or other concert hall situations. The instruments originally marketed to "hillbilly" or folk players, who had little money and usually entertained in intimate settings, were cheap products, often sold via mail-order catalogs. Only when the superior instruments temporarily fell out of fashion did they turn up where country people could find and afford them: in used instrument stores, pawnshops, newspaper ads — even in barbershop windows.

Bill treasured the way each note would sound "separate" on his Lloyd Loar F-5, ringing on its own. For a musician who valued the integrity of melodies and the shaping of each note, this was a fabulous quality. He would come to own others, but the July 9, 1923, Gibson Master Model F-5 serial number 73987 would forever be The Mandolin to Monroe and his fans, as inseparable from the man and his myth as Jim Bowie and his knife.

Indeed, this object was part reliable weapon, part work of art. Monroe carried it with masculine confidence, as if it were a meticulously crafted and perfectly balanced Remington 12-gauge shotgun or Colt .45 revolver. He unconsciously described it in such terms:

> If you're really in a tight spot, you've got a powerful crowd or a big auditorium, that mandolin will always come through for you. It's got plenty of volume and it carries good and if you want to soften up, it's got a beautiful tone. So it's just perfect for what we use it for.[78]

Bill's Lloyd Loar played a profound role in his music because it directly influenced his way of playing. Its quick response made him begin to play snappier arpeggios and cascade-quick triplets. Its ringing qualities caused him to use more individual notes in punctuated syncopations. Monroe commented again and again that in composing a new tune, one note he played on his mandolin would suggest or lead into another note. All the F-5s signed by Lloyd Loar in this period are wonderful instruments, but this instrument had exceptional tone and sustain, a sound that was clean yet woody, sharp yet resonant, seemingly with a halo around each vibration.

On February 13, 1945, Bill raised his F-5 to a recording microphone in a studio in Chicago's Wrigley Building[79] and hit the first jaunty notes of his introduction to "Rocky Road Blues," a jazzed-up twelve-bar blues. He not only had a new mandolin and a new band, he had a new label — Columbia Records. Charlie was still on Victor, and Bill decided to differentiate himself from the other half of the Monroe Brothers act once and for all.[80]

At the time, Art Satherley was Columbia's A&R man ("artist and repertoire," reflecting the twin responsibilities of talent handling and overall producing). Satherley was a self-assured, impeccably mannered British gentleman,[81] and many of his country artists were in awe of him. But in the studio his blend of perfectionism and politeness allowed him to get excellent performances out of his charges, and Bill was no exception.

It was the first session for Chubby Wise, Howdy Forrester's replacement. Wise, a Florida fiddle whiz who had popularized "Orange Blossom

James Buchanan Monroe, Bill's father *(Country Music Foundation)*

Malissa Vandiver Monroe by the new farmhouse with two grandchildren and, behind her, Bertha and Bill, circa 1920 *(Country Music Foundation)*

Pendleton Vandiver, Bill's beloved "Uncle Pen" *(courtesy Sara McNulty Crowder and* Bluegrass Unlimited*)*

Arnold Shultz, left, with Rosine resident Clarence Wilson *(courtesy John Edwards Memorial Foundation)*

Show poster of the Monroe Brothers with comedians Gladys and Rusty Scott. Bill's treatment of real African Americans was much different *(Bluegrass Unlimited)*

Carolyn, Bill, and Melissa, late 1936 or early 1937 (Bluegrass Star, *courtesy* Bluegrass Unlimited)

The original Blue Grass Boys, 1939: Art Wooten, Bill Monroe, Cleo Davis, and Amos Garen (Bluegrass Unlimited)

Tent show music and baseball barnstormers Howard Watts, Chubby Wise, Dave "Stringbean" Akeman, Clyde Moody, and Bill Monroe *(Bluegrass Unlimited)*

Bill with Chubby Wise, Lester Flatt, Earl Scruggs, and Birch Monroe in the band's speedy, high-profile stretch limo, circa 1947 *(Bluegrass Unlimited)*

First despised imitators, later Bill's treasured friends: Ralph and Carter, the Stanley Brothers *(Bluegrass Unlimited)*

Monroe and Jimmy Martin bring their "high lonesome" sound to a quartet at the Ryman Auditorium with Charlie Cline and Jim Smoak (hidden) plus Buddy Killen and son Slocum *(Grannis Photo)*

The handsome, confident country music star: studio portrait, circa 1951 *(courtesy Douglas B. Green)*

In traction after his near-fatal wreck, Bill receives benefit concert money from Carl Smith, Eddie Hill, Opry director Jim Denny and stage manager Vito Pellettieri, Roy Acuff, and Ernest Tubb *(Country Music Foundation)*

Former sidemen, now
polished showmen: Lester
Flatt and Earl Scruggs, late
1950s *(Les Leverett/WSM0)*

The spark and sparkle that kept them together: Bill Monroe and Bessie Lee Mauldin
(courtesy Bill Price)

Special," built on Forrester's work and brought his own genius to the Blue Grass Boys. He could be soulful and spirited, yet his bowing was smooth, his tone sweet. He could really hang on to a note and make it sing. Indeed, he was like a singer with his fiddle.

The band's beat was slightly different now, still crisp but with more of a bounce than a surge. The Blue Grass Boys of this period sounded closer to a western swing outfit than a square dance band, in part due to Sally Ann Forrester's rhythm vamps on the accordion. Another factor was the lack of bite in the banjo picking of Stringbean, whose greater strengths lay in his comedy. But the sound perfectly suited the material, which included "Kentucky Waltz," a wistfully sentimental vocal credited to Monroe as composer, as well as the strutting "Rocky Road Blues."[82]

Bill sang with rousing defiance about how the road wouldn't be rocky for long even though another man had taken his woman and gone. And that — the unthinkable — was precisely what had happened.

Bessie Lee Mauldin had left him for another man. Their relationship would cause Bill Monroe to write some of the most searing, agonized, and wonderful music of his life.

Nelson Campbell Gann was born in Lebanon, Tennessee, in Wilson County, east of Nashville, on September 22, 1921.[83] Although Gann was ten years younger than Monroe, the similarities in the backgrounds of these rivals are amazing.

Both came from farming families. Arthur W. Gann, Nelson's father, was a cattle dealer. Like Bill, Nelson was a youngest child, having three older sisters and a brother. The year before Nelson's birth, the 1920 census also found that living at the Gann farm were two boarders and (shades of Uncle Pen) Arthur's brother-in-law.

Astrology devotees will no doubt notice that both men were Virgos. But of truer developmental significance is that both were born to middle-aged parents (Arthur and his wife Sula Jones Gann were forty-three at Nelson's birth) and that both lost parents while young (Sula dying in 1925, when Nelson was four; her headstone records that she was the widow of A. W. Gann, indicating that Nelson lost his father even before his mother).

Who raised Nelson is unknown. His oldest sister was only about twenty at the time of their mother's death. But it appears that when he turned eighteen, he left Lebanon and headed for Nashville, much as Bill had left Rosine and moved to greater Chicago. Nelson did not find work in a factory or refinery, however; he appears to be the same Nelson Gann listed in the 1940 city directory as working as a clerk at Foxall Moon Drug Company, a pharmacy with three Nashville locations.

Also unknown is how Nelson and Bessie Lee met.[84] But if Bessie was already experiencing the illnesses (including heart problems and diabetes) that would plague her later in life, she might have been a customer at the drugstore where Gann was employed.

Nelson Gann was handsome and dashing, every inch a man.[85] During World War II, he served in the navy as a petty officer and by 1943 or 1944 was stationed in Piedmont, California.[86] Bessie Lee soon joined him on the West Coast, because by now they were married. She must have known that Bill was not about to leave his wife and children, and she must have also known that he had other women. She had every reason to take up with Gann.

Bill, of course, had a personal rule about not fooling around with married women. But in this case, the rule had its exception. Bill Monroe believed — deeply, fiercely — that Bessie Lee Mauldin was his. And always would be.

Betrayal. A love that has proven untrue. A man left blue and alone.

Bill was on tour, driving back up from Florida, when he saw a particularly large full moon over the highway.[87] It reminded him of the moons he had seen in Kentucky, and he wanted to write about it. The best poetic device, he decided, was to bring a girl into the song. It will never be known if Bill was thinking about Bessie or any actual woman, but thus was born his most famous composition, "Blue Moon of Kentucky." This wistful waltz, its lyrics full of sad resignation as the singer calls on the moon to shine upon his false lover, would of course have a second rising thanks to the young Elvis Presley's first commercial recording.

The song's metaphor was perfect, more so than Bill realized. When two full moons appear within the same month, the second is called a "blue moon." This infrequent event gave rise to the expression "once in a blue moon." Of course, the second moon does not actually have a bluish tinge. "Blue" probably comes from the Old English word "belewe" meaning "to betray," reflecting the ancient belief that rare astronomical events are inauspicious.[88] Monroe knew nothing of this, making his choice of a blue moon for a song about betrayal even more striking.

Fiddler Jimmy Shumate had been playing over WHKY in Hickory, North Carolina, on a noontime show with Dan Walker & the Blue Ridge Boys. One day in late 1944, the phone rang at his family's farm. It was Bill Monroe. Howdy Forrester was still in the navy and Chubby Wise had temporarily left the Blue Grass Boys.

"Your style would fit mine," Monroe said.[89] "I'd like you to come play on the Grand Ole Opry." Shumate accepted with alacrity, but then wondered: How in the world did Monroe know about me?

Numerous musicians, flattered but curious, would ask themselves the same question in the years ahead. Shumate learned this: During Monroe's hundreds of days of touring each year, the radio in the Blue Grass Special was often kept playing. While his sidemen simply enjoyed the diverting music being broadcast live from stations across the South, Monroe was in the backseat, listening attentively and discerningly, quietly filing away in his mind pickers, fiddlers, and singers, their names and locations, their styles, strengths, and weaknesses. When he needed a new band member, he would simply call a station, introduce himself, and get the appropriate musician's home phone number.

It was all so consistent with Monroe's life: A lover of baseball, he was like a coach or a talent scout who keeps a depth chart of players to fill positions on the team. A lover of women, his list of sidemen was probably more extensive than any black book he may have kept of girlfriends. Both of course served a similar purpose for the man who had known bitter childhood loneliness: If someone left him, he wouldn't have to suffer the loss for long. A replacement was just a phone call away.

Shumate the rookie was eager to be a team player. Late one night, the touring limo had a flat. Jimmy immediately got out the spare tire and began rolling it over to be put on. There had been some tree cutting along that stretch of road, and in the dark Shumate ran into a log by the side of the road.

Or so he thought.

Shumate was struggling, pushing and ramming to get the tire over the tree, when suddenly the object spoke to him: "Jimmy, is that you rolling that wheel over me?"

It was Bill. He had been lying on the ground taking the lug nuts off. So hard and muscular was Monroe's torso that Shumate had mistaken it for wood.

"Bill, why didn't you tell me it was you?" he exclaimed.

Monroe chuckled in the dark. "I knew you was going to do it, I just wanted to see you do it."[90]

There was once a boy from Tennessee who tried to play the fiddle but only produced squawks.[91] He turned to the banjo, but one of his older sisters played the five-string almost effortlessly, and he got mad that she could master it and he couldn't. So he took up the guitar. Like Bill Monroe, Lester Flatt had selected the instrument of his destiny by default.

Lester Raymond Flatt was born June 19, 1914, in Overton County, the seventh of the nine children of Isaac and Nancy Flatt. His father worked at various times as a sharecropper, logger, and sawmill hand.

Lester worked for a time in a sawmill. At age seventeen, he married sixteen-year-old Gladys Stacey of Sparta. They later worked at various textile mills in Tennessee and Virginia.

Lester kept up his hobbyist singing and guitar strumming, showing professional promise. In 1939, he made his radio debut as a member of Charlie Scott's Harmonizers on WDBJ in Roanoke, Virginia. He eventually came to the attention of Charlie Monroe, and in 1943 Lester and Gladys (also a singer-guitarist) accepted an offer to join the Kentucky Pardners. Gladys used the stage name "Bobbie Jean," joining a second woman in the band, banjo-playing Helen "Katy Hill" Osborne.

But by 1944, Lester had tired of the grueling life of a Charlie Monroe sideman, which often meant playing three or four shows a day for a flat per-day rate. He and Gladys left the act. Flatt bought a truck and went into the hauling business. But that too wore thin. Lester soon returned to music and in March 1945 was offered a radio show in Raleigh, North Carolina.

Gladys was packing to join her husband when a telegram arrived. Bill Monroe had heard that Lester was at liberty and wanted him to head straight for Nashville and start with the Blue Grass Boys on the band's next Saturday night Opry appearance. Gladys knew that Bill still had Sally Ann Forrester in the act and, unlike Charlie, wouldn't use a second girl musician. But she telephoned Lester immediately. He went straight to Nashville.

Flatt's duties as a Blue Grass Boy included acting as master of ceremonies. Bill's style in those days was to have the singer-guitarist come out with the band, do a few numbers to open the show. (Bill's avoidance of emcee work was a measure of his lingering shyness. The jovial Charlie, by contrast, always opened his own shows.)

The deal soon involved songwriting. Bill had yet to hit his stride as a composer, but Lester was writing successfully and eager to find an outlet for his material. Flatt had been unable to land a recording contract on his own, and he knew that writing for Bill was a golden opportunity. They came to an agreement: Bill would share half the songwriting credits and rights for any original material of Lester's that they recorded together. Flatt welcomed the deal,[92] and under this arrangement he composed "Will You Be Loving Another Man" (inspired by the theme of separation during World War II),[93] "Little Cabin Home on the Hill," and other Monroe classics.

Flatt served as a further bridge to Monroe's own songwriting. One day, Bill struck up a conversation with a black man (by varying accounts a shoeshiner or a newspaper seller).[94] Asked how he was doing, the man replied sadly, "Oh, it's mighty dark to travel." Knowing there was a song there, Monroe told Flatt about his encounter, providing the idea and title — "Mighty Dark to Travel" — for one of their best numbers. In the years ahead, even as Monroe gained enough confidence in his own writing to dispense with songwriting arrangements like this, he would still toss out a song idea to his sidemen. The most creative would toss it back, spun with more ideas, in a game of musical catch.

*   *   *

Lester Flatt enjoyed his job with the Blue Grass Boys. His duets with Bill were blending better and better, and he was now a featured vocalist on the nationally famous *Grand Ole Opry*. Still, Lester was frustrated. And it was all about the banjo.

As much as he liked Dave Akeman personally, Stringbean was not a fast picker. He was dragging down the group's rhythm on the uptempo numbers. Flatt was an extraordinary fluid rhythm guitarist, scrupulous about timing. Stringbean was a lively, crowd-pleasing frailer as a comedian, but when he played within the ensemble he picked with his thumb and forefinger and barely kept up. Lester Flatt was growing quite weary of the banjo.[95]

But better banjo playing — swift, sure, and so very exciting — was available.

One night in 1943, Monroe had gotten into a jam session at a Spartanburg, South Carolina, hotel with a five-string banjo picker. Unlike Stringbean, this fellow played with his thumb, forefinger, and middle finger in a musical maelstrom, a syncopated whirl of percussive notes. Bill had never heard anything like it.

Although born right there in Spartanburg in 1926, Don Reno was the child of parents residing in North Carolina, a state in which surprisingly sophisticated three-finger banjo picking styles had evolved.[96] Don started playing the banjo at age five, heavily influenced by DeWitt "Snuffy" Jenkins, a North Carolinian with a well-developed three-finger roll. By age twelve, Reno had played his first professional gig.

After the jam session, Monroe offered Reno a job. It seemed that history was about to be made. The driving syncopations of North Carolina–style banjo picking were about to be melded with Monroe's surging rhythms, advanced fiddling, and stirring tenor singing. But greater historical forces intervened. World War II was still being fought, and Reno was inducted into the army.

In late 1945, Stringbean decided to start a duo act with musician-comedian-dancer Lew Childre. Bill wanted to keep the five-string in his band, but Reno was still in the service.

"We need another banjo player," Bill told Jimmy Shumate. "Do you know anyone?"

Shumate did indeed. An exceptional young musician had come to Nashville with Lost John Miller of Knoxville. Miller's group had tried unsuccessfully to get on the Opry and was now disbanding. In fact, Jimmy had already been urging the young man to audition for Monroe.

"Yes, I know a banjo picker from North Carolina, a good boy," Shumate replied. "He don't play like String, but he picks a whole lot of banjo."

Monroe asked Jimmy to contact this fellow. And what was his name?

The young man's name, Shumate said, was Earl Scruggs.[97]

CHAPTER 4

BLUEGRASS

(1945 TO 1953)

When you want genuine music — music that will come right home
to you like a bad quarter, suffuse your system like strychnine whiskey,
go right through you like Brandreth's pills, ramify your whole constitution like the measles, and break out on your hide like the pinfeather
pimples on a picked goose — when you want all this, just smash your
piano, and invoke the glory-beaming banjo! — Mark Twain, "Enthusiastic Eloquence," in the *San Francisco Dramatic Chronicle*, June 23,
1865

When Lester Flatt heard that a new banjo player was being
auditioned, he grimaced. The group had been banjoless for
about two months, and Lester was happy not being shackled to a clunky
five-string.

"As far as I'm concerned," Flatt told Monroe, "this Scruggs fellow can
leave his banjo in its case."[1]

Given what Flatt and Scruggs would one day accomplish together, it
was as if Rodgers had not wanted to meet Hammerstein, Bogart and
Bacall had decided they just didn't have any chemistry, or Lennon had
taken an immediate dislike to McCartney.

Monroe, Shumate, and Howdy Forrester (back from the navy and
about to resume his old job with the Blue Grass Boys) got together with
Scruggs at the Tulane Hotel.[2] He proved to be a phenomenal exponent of

the athletic North Carolina style of syncopated three-finger banjo pick-ing. Monroe was impressed. Once Flatt heard Scruggs, he too realized the possibilities. Lester told Bill, "Hire him no matter what it costs."[3]

And what did it cost? Monroe told Scruggs the salary was "sixty dollars a week and ten dollars extra if you work Sunday." Lost John Miller had only been paying $50 a week.[4] Earl signed on.

But the Blue Grass Boys had to pay for their own room and board. So they ate in cheap restaurants and doubled up on hotel beds.[5] Not that they often had time to even sleep in beds: Earl Scruggs, the farmboy from Flint Hill, North Carolina, plunged into the life of a professional musi-cian, a life much different from that of his raising.

Born January 6, 1924, Earl Eugene Scruggs was one of six children in a musical family.[6] His mother read shape notes and played pump organ in church. His father played the banjo in both the frailing and two-finger styles. There was a guitar, fiddle, banjo, and dulcimer in the house and (with exception of a stepsister) everyone learned to play a little on each one. The tunes played around the Scruggs home would one day become five-string standards, thanks to Earl: "Cumberland Gap," "Cripple Creek," "Sally Goodin'," and "Sally Ann." (The last two were his uncle Sid Ruppe's favorites; if you played one, Uncle Sid would always say, "Now play her sister!") Earl had fun with music, but it also became a very per-sonal, even sacred thing for him.

His childhood was happy but by no means idyllic. When Earl was four, his father died, and he came to awareness of the world just as the Great Depression hit in full force. He was discouraged to find how farm chores hurt his music. His hands got tired, sore, and callused, and in the evenings it always took a while to get them adjusted to playing an instrument.

Interestingly, just as Bill had taken up the mandolin about the time his mother died, Earl started picking the banjo near the time of his father's death (literally resting its heavy drum on the floor next to him and prop-ping up the neck). And just as Birch, Charlie, and Bill Monroe had been hired to play by Rosine neighbors, some of Earl's older brothers got seri-ous enough to stage local shows, distributing handbills and collecting a quarter admission at the door. Nearly the entire family had the talent to go professional, but didn't know how to go about it. Anyway, they were too poor to scrape together the stake money they would need. So music remained a parlor affair, diverting and bonding the Scruggs clan.

This part of North Carolina was an anomaly. In most parts of the South, the fiddle was the rule and the banjo the exception among local musicians. Here it was the opposite: The banjo was king. One day, Earl was trying to work out "Lonesome Reuben" (also known as "Reuben's Train") using a three-finger picking approach. What happened next was worthy of a sentimental Hollywood musical biography: Earl's fingers magically fell into sequence. They rolled and rolled, beautifully. He had it.

Earl was a true prodigy. Like many prodigies, he started getting flashy and a bit rococo. Then a simple criticism from his mother put him onto a higher path. "I can't hear the melody," Mrs. Scruggs said one day.[7] "I want to be able to hear the melody."

And so Earl concentrated on getting it out, usually hitting the melody notes with his strong thumb to emphasize them. The wonder, indeed the miracle, of "Scruggs-style" banjo picking is that amidst a shower of sound — usually two or three accompanying notes for every melody note — the main theme clearly registers on the listener's ear, like the raised image on a beautifully cast silver box still stands out to the eye even if rain pours upon it.

Earl's mastery and reputation grew. He won a banjo contest sponsored by the local chapter of Future Farmers of America. The tiny trophy looked huge to him. A basically shy person, he learned to concentrate on his playing as a way of blocking out self-consciousness and stage fright.

Earl began to play on a professional level. He joined various bands on radio shows in the Carolinas. But Scruggs was as straight as he was shy. The rowdy side of the entertainment business frightened him, especially the heavy alcohol use of many musicians. For a time, this held him back from delving into music as a career. He got a cotton mill job and during World War II received a dependency deferment to support his widowed mother.

After the war, he had asked his mother's blessing to try music again. Bill Monroe was a major Opry star with lots of work, paying well for the times. And Bill was a sober man who expected the same of his employees. That was just fine with Earl.

For Earl's first night on the Opry, Monroe picked out a fast number that would show off the newcomer's dazzling style — "White House Blues," an old song recounting the 1901 William McKinley assassination.[8] It was a perfect selection. Scruggs stepped up to the microphone with apprehension, knowing that nothing like this had been heard to date on the Opry or even over WSM radio.

Used to the banjo as a country comedian's prop, or hearing it picked or strummed in one of the quaint old styles, the audience was totally unprepared for the speedy, leaping avalanche of notes that issued from the five-string in the hands of this twenty-one-year-old from North Carolina.

They went wild.

Transcriptions of Opry broadcasts circa 1946 show that Scruggs's playing was at first quite rudimentary compared to what it would soon become. Additionally, although the Gibson banjo Scruggs played was a fine instrument, its sound was often primitive: In these days before plastic banjo drum heads, calfskin was vulnerable to stretching and sagging in heat and humidity, particularly in the uncooled Ryman. Sometimes his banjo sounded more clunky than bright.

Yet Earl Scruggs electrified audiences. Monroe fully showcased his new find. On some numbers, Bill sang, but he had Earl take all the instrumental breaks. Monroe and Opry host George D. Hay both knew they had a huge new attraction. Hay would announce, "Here's Bill and Earl Scruggs and that fancy banjo."[9]

Listeners would physically come out of their seats in excitement. "Oh, that's got 'em," Hay would exclaim, the Solemn Old Judge losing all semblance of solemnity. "That has got 'em!"[10]

Years later, during an interview for the Country Music Foundation's oral history project, Earl Scruggs told Douglas B. Green:

Well, they hadn't heard [anything] like me, for instance . . . So it wasn't overexposed to say the least, the whole sound was new. When I first started, the dressing room would pack up with people who'd come and listen to Bill practice, because they'd never heard, you know, the banjo, this style banjo. . . . This band, the musicians themselves, was altogether a new sound. . . .

Uncle Dave Macon, who had mastered some nineteen different old-time banjo picking styles, was outright jealous of the newcomer, whom he insisted on calling "Ernest" instead of Earl. "Ernest sounds pretty good in the band, but I bet he can't sing a lick," Macon scoffed.[11] Actually, Scruggs could sing, providing a pleasant baritone and occasional bass to the gospel quartets. Macon then fell back onto the pseudoprincipled position that banjo players should be able to do comedy. "Ernest is pretty good on that banjo, but he ain't a damn bit funny," he gibed.[12]

Macon was wrong there, too. Onstage, Earl was straitlaced, allowing himself only an occasional modest smile as audiences thundered their approval of his playing. But offstage, he revealed a wicked if deadpan sense of humor that Lester Flatt relished. He began to take to Earl as a person and enjoyed touring with him. A friendship grew between the two sidemen.

Scruggs learned professionalism from Bill Monroe.[13] Sometimes Earl didn't feel up to picking and hated to perform when he knew he was less than his best. But he quickly grasped his obligations to the audience, learning how to find energy onstage even when he was exhausted, how to act fresh even when he was wilting.

The band was so busy that it would literally leave the Ryman immediately after the Saturday night Opry, drive straight to their next gig, play it, get back in their 1941 Chevy stretch limo, sleep in the car en route to the next job, play it, get back in the limo. . . .

Space was scarce even in the monster Chevy, so the musicians packed paper bags instead of suitcases and wore their hats in the car to keep them from getting crushed. On occasion, the band would stop at a one-hour dry cleaning service, hand their suits out of a changing room, then sit in their underwear until the clothes were ready.[14]

Around March 1946, the Forresters returned to Texas as had long been their plan. Chubby Wise came back to fiddle with Monroe. The bass player now was Howard Watts,[15] a.k.a. "Cedric Rainwater," a musician-comedian who had worked with Wise in Florida. On September 16 and 17, 1946, Monroe finally got his band into Columbia's Chicago studio. By then, Scruggs — indeed, the entire ensemble — had improved exponentially. It would be, in retrospect, an all-star lineup playing on some of the most innovative and important recordings of Bill Monroe's career.

The back-to-back sessions produced classic after classic. Monroe's songwriting arrangement with Lester Flatt proved to have been a highly beneficial deal for both men: Lester's country crooning — enhanced in the choruses by Bill's beautifully blended tenor harmonies — absolutely shone on "Why Did You Wander?," "Toy Heart," "Mansions for Me," "Will You Be Loving Another Man?," and others for which Monroe purchased or shared composer credit. The Blue Grass Boys gospel quartet was stronger than ever, with Flatt and Monroe joined by Earl (baritone) and Birch Monroe (bass) on "Wicked Path of Sin," the first gospel number that Bill had ever written.[16] (Birch would later play bass with Bill on tour after Watts departed the band.)

The superb singing was matched by the pulse-quickening picking. Monroe always played his best when challenged, and now he was positively surrounded by outstanding instrumentalists. Chubby Wise was firmly establishing the bluegrass style of fiddling. Chubby took his cues from the vocals, producing music that was incisive yet not harsh, powerful yet tender.[17] Scruggs's banjo was dynamic, perfectly complementing every other instrument while making its own insistent statements. Monroe's mandolin could sweetly plaudit or sassily strut, his playing a masterful mixture of tight tremolos, rapid runs, leaping and punctuated single notes, and tight, astonishing triplets.

But topping it all was the voice of Bill Monroe: as high as a woman's but totally masculine, as sharp as a razor but as friendly as a handshake, as crystalline as an icicle but as warm as beaming sunshine. This voice was not hampered by the primitive radio or record players of the day. From the WSM signal or the grooves of a Columbia 78, this voice emerged to thrill.

A distinctive style of American music was coalescing and its esthetic was being formalized. At these and later recording sessions, the great bluegrass-style solos on the fiddle, mandolin, and banjo were exhibiting a brilliant melding of lively improvisation within a structured symmetry.

Things that a musician played in the first half of a solo generally set up things played during the second half. First, the melody was clearly stated. (Here was made manifest the loyalty to melody instilled in Bill by Uncle Pen and in Earl by his mother.) Then — during what would be, if sung, long notes held at the ends of lyrics — a scale was improvised leading up to the beginning of the next melody passage. Soloists might throw in a final improvisational flourish, but they invariably ended squarely on the root note of the tonic chord.

All the great bluegrass soloists — Monroe, Shumate, Forrester, Wise, Scruggs, Reno, and those who followed them — figured out this approach as the most pleasing way to structure their flights of fancy. Even if they could not always articulate it, they recognized the concept of symmetry. Monroe once complimented a young fiddler by saying: "You play it right because you make it go in a circle."[18]

A year later, on October 27 and 28, 1947,[19] more classics were added to the repertoire of what was becoming a truly classical style of country music. The Flatt-Monroe team got on acetate "I'm Going Back to Old Kentucky," "Little Cabin Home on the Hill," and "It's Mighty Dark to Travel." The quartet (this time with Watts singing bass) recorded such spirited and spiritually uplifting originals as "Remember the Cross" (co-credited to Watts) and "Little Community Church."

Still powerfully showcasing the banjo, Monroe turned Earl loose on "Molly and Tenbrooks." The song, which Bill first heard as a boy, celebrated a famous 1878 race in Louisville between Kentucky Thorough-bred Ten Broeck and California mare Mollie McCarthy in which the local favorite bested the swift competitor.[20] Although the song was always played speedily, Monroe urged his banjo pickers never to rush it: He instructed them to visualize the smooth back-and-forth head/neck movement of a Thoroughbred at full gallop as their guide to the proper tempo.[21]

However, Bill Monroe had only placed when it came to releasing "Molly and Tenbrooks." The Stanley Brothers got it out first.

And Bill was furious.

*   *   *

The Stanleys were from Dickenson County, Virginia, in the Clinch Mountains, the sons of a farmer and mobile saw mill operator.[22] Their mother played traditional mountain music on the banjo. Carter, the elder son, became a guitarist and a singer-songwriter of style and conviction. Ralph developed a strong and flavorful banjo technique.

Turning professional at the end of 1946, they collaborated with mandolinist-vocalist Pee Wee Lambert, a Monroe devotee to the stylistic point of being a Bill clone. The Stanley Brothers & the Clinch Mountain Boys were soon hired to perform on the popular *Farm and Fun Time* show at WCYB in Bristol, Tennessee, heard over a five-state area in prime time — the noon hour when farm families and hired hands came in for their midday meals.

Revering Monroe, the Stanleys began performing songs they heard him play on the Opry. It almost got to the point where, if Monroe played a new song on WSM on Saturday night, the Stanleys and Lambert were performing it on WCYB by Monday afternoon.[23] To them, imitation was the sincerest form of flattery. To Monroe, it was the baldest kind of theft.

In fairness to the Stanleys, they had no idea that Monroe had not yet released "Molly and Tenbrooks."[24] And their version for Rich-R-Tone Records, an independent label based in nearby Johnson City, Tennessee, became one of the most important in bluegrass history. It wasn't necessarily better than the one Monroe recorded, but it proved that Bill's music had gone beyond being the sound of just one band. It was now a true, recognizable genre.

If Bill had hit the Opry just at the right time in the show's history (not to mention two weeks before Charlie's planned audition), his lucky timing continued. World War II was over. Service people were returning, the economy was ready to boom, life was getting back to normal — and people were starved for entertainment. Southerners were delighted to hear lively country music, and that's exactly what Bill Monroe provided.

More than that, country music continued to reinforce the cultural identities of southerners who had left their homes, to find work during the depression or because of military service and defense industry employment during the war. Between 1920 and 1950, the number of

Americans living on farms experienced a net decline of 22.9 million.[25] During the war years, the loss was more than a million persons annually. When the Blue Sky Boys sang "Are You from Dixie?" about a southerner's delight in encountering a kindred soul in a faraway place, hundreds of thousands nodded their heads knowingly while tapping their feet.

But Monroe's music was more than a nostalgia trip. It was familiar but it was novel. It was comfortable yet exciting. Bill Monroe the showman was constantly refining his presentation, retaining ideas with audience appeal. One delectable gimmick was to go for a high falsetto note at the end of "Blue Yodel No. 3" and apparently fail, his voice cracking.[26] He would vamp time until the laughter subsided — then go for an even higher note and absolutely nail it.

In Monroe's audiences in those days were future stars of country music, then mere youths, people like Johnny Cash and Porter Wagoner.[27] Charley Pride, a black youngster with a fervent love of country music, stood outside Monroe's tent show near Sledge, Mississippi, peering in past the all-white audience and listening happily.[28] Down in Littlefield, Texas, Waylon Jennings, a future star of "outlaw"-style country music, spent happy Saturday nights listening with his father to *The Grand Ole Opry* and his dad's favorite singer, Bill Monroe.[29]

Even a future rock star was enthralled. Levon Helm would one day be a mainstay of The Band, the rock-country-folk fusion group that backed Bob Dylan in the late 1960s and had such top-40 hits as "The Night They Drove Old Dixie Down." He was a six-year-old West Virginia farm kid in the summer of 1946 when he attended his first live music show with his family — Bill Monroe & His Blue Grass Boys.

As Helm recalled in his autobiography *This Wheel's on Fire*, it changed his life.

Boy, *this really tattooed my brain.* I've never forgotten it: Bill had a real good five piece band. They took that old hillbilly music, sped it up, and basically invented what is now known as bluegrass music: the bass in its place, the mandolin above it, the guitar tying the two together, and the violin on top, playing the long notes to make it sing. The banjo backed everything up, answering everybody. . . . That was the end of cowboys and Indians for me. When I got home I held the broom sideward and strutted past the barn, around the pump, and out to the watermelon patch, pretending to play the guitar. I was hooked.[30]

One night in Boone, North Carolina, during this period, Bill was lying in the limo while the rest of the band was in the tent, desperately trying to cobble a show together.[31]

A local musician in his early twenties was led to the vehicle by a friend and musical partner named "Frog" Greene. Led, because he was blind. He and Bill shook hands.

"Bill, they tell me you're feeling pretty bad, my friend," said the young man.

"I'm pretty sick," Monroe admitted. "I think I got hold of some bad sausage."

The two locals made their way to the back of the tent and found Lester Flatt. "Lester, could me and my buddy here play a tune on the show?" the blind boy asked. "Seems like you're shorthanded a little bit."

Flatt was delighted. If these guys worked out, there might be enough entertainment to fill the program, and of course the crowd would take kindly to seeing some of their own on stage. The two were loaned guitars, passed a quick audition, and ended up performing some Eddy Arnold songs.

The blind singer's name was Arthel Watson. He was born in 1923, in the Deep Gap section of Stony Fork Township, North Carolina. An eye infection in infancy had cost him his vision except for the very dimmest of light sensitivity. He loved electronics and had shown a surprising aptitude for hooking up wires and using tools. But his only real chance to earn money was to pursue his love of music, and this he had done.

When a radio show announcer had feared he'd have trouble pronouncing Arthel, someone suggested, "Call him Doc," perhaps thinking of Sherlock Holmes's friend Dr. Watson. The name stuck. He was now known as Doc Watson. Bill, Lester, and Earl had not heard the last of him.

By 1947, Bill Monroe had become one of *The Grand Ole Opry*'s biggest stars and in those days — given the huge listenership for the program — an *Opry* star was almost like a movie star. Only Eddy Arnold, the Bailes

Brothers, and Ernest Tubb excelled him in popularity.[32] (Roy Acuff had temporarily gone off to Hollywood to make films.) In 1946, Bill's recordings of "Kentucky Waltz" and "Footprints in the Snow" became major hits, respectively reaching numbers 3 and 5 on the *Billboard* "Most Played Juke Box Folk Records" charts.[33]

Yet at the time Monroe's recordings were not the greatest source of his fame. In fact, Columbia only put out ten sides of the classic 1946–1948 band while it was actually still together, releasing the rest slowly through September 1949.[34] Bill Monroe was a star because of his in-person appearances and the weekly broadcasts of the widely heard *Grand Ole Opry*.

So hectic did Bill's touring schedule become that he and Carolyn needed help maintaining their forty-four-acre Nashville farm. Bill brought brother Speed and his family down from Kentucky. Bill had developed a good relationship with Speed and often told his daughter Rosetta that he had written "My Rose of Old Kentucky" for her.[35] (Although ostensibly a love song, the lyrics are so gentle and general that it could well have been inspired by avuncular affection.) Bill's extended family was a source of happiness and even inspiration to him.

One day, he was relaxing at his farm on a rare day off when his daughter Melissa returned from school.[36] She waved to her father as she approached. Bill's heart was gladdened by this all-too-rare sight of his daughter coming up the lane.

Then anxiety seized him. What if he lost her? What if a sudden illness claimed her?

Bill was moved to write "I Hear a Sweet Voice Calling," in which a girl is taken ill walking home from school and soon lies on her deathbed. There she comforts her parents, saying that heavenly voices are assuring her a place with God. Monroe recorded it on October 27, 1947, singing lead on the verses and then providing an absolutely ethereal tenor harmony for the chorus trio, while all the instruments except the rhythm guitar faded away — a breathtaking arrangement depicting the ebbing of the girl's life.

On another occasion at the farm, Speed's other daughter, Erroldean, was bitten by a snake.[37] The reptile was not poisonous, but Bill again got to thinking about the death of a youngster. The result was "The Little

Girl and the Dreadful Snake" (which Bill waited until 1952 to record, a growing pattern in which he would hold back songs, sometimes for years, until he found the near-perfect match of musicians and material). Despite its penny-dreadful title and melodramatic plot — child allowed to stray away in "dark and weary" woods; bitten by poisonous serpent; screams; reached too late by parents; dies with things "getting dark" around her — it proved a captivating work.

Surprisingly, there has been no critical notice to date of the deeper meaning of songs like "I Hear a Sweet Voice Calling" and "The Little Girl and the Dreadful Snake."[38] Monroe recorded a significant body of material thematically united by the concepts of dying, suffering, or abandoned children, including "I Was Left on the Street," "Little Joe," "Jimmy Brown the Newsboy," "Put My Little Shoes Away" (and the nearly identical "Put My Rubber Doll Away"), and "There Was Nothing We Could Do."

Abandonment and childhood suffering were huge psychological issues for Bill Monroe. His attempts to relieve his own lingering childhood pain were reflected in his kindnesses to youngsters, his habit of adopting animals, and in his beautiful although disquieting songs about dying or neglected children.

Soon another Monroe contribution to this genre — "My Little Georgia Rose" — would deal with abandonment in a very personal way.

Of course, Bill was now often abandoning his own children because of the demands of touring. Melissa and James, who adored their father, would spend hours on Saturday meticulously shining his boots so he would look better than anyone on the Opry that evening.[39] When Monroe left for the road, Jimmy would sometimes chase after him, grab on to his legs, and hold him and beg to be taken along. Bill would shake the boy off.[40] His own father had been busy and not been able to take him along. Now he was busy.

Carolyn Monroe was busy, too.[41] She was taking care of Bill's house and his children and also his business affairs. She would cook hearty meals for the band members when they came over to rehearse. If shows were booked fairly close to Nashville, Carolyn would personally do the advance work, getting the necessary permits, hanging posters in shop windows, and tacking handbills to telephone poles. Carolyn was motivated and could display a winning personality. Seldom was she refused permission to set a poster or get a license. Sometimes she brought along Melissa and Rosetta. They would ride and chat and laugh and get their tasks accomplished, then stop for lunch or soda pop before traveling some more; three high-spirited young women having fun together, enjoying their roles in show business, and working for a man they adored.

Before heading out on tour, Bill and the band would occasionally stop by the trailer in which Lester and Gladys were living. Gladys would have a supper ready of fried chicken and gravy (one of Bill's favorite meals) and of course biscuits, the great southern staple.

The biscuits that Bill and the boys ate were made with Martha White brand flour.[42] At the time, no one could have foreseen the incredible irony in Mrs. Flatt's choice of ingredients.

Gladys Flatt had rarely been apart from Lester, and the separations were difficult for her. Sympathetic, Bill found a place for her in the touring show.[43] She ran the concession stand for nearly a year, selling Cokes, popcorn, and candy. She received a regular salary.

Like Sally Ann Forrester, Gladys was always treated by Bill with complete respect and was never the object of any romantic advances. And like Sally Ann, Gladys frequently found herself holding large sums of cash that had accumulated over the course of several nights. The problem was that Bill often couldn't be found after the shows, having already gone off with a woman.[44]

There is a story that Monroe had so many bags of cash lying around his house that one day Earl Scruggs suggested Bill take the money to the bank and open savings and checking accounts, which would not only be more secure but allow better record keeping.[45] Bill thought this was a good idea and sent Earl to do it. A few weeks later, Bill needed some money and, so the story goes, asked Earl, "Why don't you go down to the bank and get one of those bags out?"

The story is probably apocryphal. J. B. Monroe had kept detailed account books and written checks, so his son was doubtless familiar with the basic principles of banking. But throughout his life, Bill Monroe dealt almost entirely in cash. He was not attempting to hide earnings from the tax man: Bill was culturally a product of the 1800s, and the nineteenth century was a cash-and-carry world.

One thing is certain: Earl Scruggs was starting to notice how much money a popular band could make.

Bill Monroe now had success, a trend-setting group, and a happy home life. But he still had the need for extramarital liaisons. Had these affairs remained limited to brief flings on the road, he might have been able to find some kind of contentment and stability with Carolyn.

But another woman had been more than a fling. And now she was back in his life.

The war over, Bessie Lee and Nelson Gann had returned from California. In retrospect, given Bessie and Bill's strong attachments, it was foolhardy for the Ganns to resume life in Nashville. But Nelson was probably as proud as Bill and just as determined not to fear anyone.

After another stint as a drugstore clerk, Gann was accepted for service in the Tennessee Highway Patrol,[46] a division of the Department of Safety established in 1929 to enforce traffic laws, catch bootleggers, and apprehend lawbreakers trying to evade arrest by escaping over county lines. The troopers were tough men who commanded respect. Bill Monroe could not have found a more formidable rival than Nelson C. Gann. But Bill was the consummate competitor, in love as well as music. He would not rest until he had won Bessie back.

Carolyn knew of Bill's relations with Bessie, and now she was obviously aware that their affair had been renewed. One night out at the Monroe farm, the situation exploded.[47]

Carolyn had played the long-suffering wife long enough. She quarreled with Bill all night through and well into the early morning hours. After a time, Bill probably just started ignoring her. That was his pattern when he got angry; not to lash out physically or even verbally but to ignore people, to shut them out of his life. But after the pain and humiliation of Bill's blatant long-term affair with Bessie, Carolyn was not to be denied. She blew up, grabbed an ice pick, and stabbed him in the leg.

Bill stumbled out of the house, stanched his bleeding, and escaped into town. He checked into a hotel, and there wrote one of his earliest and most compelling autobiographical — or, as he called them, "true" — songs, "Along About Daybreak."

Given the story behind it, the composition is puzzling. The singer is clearly worried that his marriage is over. In the final verse he appeals to his wife to take care of their children and teach them to pray for their daddy. But the first verse is seemingly written from Carolyn's perspective, about a relationship that was perhaps not based on love at all, about a life full of regrets, about "another."

There is no evidence that Carolyn ever took a lover in response to Bill's philandering. As far as is known, she was completely faithful to her husband despite his infidelities. Was Bill projecting his own sins onto Carolyn? Or was he reproducing her words in the first verse as an act of contrition before going to his own (the man's) voice in the next lyrics?

Whatever the case, the unhappy incident was more than the inspiration for one of Bill's most powerful songs. It reflected the terrible stress and frustration Carolyn was experiencing. And it was symptomatic of the chaos in Bill's private life, upheavals that were beginning to intrude into the day-to-day activities of the band.

Earl Scruggs in particular was getting anxious about the love triangle between Bill, Bessie, and Nelson Gann.[48] There may have been at least one tense personal confrontation, because the band knew about the affair and knew Gann by name. The band's transportation — a stretch limo with the words "Bill Monroe and his Blue Grass Boys WSM 'Grand Ole Opry'" emblazoned on the side — could not have been a more high-profile vehicle. And they drove like blazes, sometimes hitting 90 mph to make their gigs. The day was going to come, Scruggs worried, when they would roar past Nelson Gann in his patrol car and get pulled over for speeding. If so, Gann, armed and angry, would discover his wife with all of them. Bessie had absolutely no involvement with anyone in the Blue Grass Boys except Bill, but would Gann believe that in the heat of the moment?

Whether Gann would have drawn his .38 caliber service revolver and used it in anger will never be known. But he definitely knew that Bessie had taken back up with Bill, and he was incensed by it. Says Lieutenant

Colonel A. M. Lashlee, Tennessee Highway Patrol (ret.), who served with
Gann as a trooper stationed in Gallatin:

> When Nelson was still working there, the general talk was that he was
> very upset about Bill Monroe fooling around with his wife.[49]

Scruggs began to think about quitting. The continual stress caused by
Bill's affair with Bessie was only one factor. There were the grueling days
and nights of travel and performing. In particular, Earl felt a responsibility
to provide the best possible life for his mother, and he knew he could
make much more money as the leader of his own group.[50]

Flatt didn't talk much at home about the situation with Bessie Lee.[51]
But he clearly harbored his own dissatisfactions. He knew he was a multi-
talented singer, guitarist, songwriter, and emcee. And he wanted to be
able to enjoy something of a home life, to sit down to a nice Sunday dinner occasionally without always being on the road. Lester was eager to
start working for himself.

Flatt and Scruggs turned in their notices about two weeks apart, Earl
in late February 1948, Lester in early March.[52] In later years, they independently claimed that it was a coincidence. They had both tired of Monroe's exhausting touring schedule, they said, gone their separate ways,
then gotten together for a little picking and decided maybe they'd put
together a band.

According to this version, what became a tremendously successful
partnership began almost casually. In fact, Lester and Earl had planned
their move together. Says Gladys Flatt:

> Oh, yes. They had talked it over and [decided] they'd like to try it on
> their own.[53]

If Lester and Earl dissembled about the manner in which they left Bill
Monroe, their motives were generous. Knowing how sensitive Bill was to
being deserted — and in the aftermath of what became the most famous
feud in country music history — they obviously wanted to spare the feelings of a man they truly admired.

Bill tried to convince Lester to stay, warning him about the cruel world of professional music making.

"Lester, I need you and you need me," he argued.[54] "You will never make it."

It was nearly the identical argument Bill had presented to Charlie. But Charlie hadn't worried about starving without Bill, and now neither did Lester Flatt.

"I'll never know 'til I try," Flatt replied.

Bill offered him a raise.

"No," said Lester. "If I have to quit to get a raise, I'm still goin'."

Monroe then did exactly what would be expected for someone who had always found more sympathy from women than from men: He tried to enlist the aid of Lester's wife.

"Will you beg Lester to stay with me?" Bill asked Gladys. "Oh, please do. I need him so bad and I think he needs me."

"Bill, I think a lot of you," Gladys replied. "But I don't want to do that. Lester thinks he can make it on his own. He wants to try it. We've saved the money to do it. If we go broke, all right. And if he makes it, that's fine."

Faced with Gladys's support of her husband, Monroe gave up.

Flatt and Scruggs formed a band called the Foggy Mountain Boys, taking its name from "Foggy Mountain Top," a Carter Family favorite they decided to use as their theme song.[55] They had already discussed where to get bookings. Earl was from North Carolina, and he knew a lot of auditoriums and schools there. So the new band found its first home at WDVA, just across the border in Danville, Virginia. They soon moved into North Carolina proper and played at WHKY in Hickory. Now joining them were two other former Blue Grass Boys: fiddler Jimmy Shumate and bassist–baggy pants comedian Howard Watts. If Monroe later objected to Lester and Earl appropriating his sound, no wonder — they were even using his former sidemen.[56]

By late 1948, Lester and Earl joined the WCYB *Farm and Fun Time* show in Bristol, Tennessee. They were helping firmly establish Monroe-style band music away from Kentucky (Bill's home state) and central Tennessee (his base of operations), east to the Appalachian region. It would prove to be a stronghold for bluegrass, both as an audience base and talent source.

But around this time, probably just before the move to WCYB, they went back to WSM in hopes of getting on the Opry.[57] They didn't even get to audition. Learning of their plans, Monroe quietly convinced Opry manager Jim Denny (who had recently replaced the ailing George D. Hay) not to add them to the lineup.

Monroe presented a reasonable objection.[58] The Opry had one of every kind of act: one Roy Acuff, one Ernest Tubb, and one Bill Monroe, each with his own style and sound. Adding Flatt and Scruggs to the roster would be like adding a second Bill Monroe. Of course, Bill's rational veneer thinly covered his discomfort at having such strong rivals competing for the love of his audience. But Denny had agreed, and Flatt and Scruggs were kept off the Opry. For the time being.

One of the great myths attached to the Bill Monroe saga is that Monroe started feuding with Lester and Earl as soon as they left his band and refused to speak with them for more than twenty years. In fact, relations between Monroe and the former sidemen were quite cordial at first.

It was a common practice in these days for touring country musicians to perform as guests on the local radio programs of their colleagues. This professional courtesy was a win-win situation for all concerned. Touring artists were able to plug their regional appearances, they provided variety to a program's usual lineup, and the prospect of hearing surprise guest stars boosted a show's appeal.

In the fall of 1948, Monroe came to Bristol to play a local theater and appeared on Flatt and Scruggs's segment of *Farm and Fun Time*.[59] Monroe entered the studios and greeted Lester and Earl warmly. However, it quickly became clear that Bill was feuding with the Stanley Brothers, whom he pointedly ignored.

At first, Monroe's appearance went smoothly. Then Bill caused a moment of tension. He complimented Mac Wiseman, the Foggy Mountain Boys' tenor singer and second guitarist, and said — right on the air — "If you ever need a job, come to Nashville."

Wiseman cringed. Flatt was obviously angered at Monroe's making a public overture to one of his sidemen, but said nothing and let the incident go. Still, Mac's curiosity was piqued. Later he took Scruggs aside.

"How'd he know about me?" he asked.

Earl revealed that Monroe had long been a fan of Mac's genial but powerful vocalizations. In 1947, Wiseman had an early morning show on WCYB performing as a solo act. On tour, Bill would instruct the driver, "When we get up around Bristol, wake me up. I want to hear that boy on WCYB." Wiseman — like Jimmy Shumate and others — realized that Monroe had a filing-system memory for talent.

Wiseman left Lester and Earl at Christmas 1948, going to the WSB *Barn Dance* in Atlanta. When the *Barn Dance* folded the following spring, Wiseman called Monroe and asked if the job offer was still open. It was. For a time, the Blue Grass Boys featured the formidable talents of both Wiseman and Don Reno, Earl Scruggs's great friendly five-string rival, who had finally completed his military service.

A new attraction was added in the summer of 1949: the Shenandoah Valley Trio. Monroe initially formed the vocal subgroup as something of a minor league that provided second-string singers in case anyone in the regular band had a sore throat and had to be put on the musical equivalent of the injured reserve.[60] Yet again, it was Monroe as coach. Although Monroe did not carry the tent show at this time, he still had the ball club and he still needed major league transportation. So he bought a used Miami city bus as a tour vehicle to transport his motley collection of musicians, athletes, instruments, bats, gloves, and everyone's luggage. Unfortunately, the penny-wise, pound-foolish, and thoroughly ascetic Monroe never modified the interior. The original seats stayed, with their thin padding and steel handrails, miserably uncomfortable places to get a night's sleep. A car seat would have been luxurious by comparison.

If the road was tiring, it was art-friendly, a pressure cooker for performers but an incubator of creativity. Bill shaped up new songs during tours, Mac Wiseman says.

> He'd change them. He'd have an idea for one, a verse and a chorus or a few lines or something. Maybe we'd be standing around noodling in the dressing room or on the bus, and he'd say, "How do you like this?"

Sometimes I'd add a line to it or suggest a line. Sometimes he'd work on one and get part of it and go blank and it would be years later before he finished it.[61]

As Bill neared his forties, he began a practice that would characterize the rest of his creative life: commemorating the past, and perhaps reclaiming it, in song. "I'm on My Way to the Old Home" was written during this period, with Wiseman contributing the final verse.[62] Mac had a rich, strong voice that Bill could lay a hard tenor against. Wiseman's lead provided the pedestal for some of Monroe's truly monumental love songs.

On October 22, 1949, Bill entered the Castle Studios in Nashville's Tulane Hotel. Don Reno had gone out on his own before he had a chance to record with Monroe, and in his place was Rudy Lyle, a picker so strong and driving that he sounded like he was going to pull the strings off the banjo, yet a tasteful musician whose work beautifully fit any type of material.

It was Bill's first recording session in Nashville, which was finally on the verge of becoming a true music center. It was also his last for Columbia. Monroe was irked because Columbia had rewarded the Stanley Brothers, his first professional imitators, with a contract.[63] Owing Columbia four more sides, Bill waited until just two days before his contract expired to record them.[64]

As ever, it was the cold shoulder treatment he gave anyone who angered him. And as ever, he had a backup: Paul Cohen, head of the country music division of Decca Records, had been actively courting Monroe for his label. They had closed a deal with a handshake in one of the few places were Cohen could find Monroe and have a discreet chat with him — a men's room at the WSM studios.[65]

Bill opened the session with "Can't You Hear Me Callin'." There can be little doubt as to who was the inspiration for this monumental love song, a masterpiece of passion and pathos, exultation and despair, defiance and contrition.

Mac Wiseman sang the second line of the chorus as "a million times I've loved you best" to provide a rhyme for the final line "come back to

me is my request." Wiseman doesn't think the song is specifically about
Bessie Lee Mauldin; at least Monroe never discussed with Mac the circumstances that inspired it.[66] However, in later years Monroe specifically
instructed singers that the words were "a million times I've loved you,
Bess."[67] The internal evidence — the singer's proud declaration of his
love, his mournful pleading of his loneliness, his humble confession that
he has mistreated his beloved, his plea for her return — also bespeak
Bill's relation with Bessie Lee Mauldin.

Monroe devised one of his most ingenious tenor harmonies for the
chorus, singing an arresting B-flat against Wiseman's G note at one
moment, then an F against a Wiseman C, raw, poignant effects. It
sounded as if Bill was taking a razor to an emotional vein.

And he was. Because before "Can't You Hear Me Callin'" was
recorded, Bessie Lee had indeed left him again for Nelson Gann.

Bessie and Nelson had reconciled. On February 7, 1948, they had slipped
over the state border and traveled to Franklin, Kentucky.[68] There, taking
advantage of some of the most liberal residency laws this side of Las
Vegas, they had remarried.

They wed in secret so Bessie could hold on to a job she feared she'd
lose if her employer discovered she had a husband capable of supporting
her.[69] And of course, a public ceremony might attract a certain unwanted
guest.

Hank Williams is often heralded as the father of autobiographical
country songs, and the influence of his wrenchingly personal compositions cannot be denied.[70] But it is notable that Bill Monroe's "Along
About Daybreak" was released as a single in 1949, and "Can't You Hear
Me Callin'" released in 1950. By contrast, Williams's "Cold, Cold Heart"
and "I Can't Help It (If I'm Still in Love with You)" were not released
until 1951, and "Your Cheatin' Heart" until 1953.

Bill Monroe's most powerful "true songs" therefore predate those of
Hank Williams. But Bill's personal life, although highly dramatic, was
never the high-profile soap opera that Hank's became nor was his end so
tragic. It is probably for these reasons, as much as comparisons of mere
record sales figures, that Monroe has never received the recognition due
him as a pioneering autobiographical singer-songwriter.

But even without the alcohol and drugs that destroyed Hank, Bill's private life had enough fuel to create searing compositions. His next great lead singer would prove both colleague and confidant, a friend in the dark times and the musician who would help him fully define the bluegrass sound.

James Henry Martin was born on August 10, 1927, in Sneedville, Tennessee.[71] As a boy, Jimmy had worked all summer plowing corn for a neighbor after his own chores were done to earn seven dollars to buy a Gene Autry guitar. As a teen, his family too poor to afford a radio, he had walked into town on Saturday nights and convinced auto owners to tune in WSM for him on their car radios so he could hear Bill Monroe.

Now, in the autumn of 1949, barely twenty-two and a mixed bag of brass and deference, Martin had managed to get backstage at the Ryman Auditorium to audition for Monroe. Intrigued, Bill agreed to hear him. They sang "The Old Cross Road" together, and Jimmy backed Chubby Wise on "Orange Blossom Special." Monroe and Wise relished Martin's lively voice and punctuating guitar runs. He was hired for the Shenandoah Trio. In December 1949, when Wiseman left the Blue Grass Boys to resume his solo career, Jimmy was promoted to lead singer.

Meanwhile, the Ganns' second marriage had run into trouble, again in the form of Nelson's determined rival from Kentucky. Bessie returned to Bill — for the time being at least — and in the latter part of 1949 Bill informed Carolyn that he was leaving her.[72] She and the children were left at the forty-four-acre property on Dickerson Road.

Bill did not sever ties to his family. He and Carolyn maintained surprisingly cordial relations, and he visited his children and gave Carolyn money for their support.[73] James was still too young to join his father on the road, but occasionally Melissa would. When she traveled with him, Bessie did not, and vice versa.

And for parts of two summers, in 1949 and 1950, when Bessie came along on tour another female did, too — a young, pretty, golden-haired girl.

She was Bessie and Bill's daughter, a love child Bessie had gone to have in Georgia and left for adoption by friends.[74] Jimmy Martin knew about the situation and was kind to the girl, treating her like a niece or cousin. The band was now back to using a touring car, a big Chrysler, and as it rolled along the girl sang with her father some of his old songs. Bill called her his little sweetheart, and she smiled at him. These tender moments inspired the lyrics of one of Bill's most beloved compositions, a number now in the repertoire of nearly every bluegrass band in the world — "My Little Georgia Rose."

The story behind this classic Monroe song has not previously been told, although in its opening lines Bill declared it to be "a story that I know is true," codewords for an autobiographical composition.

Sometime in the late 1930s or early 1940s, Bessie Lee Mauldin had lived in northeastern Georgia, by some accounts in the town of Clayton just three miles south of the North Carolina border,[75] by others in Toccoa, about twenty miles farther south.[76] (Indeed, although Bessie was born in North Carolina and later performed as "The Carolina Songbird," her connection to Georgia was so strong that some musicians who knew her are still under the mistaken impression that she had been born there.) Clayton and Toccoa are both in the Blue Ridge Mountains where the tall pines grow — the setting described in the song as the home of the Little Georgia Rose.

Bessie seems to have quietly moved to Georgia to have the child, a girl. The baby was given up for adoption — "Her mother left her with another," the song reports — perhaps by friends that Bessie had there.

Like so much in Bill's life, his attitude toward this girl and the circumstances of her birth was maddeningly contradictory. Clearly he loved her and knew she was his issue. Yet somehow he looked on her as Bessie's daughter and not his own, refusing to recognize his own role as a parent to this girl. The second verse of "My Little Georgia Rose" reflects an undisguised anger toward Bessie, speaking of a mother who left the child with others in order to pursue a "carefree" life, further asserting that the girl was someone her mother "couldn't stand." It was a cruel dig. What was Bessie to do? She had borne the infant in an era when unwed mothers and their children were not as blithely accepted as they are today.

It is not known whether Bill ever contributed to the Little Georgia Rose's support, but given his great generosity toward those he loved, he

almost certainly did. Bill's embracing of this love child, his distancing
from her, his self-righteous criticism of the anonymous Bessie — all were
manifestations of his conflicted feelings.

At the time of this writing the Georgia Rose, who would be nearly
sixty now, has never publicly identified herself.[77] Her present where-
abouts are unknown.

Jimmy Martin's talents continued to develop and in the process heavily
flavored his employer's music. Martin had a country voice, more
descended from the lineage of the new commercial singers than the first
generation of rural musicians. Yet it was a voice of controlled dynamism.
Martin could hit notes dead on but also loved to slide into them in much
the same way that a fiddler might subtly slide into a bluesy, almost quar-
tertone effect.

Hank Williams — now the hottest new vocalist on the country
scene — was a major influence. Williams had a way of throwing a "break"
into his voice, a minisecond yodel, a subtle passing sob. Martin adopted
this technique and Monroe responded to it immediately.[78]

"That's good," Bill said. Ever striving to blend closely with his lead
singers, he began ornamenting his harmonies to match Martin's leads.
Jimmy, in turn, worked to match the timbre of his voice to Monroe's.
What would one day be termed Bill Monroe's trademark "high lonesome
sound" was being structured by two musical craftsmen.

Williams himself noticed this haunting coloration in Monroe's music
and reinforced it. Hank and Bill were part of a package tour in 1949,
spending three weeks traveling through Texas. One day on the tour bus,
Williams told Monroe that he had written a song for him to record and
then sang it for him: "I'm Blue, I'm Lonesome."[79]

Williams's new creation, with its high, yearning lead line and poetic
images of passing, sighing trains, fit Monroe's evolving style perfectly. Bill
recorded it on February 3, 1950, during his first session for Decca
Records.

In later years, Monroe would claim that they had jointly composed the
number during backstage jams, Monroe creating the melody and
Williams putting lyrics to it.[80] But Jimmy Martin insists that the song was
fully composed when Hank first sang it for him and Bill on the bus.[81] It

appears that "I'm Blue, I'm Lonesome," one of the most compelling of the Monroe high-lonesome oeuvre, is another example of Bill appropriating work to which he felt he had contributed.

And Monroe's contribution was very real: The song would not be the same without its distinctive tenor harmony line, and that was all Bill Monroe. That Hank Williams would write a song like "I'm Blue, I'm Lonesome" for Bill Monroe was further affirmation that the Kentuckian had developed a distinctive style emphasizing high leads, poignant bluesy harmonies, and themes of mournful isolation — all of it far removed from his sound of just a few years earlier. It is hard to imagine the 1946–1948 Blue Grass Boys with Lester Flatt assaying "I'm Blue, I'm Lonesome."

The first Decca session was highly successful. Monroe was in good hands. Paul Cohen, whose work and influence helped turn Nashville into a major recording center, was a man of taste and restraint. So was Owen Bradley, then a leading WSM staff musician moonlighting as a recording engineer. Bradley became de facto producer on most of Monroe's early Decca sessions because Cohen was physically based in Decca's New York office. Monroe enjoyed a long, happy relationship with both men.

"My Little Georgia Rose" was recorded at this session (and rerecorded in a more ambitious arrangement on June 26, 1954, with triple harmony fiddles, another Monroe innovation that soon greatly influenced the rest of country music). So was the plaintive "Memories of You," surely a product of the misery caused by the Mauldin-Gann relationship, with its reference to the lovers foolishly letting "other people" tear them apart. There is no telling how many other songs Bill wrote specifically about Bessie. There are many candidates, including two trios recorded on January 25, 1954: "On and On," which declares that the singer must follow his beloved because it is his destination (read, destiny) to be by her side; and "I Believed in You Darling," the accusatory lament of a man betrayed.

One of the greatest Bessie songs was inspired by a "Dear John" letter. Having a wife and a girlfriend was not enough for Bill. The enjoyment and ego gratification of having other women, likely fueled by a persistent narcissism and a consuming need for contact and reassurance, gave rise to multiple affairs. Just as Monroe kept track of potential sidemen around the country, he kept track of potential companions and always had phone numbers to call. Some of these girlfriends enjoyed a surprisingly high profile: One, a schoolteacher from Ashland, Kentucky, would come up onstage and sing when Bill was in town.[82] Bessie knew all too well what was going on. Like Carolyn, she was willing to look the other way. Up to a point.

One day toward the end of 1950, Bill went to the Andrew Jackson Hotel to see Bessie. She was gone. She had left him a letter written on hotel stationery, a cry from the heart declaring that he could never be true to her. It was signed, "I love you so, Bessie."

Heartbroken, Monroe showed Jimmy Martin the missive. "I can't answer it, 'cause there ain't no address on it," Bill said.[83]

"Well," Jimmy replied, "that's a good song there: 'I can't answer her letter, for she left me no address.'"

The two sat down. "Letter from My Darlin'" simply poured out of them. It was an answering cry from Monroe, his response to Bessie's despairing (although certainly justified) accusations. If Bill lacked an address for Bessie, he did have access to the nation's jukeboxes and he got his reply out at his next recording session on January 20, 1951. ("It wasn't too long after we wrote it," says Martin. "Bill wanted that recorded real quick.") Monroe's agony was expressed in one of the most brooding, evocative mandolin solos he ever recorded.

Maybe this declaration of love helped, because Bessie came back, yet again. Sometimes their blowups were more commedia dell'arte than grand opera. They got into it once just as they were leaving town. Not wanting to endure hundreds of miles of this, Bill had the car stopped and told Bessie to get out.

She refused. Bill declared he'd throw her out.

"You wouldn't do that to a lady!" Bessie exclaimed.[84]

"To a lady, no!" Bill retorted. A moment later, Bessie's backside hit the pavement. A moment after that, her suitcase hit a nearby wall.

They would feud and fuss and she would leave. And then she would come back.

*   *   *

Monroe's fiddlers during this period — men like Vassar Clements, Merle "Red" Taylor, and Charlie Cline — were further defining the bluegrass style, playing bluesy slides with virtuoso technique and exploding with raw, slicing bow strokes. Meanwhile, Bill was refining his own playing. He began to evolve a strategy for improvisation in which he would stay close to the melody but at the end throw in an unexpected, even flashy variation.[85] The sudden contrast was much more striking than straight melody or pure improvisation alone.

And in this period Monroe perfected his rhythm "chop," in which he would sharply strum the mandolin on the offbeat, then quickly mute the strings by slightly easing the pressure exerted by the fingers of his left hand. The effect was similar to the "sock chords" played by jazz and swing guitarists. It soon became a hallmark of his style.

Martin's snapping guitar runs had helped inspire the competitive Monroe to develop his mandolin chop by way of response. Sometimes, they inspired him to more.

Bill was now touring in a Flxible bus with a straight-six Buick engine. Some seats faced each other and Monroe, Martin, and other band members would sit together over the miles and play, their jams turning into complete compositions.[86]

One day Monroe was fooling around with a scalding instrumental in the key of C. He threw out riffs. Jimmy punctuated them with individual notes that suggested entire chords to Bill, who devised a cunning and potent progression.

"What should we name that?" Monroe asked.

"Let's call it 'Big Mac,'" said banjo picker Rudy Lyle, in a droll reference to hefty Mac Wiseman.

Instead, Monroe named his masterpiece after a western that had starred cowboy actor-singer Max Terhune, an acquaintance from his WLS radio days — "Raw Hide."[87] It became Bill's mandolin piece de resistance.

One day, fiddler Red Taylor composed an engaging melody in the key of A, its ascending and descending lines similar to the traditional tune "Gray Eagle." But the second part leaped into a sit-up-and-take-notice subdominant D chord.

Monroe certainly took notice. At their previous recording session, Paul Cohen had suggested that Bill record "The Old Fiddler"[88] by Hugh Ashley and Ira Wright, a tribute to a spry old-timer in much demand at "all the good quadrilles." Monroe had sung it with verve. There can be no doubt of which old fiddler it reminded him.

In typical fashion, Bill was ready to go the world one better. By his next session, on October 15, 1950, Monroe had set words to Red Taylor's tune and created his own tribute to a fiddler — "Uncle Pen." It became one of his most requested songs.

Paul Cohen had provided the impetus, the uncredited Red Taylor had provided the melody (which Monroe had simplified while singing the lyrics), Pendleton Vandiver had provided the inspiration. And, as ever, it was Bill Monroe the synthesizing creator who had brought it all together.

But Monroe's use of uncredited material soon caused him trouble. On April 14, 1951, he was served with a summons in a lawsuit being brought by songwriter Tomie Thompson.[89] Thompson alleged that he had written the lyrics to Bill's popular "Kentucky Waltz" for which Monroe promised him half the income from the song. But instead, Tomie claimed, Monroe had sold the rights to Peer International, a major New York–based music publisher, for $3,000 and certain royalties. Monroe admitted asking Tomie to write the lyrics but claimed he had purchased them outright.

On the very day Monroe was served with the summons, Eddy Arnold's recording of "Kentucky Waltz," which had been gaining momentum, hit the *Billboard* country charts, eventually spending three weeks at number 1. How the lawsuit turned out is now unknown.

"Kentucky Waltz" was more than just a success for Monroe and Eddy Arnold. It directly inspired one of the biggest crossover hits in history. One night in 1948, Pee Wee King and Redd Stewart were driving back to Nashville after a tour and heard Monroe's version on the radio. "It's odd no one ever did a 'Tennessee Waltz,'" Stewart observed.[90] The duo's subsequent composition "Tennessee Waltz" became a pop smash when recorded by Patti Page and inspired the craze for "state" waltzes. It stands as yet another example of Monroe's broad influence on American popular music, but it also stands at the threshold of the dark and thorny path toward sorting out just who wrote all those "Bill Monroe" songs.[91]

There is absolutely no question that Monroe was a gifted artist who wrote much of his own material. The evidence is overwhelming in terms of first-person accounts of people who were present when Monroe created songs. But there is also no question that — like many bandleaders or star vocalists of his time — Monroe additionally purchased rights to songs created by professional songwriters or assumed rights to material written by his sidemen, then listed himself as the composer on the recordings.

To put the matter in perspective, sharing or outright sale of song rights was common practice in the 1920s through 1940s and beyond. (For example, Ray Whitley wholly composed Gene Autry's theme "Back in the Saddle Again," although Autry shared composer credit.)[92] It was a common attitude that work done by sidemen was the property of the bandleader. Only later, when songwriters and creative sidemen began to retain their rights, did such attitudes seem exploitative. Bill Monroe remained of the old school. Therefore in retrospect he is vulnerable to criticism on "Kentucky Waltz" and many other songs that he claimed as his own.

At this juncture, it is fitting to consider the greater question that divides and vexes lovers of bluegrass: Who actually started the music?

Of course, the most common response is that Bill Monroe was "the Father of Bluegrass" and its true creator. It was his melding of a band sound around fiddle playing, his high singing, his revolutionary mandolin stylings, and his distinctive surging rhythm that set bluegrass apart from the rest of country or folk music.

But dissenters claim that the music we now call bluegrass really began with the addition of the syncopated five-string banjo as played by Earl Scruggs. They point out that bluegrass is firmly associated in the public mind with this banjo sound. Without Scruggs (or at least without Don Reno or someone like them), they say, Monroe's music would have been just a lively chapter in southern string band history, not the internationally renowned genre that bluegrass is today.

Along these lines is the radical view that the 1946–1948 Blue Grass Boys — that is, Monroe's sidemen — were the true sound of bluegrass. Thus Scruggs (banjo), Wise (fiddle), and Flatt (vocals/guitar) were each equal contributors with Monroe (vocals/mandolin) to what became "bluegrass." According to this theory, their total contributions outweighed Monroe's: Monroe was the star but Lester and Earl were the band, and the band was bluegrass.

Yet one must come back to Bill Monroe's unique rhythm, a keystone of bluegrass. As powerful as Scruggs's syncopated banjo picking was, it was Monroe's beat and timing that set it off to best advantage.[93] Other early three-finger style pickers, such as Snuffy Jenkins, never made the impression that Earl did. It was not just that Scruggs was a more advanced player than Jenkins: Snuffy didn't have anything like Monroe's Blue Grass Boys driving him.

Moreover, champions of the view that bluegrass began with the 1946–1948 band are guilty of selective memory. The raw, sliding, high-lonesome duets; the mournful themes; even Bill's trademark rhythm chop on the mandolin — all were essentially absent from that band's music. The most striking hallmarks of so-called traditional bluegrass were fully defined during the Jimmy Martin years, long after Flatt and Scruggs had left the Blue Grass Boys.

If Bill Monroe started bluegrass, Earl Scruggs certainly made it as popular as it is today. But it is crucial to recognize that Monroe was the prime creative organizer and artistic guiding force behind bluegrass. He was very much like the director of a major motion picture: A director does not do all the script writing, acting, cinematography, sound recording, and editing by him/herself. But the director brings everything together in accordance with his/her own vision of the final film.

In this sense, Bill Monroe was (to borrow a term from film criticism) the "auteur" or author of bluegrass, a great synthesizer.[94] If he heard a song, a sound, or musician he liked, he used them. If not, they were not used. He was the bandleader, the man in charge. It was not as if skinny, shy Earl Scruggs had bullied his way into the Blue Grass Boys and forced the banjo upon strapping, steel-willed Monroe. Bill wanted the banjo sound in his group long before he heard Earl's revolutionary stylings.

The debate on who started bluegrass or who made the most crucial contributions to its development will go on forever. It bespeaks the vitality of this vibrant American art form. What should never be forgotten are the breathtaking talents and sheer genius of those who were present at its creation.

Ironically, as Bill Monroe's creative powers were approaching their zenith, his career was beginning to go into decline.

Tastes were changing. Country stars like Ernest Tubb were featuring electric guitar and lap steel, deemphasizing the fiddle, and having big hits. Bar and club patrons were preferring dance records in their jukeboxes, and except for his waltzes Bill's was essentially a listening music. And it was no longer sunny and accessible as it had been in the Flatt and Scruggs period. His songs were still powerful, but now had a more personal edge and darker undertones.

Like a once-famous actor who retains drawing power but is only offered parts in B-movies, Monroe went on the circuit of booking agent T. D. Kemp, thirteen-week stretches of playing theaters.[95] The work was steady but hard. A band followed every showing of a movie; as soon as "The End" appeared on screen, they were onstage playing their opening theme. The Blue Grass Boys would perform for fifteen or twenty minutes, then bring out Monroe as the star. Bill might play as many as five shows a day. But the early shows would often have a few people and he was paid strictly on percentage, usually about 60 percent of the door.[96]

The Blue Grass Boys played schoolhouses in which the only backdrop was a blackboard. They played drive-in theaters, standing on top of the concession stand. The money softened, but the traveling life remained hard, as Jimmy Martin recalls.

What if you had to ride and sleep on each other's shoulders? Many times I've rode in the backseat and I'd have my head leaning on the left side of the guy next to me. We'd ride like that for miles. Then we'd wake up and say, "Well, time for us to change sides," and then we'd lean to the right and sleep like that. But there was not too much bitching about it being hard, because you didn't want to go back to digging ditches and stuff on the farm. At least I was getting to travel and sing and play.[97]

Now began an almost cancerous pattern. Bill would have bookings but not be able to pay a regular band at full salary. "How much can you get by on this week?" was an increasingly frequent question. After Flatt, Scruggs, and Wise had left, he had been blessed with exceptionally talented replacements. Now strapped for cash, Bill began settling for pickup musicians who were familiar with his records and could put on a halfway decent show. Says Martin:

> I've left town with just him and me and the bass player and pick up a banjo picker from Cas Walker's show in Knoxville. He'd say, "Who's this guy you've got?" "Well, it's Jim Smoak, he's pretty good, I think he can do the job." Bill would introduce a boy on the show, and look at the guy and say, "What was your name, now?"
>
> Bill didn't want it that way. There just wasn't nothing he could do about it.[98]

Monroe recorded again on March 17 and April 23, 1951. But gone were the Blue Grass Boys (with the exception of Rudy Lyle, playing nearly inaudible banjo on the second session). The unthinkable had happened: Bill Monroe was being backed by a contemporary country ensemble of studio musicians playing drums, piano, and electric guitar.

Paul Cohen of Decca was taking a realistic view of Monroe's sagging record sales.[99] He hadn't had a hit since 1949 when "Toy Heart" and "When You Are Lonely" both hit number 12 on, respectively, the *Billboard* country best seller and jukebox charts. And this was old Lester Flatt–era material on Columbia.

So Paul decided to modernize Bill's sound, and he had a specific plan: The music of the late Jimmie Rodgers was enjoying a resurgence, being recorded by such Rodgers devotees and major country stars as Ernest Tubb, Hank Snow, and Lefty Frizzell.[100] Nashville was getting back on the Singing Brakeman's train, so why not put Bill Monroe on board, too? Bill wasn't enthusiastic about this experiment, but he trusted Paul and was willing to try.

The results were a near disaster, with none of the sass and assurance that had transformed Rodgers's "Mule Skinner Blues" into Bill's first major solo vehicle. Then–Decca producer Owen Bradley, who also played key-boards on one session, well recalls these uncomfortable sessions:

> All that stuff was not really fun to make with Bill, because we were all walking on eggs, and I know he was too. We had no idea what the hell we were doing, to be honest. I think Bill was as bewildered as we were.[101]

Today, some Monroevians proudly point to these sessions as proof of Bill's willingness to experiment. Others decry them as evidence that the country music industry was eager to compromise his artistic integrity. Bradley takes a more measured view of this bizarre episode in Monroe's recording career:

> The bluegrass thing was not as sacred as it is now. If Bill was selling 55 [thousand records] or 75 or 105 and if you could do something else and get him selling 200,000 without ruining him, everybody would feel like they ought to do it. They might not feel that way today. Today, forty or fifty years later, people might look back and say we were ruin-ing him, and that's easy to say. But we're talking about a time when things weren't going that great.[102]

Not all of Bill's studio experiments were disasters. Benjamin "Tex" Logan, a fiddler and a fan of Bill's, had put together "Christmas Time's A-Coming," which Bill recorded on October 28, 1951. It became a perennial favorite, covered by numerous country singers. Owen Bradley had a little set of vibes which Paul Cohen suggested he play for a cheery holiday effect.

Vibes on a Monroe record? The drums/electric guitar business had been bad enough.

"Bill and Paul, don't you think I should just lay out on this?" Bradley asked.[103] "I feel like this is going to ruin Bill Monroe."

"No, I think it's beautiful," Monroe said. "Just play it." Bradley did.

For the most part, Cohen and Bradley took a laissez faire attitude toward Bill. He knew what he wanted. They just helped him get it.

Recording was still done in the old style, with musicians mixing it themselves by moving in and out around a single, omnidirectional mike.

("They'd leap into the mike," Bradley recalls.) Owen found Bill easy and economical to work with: Three-hour sessions often yielded three or even four good songs.

By now, another Monroe was on records. Melissa had a strong, attractive voice, and at a mere thirteen years of age she landed a contract with Columbia. She recorded four sides on August 6, 1950, and four more almost exactly a year later, on August 5, 1951.[104]

Her first session was the best. Melissa's cover of the Pete Cassell hit "Oh, How I Miss You" enjoyed modest success and earned her some attention. A charming surprise was "Peppermint Sticks and Lemon Drops," a novelty love song that Melissa sang with pleasing pertness.

When Melissa was about sixteen, she and Jimmy Martin dated.[105] Appearing with the Blue Grass Boys, she would sometimes look at him when she sang "Oh, How I Miss You."

"Look at the crowd, Melissa!" Bill would whisper forcefully. "That's who you're singing to!"

No, it wasn't. She was smitten with the spirited and boyishly handsome singer and wanted to marry him. Bill refused to sign the papers giving her as a minor permission to wed. Since this was really Melissa's idea and since her dad frowned on the relationship, Jimmy didn't press the issue.[106]

Despite Melissa's potential, her career stalled. And now circumstances were preventing her from touring regularly with her father. Once again, Bessie Lee had been coaxed away from her husband. Melissa and her mother understandably looked on Bessie as a homewrecker, so it was out of the question for Melissa to tour with Bill whenever Bessie was along.

On September 25, 1951, Nelson C. Gann and Bessie Lee Mauldin separated for the last time.[107] Gann was obviously fed up, and on this particular night he simply didn't come home. They divided their property, including their interest in a small house in Cherokee Park in the West End section of Nashville. Bessie's suit for divorce was granted on November 28. Years later, she would bitterly claim that Bill's interference had thwarted every attempt to salvage their marriage.[108]

Gann stayed with the Tennessee Highway Patrol until 1952, when he became a Nashville city policeman.[109] Around 1955, he left the force, remarried, and worked for an electrical manufacturing company. In the mid-1960s, he managed the Music City Dinner Club, a short-lived bar on 16th Avenue South, then worked in the furniture business. He died in September 1987 in the northern Nashville suburb of Goodlettsville. (The final ironic parallel in the lives of the rivals: Monroe was also a Goodlettsville resident at this time.) Gann's role in inspiring all those powerful love songs remained known to but a few.

If relations between Bill and Carolyn remained unsettled, Bill was actually getting along with another relation — his brother Charlie. In 1951, they reunited as the Monroe Brothers in Corbin, Kentucky, their first public performance in thirteen years.[110] Fans literally came from hundreds of miles to hear them.

But Bill was by no means mellowing, as the Gibson musical instrument company was about to discover.

Bill's F-5 mandolin was no longer the pristine orchestral instrument that had been displayed in the Florida barbershop window. It was well scratched from years of heavy use, and the curlicue on the headstock had been broken off. (Monroe carried around the piece for several years but lost it before a repair was made.) Bill occasionally sent the instrument back to the Gibson factory for work. With the amount of playing he did and the pressure his strong hands exerted on the instrument, new frets and even new fingerboards were often needed.

Around 1950, Bill had a long list of repairs:[111] resetting of the neck; new frets and fingerboard; new tuning pegs; a new bridge; and refinishing. Gibson kept it about four months, for Monroe a difficult separation during which he had to make do with other instruments. (Whatever happened to the F-7 mandolin, Bill's original professional instrument, is a mystery. It seems to have been sold or given away by this time.)

When the mandolin came back, only the neck had been reset. Aggravated, Bill thought of all the people inspired by his music to take up the mandolin and how most of them had purchased Gibsons because he played one. Looking down at the headstock, he decided he had given the company enough free advertising. He unfolded his pocket knife, sat down, and gouged the inlaid mother-of-pearl "Gibson" out of the headstock, leaving only "The" above a raw red wound in the wood.

*   *   *

Like other Monroe lead singers before him, Jimmy Martin was ready to start striking out on his own. He came and went several times between mid-1951 and early 1954. One of his first replacements was none other than Carter Stanley of the Stanley Brothers.

By now, Carter and Ralph had matured from being Monroe imitators to establishing a true "Stanley sound" with flavorings of contemporary country and healthy doses of old-time mountain music. Monroe had also got to know the brothers, and he genuinely liked them.

Tired of the road, Ralph had temporarily returned to the family farm. Carter jumped at the chance to perform with Monroe. Not long afterward, Monroe found he would be between banjo players for a week. Would Ralph fill in? He agreed and went on the road with Carter and Bill.

At the end of the week, Bill completely surprised the young Virginians by asking them to join his band. If they did, he said, he would drop the name "Blue Grass Boys." Henceforth the act would be known as "Bill Monroe & the Stanley Brothers."[112]

Perhaps Monroe — now without Jimmy Martin and Rudy Lyle and thus feeling the loss of Flatt and Scruggs even more keenly — was eager to latch on to a strong singer-guitarist/banjo duo. And having the Stanleys would mean having two name acts in one. (Ralph Stanley says he has often wondered about this but cannot say for sure why Bill made the offer.)

Carter was all for it. Ralph was honored, but knew that Bill had an even more grueling touring schedule than the one he'd just escaped. Ralph said he'd think it over. Then he drove back to McClure, Virginia, with Pee Wee Lambert, who had come to the show.

At about 7:45 the next morning, just south of Raleigh, North Carolina, Pee Wee fell asleep at the wheel and had a head-on collision with another vehicle. No one was killed, but Ralph spent months recovering. The ultimate fatality was the concept of Bill Monroe and the Stanley Brothers.

Carter decided to stick with his brother. Monroe found another outstanding singer, one of the few men who actually awed Bill.

Born in 1926 near Dawn, Texas, about thirty miles southwest of Amarillo, Thomas Edward "Edd" Mayfield was the real deal — not a spangled, softhanded pseudocowboy but a handsome, tough-as-barbed-wire cowpuncher who literally grew up on a ranch, who could ride hard, lasso accurately, and literally toss and tie up a bull.[113] Mayfield had the wiry strength of a gymnast and in some respects was stronger even than Monroe: His favorite trick was to climb a rope without using his feet — while holding his arms straight out.

Edd was an equally powerful singer-guitarist, who with his brothers Herb and Smokey had formed the nucleus of an early Texas bluegrass band, the Green Valley Boys. Edd played with Bill over the next few years in general sync with the goings and returnings of Jimmy Martin. One of the few Monroe guitarists who played with a thumbpick, Edd, like Charlie Monroe, put out booming backing notes. As a vocalist, his strength of voice matching that of his limbs, the Texan was a fine partner for the Kentuckian.

One night in December 1952, word circulated backstage at the Opry that Hank Williams was in the alley behind the Ryman, sitting in his car.[114]

"Is he sober?" was the immediate question. The answer, of course, was no. So none of the Opry stars went out to greet him.

With one exception. Bill Monroe ventured out into the winter cold. The windows of the Cadillac were fogged up, but Williams, who was sitting in the backseat, recognized Monroe and rolled down the window. Monroe was shocked at what he saw. Williams was so tiny that he looked as if he was all folded up, a wasted man, nothing but bones. His ashen face seemed no bigger than the hand that Monroe extended to him.

"Bill," said Hank, shaking hands, "I ain't got a friend at the Grand Ole Opry. Nobody but you. Nobody here cares about me."

Within a few weeks, Williams was dead in the backseat of that car. The Opry stars who had spurned Williams that December night were soon out in force at his funeral, singing his praises.

Although Bill's fortunes had declined, he still had a slightly positive cash flow and the drive to entertain. Now he found a venue of his own.[115] In 1951, he and brother Birch began purchasing (and in 1959 formally acquired title to) the Brown County Jamboree, a beloved but rather run-down country music park in the tiny community of Bean Blossom, Indi-

ana. Started in the 1930s by a local entrepreneur, the Jamboree was originally just a big tent in former farm fields. In the early 1940s a long single-
story building (affectionately called "the barn") had been erected to serve
as the main concert site.

Monroe was popular here. Well-advertised shows with a big-name
country headliner could draw audiences from across the Midwest. Birch
served as manager, and the concerts were presented on Sunday, a good
day for Opry performers after their Saturday night obligations in
Nashville.

The park in Bean Blossom was not just a professional venture. In the
unsettled times with Carolyn, it became a home away from home in a
setting not unlike Ohio County, Kentucky. Bill even built some cabins on
the site.

Maybe now — with the park operating, his romantic rival finally out
of the picture, and Bessie at his side — he could find contentment.

At about 3 A.M. on January 16, 1953, Bill was driving back into Nashville
after an enjoyable evening of foxhunting. He was scheduled to do a
5 A.M. radio show on WSM. Bessie Lee was with him.

On Highway 31-W near the little town of White House, Bessie
noticed an oncoming vehicle drifting toward them.

"Bill," she warned, "he's coming into our lane, get over."

Monroe was in the right, and he knew it.

"Let him get over!" he snapped.

The crash was horrific.[116]

CHAPTER 5

IMPACTS: ROCK 'N' ROLL, FLATT AND SCRUGGS, FOLK MUSIC

(1953 TO 1961)

I will instruct my sorrows to be proud. — Shakespeare, *King John*

B essie Lee ducked down at the last moment. Her injuries were relatively minor. Bill's were not.

The vehicles collided, and Monroe cannoned into the steering wheel. In a split second, he sustained some nineteen broken bones including a broken pelvis, a fractured spine, a compound fracture of the leg, and skull fractures. He had a broken nose and a concussion. The force evulsed one eye out of its socket.[1] The occupants of the other car, two men, were also critically injured.[2]

Bill's strength and willpower now exceeded even the superhuman ego that had contributed to this catastrophe. He managed to extract himself from the wreck, then by holding on to the car, walk around to reach Bessie. He pulled her free and carried her off the road despite his own horrible injuries.[3]

What happened next is uncertain, whether Bill reached a nearby home or passing motorists called for help. What is certain is that Jimmy Martin and the band were waiting at the WSM studios for the early morning broadcast when they heard the sickening news.

The band played the show, then Martin rushed to Nashville Memorial Hospital. There he got past the nurses as singlemindedly as he had gotten past the Ryman security guards the night he auditioned for Bill. He found Bill "broken all to pieces, really tore up"[4] and barely conscious.

Jimmy took his hand. "Bill, do you know who this is?"

Monroe stirred. "It's Jimmy Martin."

After a few hours, Bill regained full consciousness. He asked Jimmy to go to Gary's Garage in Nashville and see about his mandolin and a fox-hound that had been in the car. Both the instrument and the animal survived. (Monroe hadn't wanted the dog soiling the backseat, so it had been in the trunk.) Bessie had been taken to a different hospital. Jimmy checked on her.

Bill's eye was eased back into its socket, and he was put into a body cast to hold his spine and pelvis straight while they healed. He lay on his back in the hospital for nearly three months.[5]

Family, friends, and colleagues rallied around. Owen Bradley and Paul Cohen went to see him. "I'm sure they gave you something to keep you from suffering," Bradley said solicitously.[6]

"I won't take an aspirin!" Bill replied defiantly. "They ain't gonna make a dope fiend out of me." Bradley and Cohen realized that Monroe was lying there with terrible injuries yet refusing painkillers.

The accident could not have come at a worse time. Monroe was receiving some record and song royalties, but his main source of income was from performing. That income had been dwindling; now it was shut off. After Bill left the hospital, he was unable to return to touring until May. Even then he had to wear a brace and was in such pain that at one of his first shows after the accident he nearly collapsed.[7]

On February 22, 1953, a benefit concert was held at the National Guard Armory in Louisville, Kentucky.[8] Numerous country stars participated: Ernest Tubb, Hank Snow, Red Foley, Carl Smith, Pee Wee King, Maybelle Carter & the Carter Sisters, Lew Childre, and Geri Carr & Her

All-Girl Band. Nearly $9,000 of badly needed money was raised, a huge sum in those days. The country music community held Bill Monroe in high esteem, even though to many of his Opry costars he was still an intimidating figure.

The accident hardened Bill's appearance — afterward he was still handsome but no longer had his boyish good looks — but it softened the face he turned toward the world. In addition to a rude reminder of his own mortality, he had learned that he was widely loved and respected.

Owen Bradley noticed that Bill started connecting more with other people.

> He became a lot more open, easier to talk to. He began to take better care of himself. He began to wear his glasses more in public. The funny thing, we kind of found out that one of the reasons he was [standoffish] was that he couldn't see you. You might pass by and maybe he wouldn't talk to you because he didn't know who in the heck you were. He seemed to be much more cordial and easier to get along with. He probably changed a lot of things because he had had a pretty good lick.[9]

Still, the accident was a disaster. Any momentum he had with the powerful high-lonesome ensemble of Martin and the others was broken. Meanwhile he was getting more and more competition from other bands playing in his style — Flatt and Scruggs, Jim and Jesse, Reno and Smiley, and the Stanley Brothers. Indeed, audiences and the emerging class of record-spinning disk jockeys (whose programs were beginning to replace live music) were starting to recognize that this was a genre of banjo/ fiddle/mandolin-driven, high-vocal-crowned music distinctive from the rest of country music; the label "bluegrass" seems to have been coming into use around this time.

At the precise moment in history when bluegrass was developing an identity, its progenitor was trapped in a hospital bed.

Flatt and Scruggs in particular were going from strength to strength in artistry and popularity. Now they were about to acquire the final element that would allow them to rise to the top levels of country music — a powerful sponsor.

Martha White Mills was a growing producer of flour. Its president, Cohen T. Williams, was a go-getter who had a sign in his office that read "Early to Bed, Early to Rise, Work Like Hell and Advertise."[10] Now in May 1953, Efford Burke, one of Cohen's top salesmen, was in that office urging a new strategy for advertising to their core customers: the southern farm families who worked hard, rose early, and ate a lot of biscuits.

Sopped with gravy, biscuits were a staple of the breakfasts and midday dinners that were eaten while the kitchen radio was tuned to country music programs. Burke had attended a Flatt and Scruggs concert. He came away deeply impressed by their professionalism and the clean, entertaining show that contrasted with the growing honky-tonkism of contemporary country and western.

Williams went to see the act and immediately agreed. His shareholder relatives cringed at the idea of hillbilly musicians as Martha White spokesmen, but Cohen prevailed. Once it worked, the family thought he was the smartest guy ever.

The synergy worked for Flatt and Scruggs as well. The Martha White deal provided enough cash flow to allow them to pay their Foggy Mountain Boys a regular weekly salary. So in contrast to the Blue Grass Boys (who were being paid only if there was work, day by sporadic day), there was little turnover in Flatt and Scruggs's outfit. Their band kept getting more polished as the years went on.

The great irony was Martha White flour had been the chief ingredient in Gladys Flatt's biscuits, the ones Bill had consumed with such gusto in 1946. Now, in an unpleasantly symbolic way, Martha White was eating up Bill Monroe.

Monroe was never a candidate for such full-time corporate sponsorship. Although a compelling stage figure, he was a pathetic pitchman. Not only was he aloof, he had only the vaguest conception of how commercials are done. On one occasion, Bill was handed a short product endorsement script just before doing a radio show.[11] When it came time to read the spot, the host gave Bill an intro and cued him, then stood in helpless horror as Bill said, right on the air, "I left my glasses at home this morning, I believe I'll have this boy read this" — and handed the sheet to his banjo player.

The day inevitably came when Flatt and Scruggs were asked to make a guest appearance on the Opry.[12] Backstage at the Ryman, Flatt saw Monroe. After their pleasant visits in Bristol, he had no reason to suspect anything was wrong.

"Hi, Bill!" Lester greeted his old employer.

Monroe walked right by him.

Lester immediately thought: Well, he's got that bad eye, he might not have seen me.

But later in the evening, their paths crossed again. The same "Hi, Bill," the same nonresponse. The truth washed bitterly over Lester Flatt: He was being rudely snubbed. Later he told a friend, "I made up my mind from then on, that if there was any speaking done between me and him, by God, he'd be the first to do it." Flatt stuck to his principles on the matter, and Monroe stuck to his. For years.

But forced together in the close confines of the WSM radio studios or backstage at the Opry, band members would speak to each other. The effusive Jimmy Martin often greeted Lester and Earl. It was clear they regretted the estrangement, and on at least one occasion told Jimmy how much they still loved Bill.[13]

Monroe remained at the height of his creative and performing powers. His combined talents as a singer-instrumentalist-composer were unrivaled in country music. Yet in truth, Flatt and Scruggs simply had a much more polished and entertaining band at this stage.

Mac Wiseman, who played in both the Blue Grass Boys and the Foggy Mountain Boys, saw the differences:

> Flatt and Scruggs didn't have as much turnover as Bill. We did rehearsals with Flatt and Scruggs and learned our parts and were more closely knit probably than Bill's band. With Bill, it was kind of learn-on-your-own. If you had questions, he wasn't standoffish. He wouldn't try not to answer them. But it was pretty much up to you how quickly you

wanted to learn it and play catch-up. So he was more loose, but he was very strict in wanting it his way.

Although Monroe had tightly rehearsed his first edition of the Blue Grass Boys prior to auditioning at WSM, a decade later his style as a band-leader seemed to be influenced, probably subconsciously, by his own experiences working as a youth on the family farm. Little Willie, shunted aside in the hustle and bustle of life, had rarely been taught various chores and skills directly. He had typically learned by watching his father. Now Bill, the boss of his own musical farm system, was expecting his employees to do the same: show interest, watch and listen closely, learn on their own.

Monroe continued to give 100 percent as an individual performer, but his shows were becoming too informal in comparison with the polished offerings of Flatt and Scruggs. Bill seemed to be acting like a pouting schoolchild who refuses to do homework. Mac Wiseman agrees that as great as Monroe was, in the aftermath of Flatt and Scruggs's departure he allowed himself to suffer a letdown.

> I firmly believe that he wouldn't have had a dry spell at all when Flatt and Scruggs left him if he'd just got him two or three more good guys and kicked ass. I just feel he didn't concentrate on putting his unit back together as tight as it was when Flatt and Scruggs were with him. It would have took [Flatt and Scruggs] a lot longer to get established [if Bill had kept a polished act]. But it was Bill's nature. He felt like they'd done him wrong, and he felt kind of sorry for himself and pouted around for a while, and the first thing he knew they were breathing down his neck.[14]

On January 21, 1954 — almost exactly one year after his near-fatal wreck — Bill Monroe did make one significant new start: He purchased a 288-acre farm in Sumner County, Tennessee, near Goodlettsville, just over the line from Davidson County, whose seat is Nashville.[15] This farm was for Bill and Bessie. Carolyn and the children stayed at the Dickerson Road property.

Even if Bill had recovered physically from the car crash, he had not recovered from its financial aftereffects. In 1943, he and Carolyn had put down $11,000 cash to buy their little farm. Now a decade later, he could only afford to put down $10 cash as a goodwill payment on this new property. It was bought in sixty installments of $261, including principal and interest, for a final total of $15,660.

It is of no small significance that this corner of Sumner County closely resembles the terrain in Ohio County, Kentucky, nor that Bill would raise Black Angus cattle, foxhounds, and gaming chickens here, and plow, cut hay, and haul materials using old-fashioned horse and mule teams whenever possible.[16] Monroe's new farm was clearly a reinvention of the world of his childhood; only now he was safe and secure, the master of the place.

Bill Price was in 1954 one of the talented young singers who followed Jimmy Martin. Born of a farming family in (fittingly enough) Monroe, North Carolina, he later landed a contract with RCA and became the first bluegrass musician to record in high fidelity. Price saw a post-accident Bill Monroe who was enjoying life and taking time to smell the flowers — or in Bill's case, the skunks.

> Bill would do crazy things. In the winter, if it was snowing, he'd lay out and let it snow on him. If he smelled a skunk, he'd get out [of the car] and smell it, saying it was good for you, that smelling it would make you strong. If he saw some old man plowing in the field with a double shovel and a two-horse team, he'd stop, get out, and tell the man who he was and ask if he could plow awhile. He'd plow for thirty minutes and get his exercise. We'd set there, take a nap, or get out and talk. I wasn't interested in plowing. I'd had enough of that!
>
> Bessie would carry a tablecloth and sometimes when we'd pass a [farm] field, she'd go into the house and ask if we could take a watermelon, cantaloupe, or tomatoes, then cut them up and put the cloth on the hood and we'd have a picnic. Bill would peel cucumbers with his pocket knife, then put on salt and pepper. And we'd have the best times in the world.[17]

Bill and Bessie would visit each other's kinfolk, the Monroes in Rosine, the Mauldins in Norwood. Lee Mauldin, Bessie's father, thought highly of Bill and vice versa.[18] Lee was of course a master repairman, and the two shared an interest in tools. But back in Nashville, Bill's decision to leave his family and live openly with Bessie was not going to go unchallenged.

One Saturday night in late 1954 or early 1955, Bill exited the Opry as he often did, with Bessie Lee on his arm.[19] Stepping through the performers' door and into the alley, they were confronted by surprise visitors — Carolyn, Melissa, and James.

The Monroes glared at the woman they hated as a homewrecker. Suddenly, Melissa jumped Bessie. She pulled her hair and pummeled her in a fury. Bill tried to intervene, but Carolyn got in his way.

"Somebody get her off Bessie!" Bill yelled.

Carolyn yanked off a high heel and brandished it at the startled onlookers. "If you bother Melissa, I'll hit you!" she screamed, while Melissa finished the job.

Melissa's whupping of Bessie became the talk of the Opry and beyond. And it had one decided effect on Bill's performing career: At about this time, Bessie Lee was taking up the bass, her first serious foray into music making. She would be Bill's bass player for a decade and also sing on his shows as "The Carolina Songbird." Yet although she jammed backstage at the Ryman, as best as can be determined Bessie Lee Mauldin never played on the Grand Ole Opry.

Despite Bill's intractable womanizing, he had some sense of proprieties. The entire Opry knew of his affair with Bessie, but he was not going to use country music's highest-profile show to rub it in Carolyn's face. Bill was also a realist: If his family knew they could find Bessie at the Ryman every Saturday night, more blond hair would litter the alley. Bessie knew that, too.[20]

Monroe family brawls at the Ryman were nothing. A real bloodbath was beginning for country music. Elvis Aron Presley from Tupelo, Mississippi, by way of Memphis, Tennessee, had recorded his debut single for Sun Records.

Sun owner-producer Sam Phillips had been sitting in the control room listening to what Elvis, bassist Bill Black, and guitarist Scotty Moore had done to "Blue Moon of Kentucky." He exulted, "That's fine. Hell, that's different! That's a pop song now, nearly 'bout."[21]

It was more than that. The whole world was about to change.

On July 19, 1954, Phillips released Sun No. 209, "That's All Right" backed with "Blue Moon of Kentucky." A *Billboard* reviewer praised Presley as "a strong new talent" and predicted that he could appeal to fans of both country music and rhythm and blues.[22]

The reviewer was quite right. The recording was a strong seller through the South. This "Blue Moon of Kentucky" was not a Monroe-style version by any means, but Presley's quick shifts into high passages and his way of attacking certain words and dropping others showed Bill's influence. (Actually, Presley was afraid that he might be attacked and dropped with a punch by Bill for what he had done. Sam Phillips even heard a rumor that Monroe had vowed to break Sam's jaw for producing a desecration of his song.[23] Of course, the night Presley guested at the Opry, Monroe was gracious and even complimentary.)

Bill Monroe and Jimmy Martin were listening to the car radio en route to a show when they first heard the hopped-up "Blue Moon of Kentucky."[24] Jimmy turned to Bill and said, "That guy's gonna tear this country up."

Monroe had an equally keen ear and an eye on the charts. On September 4, 1954 — just a month and a half after the release of Presley's single — Bill was back in the studio with a single purpose: to rerecord "Blue Moon of Kentucky." No other number was done that day.

Monroe did the introduction and 32 bars in 3/4 time, then shifted to 64 bars of rapid 2/4 time. Monroe's competitive fires were evidently stoked by the Presley hit: The 2/4 time segment was played even faster than Presley's. It proved a brilliant balance of old and new. (Interestingly, many rockabillies began recording the song not like Presley but like Monroe, with the waltz to straight time segue.)[25] Monroe used triple fiddles to further stoke up his new arrangement.

He urged the Stanley Brothers to cover "Blue Moon of Kentucky" as a wise career move. They took his advice, and Bill attended the session.[26] Soon, songwriting royalties on Presley's version began to come in. "They was powerful checks," Bill later observed. "Powerful checks."[27]

*   *   *

Another rising rockabilly had perked up Monroe's waltz, although not in a recording studio. Carl Perkins of Tiptonville, Tennessee, the future composer of "Blue Suede Shoes," had grown up loving country music, especially Bill Monroe's.[28] His father faithfully tuned into the Opry every Saturday night. Little Carl enjoyed Roy Acuff, too, but he was captivated by Monroe's high lonesome singing. His brother Jay became an Ernest Tubb fan with precious little use for Monroe's keening tenor or its influence on his brother.

"Man," Jay would scoff, "those low notes that Ernest hits, that's a whole lot better than that ol' high stuff you do."

"I'll tell you one thing," Carl would shoot back. "Bill can whip Ernest." These exchanges would end in competitive brotherly wrestling matches. Monroe would have been proud.

The Perkins boys never aspired to play exactly like Monroe, Acuff, or Tubb; in 1947, they organized a band with pronounced rhythm and blues influences. But they dreamed of playing the Grand Ole Opry and they performed "Blue Moon of Kentucky" in a fast 2/4 time. Then in the summer of 1954, Carl heard another clearly Monroe-influenced singer doing that same number in the same meter — someone named Elvis Presley.

Carl and Jay Perkins first saw Presley play in a high school gym near their hometown. They met him after the show, and Carl's take on Presley's musical influences was confirmed. As Perkins later recalled:

> I loved the blues and I loved bluegrass. . . . I heard this "Blue Moon of Kentucky" by Elvis, and I said, "Whoa!" Believe me, I played the song *that* way. It was Bill Monroe–influenced bluegrass, that uptempo sound, that turned me around in country music.
>
> Upon meeting Elvis — and here's the historical fact — Elvis said to me, "You like Mr. Bill Monroe?" I said, "I love Mr. Bill Monroe." Elvis said, "Man, I do, too." I said, "I knew you did. I could tell it by the first record."
>
> Rock & roll music is a derivative of rockabilly music; rockabilly music is Bill Monroe and the blues tied together. That's it.[29]

When Carl Perkins's career took off in 1956, he fulfilled his dream of guesting on the Grand Ole Opry and meeting his idols Monroe and

Acuff.[30] That same year, Perkins found himself touring with another dedicated, if unlikely, Bill Monroe fan — a black guitar player, singer, and songwriter from Saint Louis named Chuck Berry.

Just as Presley and Perkins had listened appreciatively to black rhythm and blues, the singer-composer of the pop/R&B classics "Maybellene" and "Roll Over Beethoven" was an unashamed fan of white country. Berry knew every one of the blue yodel songs recorded by Jimmie Rodgers and most of Bill Monroe's songs, too. He and Perkins would spend miles riding together and harmonizing on "Knoxville Girl" and "Blue Moon of Kentucky."[31]

Johnny Cash loved Monroe's music. "I could sing his songs when I was a kid with a high tenor, before my voice broke," Cash recalled in his autobiography.[32] When, on December 4, 1956, Carl Perkins was scheduled for a recording session at Sun Studios, Cash was there to watch. In midafternoon, Elvis and his girlfriend stopped by. The general cutting-up turned into some jamming.

Elvis sat down at the piano, and he, Cash, and Perkins started singing gospel songs, then some Bill Monroe numbers.[33] They tried (with varying degrees of success) to do such Bill Monroe classics as "Little Cabin Home on the Hill," "Summertime Is Past and Gone," "I Hear a Sweet Voice Calling," and "Sweetheart You Done Me Wrong."

Buddy Holly had grown up in Lubbock, Texas, idolizing Edd Mayfield and his brothers and, as a result, their hero Bill Monroe.[34] Holly had a little bluegrass band around town before bursting onto the national scene with "Peggy Sue." Buddy put a little high-pitched yodel ornamentation at the end of lines in his big hit ("Uh-oh! Peggy Sue!"), certainly a very Monroe-like effect, and his strumming, driving guitar solo was reminiscent of Bill's mandolin work on "Blue Grass Breakdown."

The early rockers and rockabillies — Presley, Holly, Perkins, Cash, and all the rest — adored Monroe, and small wonder. He wasn't a soft, sappy kind of country singer. He played his mandolin like a rock guitar and he had attitude in abundance. Even where his influence wasn't direct, it was still pervasive: It can hardly be a coincidence that the beat and general groove of Bill Haley's "Rock Around the Clock" is so similar to Bill Monroe's "Rocky Road Blues."

The bitter irony, of course, was that the same young musicians who stood in awe of Bill Monroe were about to push him, and others like him, off the stage. Rock 'n' roll began to take the youth audience away from country music. And that was a disaster.

As in any times of crisis, be it during wars or ecological upheavals, survival is found in niches. Now was no exception. Little family-oriented country music parks scattered throughout the South, Midwest, and Midatlantic provided an informal circuit for acts like Monroe's. These quaint venues had open spaces for "dinner on the ground" (picnics), concert areas with a roofed-over stage, benches and rudimentary sound systems, and few other amenities. But there was down-home atmosphere in abundance. Their delightful names alone evoke the feeling of hearing the real stuff in the real context: Mockingbird Hill Park in Anderson, Indiana; Frontier Ranch in Kirkersville, Ohio; Himmelreich's Grove in Womelsdorf, Pennsylvania; Valley View Park in Hallam, Pennsylvania. The names now sound like apartment complexes or shopping malls. Sadly, that is what many of the properties have become.

Although independently booked, they operated like a circuit. In the years when rock 'n' roll first swept up vast segments of the national audience for music, these parks helped keep country, including its bluegrass and old-time substyles, alive by attracting families — and a growing subculture of northern enthusiasts — from long distances.

On May 8, 1955, the fields that served as parking lots for New River Ranch in Rising Sun, Maryland, were filled to capacity. Latecomers were forced to leave their cars along the road and walk in. The attraction — believed to be the biggest in the park's history — was a reunion of the Monroe Brothers.

This reunion had been masterminded by Don Owens, a promoter, singer, and deejay with a show on WARL in Arlington, Virginia. Owens successfully pitched the idea of having Charlie perform with the Kentucky Pardners and Bill with his Blue Grass Boys, then as a grand finale having the two appear as the Monroe Brothers.

They reprised at New River Ranch on July 31. Bill showed up with his left arm in a sling. He had slipped in a bathtub while touring in

Vermont and suffered a broken collarbone.[35] Blue Grass Boys Charlie Cline and Bobby Hicks had been taking over on the mandolin during this period, and today it was Cline's mixed glory to play the instrument. (He was of course mercilessly kidded onstage by Bill whenever he made a mistake.) Otherwise the event was another triumph. The brothers seemed to genuinely enjoy performing together again.

"You Blue Grass Boys go off and take a rest," Charlie instructed.[36] "Brother Bill and I will take care of it from now on." The happy arrogance had not died.

The shows were not their first public appearance since that day in 1938 when Charlie had hitched up his trailer and Bill had stayed put. They had ridden together to the first Jimmie Rodgers Day in Meridian, Mississippi, on May 26, 1953, and performed as the Monroe Brothers.[37] ("You never heared such a holler," says Jimmy Martin of the crowd's reaction.) Yet strangely, despite the success of these reunions, there was apparently no attempt to further capitalize on the immense popularity of the duo.

Lester Flatt and Earl Scruggs & the Foggy Mountain Boys were certainly capitalizing on their own immense popularity. By May 1954, they were based at WSVS in Crewe, Virginia, and also appearing on WRVA in Richmond weekdays (with a 5:15 A.M. show) and Saturday nights (on the WRVA *Old Dominion Barn Dance*).[38] But they were also taping an early morning radio show sponsored by Martha White and broadcast over WSM in Nashville.

They were working hard and drawing inexorably closer to their ultimate goal — full membership on the Grand Ole Opry. They made the big move to Nashville and WSM,[39] doing early morning radio and three television shows a week, and began guesting at the Opry. They had left Mercury and were quickly in a Nashville recording studio for the Columbia label.

Lester Flatt and Earl Scruggs & the Foggy Mountain Boys became one of the most effective acts in American music history. Lester had the great voice and genial emcee skills, Earl had the captivating banjo. They had a tight and truly versatile band, the perfect sponsor, and they also had one of the best agents around — Earl's wife, Louise Certain Scruggs.[40]

Louise Scruggs was a pioneer of women in country music promotion. She became one of the best managers and booking agents, male or female, in the industry, thanks to her thoroughness and dedication. Says Lance LeRoy, a country music historian and head of the Lancer Agency in Nashville:

> Back in those days, booking a band was a thankless job. Nobody wanted it and nobody did it good. Louise was the exception. She did every-thing that needed to be done, she was right there full time. She worked with Martha White about the advertising of the shows and followed up on things. A lot of bands would work without a contract. Things were verbal — "When's that? Oh, May 6, yeah, we'll be there" — and bands wouldn't be there because they got the dates mixed up. But that didn't happen with Flatt and Scruggs, because they had Louise.[41]

It is part of the modern mythos of bluegrass that the music is a pure, folk-roots art form that would be much more successful if the country music establishment hadn't actively repressed it in favor of an increas-ingly sequiny, electrified commercial product. While it is certainly true that Nashville later treated bluegrass like a poor relative, many bluegrass performers were choosing to live in the backwoods of business, as LeRoy notes:

> The business level just about didn't exist. Bluegrass is such a music of the hills. Many of the first-generation people were born back in the coun-try. I'm not saying they were ignorant, certainly not. They were smart people, they knew how to make money and they knew how to conduct themselves and put on a show. They were great musicians. But it was not part of their heritage to look after the paperwork end of things.[42]

With each new Flatt and Scruggs success, Opry cast members could see that Bill was truly, if silently, irked. Some began to tease him: "Say, that Lester and Earl are gettin' real popular,"[43] and "I believe them boys is gonna be asked to join the Opry."

That pushed Monroe's buttons. "If they ever come back here," he declared, "it will be as members of the Blue Grass Boys."[44] Monroe expressed that sentiment openly and on more than one occasion. Word started getting back to the Foggy Mountain Boys that Monroe was even sneering that they would soon be holding tin cups and begging on the street.[45]

In fact, it was Bill who was in danger of begging. He was paying scant attention to business matters, playing a patchwork of low-paying percentage-only jobs, and often letting the pleasures (as well as the chaos) of his love life intrude on his professional activities.

Stung by the teasing, Monroe — usually a man of carefully chosen words — had worked himself into a corner. He couldn't back down without losing face, so he made a final desperate effort to stave off his former sidemen: He circulated a petition among the Opry cast opposing the hiring of Flatt and Scruggs.[46]

Monroe continued to make his reasoned case that the Opry had one Roy Acuff, one Ernest Tubb, one Bill Monroe, each with a distinctive sound. The Opry wouldn't hire Acuff or Tubb imitators. Why should it hire Monroe imitators? So it was to Acuff and Tubb — who, in Bill's mind, formed with him the great triumvirate of Opry vocalist-stars — that he now turned. Acuff signed the petition, but then thought better of it and insisted that Monroe scratch his name off the paper. Monroe approached Tubb, who declined outright.

"Well, Bill," Ernest said, "I like Lester and Earl. They're mighty good boys, and I think they'd be good for the Opry. I think they have a right to play here just like the rest of us."[47]

Knowing that Lester and Earl were deserving, Cohen T. Williams of Martha White went to Opry director Jim Denny and told him very clearly that if membership was withheld, Martha White — a major WSM sponsor since 1948 — would pull its advertising.[48] Denny relented.

In January 1955, Flatt and Scruggs officially joined the show. Opry fans cheered the new additions, having no idea of the bitter power struggle that had been played out behind the Ryman's folksy advertising backdrops. Often the rivals would be on the Opry the same night. Backstage, they would pointedly ignore each other.[49] Monroe even asked his sidemen not to hang out with or even speak to members of the Foggy Mountain Boys.[50]

As the years went by, other bluegrass musicians came to believe that Monroe had actively opposed their addition to the Opry. Jimmy Martin was one of them. Martin's brash and occasionally abrasive personality was not winning him many friends backstage during his Opry guest appearances. However there is no question that the faithful Jimmy, now independently successful, was being exposed to Bill's absolute-zero chill:

> I really loved singing with Bill and working with him, and he was real good to me. Me and Bill Monroe, I would say, were as close as any two musicians ever have been when I was a Blue Grass Boy. But when I went out on my own and my records started getting up on the charts, he started to ignore me and wouldn't even talk to me. It seemed like the more popular I was, the less he cared for me.
>
> I hated that. I wanted so bad for it to be like it used to be with us.[51]

Lance LeRoy, who became good friends with Bill and even did business with him, expresses a widely held sentiment:

> I found a lot to like about Bill. It was just one of those mixed bags. Bill was an intensely jealous person. It was just ingrained in him. He was jealous of other bands. And no one could hurt him — he certainly was not jealous because he thought someone was better than he was.
>
> In my opinion, the root of the whole thing was that Bill thought of bluegrass as his music, and that anyone who did it after him was an imitator, that they were trying to steal something from him. But you invent a machine; you don't invent a music.[52]

Bill was genuinely puzzled that some audiences preferred the Flatt and Scruggs brand of bluegrass to his. "They just don't play it right," he once said, shaking his head in bewilderment.[53] Added to his dogged competitiveness was his militant territoriality. It is highly significant that his favorite farm chore was working on his fence lines.[54] Monroe had a fierce sense of boundaries, both personal and professional. Even late in life, he was offended if someone began dating one of his former girlfriends.[55] At some level, Monroe felt that certain people and places were always his. And he tolerated no intrusions on his turf.

Lester Flatt and Earl Scruggs had unwittingly pushed Bill Monroe's most sensitive buttons: They had left him; they had begun competing with him; and they had come into his backyard, the Grand Ole Opry. As long as former Blue Grass Boys stayed in the hinterlands, Bill was tolerant of them, even cordial. But once they tried to become an Opry peer, it was war, a cold war of stony silences.

On September 16, 1955, recovered from his broken collarbone, Bill was back in the studio. It was a noteworthy session on several counts. It featured triple fiddles — a true dream team of Vassar Clements, Bobby Hicks, and Gordon Terry — and a new bass player, Bessie Lee Mauldin.

Bessie had come to performing music late in life. (She was now thirty-four.) But she would play with Bill on a total of 31 sessions and 99 cuts, more than any other bass player (indeed, more than any musician with the exception of fiddler Kenny Baker). Onstage, she was a glamorous figure, heavyset but pretty with bleached blond hair, wearing colorful, shiny dresses and lots of makeup and jewelry. She could be bossy, and she had a temper. She could be generous, too, and loved buying presents for the children of Bill's favorite sidemen.[56] She had style and charisma. In many ways, she was a female Bill Monroe.

In addition to the yearning love songs she had inspired, Bessie was directly or indirectly responsible for at least three other Monroe classics.[57] On one return visit to her hometown of Norwood, Bessie had introduced Bill to the Tysons, a black family. Elizabeth Tyson worked for the Mauldins as a domestic. Her husband, a preacher, was a fan of Monroe's. Mr. Tyson invited Bill to supper and taught him "Walking in Jerusalem Just Like John."

Bessie also claimed that she had written or provided the concept for "Cheyenne," an adventurous instrumental with an American Indian flavor, and that she wholly wrote "A Voice from On High," an expansive gospel quartet. (Her claims for the latter are supported by the composer's credit she shared with Monroe and the fact that she sometimes sang solo lead on the song in concert.)

Bessie's occasionally bossy behavior came in handy. She began to act as

Bill's de facto road manager, sitting in the front seat of the car, road atlas in hand, getting the Blue Grass Boys around to their dates.[58]

Some kind of organization was needed, because Bill and other country acts were desperately trying to ride out the rock 'n' roll boom.

Backstage at the Opry, gloom and doom prevailed. Stars and sidemen alike groused that country music was done, finished, over.

"Yeah, I believe it's about over," Lester Flatt would say with an absolutely straight face, then get on the Martha White bus for another tour during which the Foggy Mountain Boys would often work two shows a day.[59] Lester and Earl were the most booked Opry act at this time.[60]

Soon, Nashville started to mount a concerted response to the rock challenge. Some mainstream country recordings began using slick pop-style arrangements. Crossovers into mainstream pop became easier and more frequent. The versatile, insinuating pedal steel guitar had largely replaced the fiddle as a lead instrument; now it was giving way to mellow electric guitar, grace-note accented piano, even lush orchestrations. It was all part of "the Nashville sound," masterminded by such figures as Chet Atkins (guitar legend turned RCA A&R director) and Bill Monroe's own producer-recordist Owen Bradley, who in 1958 became head of Decca's country division after Paul Cohen moved on. Vilified today by purists for selling Nashville's soul to commercial interests, Atkins, Bradley, and company were simply fighting to help country music evolve and survive in a Darwinian cultural climate.

The implications for bluegrass were devastating. As country music adopted a more urbane image, it had little room for roots sounds. It was as if traditional-style string band music had survived the initial rock 'n' roll bombing only to be locked out of the bomb shelter. As Mac Wiseman notes:

> The [radio] stations, and a lot of these little music directors and pro-
> gram directors, they all visualized bluegrass as the hillbilly barefoot and
> in overalls. Consequently, they said, "We can't play that." Ironically,
> that was the image Monroe was trying to fight, the barefoot musician

and everybody in a different checkered shirt. It was just another country record before it was called bluegrass. To me, that was the only damage that came out of the bluegrass movement, that it segregated us
within the industry.[61]

There was also a clash of sounds. By the late 1950s, the contrasts were
just too great for a Bill Monroe record to be played on radio back-to-back
with chart-topping singles by Patsy Cline, Eddy Arnold, Don Gibson, or
Jim Reeves. It was the searing versus the smooth; the lonesome fiddle
contrasted to the lush string section; the chopping mandolin against the
brushed snare drum.

There were other changes in the music business. It was the era now of the
long-playing, 33⅓ album. In 1957, Monroe set about recording his first,
and it proved to be a masterpiece — *Knee Deep in Blue Grass.*

There were no straight instrumentals and only one trio harmony.
Otherwise the material had a pleasing variety. Again, he featured triple
fiddles, the dense yet gorgeously fluid sound that he helped bring into
the Nashville mainstream.[62] Monroe opened the record with a searing solo on "Cry Cry Darlin'," a cover of a hit by fellow Opry star Jimmy
Newman. He rerecorded his classic racehorse song "Molly and Tenbrooks," with Don Stover ably following in Earl Scruggs's pick patterns. "In Despair," the album's only cut with harmony, was topped by
an impassioned Monroe chorus high harmony. (This number was another
of Bill's autobiographical songs:[63] Monroe had a girlfriend in Burling-
ton, North Carolina, and one day, while in the area, decided to pay her
a surprise visit. It was Bill who got the surprise. There was a car in the
driveway, which he recognized as belonging to another man who had
been courting this lady. Bill drove on and never returned, later writing
the song about the experience of calling on this lover and finding another
there.)

Perhaps the biggest surprises were two rockabilly-style numbers recorded with Doug Kershaw on guitar. On the night of December 15,
Kershaw (the original "Ragin' Cajun" from Louisiana) had been madly
strumming away backstage at the Opry on something he had just written

called "Sally-Jo." Someone tapped him on the shoulder. It was Monroe. "I want to record that tomorrow for Decca Records," Bill said.[64] And perhaps to show the rock 'n' rollers a thing or two, at the session Bill recorded a mandolin kickoff to "Brand New Shoes" that would have blown even Chuck Berry out of the studio. These two tracks were among the most arresting — and most unbluegrassy — that Monroe ever recorded, further proof of his astonishing versatility.

The unbowed Monroe was still capable of surprising with big-selling singles. "Scotland" featured the twin fiddles of Kenny Baker and Bobby Hicks providing bagpipe-like airs. Released in November 1958, the stirring instrumental marched onto the *Billboard* country charts and peaked at number 27. It was Monroe's first top-30 hit in nine years.

In December, Bill covered the strutting "Gotta Travel On," which had been a hit for the Weavers folk music group and country singer Billy Grammer. Released in March 1959, this too became a major seller for Monroe, reaching number 15 on the country charts.

Bill also continued to record his powerful but more esoteric music. Fiddler Charlie Smith composed the haunting instrumental "Stoney Lonesome," using a jarring, staccato-accented opening theme given him by Monroe.[65] It was titled after a town in southern Indiana that Monroe would pass through en route to the Brown County Jamboree, a name with immediate resonance for Bill. Bobby Hicks, a genius at devising fiddle harmonies, played flatted harmonies that should have caused dissonance but instead created chilling beauty. With Smith and Hicks's lines almost impossibly intertwined like a musical Möbius strip, "Stoney Lonesome" was exquisite, perhaps the most underrated of all Monroe's instrumental recordings.

Despite such creative triumphs, Bill was still on hard times. His music had helped define early rock and country; now trends in those mainstream genres were diverging from his roots-based sound. The bottom line showed it.

Unable to maintain a bus, he started using Bessie Lee Mauldin's white 1958 Oldsmobile station wagon as the band's touring vehicle. He needed it badly. In July 1958, the General Motors Acceptance Corporation had repossessed Bill's 1956 Cadillac.[66] He still owed $3,200.37 on the $6,989 automobile. To make matters worse, GMAC claimed it could only get $1,209.31 in resale for the used car and sued Bill in chancery court for the difference of $1,991.06.

The repossession of the Cadillac was a mild loss compared to a very personal one Bill suffered that summer.

Edd Mayfield, the cowpunching, rope-climbing Texan, had been riding the rodeo circuit when he decided to return to Nashville and show business.[67] In February and March 1958, he participated in the sessions that produced the *I Saw the Light* gospel album. This banjoless, fiddleless album would not have succeeded had not Edd been a solid guitarist who melded with Bill's inspired mandolin lines. In April, during the recording of the instrumental "Panhandle Country," Mayfield provided a rousing and rare guitar solo.

Like Bill, Edd was tough and didn't complain if he took sick. When the Blue Grass Boys left for a tour in July, Monroe sensed that Mayfield wasn't feeling well. Edd's condition noticeably worsened by the time they arrived in Pulaski, Virginia, but there was a delay in getting him admitted to the local hospital.

The band pushed on to Bluefield, West Virginia, where a doctor examined the ailing guitarist, immediately hospitalized him, and then delivered the terrible diagnosis — Edd Mayfield had advanced leukemia and would probably live only another three days.

Monroe immediately called Edd's wife, Jody, in Nashville and every Mayfield friend and relation he could think of. He refused to leave Edd's side. Jody and their sons finally arrived and visited with him. Then Edd softly requested, "You're just going to have to let me rest," and gazed up to a corner of the room.

Twenty minutes later he was dead. Edd Mayfield was just thirty-two. The sudden demise of this man — so strong and vital, someone who also loved "Mother Nature," a superb musician and a favorite traveling companion — shook Bill Monroe like few other events in his life. Although he never stopped visiting sick friends, forever after when he walked into a hospital he was haunted by the memory of watching his Texas cowboy friend die.[68]

As Bill was struggling in his career, a national entertainment craze held the promise of providing huge new audiences for southern string band music. The folk song revival or "hootenanny" movement had begun.

Mini-revivals had seeded the fields for this late-fifties flowering of folk. Field recordings of folk music done in the early 1930s for the Library of Congress (notably those by the father and son song collecting team of John and Alan Lomax) documented America's rich store of folk sounds and gained respectability for indigenous music. The labor movement employed topical folk songs to rally its members. In the early 1950s came the first crossings into the commercial mainstream: the Weavers' pop chart successes with Leadbelly's "Goodnight, Irene" and Woody Guthrie's "So Long, It's Been Good to Know You," and balladeer Burl Ives's recording of "Goober Peas," which earned more than the peanuts celebrated in the song.

Then in 1952 appeared the folk music collection to begin all such collections: *The Anthology of American Folk Music,* a compilation of old 78 "string band" and "race" records that had preserved the best of mountain music, old-time gospel, and the blues. Produced by the avant garde filmmaker, amateur ethnologist, and world-class eccentric Harry Smith, the anthology stunned listeners with sounds that were raw, gentle, bizarre, familiar, primitive, and sophisticated all at once. The Monroe Brothers were not included (the material on the three *Anthology* disks released by Folkways Records only went through 1933) but many of their contemporaries were: Uncle Dave Macon, Charlie Poole & the North Carolina Ramblers, the Carter Family. The impact of the *Anthology* was profound, reviving interest in both black and white rural music.

In the late 1950s, folk music exploded. Where had all the flowers gone? From the grassroots into receptive cracks in the urban/suburban culture. For those unhappy with modern society, folk music suggested the colors, scents, and textures of a more authentic time. The folk scene offered a purer cultural identity, or at least the fantasy of one.

In 1958, the Kingston Trio recorded "Tom Dooley," an old ballad that had been taught by North Carolina traditional singer Frank Profitt to New York City folkie Frank Warner.[69] It went straight to number 1 on the *Billboard* charts. More million-selling hits followed by the Kingston Trio, the Limelighters, the Chad Mitchell Trio, and, later, Peter, Paul, and Mary.

It didn't take long for the hootenanny movement to discover bluegrass. Its core repertoire included many old mountain ballads and it was played on nonelectric folk instruments. Pretty Pollys, handsome Mollys, and little Maggies were characters in its songs. The settings were romantic hills and hollows and mountains and farms.

And bluegrass was just plain exciting. Prominent folklorist Alan Lomax tapped into this feeling while endorsing the music in "Bluegrass Underground: Folk Music with Overdrive" in the October 1959 *Esquire*. Lomax raised the intriguing parallels between bluegrass and jazz — and specifically praised Bill Monroe and Earl Scruggs:

> Out of the torrent of folk music that is the backbone of the record business today, the freshest sound comes from the so-called Bluegrass band — a sort of mountain Dixieland combo in which the five-string banjo, America's only indigenous folk instrument, carries the lead like a hot clarinet. The mandolin plays bursts reminiscent of jazz trumpet choruses; a heavily bowed fiddle supplies trombone-like hoedown solos; while a framed guitar and slapped bass make up the rhythm section. Everything goes at top volume, with harmonized choruses behind a lead singer who hollers in the high, lonesome style beloved in the American backwoods. . . .
>
> Bluegrass style began in 1945 when Bill Monroe, of the Monroe Brothers, recruited a quintet that included Earl Scruggs (who had perfected a three-finger banjo style now known as "picking scruggs") and Lester Flatt (a Tennessee guitar picker and singer); Bill led the group with mandolin and a countertenor voice that hits high notes with the impact of a Louis Armstrong trumpet.[70]

Louise Scruggs made sure that Lomax's mentions of Lester and Earl — plus the catchy phrase "folk music with overdrive" — quickly found a place in their press material. But the Monroe camp did absolutely nothing with this tremendous publicity, although Bill desperately needed it. His profile was so low that many northern converts to bluegrass assumed he had retired. Some even thought he was dead.[71]

Much of the folk revival was banjo-driven. David Guard's rudimentary banjo playing with the Kingston Trio had given the five-string a plunky popularity, and thousands were taking up the instrument. Soon, folkie pickers began hearing about bluegrass-style banjo and a musical god named Earl Scruggs.

On July 12, 1959, Scruggs appeared at the inaugural Newport Folk Festival in Rhode Island, backed by guitarist-vocalist Hylo Brown and his group, The Timberliners. (Since Scruggs and his banjo were what the folkies wanted to hear, Earl appeared this time without his usual band.)

Scruggs was a cult figure, and his northern acolytes were out in force to worship him. For new listeners, it was conversion. As tasteful and versatile as Pete Seeger was, as widely heard as the Kingston Trio's records had made David Guard, none of their playing prepared the uninitiated for the staggering virtuosity, the seamless melding of lead lines and backup counterpoints, the sheer avalanche of excitement that was the music of Earl Scruggs.

"It was fabulous," recalls Clarence "Tater" Tate, who was playing fiddle with Hylo Brown that day.[72] "They wouldn't hardly let him leave. He could have encored all night." The rolling entry of bluegrass banjo into the folk music revival is dated from the moment that Scruggs stepped up to a microphone at Newport and put pick to string.

The next year, the complete ensemble of Flatt and Scruggs & the Foggy Mountain Boys played the festival. They started doing regular tours up north and at folk music–friendly colleges. Meanwhile, Monroe continued to perform in relative obscurity on the southern country music circuit. And he was faltering creatively.

Monroe returned to the studio on November 25, 1959. Harry Silverstein of Decca, an assistant to Owen Bradley, was now handling Monroe's sessions and trying to follow up on the success of "Gotta Travel On." Oblivious to the market for folk music, he urged Bill to record more country-style material. Monroe agreed, and the session yielded three rather bland cuts.[73]

Silverstein was bemused by how much coaxing it could take to get Bill into the studio.[74] Sometimes it proved impossible to reach Monroe at home, so Harry was forced to leave messages at Bill's favorite gas station or grocery store. He concluded that Monroe was truly of the old school: first and foremost a live, in-concert performer for whom records were of secondary interest.

Monroe was so far out of the folk music loop that he wasn't even invited to Newport. But he was invited by folklorist Alan Lomax to the "Folk Song '59" concert at New York's Carnegie Hall. The April 3 event was to folk music what John Hammond's landmark 1938 "Spirituals to Swing" program had been to African-American gospel, blues, and jazz. In both cases, music previously dismissed as déclassé was now being revealed at the nation's most prestigious concert space as vital American art.

Incredibly, Monroe turned Lomax down.

Lomax was a northern intellectual and folk song collector outside the commercial country music circuit. Monroe also associated him with left-wing politics.[75] (Although the Lomaxes had worked with some folk singers who had been affiliated with the American Communist Party, this characterization was certainly unfair.) Overall, the folk music scene was an alien world to Bill.

In any event, it was a colossal blunder, a missed opportunity for Monroe to jump-start his stalled career. Lomax then attempted to get Flatt and Scruggs, but delayed the process by calling Flatt. By the time Louise Scruggs got back to him, Lomax had already hired Earl Taylor & the Stoney Mountain Boys. The Baltimore-based Taylor was a solid mandolinist-vocalist but he was no Bill Monroe; in fact, he was a second-tier blue-grasser. Yet the Carnegie Hall crowd went wild for him. Taylor recalled that when his band ended a number "it would take five minutes before we could go into another one — that was how much rarin' and screamin' and hair-pullin' there was."[76] This was the adulation that Bill Monroe missed; plus the Stoney Mountain Boys earned the eternal distinction of being the first bluegrass musicians to perform at Carnegie Hall.

Then, at the end of 1959, Bill Monroe received yet another invitation. This one he could not refuse.

*   *   *

On the evening of Saturday, December 12, Monroe was approached at the Opry by a man holding a piece of paper.[77] He was not an autograph seeker.

Three days earlier, a court summons had been issued. Now it was being served. After two decades of infidelities and years of actual desertion, Carolyn filed for divorce in the Fourth Circuit Court of Davidson County, Tennessee, in the county seat of Nashville.

Despite the vagaries of Bill's touring schedule, she knew there was one sure place to locate him and serve the papers, and the summons contained that information: "Deft. [defendant] can be found at Grand Ole Opera [sic] Sat. Night 8:30."

Carolyn's divorce petition — written by her attorney in no-nonsense southern prose — poured out the details of the tumultuous marriage.

Carolyn claimed that she and Bill "got along fine the first few years of their married life" but that after the birth of their second child, "the defendant lost interest in her and commenced running around with other women. He would constantly be after women or them after him. He would spend the greater portion of his money on women and on carousing."

Of course, a certain woman was specifically named: "About the latter part of 1941, he took up with one Bessie Mauldin and has been going with her since. They are now living together at Goodlettsville, Tennessee on Allen Road, as man and wife. . . . She would make trips with him and he would spend his money upon her and other women." The claim that Bill and Bessie were living together as man and wife was a damaging legal point that would come back one day to haunt Bill.

Carolyn alleged that she and the children did not even have a phone, could not afford furniture, and had been "almost without necessities," living in near squalor in a rundown house: "The plaster has fallen in the living room. The bedroom leaks until they have to move their bed when it rains. The outside is sorely in need of repair and gives the impression of direst poverty." It was a far cry from the genial domicile George D. Hay had described in 1945 as "a very comfortable American home, the kind one reads about but seldom sees."

Meanwhile, Carolyn claimed, Bill had "been stingy and miserly, giving them probably less than $100 per month, while he was making big money as an entertainer of national renown. . . . On one occasion after the separation Defendant came out arguing and struck her. Usually when he comes out to their place, he commences arguing — always about money, as he resents the very small amounts that Petitioner and the children have cost him." She received an injunction enjoining Bill from coming near her.

Given the late-1940s incident where Carolyn "quarreled at" Bill the whole night through, finally stabbing him in the leg and inspiring the painfully autobiographical "Along About Daybreak," and given the incident in the alley outside the Ryman Auditorium in the early 1950s during which Carolyn aided Melissa's assault on Bessie Lee, Carolyn could hardly be considered a blameless party in Monroe marital squabbles. And she was under no real threat of bodily harm: Bill certainly had a temper and it is possible that he did indeed shove or strike Carolyn during the incident she mentioned. But Bill Monroe was not a wife beater. The issue was not abuse, it was abandonment. This was thoroughly consistent with Bill's behavior throughout his life. If he became angry with someone he would not threaten them or strike them or even sue them; he would pointedly ignore them.

Carolyn petitioned the court for an absolute divorce on the basis of adultery, abandonment, and "willful or malicious desertion and/or absence." She asked for custody of James, who was then still a minor. And she pointedly asked for a full disclosure of Bill's financial situation.

A special master appointed by the court gathered information on the assets of the parties. The results document that Monroe's fortunes at this stage of his career were nowhere near those of the golden 1940s.

The 44-acre farm on Dickerson Road (where Carolyn and the children had been left) was valued at $32,500 but was encumbered by a mortgage in the principal of $10,550.50 plus interest, and subject to taxes, accrued costs, and penalties. The 270-acre farm in Sumner County (where Bill and Bessie were keeping house) was valued at $14,500 and was without encumbrances. However, there were delinquent taxes on this property for the proceeding years of 1958 and 1959 of $204, plus costs, penalties, and current taxes. In 1957, Monroe had net earnings of $2,621.30 from appearances of his band; in 1958, a loss of $373.91; and in 1959, earnings of $2,103.21.

"All the foregoing payments are by cash or its equivalent from those sponsoring said appearances," the court officer wrote. Monroe, as always, was a cash-and-carry performer.

There are no replies in the case file. The divorce was probably uncontested. Carolyn was granted her divorce on August 12, 1960. An alimony settlement was reached, which included the sale of the farm on Dickerson Road.

Then the court dropped a bombshell. In finding Bill guilty of adultery with Bessie, the judge ruled: "The Defendant William S. Monroe is enjoined from marrying Bessie Mauldin during the life of the Petitioner, Carolyn Monroe."

Bill did not tell Bessie Lee about this order.[78] That too would come back to haunt him.

Just two days after the divorce was finalized, on the afternoon of Sunday, August 14, Bill Monroe & His Blue Grass Boys played a show in Virginia.[79] It was not just any show. It was the first of its kind, a landmark standing at the gateway to a new golden era for bluegrass. But no one, least of all Monroe, realized it at the time.

Don Owens, who had promoted the 1955 reunion of the Monroe Brothers at New River Ranch, was now master of ceremonies at Watermelon Park in Berryville, sixty-five miles west of Washington. Owens and park owner John U. Miller Sr. had an idea: Why not do an all-bluegrass program? Bluegrass had a good following in northern Virginia and nearby D.C., and a lineup of top acts could be assembled cheaply.

Monroe agreed to participate despite a tight touring schedule. (He flew in with one Blue Grass Boy, all-around man Joe Stuart, and they performed with a pickup band). Bill was not the headliner, another telling indication of how far his fortunes had declined. That honor went to Mac Wiseman, followed by the Osborne Brothers and ace fiddler Scotty Stoneman. Monroe was listed next in the ads in smaller type, then popular Virginia-based musicians Don Reno and Red Smiley, Buck Ryan and Smitty Irvin, and Bill Harrell. The program was a huge success. Traffic was backed up some three miles to get into the park.

New research by country music historian and WSM *Grand Ole Opry* announcer Eddie Stubbs has documented that this was the first all-day, all-bluegrass show featuring multiple bands. It was a harbinger of the week-end-long bluegrass festivals that would sprout up prolifically in just a few years. There was another sign of things to come: Owens was a New York City native who had grown up near Rochester and, later, Silver Spring, Maryland. His involvement foreshadowed the central roles nonsoutherners would soon play in bluegrass. Surprisingly, Owens and Miller did not follow up on the show's success. But the next summer Bill Clifton did.

Clifton was the scion of an old-money family that had made its fortune in tobacco. He attended private schools in New England and Florida and then the University of Virginia, where he was introduced to folk music. He began performing country music professionally and changed his name (he was born William August Marburg in 1931) to avoid embarrassing his family. With his background, his love of hillbilly music, and his performances of folk songs in a bluegrass band context, Clifton was the first of the "citybillies."[80]

In 1961, Clifton was show producer at Oak Leaf Park, in Luray, Virginia, seventy-five miles west of Washington, where bluegrass bands drew good crowds. For an all-bluegrass show on July 4, he signed up Monroe, the Stanley Brothers, Mac Wiseman, Jim and Jesse, and Washington's hot new progressive bluegrass band, the Country Gentlemen. Clifton also performed himself.

Flatt and Scruggs declined to appear. The issue was not money. Louise Scruggs informed Clifton that they would not appear if Bill Monroe was there.[81] When Clifton persisted, he was told that working with the Stanley Brothers was also unacceptable. Having no desire to take sides, Clifton booked Flatt and Scruggs for later in the season.

The promotion attracted fans not only from the D.C./Baltimore/Northern Virginia region but from as far away as New York City and Boston, many of them bluegrass-curious folkies. Israel Young later wrote in Sing Out!, the leading folk music publication, "By the end of the day I wasn't sure yet of a definition of Bluegrass Music, but I realized, to my great satisfaction, that it is a modern offshoot of traditional music. . . ."[82]

During his set, Monroe featured one of his occasional reunions with former Blue Grass Boys, this time inviting Carter Stanley to join him for duets like "Sugar Coated Love."[83] What happened next became one of the most notorious incidents in bluegrass history.

Clifton had provided some backstage hospitality in the form of a spiked punch. That was a mistake, considering that Carter had a serious problem with alcohol. By the time Carter joined Monroe onstage he was merry and feisty. Then Monroe made his own error in judgment. He couldn't resist a dig at the former sidemen who had refused to share a stage with him.

"It's a shame," Monroe said to the crowd, "a lot of bluegrass people you know think they are . . . they don't want to be on a show with you or something, if the folks will think you started them. Well, it's the truth, so they shouldn't a-mind that, and they should be glad they got a start, they'd-a probably had to plow a lot of furrows if they hadn't-a been in bluegrass music."[84]

Monroe seemed satisfied with this. He had not-so-subtly declared himself the originating and mentoring figure in bluegrass and had expressed irritation at his famous protégés without publicly identifying them. But that just set off the lubricated Carter, who had his own ax to grind.

"I guess I'll just break into this kindly blunt like," said Carter, stepping up to the microphone. "I understand they was a group that some of the folks asked to come in here today. They said no, they didn't want to play here because Bill Monroe and the Stanley Brothers was gonna be here. And that was Flatt and Scruggs. You know, we missed 'em a heck of a lot, ain't we?"

The gibe elicited laughter and applause from the crowd. Now that names had been named, Monroe decided to be more specific.

"Well, you're talking about Lester and Earl," he said. "Now I started the two boys on the Grand Ole Opry, and they shouldn't be ashamed to come on the show and work with us." After more laughter and applause, Monroe added, "And I am sure I wouldn't hurt either one of them."

It was Monroe who could be hurt, and hurt badly, by this joking banter between a slightly drunken man and a sober but prideful one. Within a year, there was the prospect of a major lawsuit and the loss of his cherished berth on the Opry. The aftermath of this incident even threatened to derail the best chance Bill Monroe had to get his career back on track.

But for the time being, the comments caused only titillation in bluegrass circles. The bands went their separate ways. One attendee, country

music promoter Carlton Haney, looked around at the successful event —
it drew about 2,200 people, not bad for a country music show anywhere
in these days, especially one held on a major holiday[85] — did the math
and pondered the possibilities.

The following year Bill Clifton was named to the newly organized
Newport Folk Foundation that was revitalizing the major folk festival
held in that Rhode Island resort. With this and business commitments,
Clifton was unable to do any more work at Oak Leaf Park.[86] Don Owens
also made no further contribution to the fledgling bluegrass festival
movement: He was killed in a car crash in the early morning hours of
Sunday, April 21, 1963, at age thirty-two.[87]

So for now, the potential of all-bluegrass shows went unrealized. Bill
Monroe & His Blue Grass Boys continued to play a patchwork of jobs.
There was always the WSM *Friday Night Frolic* and the official Grand Ole
Opry on Saturday night for union scale and a few moments of prestige.
Otherwise the Blue Grass Boys performed at the little country music
parks, as a pre-dusk act at drive-in theaters, in high school auditoriums,
courthouses, and American Legion halls. They even played for square
dances if someone would hire them.

Most acts were still contractually required to provide the local promoter with advertising posters. If Monroe did not have posters made up
by Hatch Show Print in Nashville, did not mail them in time, or (as happened all too frequently) a lazy local simply failed to put them up, there
would be scanty crowds and little money.[88]

Tater Tate, who occasionally played fiddle with the Blue Grass Boys in
the 1950s, saw at firsthand the result of poor promotion — and Monroe's
response to it.

Bill just loved the music. If he had a fifteen dollar crowd, he'd play to
them just as long and do just as good as if he had fifteen thousand. He
never worried about the money. He got by.

We worked a show, it was some place in Georgia. We played in a
courthouse in a little town. It was me, Joe Stuart and Bobby Hicks, and
I believe Jackie Phelps. And Bessie Mauldin played bass. Well, me and
Joe and the boys went walking around. The show was supposed to start
at 7:30. Bessie was at the door to sell tickets. We got back to get up

there for the show and Bessie said, "Well, I guess we'll be taking down the PA stuff. There ain't nobody here." There were only two people in there, a man and his wife. "Well," we just said, "let's give them their money back and take the stuff down and go home." Well, we got up on the stage and started to take the PA set down, and Bill got up there on the microphone with his mandolin and said, "Let's go, boys!" Nobody else even had an instrument out of the case. But we got them out and played a whole show. [Bill] said, "Those people came to see us, and they paid their money, and we're going to work." So we did. I mean, the full thing, an hour and a half. That was Bill Monroe. It wasn't the money. He loved the music and he wanted to do everybody right. I appreciate it now, but back then I thought, "What's wrong with him?"[89]

Monroe's grim slide into obscurity constituted only one aspect of his career problems. He was starting to go adrift artistically. This became painfully obvious during recording sessions.

Gone was the musical Caesar who had forged masterpieces during touring campaigns and brought them triumphantly home to the forum of the studio. Monroe now typically lacked much of a plan or even sufficient material to record the usual three or four songs. He might have a slip of paper with him and sit very quietly for a few minutes looking at it. Finally, somebody would say, "Well, Bill, what are we going to do?"

Bill would respond, "Well, I've got this song here, I think that maybe we ought to do this."[90] He'd run through it with his mandolin and voice. The band would learn the song quickly — the clock was ticking; sessions were scheduled for just three hours — and then record it. For the most part, says Paul Anthony "Tony" Ellis, who recorded on banjo with Monroe between December 1960 and May 1962, "when we would go into a session we would have no idea what we were going to do. He wouldn't tell us or rehearse ahead of time."

Owen Bradley was now the dean of Nashville recorders and producers. He had been working with such high-powered stars as Patsy Cline and Kitty Wells, but he remained committed to doing the best job he could for Bill, no matter how minor a performer he had become. With care and sensitivity, Bradley undertook the tricky task of getting Monroe to record music that had commercial appeal without deviating from his trademark sound.

Monroe needed a fourth song to fill out a December 3, 1960, session and had nothing planned. Bradley suggested doing a rockabilly-style number. On the spot, Monroe threw together a rocking little mandolin instrumental in the key of G. "We'll just call it 'Bluegrass Part One,'" he said.[91] (It was released as "Bluegrass Part One (Twist)," a nod to the gyrating dance craze then sweeping the nation, making this recording truly a bizarre twist in Monroe's studio output.)

At the time, the thirteenth fret on Monroe's well-worn mandolin had slipped from its groove and was protruding slightly from the neck. The outside E or first string got momentarily snagged on it, causing a high F-sharp note. It actually fit perfectly with the bluesy G7 chords Monroe was playing and created some intriguing dissonances.

"Well, it sounds good, leave it alone," said Monroe upon hearing the playback.[92] Generations of Monroevians, not knowing about the faulty fret, have spent fruitless hours trying to reproduce the funky sound.

By now Bradley's studio had stereo, an early three-track system. The technology really opened up the sound of records. On one occasion, it captured the almost mystical resonances of Bill Monroe's mandolin.

When recording the Blue Grass Boys in this early format, Bradley would put Monroe in the middle by himself, singing and playing his mandolin into one microphone. The remaining lead instruments, banjo and fiddle, were separated on the other channels accompanied by one rhythm instrument (guitar or bass) each. (In the final mixes, the central track was usually mixed equally between the two channels.) During playbacks, Bill could be turned up and isolated on the large, finely tuned "Voice of the Theater" speakers in the studio. On one occasion, Monroe, Bradley, and the others noticed an odd but captivating overtone coming from the mandolin.

"Finally, I heard it and I can prove it!" Monroe declared.[93] "I've been telling people about that for years, and now I can prove it!"

Bill had been strumming powerfully on his mandolin in the key of G and there was a B-flat overtone just sticking out. Bill had heard it before — he called it the "ghost note" — now everyone else could, too.

*   *   *

The touring grind brought out the best and worst in everyone in the band. Bessie had two Pekingese dogs, Chappie and Cupid, who often traveled with the band. They were notorious. Cupid was a sweet little dog; Chappie was just plain mean.[94] Chappie liked to ride in the front seat and snuggle up to the driver. If the driver tried to be friendly and pet him, Chappie would growl and snap.

Bessie could snap, too, and one day she did at banjo picker Tony Ellis over some minor matter. Bill demonstrated his support for Ellis by swatting Bessie alongside the head with a newspaper he was reading.[95] ("He swatted her pretty hard, too," Ellis recalls.)

But there could be moments of levity. Lead singer Frank Buchanan had a voice similar to Lester Flatt's, and was perhaps Monroe's best lead singer since the death of Edd Mayfield. But one night he gave into his great gustatory passion: a hamburger topped with a thick slice of raw onion. After an evening of duets sung in close proximity on a single mike, Bill practically stumbled off the stage, his eyes watering, declaring that Frank had nearly killed him.[96]

The band always tried to make it back for the Opry. Backstage, Monroe and the Flatt and Scruggs contingents avoided each other. But Tony Ellis, constantly seeking to improve his picking, would ask Earl how he played certain tunes or passages. Earl would obligingly give him pointers. One night, Monroe came in from getting coffee at Linebaugh's restaurant to discover his banjo player in close conference with Scruggs.

Later, Monroe approached Ellis. "What was you doin' there talkin' to him?" he asked testily.[97]

"Well, Bill, he was showing me some stuff," Ellis explained.

"Well, it don't look good," said Monroe. "It just don't look good."

"Bill, nobody cares. And he's the best banjo player in the whole world, and if he's willing to show me some stuff to help my playing, I'm sure gonna listen to him."

"Well, I don't care, it just don't look good."

Ellis realized that Earl must be silently laughing to himself, knowing Bill was getting ruffled.

*   *   *

At the end of 1961, Bill Monroe finally went into the studio and struck gold in the form of folk music. But he was not prospecting for it, and he and Decca Records treated it like mere zinc.

During sessions on November 9 and 10, and December 1 and 4, Bill had again entered Owen Bradley's studio with no clear plan. Band members suggested folk songs like "Little Maggie," "Shady Grove," and "Nine Pound Hammer" because audiences had been requesting them lately. "Cotton Fields," from the bulging songbag of legendary black folk singer and twelve-string guitar player Leadbelly (Huddie Ledbetter), was suggested on the spur of the moment by fiddler Bobby Joe Lester, who was performing it in a side group he had with Tony Ellis.[98]

"Danny Boy," a contemporary composition by Fred Weatherly based on the traditional Irish ballad "The Londonderry Air," was urged by Bradley. The number had long been a favorite of Irish tenors, and in 1959 Conway Twitty had taken it to number 7 on the pop charts.[99] Monroe's high lonesome vocals brought a new dimension to the song.

To his credit, Bill rose to the challenge of these largely unfamiliar tunes. The recordings — some of his best and most vibrant in years — were released the following June on *Bluegrass Ramble*. The album's title reflected the recognition that there was a "bluegrass" style of country music, but no attempt was made to promote the material to the lucrative hootenanny market. Then Bill got even further away from folk by starting work on a gospel LP.

Unlike the Osborne Brothers or Jimmy Martin & the Sunny Mountain Boys — Decca bluegrass artists who were decidedly more country in their approaches — Bill Monroe's ballad, blues, and fiddle tune–oriented music had tremendous potential with the hootenanny crowd. Meanwhile, Columbia was heavily promoting Flatt and Scruggs & the Foggy Mountain Boys to folk enthusiasts. In 1961, it released *Songs of the Famous Carter Family*, which appealed to folkies as well as long-time country music fans of the Carters, and in 1962 the calculatedly conceived *Folk Songs of Our Land*.

Even small independents were ahead of Decca in recognizing the new market: In 1962, Starday released Hylo Brown's *Bluegrass Goes to College — American Mountain Music with 5-String Banjo*, while King presented the Stanley Brothers as *Award Winners at the Folk Song Festival*.

Culturally and politically, Nashville and the South were far removed from the campuses and coffeehouses of the Northeast and California, where the folk music revival was at its most vibrant. But Columbia, hugely successful with Bob Dylan and other folk artists, was in tune with the music's potential. Small independents were more flexible than Decca as business entities, quicker to package bluegrass for the folk boom.

Overall, Decca as a corporation was slow to react to trends.[100] (Country singer Bill Anderson recalls watching for nearly four months as his recording of "Still" got hotter and hotter until Decca finally realized it had a major hit.) Decca was also heavy with country stars, its roster unmatched before or since: Anderson, Ernest Tubb, Red Foley, Webb Pierce, Kitty Wells, Loretta Lynn, the Wilburn Brothers . . . the list went on and on. Not all could get individual promotion, especially a fading star like Bill Monroe who was selling 20,000 to 40,000 records a year, profitable but not a money press.[101] Ironically, being on a major label like Decca now put Monroe at a disadvantage.

Decca's ineptitude was compounded by Monroe's lax approach to recording during this stage of his career. This otherwise singleminded artist was indecisive and at a creative low point.

Why? Monroe may have been experiencing a burnout fueled by lingering bitterness about his lagging fortunes and the triumph of Flatt and Scruggs. He was now recording largely to fulfill contractual obligations and earn a few dollars of session pay. And Monroe's lack of creative motivation coincided almost precisely with Carolyn's preparation and execution of her divorce filing. Despite his love for Bessie, Bill continued to have deep feelings for his wife and the children. Desertion had been a painful personal issue for him since childhood; the divorce's finality must have been hard to bear.

There were exciting new opportunities for bluegrass among the folk revivalists and a new audience that specifically identified themselves as bluegrass fans. The music could finally shake off its post-Presley doldrums.

But like a lonesome figure in one of his own songs, Bill Monroe had stayed on the platform while the train pulled out. Now he was being left farther and farther behind.

★ CHAPTER 6 ★

RENAISSANCE:
FOLKIES AND YANKEES
(1962 TO 1965)

Most men are like the magnet; they have a side which repels and
another which attracts. — Voltaire, *Notebooks*

A s 1962 opened, it offered a mixture of hope and woes. Bill Monroe & His Blue Grass Boys had belatedly made their Carnegie
Hall debut on November 29, 1961, as part of an Opry package show
headlined by Patsy Cline, Jim Reeves, and Faron Young.[1] Now a two-
week trip in January sent them through the Midwest and into Canada as
part of another package show with Cline, George Jones, Johnny Cash,
and Bill's rockabilly admirer Carl Perkins.[2]

Big package shows were proving a wise response to the rock 'n' roll
challenge, drawing droves of country fans to major venues. Monroe was
getting booked on them through the powerful Jim Denny Agency. But
they were a mixed blessing. The Blue Grass Boys were essentially a token
old-timey act to provide variety on the bill, and in contrast to the elec-

tronically amplified country and western groups, they were not show-cased to any advantage, as Opry star Bill Anderson recalls:

> Let me tell you what hurt him and all the bluegrass acts in those big coliseums. They made these places for ice hockey and basketball, and they put concerts in them kind of as an afterthought. These were the days before the big sound [system] companies. A lot of times — many times — the bluegrass acts would get lost playing on a little dinky sound system, maybe one or two microphones.
>
> The people had already heard two or three — I heard Monroe call them — "plug-in bands" [and] if they couldn't hear well, they would get rowdy and start yelling things out. It was easy to lose control of an audience in those places.[3]

After briefly sharing the package spotlight, it was back to Monroe's own schedule of widely spaced solo gigs. He'd be heard better, but at smaller venues he'd play for a percentage of the door with no guarantees.

Bessie Lee Mauldin's 1958 Oldsmobile station wagon continued to serve as the band's tour bus. With nearly 200,000 miles on its odometer, it would occasionally break down and require quick repairs to get it going again. The vehicle was almost a metaphor for Bill and Bessie's relationship: somehow surviving despite the years, the blowups and breakdowns and fixes.

Yet there were magic moments when Bill's popularity reasserted itself. In the spring, the band played a movie theater in Cleveland. The area was heavily populated by Kentuckians and West Virginians working in local factories. They had grown up listening to Bill Monroe on the Opry, and they still loved him. The Blue Grass Boys had only been hired to do two half-hour sets, but people lined up for blocks. The band did three sets that night to accommodate the crowds and still couldn't get everyone in.

The group returned the next day — truly by popular demand — and did two more shows. Monroe remarked that he hadn't seen crowds like that in years.[4]

A new type of show was being added to the mix. Bluegrass performers throughout the South were seeing the benefits of promoting events with

Monroe as the headliner and themselves as opening acts. Monroe would play these dates on a percentage basis, but everyone would do well because he'd draw big crowds.[5]

Monroe's music had huge potential and not just with country or folk music enthusiasts: A growing niche audience specifically identified itself as bluegrass lovers. In fact, the very term "bluegrass" was now commonly used to describe the Bill Monroe/Flatt and Scruggs/Stanley Brothers style of string band music.[6]

Since neither Monroe nor any of his peers started out calling it bluegrass — to them it had been just "country" music — theories abound as to how the term was first used. By the mid-1950s, radio disk jockeys and mail-order record stores were using it to differentiate Monroe-style music from the diverging country mainstream. Fans themselves may have started it by requesting Monroe material at Flatt and Scruggs shows but, aware of tensions between the rival acts, simply asking for "some of those Blue Grass songs" in reference to Lester and Earl's days as Blue Grass Boys. And as far back as 1950, Hill and Range Songs Inc., a New York–based music publisher, had produced a souvenir songbook called *Bill Monroe's Blue Grass Country Songs*. Whatever the case, Monroe had named his band in honor of the Blue Grass State of Kentucky, and the music was named in honor of his band, even if it was now being spelled as one word.

These were powerful trends. Yet few promoters in the South seemed to grasp their significance. Neither did the taciturn father of the genre.

Meanwhile, the Flatt and Scruggs juggernaut rolled on. Under Louise Scruggs's shrewd management, Monroe's former sidemen had become the bluegrass darlings of the northern folk music revival. They were being represented on the lucrative college circuit by promoter Manny Greenhill, Joan Baez's booking agent.[7] They were making the most of their contract with Columbia, and lots of their records were ending up in dorm rooms.

And with each new press release or set of album liner notes, Louise was shaping history. Many journalists were getting their first exposure to bluegrass through Flatt and Scruggs, whose promo material (which if not directly written by Louise never went out without her approval) contained no mention of a Mr. Bill Monroe. And why should it? After the way Bill had fought to keep Lester and Earl off the Opry, Mrs. Scruggs was under no obligation to act as Bill's pro bono press agent.

In 1963, Columbia released *Flatt and Scruggs Recorded Live at Vanderbilt University* with liner notes by Thomas B. Allen, the painter who was creating the band's album cover art. "I feel it appropriate to end with a thank you list," Allen wrote. He proceeded to plaudit, among other things, the British Isles "in whose heritage 'Bluegrass' has its longest roots."

So how to address the touchy matter of Bill Monroe? The conundrum was cunningly handled: "Thank you WSM Grand Ole Opry for providing the place and situation in which Lester and Earl first got together."

Not even in private correspondence would the Flatt and Scruggs camp acknowledge Monroe's existence. A Pittsburgh-based bluegrass enthusiast wrote asking whether Scruggs was the banjo player on Bill Monroe's driving instrumental "Blue Grass Breakdown" (which of course he was). Responding on the letterhead of "The Flatt and Scruggs Show," Louise Scruggs replied, "I do not know if Earl is playing on the record of Bluegrass Breakdown, since I havent [sic] heard the record. He does not record with any other artist except the Flatt and Scruggs recordings."[8]

Bill Monroe had not only been shunted aside in the history of bluegrass. He had become a virtual nonperson.

On Sunday, June 24, 1962, Bill Monroe & His Blue Grass Boys were booked at Sunset Park, the venerable outdoor country music venue in rural southeastern Pennsylvania near the town of West Grove.[9] During an intermission, Monroe was approached by a tall, slender young man with thinning blond hair, hazel eyes, and an earnest manner.

Monroe recognized him. He was one of a coterie of northerners who had been attending his shows for several years. These Yankees were of a type: obviously educated and from well-to-do families, serious but polite. They taped his shows. Many transplanted southerners did, too, in the days when few northern record stores carried bluegrass albums, but these college boys taped studiously and incessantly. And unlike the southerners, they did not request Monroe's country hits but the old-time numbers — "Pretty Polly," "Little Maggie," "Black Jack Davy."[10] Their interest in what people were calling folk songs mildly surprised Monroe, but he obliged them.

It was about folk music that the young man was now speaking. After introducing himself, he requested an interview.

He said that a folk music magazine called *Sing Out!* wanted to do an article on Monroe. There was a lot of folk music in Bill's repertoire that would interest whole new audiences. And, he said, he wanted to talk about the history of bluegrass music and Bill's role in it.

Monroe regarded the fellow evenly. "If you want to know about bluegrass," he replied, "ask Louise Scruggs." Then he turned and walked off.[11]

Bill Monroe had just spoken his first words to the man who was about to revive his career.

There could hardly have been a less likely champion of rural southern music than Ralph Charles Rinzler.[12] Or so it might have seemed.

He was born in 1934, in the city of Passaic, New Jersey, the son of Harry G. Rinzler, a doctor, and his wife, Beatrice. His family was of Russian Jewish descent. Ralph attended Swarthmore College, where he majored in French. After graduation, Ralph toured Europe.

But a fascination with folkways glowed at the core of his being and lit the path of his life. Passaic had many ethnic enclaves, and as a child Ralph loved to accompany his mother on her trips to the butchers, bakers, and grocers because it meant encountering people from other countries and experiencing the sights, sounds, and smells of different worlds. When he got older and was allowed to do something special on his birthdays, he always asked to be taken into New York's ethnic neighborhoods.[13]

As a youngster he was given a set of Library of Congress recordings of folk music. He adored it. Swarthmore had an active folk music scene, including an annual folk festival dating from the late 1940s, and Ralph got involved. He taught himself banjo, guitar, and mandolin.

After his graduation in 1956 and his European travels, Rinzler began to involve himself seriously in traditional music. He studied with prominent folklorist A. L. Lloyd and was greatly influenced by the pioneering song collecting work of John and Alan Lomax.

And like many of his generation, Rinzler was entranced by *The Anthology of American Folk Music*. While some folk revivalists began seeking out

Mississippi John Hurt, Son House, and other African-American blues players represented in Harry Smith's collection, Ralph was among those who sought its southern white string band musicians. In April 1960 at the Union Grove, North Carolina, fiddlers convention, Rinzler met a regional banjo player named Tom Ashley. Ralph asked him about Clarence Ashley, whose recordings of "The Coo Coo Bird" and "The House Carpenter" were highpoints of the collection. "Why, that's me," exclaimed Ashley, explaining that Tommy was his nickname.[14] To Rinzler's astonished Henry Morton Stanley it was like locating Dr. David Livingstone by near coincidence.

In 1961, he returned to North Carolina to record Ashley and his friends for Folkways Records. A young guitarist was recommended to him. It was Arthel "Doc" Watson — the same blind singer who had helped save the Blue Grass Boys show that night in the late 1940s when Bill was sick with food poisoning. (Rinzler did not know of the incident at the time.)

Doc had developed a flatpicking guitar style unrivaled in virtuosity by anything on the folk or country music scenes. And he was tremendously self-reliant. Ralph became his manager and started booking him on the college and coffeehouse circuit. Soon, "Watson-style" guitar became as renowned among folkies as "Scruggs-style" banjo.

Watson and his fellow North Carolinians were awed by Rinzler's academic knowledge of old-time music. More important, they took to this sincere, friendly, and energetic young Yankee. Rinzler had a rather affluent background and an advanced education. He was scholarly. He could be testy when frustrated. Yet these things became irrelevant.

"His personality cut through all that," recalls Watson.[15] "You didn't have to be with Ralph very long 'til you knew him and loved him for what he was."

Meanwhile, Rinzler was making his own reputation as a musician. He joined the Greenbriar Boys, a popular New York–based "citybilly" bluegrass band, as its mandolin player. One night, the Greenbriar Boys were headlining at Gerde's Folk City, the leading Greenwich Village folk music venue. Opening for them was an unknown and very nervous midwestern singer-songwriter making his New York debut. His name was Bob Dylan.[16]

*   *   *

By now, Rinzler's base of operations was a Greenwich Village apartment. He was a leader in the folk revival, networking with other perceptive northern lovers of then-arcane southern sounds. One of these was Mike Seeger, a scion of a prominent American music family. His parents were musicologist Charles Seeger and modernist composer Ruth Crawford Seeger; his half brother was famed folk singer Pete Seeger; and his full sister Peggy became a popular folk singer in her own right.

Ralph and Mike would soon be caught up in a remarkable phenomenon that transcended prevailing regional, class, and gender boundaries. It was an intertwining cultural grapevine that united northerners and southerners who shared a common passion for rural string band music. This network proved crucial to the survival of Bill Monroe's career and even bluegrass itself.

Mike Seeger was born in 1933 in New York City and lived in the Washington, D.C., suburbs until he was twenty-one.[17] A conscientious objector, he did alternative service in the mid-1950s as a kitchen worker at Mount Wilson State Hospital in Pikeville, Maryland, near Baltimore. There he met a tuberculosis patient and musician from West Virginia named Robert Dickens.

Just as Bill Monroe and some of his siblings had moved to the Chicago area to find work in the refineries, a Dickens branch family had relocated to Baltimore to labor in its factories and shipyards. The Dickens clan seemed to have stepped straight out of an old mountain folk song.[18] They were from a coal mining region. There were eleven children in the family. Their father was a hard-shell Baptist preacher, whose main employment was hauling timber and coal and who was also a very good old-time banjo picker. One of his youngest children, Hazel, would one day become a powerful professional singer and songwriter with the encouragement of Mike, Ralph Rinzler, and even Bill Monroe himself. But at the time she was a shy, self-doubting young woman who couldn't understand why an educated person like Mike would be so interested in the old music.

For Seeger and Rinzler, these people were a revelation. They were not abstractions from some ethnomusicological treatise on southern folkways. They were the real thing. And their music was the real thing, with all the authentic rhythms and inflections and feelings. Soon the Dickens family and their new Yankee friends were holding lively music parties, picking and singing, exchanging songs and ideas.

If the northerners got the soul of the music from the southerners, the southerners received something equally important — validation and a new self-esteem. Most were humble to the point of inferiority about their world.[19] Seeger and Rinzler revealed that the old music was great art, deeply rooted in venerable British Isles and African-American folkways. The southerners who had sung these songs for generations around the house and at community gatherings were therefore keepers of a great tradition, important people. Most had never thought of it that way.

Seeger and the Dickens family loved Bill Monroe. There were excellent opportunities to hear him at country music parks within an easy drive of Baltimore — Sunset Park in West Grove, Pennsylvania, and New River Ranch in Rising Sun, Maryland. But so intimidated were they by Monroe that they attended his shows for years without approaching him. It was, Seeger recalls, "the way he would look around with his nose slightly in the air, the sense of him holding the world and people at arm's length."[20]

The only time Seeger spoke to Bill in those days was to ask permission to record a show at New River Ranch. Monroe curtly replied that he didn't care — "I don't keer," the "keer" being almost a sneer. There was good reason to feel intimidated. Mike was about to be subjected to a classic Monroevian character test.

Monroe went on stage and strummed his mandolin into each of the microphones to determine which belonged to the sound system and which was connected to Seeger's tape recorder. Then he carefully and deliberately moved Seeger's mike off to one side of the stage.

Seeger sat patiently through the first set. Then he went back onstage and just as carefully and deliberately put his mike back where it had been. There was no exchange of words between them, and Bill Monroe never moved one of Mike Seeger's microphones again.

In 1954 at New River Ranch, through the urging of Mike Seeger, Ralph Rinzler saw and heard Bill Monroe for the first time. The ethnographer in Rinzler, who had delighted in cultural enclaves since childhood, was entranced by the scene at New River Ranch. He later declared that "it was like going into another world. I was fascinated by the totally different lifestyle — dinner on the ground, different speech patterns — a whole different way of life. The whole idea of it really astounded me — that this existed."[21]

Then Bill Monroe & His Blue Grass Boys took the stage. Despite Rinzler's enormous study of southern string band music, he was utterly unprepared for the experience.

Rinzler recognized that Monroe had incorporated many folk music elements into his style. He was especially struck by the degree to which Monroe had retained the old modality and use of pentatonic scale in his art, while most other bluegrassers were playing basically diatonic music.[22] Here was a performer whose music was both sophisticated and archaic, both modern *and* ancient.

Something else was irresistibly fascinating to this young intellectual. Bill Monroe was, as Rinzler later put it, "a unique synthesizer, a cultural figure of signal importance in our time,"[23] yet virtually nothing had been written about him.

Who was he? Where did he come from? What was his social context? How did he create such hard-hitting yet complex music? What were his influences?

Rinzler wondered what went on in Monroe's head that made him play music the way he did.[24] It was totally different from the way Ralph had heard anybody else play music, of any kind.

Such were Ralph Rinzler's cerebral assessments of Bill Monroe. His emotional response was an entirely different matter.

Ralph was sitting as close to the stage as he could get, but he couldn't sit still.[25] He was smiling from ear to ear, swaying to the music. At times, he practically lurched from his chair in joy.

"He was just jumping out of his skin," Hazel Dickens recalls. "It was like he was so excited he didn't know what to do with himself."

Monroe soon became aware of the little coterie that would set up microphones and ask him to perform old-time songs. (Bill had recorded "Little Maggie" and "Shady Grove" in 1961 because they were current in his band's repertoire because of audience requests. It is possible that Rinzler and Seeger had been the very ones calling out the requests.) Ralph and

Mike would soon receive face-to-face recognition from Bill Monroe. It would not be a happy experience.

The March 1962 issue of *Sing Out!* featured an article "Earl Scruggs — and the Sound of Bluegrass" by Pete Welding, a prominent jazz critic and Scruggs fan who had previously written about bluegrass for *Saturday Review* and *Down Beat*. "Earl Scruggs has become the undisputed master of Bluegrass music," Welding enthused.

Rinzler was furious. He demanded the opportunity to do a *Sing Out!* cover story on Monroe. Editor Irwin Silber agreed but warned that the haughty Monroe would never cooperate.[26] Rinzler was undeterred. He was righteously indignant and ready to swing into action.[27] Mike Seeger, the conscientious objector, suddenly found himself drafted as a lieutenant in Rinzler's personal campaign to reclaim recognition for Bill Monroe.

Rinzler first tried reaching Monroe by phone.[28] He was unsuccessful. Ever skilled at developing a strategy to address a need, Rinzler then decided to go to Sunset Park during Monroe's next appearance and speak with him in person.

Then came Monroe's curt rejection, full of bitterness about Louise Scruggs's spin on bluegrass history. Faced with defeat, Mike Seeger floated a brilliant suggestion.

The Stanley Brothers were at New River Ranch that very day, just a fast half-hour drive away.[29] Mike was on good terms with the Stanleys; he had followed them for years, even interviewing their mother about mountain banjo styles. His good friend Jeremy Foster had gotten the Stanleys hired for a 1961 concert at Antioch College. The Stanleys had been well paid and treated with great respect. They were grateful to the folk revivalists — and they were friends of Monroe's.

Rinzler and Seeger roared off to New River Ranch, found the Stanleys, and prevailed upon them to put in a good word with Bill. Fortunately, Monroe was still at Sunset Park when they returned. At about 10 P.M., the Stanleys, Monroe, with Bessie Lee Mauldin next to him, and the two folkies sat down on some empty benches in the park's concert area for what can only be described as an encounter group.

First, there was an attempt to find common ground with Monroe by talking about music. Rinzler was keenly interested in Monroe's historically and musically rich recording of "White House Blues," the broadside-style song about the McKinley assassination. (Monroe had been inspired by Charlie Poole & the North Carolina Ramblers' version and in the studio had played an exceedingly hot mandolin break.) Rinzler and Seeger pitched the idea of Monroe's getting recognition for what he'd done. And they said they could get him gigs on the college circuit.

Monroe would have none of this deferential small talk or even the offers of work. Ralph and Mike quickly learned that Bill Monroe was absolutely furious with them.

The cause was the infamous exchange between Monroe and Carter Stanley at Bill Clifton's 1961 bluegrass festival in Luray, Virginia, during which Monroe gibed that Flatt and Scruggs would have "plowed a lot of furrows" if it hadn't been for him. The program, including the comments, had been taped by several people including Mike — and someone had sent a copy to Earl and Louise Scruggs. Seeger was the high-profile recorder of stage shows in Bill's mind and he was friendly with Scruggs, so Monroe blamed him. Mike Seeger protested his genuine innocence.

> Bill thought it was me, and he said so. That was part of the very spirited discussion. It was a very strong — almost angry at times — exchange between Bill and Ralph and me. Not that he was on good terms with Earl Scruggs, but he was angry that someone would do that.[30]

The tape had more than embarrassed Monroe. There were rumors that Louise Scruggs was threatening Bill with a lawsuit or trying to get him kicked off the Opry. Even if the rumors were groundless (in later years, Mrs. Scruggs denied having even heard the controversial recording)[31] this sorry incident was now standing in the way of Rinzler's plan to establish Bill's place in music history and revive his fortunes.

Ralph and Carter Stanley continued to vouch for Mike and, by extension, Rinzler. They told Bill that these folk revivalists could help get him into places he'd never played before. Monroe remained unmoved.

Then Bessie Lee spoke up. "Bill! This could help you!"[32] she said, forcefully and with excitement. She began to take an active mediating role. She especially urged Bill to cooperate with Rinzler on a magazine article.

Monroe didn't agree to anything right away. But on a warm June night in an empty country music park some very thick ice had been broken. More important, Ralph Rinzler had found an invaluable ally in Bessie Lee Mauldin. As had Watson and Ashley, she liked him immediately and recognized his sincerity. And she wouldn't be afraid to tell her lover in private that he was being pigheaded.

Nearly three months of coaxing followed.[33] Rinzler finally made arrangements to meet Monroe at a fair in Galax, Virginia, in August 1962. Rinzler found Monroe, but Monroe avoided him. Rinzler was worried. Bessie Lee reassured him that Bill had promised to talk.

And so it went until they finally sat down for the first in-depth interview that Bill Monroe had ever granted. The unlikely setting for this historic event was a table next to a blaring jukebox in a local bowling alley. "Bill's demeanor," Rinzler later recalled, "was a curious combination of unmistakable reluctance coupled with an absolute commitment to keeping his word and telling the unvarnished truth."[34]

Rinzler was struck by the fact that for all its onstage spontaneity, Monroe's music wasn't intuitive. He had consciously created it and could relate exactly where he had gotten each sound, like a painter who knows exactly what colors he has used from his palette.[35] Rinzler began to see that this enigmatic man did little that he had not very deliberately decided upon.

Monroe was so candid about his life and music that Rinzler asked a final question: "Is there anything you said that you would not want to see in print?"

"It's all true," Monroe replied.[36]

Rinzler's article, entitled "Bill Monroe — The Daddy of Bluegrass Music," appeared in the February–March 1963 *Sing Out!* Ralph made an impressive case for Bill Monroe as a folk artist, succinctly covering the many elements of traditional music in bluegrass. He discussed Bill's background as a farmboy influenced by a musical mother, a fiddling uncle, and a black guitarist, then summarized Bill's career.

In the process, Rinzler politely but clearly answered Welding's portrayal of Earl Scruggs as the dominant innovator in bluegrass. He noted that Earl had followed a long North Carolina tradition of syncopated three-finger banjo picking and had perfected his style while working with Bill.

Rinzler stressed Bill's artistic integrity: "It is this conviction, as profound as a religious belief, which has enabled Monroe to resist the trends of Nashville. . . . This same conviction, imparted to other musicians and to audiences, is responsible for the endurance and significance of the traditional folk strain in commercial country music."[37]

It is widely believed that Ralph Rinzler's true masterstroke was the coining of the term "The Father of Bluegrass." In fact, the appellation did not originate with him. Monroe's biographical entry in Linnell Gentry's seminal 1961 *A History and Encyclopedia of Country, Western, and Gospel Music* opened with "Monroe, Bill, called 'The Father of Blue Grass Music.'"[38] Gentry was clearly reporting existing use of the phrase. An LP collection of Monroe's 1946–1947 recordings that had been released in October 1962 was called *The Father of Blue Grass Music.*

However, Rinzler brilliantly exploited the concept. Forevermore, Monroe's life and persona would hang on the powerful and catchy phrase "Father of Bluegrass." It honored his achievements as progenitor of this musical genre. It depicted him as a powerful elder figure with hints of cultural divinity. And it was a major improvement over his image as a distant stranger.

Rinzler's thoughtful questions about Bill's childhood and influences had implications far beyond the *Sing Out!* piece. Like Hazel Dickens and her kin, Monroe had never really thought of his roots as being historically significant. Now he began to incorporate statements about Pen Vandiver and Arnold Shultz into his stage shows.[39] The answers given the probing Rinzler provided rich material for the stories that Bill Monroe would tell audiences and journalists for the rest of his life.

On Saturday, January 5, 1963, Ralph Rinzler attended a party at the New York home of folk singer Oscar Brand.[40] Monroe, up for a rare northern trip, was there. So was fiddler Tex Logan, the composer of Bill's popular holiday song "Christmas Time's A-Comin'" and now a research mathematician at Bell Labs in New Jersey. Ralph told Tex that he wanted to approach Bill about managing him and, frankly, felt it would help his case if he walked over in Logan's company.

They crossed the room, greeted Monroe, and engaged in pleasant small talk. Then Logan found a reason to excuse himself. A few minutes later, he looked back to see Ralph and Bill seated on a sofa in close conversation.[41]

Thus did Ralph Rinzler become the manager of Bill Monroe. Working with an outsider was, in Monroe's mind, a gamble.[42] Ralph sensed his reluctance. He confided to Del McCoury, one of Monroe's musicians, "I'm moving to Nashville but I don't think he wants me to."[43]

How did Ralph Rinzler — intellectual, Jewish, a city boy, the son of a doctor from New Jersey — ever gain the trust of Bill Monroe? "I think Ralph just spilled over on Bill so much, he was like a tidal wave," says Hazel Dickens.[44] "He was just so enthusiastic and so supportive that Bill had never seen anything like this."

But it was Bessie Lee who proved decisive in assuring Monroe's cooperation.

"Bill," she told her lover, "you need him because he can book you into places you've never been before."[45]

Bill's risk was immediately rewarded. He got a February 1963 booking at the University of Chicago Folk Festival.[46] It was his first college concert. The night before the show, Ralph gave Bill and Bessie the newly published *Sing Out!* and the first Greenbriar Boys album, with Rinzler's liner notes prominently mentioning Monroe's role in the creation of bluegrass.

The next day, Rinzler and Seeger saw an amazing transformation.[47] Gone was the haughty and remote Bill Monroe. The man they encountered on this new morning was friendly, forthcoming, even intimate. Monroe spoke of the first time he ever visited Chicago, how his eyes were still crossed, how he had felt "pitiful." He solicited guidance about how to perform for this strange new audience of college students.

Later, Monroe acknowledged that he had been an intimidating figure and explained why he had played his cards so close to his chest.

> I didn't talk much, Ralph, and I guess 'cause I didn't talk much that the people thought, "Well, he don't want to be bothered." But it really wasn't that. I just had a lot to do and I worked hard and I would talk short to a lot of people. . . . Ralph, I think I've changed, you know, as

the years have gone along. Back when you was a kid around my show I was hard to get close to or next to. Back in the early days, a lot of kids that would hang around was smart alecks. Maybe they'd want to find out something to tell another entertainer. And I dodged them kind of people, you know. But it really proves that a kid like you and Mike Seeger, when you was first hanging around me, that you could grow into being really wonderful men and have come a long ways. . . . You've learned a lot about bluegrass music and nobody in the world could have helped it like you have . . . and I don't think I've got any better friend than Mike Seeger.[48]

For his part, Rinzler adored Monroe for his depth and artistic integrity as well as his glorious music.

"You think about things a lot more and a lot deeper than other people do, because that comes out in your music," he told Bill.[49] "And you just don't ever play a tune just to get through it, you play it the way you feel it."

People and events were converging in Monroe's career — more rapidly and significantly than was obvious at the time. The next leap forward came because a young man had a knack for music, mathematics, and mechanics.

Bill Keith might have seemed just as unlikely as Rinzler to become a pivotal figure in bluegrass history.[50] Born William Bradford Keith in Boston in 1939, just two months after Monroe debuted on the Opry, he went to prep school at the prestigious Phillips Exeter Academy. He graduated from Amherst in 1961 with a major in eighteenth-century French literature, and he also studied mathematics.

But one night, he pulled in the WWVA *Jamboree* on his little transistor radio and heard banjo music for the first time. An early edition of Pete Seeger's *How to Play the Five String Banjo*, with its pioneering chapter on the Scruggs style, coauthored by half brother Mike, got him started.

Keith's analytical mind soon engaged itself. He bought a copy of Flatt and Scruggs's 1957 LP *Foggy Mountain Jamboree* and transcribed Earl's banjo solos into standard music notation to examine their structure.

Then he created tablature to sort out the correct fingering patterns from the many options.

After college, Keith became acquainted with the music of June Hall, a fiddler living in West Bridgewater whose machinist husband was making parts for an antique car Keith was restoring. June and her mother were musicians from Nova Scotia, where traditional Scottish fiddling had survived. Keith began to absorb the New England/Nova Scotian fiddlers' repertoire, filled with lively and lilting tunes, many of them beautifully mathematical in their patterns.

How, he pondered, could you play these tunes on a banjo? At a party one night, Keith was watching June Hall playing fiddle and was in the act of biting into a very large chocolate chip cookie when he had his epiphany.

Why hadn't other banjo pickers been able to play complex melodies rapidly note-for-note? The basic Scruggs-style approach is to play one melody note and two or three accompanying notes in a rhythmically dense structure. This works fine for relatively simple melodies. But because the five-string banjo has a longer neck and different tuning from a violin, Scruggs-style players were unable to quickly access the needed notes for complex fiddle tunes. Simply put, no matter how fast they could pick, it was virtually impossible to place their fretting fingers on all the notes in sequence using standard first-position banjo chords. The best they could do was to simplify and approximate.

Keith's conceptual breakthrough was that there are chord patterns in second and third positions up the banjo neck in which the required notes are close together — although, counterintuitively, often in an inverted form with the higher notes found on the lower strings and vice versa. Thus, when Keith smoothly coordinated these chord "pockets" with rapid-fire Scruggs-style picking sequences, he could whip off endless arpeggios of pure melody. It was the first major development in banjo playing since Earl Scruggs appeared with Monroe in the mid-1940s and Don Reno coalesced a jazz guitar–influenced style in the 1950s.

Ironically, it was Keith's mastery of Scruggs's music, not his own revolutionary technique, that took him to Nashville and an eventual meeting with Bill Monroe. After a December 1962 Flatt and Scruggs concert in

Baltimore, Keith showed Scruggs his notebook of transcriptions and played a few under Earl's watchful eye. At the beginning of 1963, he accepted an invitation to stay with Earl and Louise and work on an instruction book Earl wanted to write. On weekends, Scruggs took Keith to the Opry, where he played in his melodic style during dressing room jam sessions.

One night Blue Grass Boys fiddler Kenny Baker heard him. Baker listened awhile, then left. A few moments later he was back, and Bill Monroe was with him.

It didn't take Monroe long to make up his mind about this Yankee with the hot new technique.[51] As Scruggs and Keith were about to leave, Baker — sent as a messenger by his employer, who didn't want to be seen going near Earl Scruggs — took Keith aside him and asked if he'd like to work with Monroe.

Surprised and honored, Keith accepted. But Monroe never called. He may have forgotten about the offer: In the interim he hired Del McCoury, a North Carolinian living in Pennsylvania, to play banjo. Eventually Ralph Rinzler managed to reconnect him. Recognizing Keith's astounding abilities and also McCoury's potential as a lead vocalist, Rinzler urged that Del be shifted over to guitar.

"If you can make it, you'll like it better," said Monroe of the lead singer's job.

McCoury was very disappointed about being taken off the banjo. Well, he thought, I'll do what he wants me to do, but I probably won't stay on.[52] McCoury proved to be a high-honed, exceptionally clear lead singer — and is now one of the most successful bluegrass vocalists.

In early March 1963, Bill Keith returned to Nashville, joined the musicians' union, and played on the Opry — all on the same day. Just two weeks later, Monroe took him into the studio.

But first, Bill Keith got a name change. "There's only one Bill in the Blue Grass Boys," Monroe declared.[53] He then shortened Keith's middle name from Bradford to Brad and started calling him that.

McCoury had a slightly different problem: Monroe's pronunciation was such that many audience members thought that Del's name was "Dale."[54] He had arrived in Nashville on the same day as Keith and even checked into the same hotel, the Clarkston on Seventh Avenue South.

The two new Blue Grass Boys settled into the less-than-glamorous life of Monroe sidemen.[55] For $14 a week, they got an inside room, gray walls, a pay radio, a view of the air shaft, and a bathroom down the hall. Their dining destination was usually Krystal's or some other Nashville hamburger joint.

At the Grand Ole Opry, Keith created a sensation. His solos got a huge response not only from the people out front but from a tougher audience: the crack corps of Opry sidemen and Nashville session musicians. They would gather in the wings and around the back of the stage, marveling at this Yankee wonder.

A broad smile would break through Monroe's stoic visage.[56] He had finally one-upped Earl Scruggs. As great as Earl still was, the Blue Grass Boys — and not the Foggy Mountain Boys — now featured the world's cutting-edge five-string banjo. And Monroe, the prescient bandleader, had known for decades that such musicianship was possible. He remarked to Roy Acuff, "I've told all them boys that could be done on the banjo. All the way from Scruggs, Reno, all of 'em, you could play every note I play on this mandolin on that banjo."[57]

Monroe took a proprietary interest in this new sound. "Now, Brad," he'd say, "don't you go showing people how to do that. Pretty soon they'll all be doing it."[58] But Keith, ready to help others, did show some pickers. Eventually, nearly every young bluegrass banjo player would have some "Keith licks" to throw into a tune, and some learned his entire approach.

Monroe quickly got Brad Keith into Owen Bradley's studio on March 20 and 27, 1963, cutting such lively and challenging instrumentals as "Sailor's Hornpipe" and "Devil's Dream." Unlike the previous offhanded sessions, Monroe approached these events with a plan and a purpose — not the least of which was getting Brad Keith together with Kenny Baker, the Kentucky-born master musician who was becoming Bill's favorite fiddler.

Baker was born June 26, 1926, in the coal mining town of Jenkins, in eastern Kentucky.[59] Like his father and his father's father, he went to school only until he was old enough to work in the mines. But his father and grandfather were fiddlers, too. Kenny first took up the guitar and became a skilled exponent of an arcane four-finger picking style. Then during World War II, he was pressed into service as a fiddler on a USO show. He had found his instrument and his ultimate career.

Back home he returned periodically to mining, but started gravitating to professional music. He worked for about two years in country star Don Gibson's band at WNOX in Knoxville, where Monroe heard him. Baker did his first stint as a Blue Grass Boy in 1956.

Baker had considerable western swing influences, but it was his knowledge of old-time fiddling and his advancement of it to a near-classical form that enraptured Monroe. Kenny had tremendous stylistic integrity, silky technique, and superb tone. Behind Bill's vocals, instead of creating counterpoints and fills like previous Monroe fiddlers, Baker would play the melody while Bill was singing it — most definitely an old string band approach. Baker was an anomaly, a truly sophisticated old-time fiddler.

All this sophistication came at a price: As Monroe leaned toward the smooth bowing and gorgeous technique of Baker, his music gained radiance but lost the thunder-and-cloudburst energy of the classic bluegrass fiddle kickoffs, the goosebump-raising blues slides, and the wailing double stops of players like Howdy Forrester, Chubby Wise, and Vassar Clements.

Baker would come to embody Bill Monroe's fiddle music. But he also came to symbolize the long-suffering Blue Grass Boy, his complaints notorious about being paid a day's wages as a musician and then being expected to paint Monroe's barn.[60] What Kenny didn't realize was that Bill put him to work on the farm because he probably just liked having him around.

Only a few weeks after doing the sessions with Monroe and Bill Keith, Baker ended his second stay with the Blue Grass Boys. He put down his paintbrush, packed up his fiddle, and went back to the mines.

Monroe never got Keith back into the studio. This puzzled both Keith and Rinzler, because as good as those March 1963 sessions were, the music got even better. Monroe always played his best when challenged, and now the melodic banjo was his happiest challenge in years.

Monroe seemed to know he could not — and indeed should not — try to match Keith and Baker note for note; so he slightly broadbrushed the themes, satisfying his commitment to melody but adding just enough variation to complement his sidemen and stand out from them. It was an approach that would characterize much of his later playing.

Meanwhile, Bessie Lee was still proving herself to be more than just arm candy for Bill or bass-playing window dressing for the band. Her dedication to Bill's career matched that of Ralph Rinzler's, although she lacked the resources and contacts to be as helpful. Still, she tried.

With Rinzler successfully introducing Monroe to new audiences, the band made a trip to California in May 1963. The highlight was a week's engagement at the Ash Grove, a popular folk music club in Hollywood. Coming by to hear the master was the local bluegrass community, notably the Dillards. These transplanted Missourians had recurring roles on *The Andy Griffith Show* as the musically gifted but intellectually challenged "Darling Boys." Bessie queried them closely about how they had gotten the parts.[61] She wasn't trying to get Bill on the Griffith show, but she was keenly interested in the high-profile medium of television.

Bessie knew that Flatt and Scruggs had a huge head start in exploiting TV. In addition to their popular shows on regional southern stations, they had now recorded the theme song for the nation's top-rated situation comedy, *The Beverly Hillbillies*. Their single of "The Ballad of Jed Clampett," released on October 12, 1962, spent twenty weeks on the *Billboard* country charts, peaking for three weeks at number 1, which made it their biggest hit. Lester and Earl occasionally appeared on the program, portraying themselves and doing an amusing job of it.

Bessie's inquiries were essentially useless at this stage. Bill had high anxieties about playing on TV.[62] The Blue Grass Boys appeared on a local show while in California, and it sounded great to everyone but Monroe. Again, his poor vision intruded on his life: Bill could not always tell which studio camera was on him and was embarrassed to later find he had been looking in the wrong direction.[63]

In addition, Bill was still thinking about his career in linear terms. He had come from the old, almost evangelistic school of entertainment where you put up a tent and had a show, or got on a radio station and promoted your local appearances. When live music was replaced by record-spinning disk jockeys, this system broke down. Artists like Flatt and Scruggs and the Dillards had opened themselves to a whole mosaic of options, including local and national television, nightclubs, and the college folk circuit. Bill had not.

Yet things seemed to be changing for the better. During earlier visits to the West Coast, Monroe had mostly played gigs at blue collar social halls that drew transplanted southerners and longtime country music fans. Now he was also playing white collar–style coffeehouses and nightclubs, which drew folk music fans and paid better. He saw his station in life being elevated, largely because of his new manager.

Bill's renaissance was still in its early days, however. Dillards bassist-emcee Mitch Jayne and mandolinist Dean Webb were helping Monroe unload the Oldsmobile when its tail gate suddenly snapped off, as Jayne vividly recalls.

> It fell off and dumped about 40 pounds of rust on Hollywood Boule-vard. Dean and I were trying to wrestle it back on so he could look as good as he could, and I was thinking, "Here's the most revered figure in bluegrass and he can't keep the ass end on his station wagon."[64]

But the trip witnessed the first collaboration of two musical giants: Monroe and Doc Watson, who was also booked at the Ash Grove thanks to Rinzler. Bill and Doc mutually decided against bolting Doc's flatpicking guitar onto the Blue Grass Boys. Instead, they revived some of the classic Monroe Brothers duets: "Midnight on the Stormy Deep," "Where Is My Sailor Boy?," "What Would You Give in Exchange for Your Soul." Doc knew the material well, and Bill loved the blues and Anglo-American ballads that Doc performed. There was an immediate musical bond between the two men.[65]

Uniting Monroe and Watson was an artistic dream come true for Ralph Rinzler. It was also part of his plan to cross-fertilize their careers by introducing Bill to Doc's emerging college and coffeehouse audiences, and introducing Doc to Bill's country music audiences.[66] The next step would be records. Rinzler planned to get Decca to allow Bill to record on Vanguard with Doc. En route to the 1963 Newport Folk Festival in Rhode Island, Rinzler stopped at Decca's New York headquarters and made his pitch in person.

He was unequivocally turned down. "Look," a Decca executive told him, "I wouldn't ask you to loan me your toothbrush. You shouldn't ask me to loan you a Decca artist."[67]

Vanguard was equally uncooperative. "The agreement with Decca had to be reciprocal," says Watson.[68] "Vanguard would not agree to me [only] going to record something with Bill in the bluegrass field." (Later, Vanguard relaxed its policy and allowed Doc to record with Flatt and Scruggs for their Columbia album *Strictly Instrumental.*)

No sessions with Bill and Doc. No further Blue Grass Boys sessions featuring Bill Keith. Rinzler was painfully aware of how much good music was slipping away.[69] Years later, he would find a way to remedy the situation. For now, it remained maddeningly frustrating.

Yet overall, Rinzler's campaign was gaining ground. If folk audiences were highly entertained by the lively Flatt and Scruggs, they were captivated by the dignified, powerful, and enigmatic Bill Monroe. The 1963 Newport Folk Festival was a triumph for Monroe and other southern string band musicians. On the opening night of July 26, Bill Monroe & His Blue Grass Boys and Doc Watson appeared at the main stage, sharing the program with the likes of Bob Dylan and Peter, Paul, and Mary. Robert Shelton of the *New York Times* later declared that Monroe and Watson's version of "the taut, Faustian white gospel song 'What Would You Give in Exchange for Your Soul'" was a high point of the weekend.[70]

Monroe never openly expressed his feelings about the folk revival. But acquaintances like Alice Gerrard, a former Californian who was part of the Rinzler-Seeger-Dickens circle and later became an acclaimed traditional-style musician, sensed initial skepticism on Bill's part.

> I think he was mildly distrustful and he wasn't about to take the whole thing on faith. Maybe one of the feelings he had was that they'd hold him up as some kind of curiosity. Eventually he really did appreciate what Ralph and others were doing with his work.[71]

Mitch Jayne of the Dillards was irked by another subtext to the folk and bluegrass revivals — their rabid anticommercialism.

We'd left our jobs, left our homes, sold everything we had, *to go make some money*. And here are all these people saying, "God, you're not playing for the money, are you?" I always wanted to say, "What the hell do you think I'm doing out here?"[72]

Ralph Rinzler was helping to save bluegrass by forging links with the folk revival. But in the process, he downplayed bluegrass's history as part of commercial country music. Bluegrass was now being promoted as a stout branch of the mighty tree of tradition, an offshoot of the trunk of old-time southern string band music that in turn had deep roots in British Isles folkways. Ralph genuinely looked on Monroe as a folk artist who happened to work within country music.

Powerful moments reinforced this view. Old-time-style musicians would come to Bill's Brown County Jamboree and participate in jam sessions.[73] Ralph recognized one as Luther Strong, who had been recorded by a Library of Congress folk music collection project in the 1930s.

If Rinzler was fascinated with these connections, he was equally disinterested in contemporary bluegrass. The greatest exponents of the modern bluegrass sound at the time were the Country Gentlemen, the Washington, D.C.–based foursome that was featuring jazzy adaptations of old ballads and modern pop songs done bluegrass style. They did not top Rinzler's list of favorite musicians, as folklorist and friend Neil Rosenberg recalls:

Ralph hated the Country Gentlemen. He *really* hated the Country Gentlemen. He would say, "I can't stand those guys." He just didn't like what they were doing. He thought it was a travesty.[74]

Monroe now had a two-pronged popularity. While he was being discovered by the folk crowd, he was still beloved by grassroots country fans.

"Bill Monroe to me is the greatest of all men in country or blue grass music," wrote one South Carolina fan, in a June 17, 1963, letter to WSM.[75] "I remember years ago when he was on for Wallrite building papper [sic] my father bought Wallrite and fixed our house with it because he was so fond of Bill Monroe's sacared [sic] songs."

Monroe's appeal extended across the ocean. On May 24, 1963, the president of the British Country and Western Society wrote a garrulous missive informing Monroe that "YOU are amongst the MOST POPULAR C&W ARTISTS here" and requesting records for the society's syndicated radio shows, "for we repeat, WE MUST HAVE YOUR WONDERFUL WORK."[76]

When Rinzler's involvement with Monroe became known, serious inquiries followed. Irv Dinkin of Willard Alexander, Inc., a New York–based entertainment management firm with additional offices in Chicago, Beverly Hills, and London, wrote to ask about Bill's freedom as far as agency affiliation was concerned.[77] Soon after Rinzler arrived in Nashville, Monroe took him around Music Row where song publishers and talent agents expressed a sincere, if belated, interest in the folk revival.[78]

Emboldened, Rinzler decided to negotiate a better deal with Bill's record company. One morning, he dressed in his best clothes and went to see Harry Silverstein, now Decca's Nashville A&R man responsible for Monroe. Rinzler had leverage: With his contacts at Vanguard (for which Doc Watson and the Greenbriar Boys recorded) and with other labels taking a keen interest in folk music, he could shop Bill Monroe & His Blue Grass Boys around.

"Ralph, I don't know what we're talking about," said Silverstein, interrupting Rinzler as soon as he started.[79] "Bill just signed a five-year contract with us last year."

Monroe had never told Rinzler about the agreement. Ralph was embarrassed and quietly furious.

At every turn, Rinzler had to cope with Monroe's fitful attention to business matters. On June 10, 1963, he was contacted by Cooke and Rose Theatrical Enterprises, Inc., of Lancaster, Pennsylvania, regarding a Monroe appearance at Sunset Park on July 7: "Kindly wire or phone me at once if this date is Okay [sic] as Sunset Park has advertised Bill and are getting concerned as they have not received their contract back."[80]

On June 27, 1963, a fan in Boaz, Alabama, wrote to Monroe neatly and respectfully on lined three-ring notebook paper: "If you recall I made a long distance telephone call to you at the Opry three weeks ago in regard to making a personal appearance here for the little league Base

Ball Club [sic]. You told me that night you could not give me any open dates but you would have your manager call me. As of now I have not received any word from him. . . ."

Rinzler and Monroe — the manager with a mission and the insouciant artist — were headed for a clash. It finally came over Bill's country music park, the Brown County Jamboree in Bean Blossom, Indiana.

The venue was continuing its schedule of Saturday night square dances and Sunday afternoon and evening country music concerts. Many locals loved the jamboree, but others saw it as an eyesore, a rundown park patronized by hillbillies.[81] Cash flow problems and a tendency to let accounts get in arrears were making it difficult to get local services. Still, it had tremendous potential as a showplace, even a moneymaker. The problem was its manager — Birch Monroe.

Bill's brother was a quiet, likable man. He had the Monroe dignity. (He would even mow the lawn in a shirt and tie.) And he was reliable in his way. But Birch was stuck in first gear. Even more than Bill, he seemed to embody the Monroes' difficulties in grasping basic business concepts.[82] He was notorious for buying just a small package of hamburger for the concession stand or a couple rolls of toilet paper for the outhouses. When the park ran out of food or tissue, Birch would of course go to the nearby store to purchase more supplies; meanwhile the patrons became hungry or quite anxious. His emphasis on minimizing cash outlays even applied to maintenance. Like Bill, Birch would spend hours straightening out old nails for reuse rather than just buy new ones.

In short, if the Brown County Jamboree was going to amount to anything, Birch needed to be replaced by someone with greater motivation and managerial skills. One night at Bean Blossom, Ralph told Bill exactly that.

Bill listened coldly, rigid and unyielding in his demeanor. Rinzler started huffing and puffing as he did when he became frustrated and upset.[83] Suddenly, Bill strode off and unexpectedly got into a car with Brad Keith and a friend who were about to drive back to Nashville.

"I'm aggravated," said Monroe. "Let's go." Monroe sat silently in the backseat for the entire ride. No one else in the car dared breathe a word.

Rinzler had taken a terrible risk by criticizing Bill's brother. Two things saved him: Bill's respect for anyone gutsy enough to stand up to him and the support of Bessie Lee Mauldin.

Bessie had never really gotten along with Birch (a friction that limited her visits to Bean Blossom). Now she also told Bill that Birch was not energetic enough in running the park and that it should be built up into something bigger. She supported Ralph's nominee for the new manager — Neil Rosenberg, then a twenty-four-year-old graduate student in folklore at nearby Indiana University.[84] Neil was also a banjo picker who had become a Brown County Jamboree regular and member of the house band. Bill finally agreed to the change. Birch continued to live locally and run the park's Saturday night square dances.

Rinzler's relation with his client/idol survived, says Rosenberg, thanks to Ralph's sincerity and work ethic.

> Ralph was obviously very devoted to him and was working for him 100 percent. That was what Bill noticed the most. If you were doing things for him, if you were on his side and working hard for him, that was what inspired his confidence in someone.[85]

Ever a conceiver of projects, Rinzler was full of plans. He was working on a Monroe discography and wanted to produce a full Monroe songbook.[86] He began doing interviews with Monroe for a major biography.[87]

Someone, probably Bessie Lee herself, must have told him the story behind "My Little Georgia Rose" because during one interview about Bill's songs Ralph knew enough to ask, diplomatically, "Was she a relative of yours?" Monroe denied it, saying, "I knew her from the time she was a baby" but she was "not my child or anything" — all the while drumming his fingertips nervously on the table.[88]

Although the books never came to fruition, Ralph convinced Decca to release collections of classic Monroe material that had been available only as singles. He wrote detailed liner notes for these albums. The result was a great trilogy of classic recordings, showcasing the breathtaking instrumental virtuosity and versatility of Bill Monroe & His Blue Grass Boys (*Bluegrass Instrumentals*, released June 1965); the intensely autobiographical "true songs" (*The High Lonesome Sound*, August 1966); and gospel material (*A Voice from On High*, June 1969, with notes from interviews by Alice Gerrard Foster).

In the process of publicizing Bill Monroe, Ralph Rinzler tirelessly promoted bluegrass in general. The numerous newspaper and magazine articles he wrote frequently contained mention of the Stanleys, Flatt and Scruggs, Reno and Smiley, and others. By contrast, Lester and Earl were not tying themselves to a wider bluegrass world nor promoting the overall music. (They had even begun to distance themselves from the term "bluegrass,"[89] perhaps fearing it too narrowly defined them or that bluegrass was again being identified with Bill Monroe.) In the act of championing Bill Monroe to the folk revival, Ralph Rinzler helped establish bluegrass as a genre.

Pleased with Rinzler's ideas, Monroe became worried that Decca wasn't picking up on them. He mentioned this on more than one occasion to Owen Bradley, who had been promoted into Paul Cohen's old job as head of Decca's country music division.

> He wanted it to be known that he was "the Father of Bluegrass." I don't know if we knew how to go about promoting it then. We would now.
>
> There wasn't nearly the promotion of records then that there is now. We'd just put the record out and if it got a great review, maybe we'd go the next step and run a little ad. And if it went to the next step, we'd get a little bigger ad. There wasn't a whole bunch of stuff that we did for our records, there really wasn't. You have to remember that the records sold for about $3.98, that's tops, retail. The company got just a little less than $2 for them wholesale. There just wasn't that much money. Now you're talking about a nice hunk of money, twelve, fourteen, fifteen dollars. It gets interesting pretty quick.[90]

In fairness to Decca, Monroe was himself frustratingly blasé about the business of record promotion. The advent of light, durable 45 singles and 33⅓ LPs was now allowing country musicians to sell product at their shows. (The old 78s had been too heavy and too fragile to carry on tour.) Fans thrilled at getting a personally autographed record as a memento, and the sales helped musicians pay traveling expenses, allowing them to save more of their appearance fees. Since Monroe had enjoyed success with his songbooks in the 1940s, he should have embraced the concept of artist-to-fan record sales. But by the early 1960s he was still not selling them at concerts.[91] Neil Rosenberg was astonished. He contacted Rinzler, urging that Bill start carrying records to sell at Bean Blossom and other personal appearances.

Bill certainly needed the money. The precariousness of his financial situation was revealed to Brad Keith by a totally innocent means: the mail drops at WSM. The station had general boxes for Opry musicians' mail divided into four big alphabetical sections. The box that contained the K's also contained the M's.

> You'd have to get all the mail out and go through it piece by piece, and in the process you'd see what everybody else was getting. Bill had lots and lots of mail from the I.R.S. Things were not in good shape.[92]

Keith eventually moved out of the Clarkston Hotel and with Rinzler found an apartment on West End Avenue. The place became a musicians' crash pad, affectionately dubbed "The Bluegrass Rest Home."[93]

One day, they were sitting around jamming with some visitors: Robert L. Jones (an early northern bluegrass devotee) and Geoff Muldaur (a member of the Jim Kweskin Jug Band and future husband of vocalist Maria Muldaur), who had stopped during a trip to California, bringing along Jim Rooney, an old musical partner of Keith's from Cambridge, Massachusetts.

Then — unannounced and unexpected — in walked Bill Monroe and Bessie Lee Mauldin. Bessie was bearing gifts of food.

Brad and Bessie had clashed over a musical matter during which Mauldin had invoked the name of Brad's greatest rival in the melodic banjo style. "Well, if you don't want to play," she had snapped, "we'll get Bobby Thompson." Keith had responded, "Bessie, whatever you feel is best for the music. If you feel he can do a better job, I'll step aside."

Brad's gentle sentiment about the greater good of Bill's music had surprised and touched Bessie. Now she was in the kitchen unloading jars of her delicious homemade mayonnaise as a peace offering.

When Monroe heard that Jones, Muldaur, and Rooney had driven all the way from Cambridge, he asked how their trip had been, striking up a conversation with the awestruck young men. He picked up a guitar and to their surprise, since they assumed he only knew the mandolin, proceeded to play it beautifully. Then he handed it to Rooney. A Monroevian test. Rooney broke into a sweat but managed to get through a song. Rooney, a lefthander, played a regularly strung guitar upside down, picking the bass runs upward with his index finger instead of downward with his thumb.

"That's good," Monroe commented. "You've got your own lick on that. Keep that up. That's good." Rooney had thought of his lefthanded approach as a handicap, not a style. Suddenly he felt a sense of accomplishment.

All this sociability on the part of Bill Monroe was highly uncharacteristic. More was to come. In late July, Monroe invited Rinzler and McCoury to come along on one of his occasional visits to Rosine.[94] The folklorist and the guitarist pulled into a parking lot in Goodlettsville, where they were supposed to rendezvous with Bill. But he was nowhere to be seen.

Ralph and Del looked around. There was only a man wearing bib overalls, a baseball cap, and thick eyeglasses. He was standing next to a pickup truck containing two foxhounds and two piglets. To their growing astonishment, they realized that this quaint character was, in fact, Bill Monroe. Out of context, accoutered in garb utterly different from his impeccable stage wear of suit, tie, and cowboy hat, they had failed to recognize him.

Yet this was the authentic Bill in more ways than one. The animals were presents: the dogs for Charlie, the piglets for Speed. Despite stories about the acrimonious breakup of the Monroe Brothers, Ralph detected no animosity between Charlie and Bill. Charlie was delighted with the hounds and insisted they be given an immediate trial run to determine their ability to "speak." Ralph and Del suddenly found themselves at an old-time, hill country foxhunt that lasted nearly until dawn.

The bedraggled outsiders got only about three hours' sleep at Charlie's house before Bill energetically roused them for breakfast. That day, he showed them his parents' graves in Rosine's "little lonesome grave-yard" and the headstone inscriptions that had inspired the chorus of "Memories of Mother and Dad."

"That was a true song, just like I told you," Bill said.

Bill also led them up the hill to the old Monroe place. He told them the story of how he had written another "I'm on My Way to the Old Home." He pointed out the overgrown path in front of the house, the old wagon road to Rosine. He told them how he would hide in the barn so passersby wouldn't make fun of him.

They went into that barn. Inside, they saw an old trunk. Its contents — his father's ledgers and various family letters and papers — were scattered across the floor. Monroe, Rinzler later recounted, "expressed a combination of rage and despair at his brothers' lack of respect for their father's documents."[95] (In fairness to Charlie and Speed, Bill's anger was misdirected. It is likely that outsiders had pilfered the trunk in an attempt to find valuables. Charlie and the others were probably unaware of the state of J.B.'s papers.)

The trio spent an hour carefully gathering everything into the trunk, which Bill then took back to his farm near Nashville. But before they left, Ralph expressed interest in two of Buck's old ledger books. Bill immediately presented them to Rinzler. Ralph later wrote of the trip, "The message that I derived from that experience with Bill was that his music was only one aspect of the deep commitment he felt to his family and regional culture."[96]

Yet there was another message — more basic and more profound — to have been derived from this trip and from Bill's surprise visit to the Bluegrass Rest Home.

Bill was initiating conversations with strangers. He was introducing outsiders to his family and the world from which he came. He was revealing more and more about his past, including deeply painful incidents. He was expressing his feelings more openly.

Bill Monroe was coming out of his shell.[97]

But all was not joy. Rinzler noticed that when Monroe visited his kinfolk he did not call on former neighbors who would be happy to greet a Grand Ole Opry star.

"People didn't know me when I left," Monroe said.[98] "Well, I don't know them now."

Rinzler was so struck by Bill's bitterness that he preserved the comment in the back of one of his ever-present datebooks.

During another visit to Rosine, Monroe recruited McCoury to drive his three-quarter-ton Chevy pickup truck. It carried another supply of piglets, which were traded to Speed for some foxhounds. They again stayed with Charlie, whose wife Betty cooked a fine supper. Afterward, the Monroes sat around talking. All seemed breezy. Then Del noticed that Bill had gone silent.

Later Bill told him, "You know, sometimes I get to thinking about how they treated me when I was little, and it just makes me mad."[99] McCoury began to realize why, from time to time, a very dark shadow darkened the face of Bill Monroe.

Not content just to write laudatory articles or line up gigs, Rinzler occasionally joined the Blue Grass Boys on the road.[100]

Monroe never drove in these years. Most of the time he rode in the seat behind the driver, reading a newspaper or paperback novel while Bessie navigated. The ensemble would travel for days without seeing a bed, sleeping during the drives. Slaphappy, the best and worst of their personalities came out during food stops. On one occasion at a restaurant, Bill vigorously shook a bottle of salad dressing. The bottle had a loose top. Monroe ended up decorating Brad Keith and the curtains, occasioning near-hysterical laughter. On another trip, Joe Stuart (the veteran Blue Grass Boys multi-instrumentalist who had replaced Kenny Baker on fiddle) got into a contest with Bill about how many raw oysters they could eat. The loser had to pay for the meal. Monroe won, a gut-busting thirteen dozen oysters later.

Monroe always remained top dog. McCoury, Monroe, and Stuart were once riding an elevator during a stop in a city. Joe and Bill were standing behind Del, and it was clear that Stuart was feeling his oats. There was the unmistakable sound of roughhousing, and Joe was heard to say, "Chief, I think I can take you this morning."

This remark was quickly followed by a thud that vibrated the elevator. When McCoury looked around, Stuart was flat on his back, Monroe's knee firmly planted on his chest.

And there were the continuing contests of will between Bill and Bessie. Once the band pulled up to an ice cream stand and got cones. Bessie sat eating one cone and, in a mood to needle Bill, didn't give him the other. When she finally did, Bill simply acted like he was passing it along to someone else. It went right out the window.

Monroe could easily lapse into one of his moody silences, for a day or two or more. On these occasions, when the band stopped to eat, Bill would make phone calls or use the rest room, then sit at a table by himself. The good-natured joking and banter that eased travel would stop. The miles could stretch out far indeed.

But sometimes, especially late at night if he wanted to ensure that a driver wouldn't fall asleep, Bill would become accessible. He would sit up front and engage in long conversations, sharing his philosophies of life or recounting old stories. If Rinzler was at the wheel, he would drink in these talks. Monroe was also taking a renewed interest in composing. He might get out his mandolin and play a melodic line over and over, the germ of a fertile idea. After he had worked up some lyrics (he often started his songwriting with a chorus), he would teach them to the lead singer. Or he might ask others to contribute to the verses or refrain.

The creation and rehearsal of new material was carried out on the road, while the cornfields and the cow pastures and the tobacco sheds and the little towns went by outside, and the sun rose and shone and set, and clouds gathered and rain pelted down on the poor rusty vehicle, and the Oldsmobile's odometer turned over and over and over.

But the road takes a terrible toll on those who are not up to its stresses. One who was unprepared was Bill's daughter Melissa.

In the summer of 1963, Bill again began taking Melissa on tour as a guest vocalist. She was still the strong singer whose potential had never been realized after her brief recordings with Columbia as a teenager. But she was not a strong person. She could be sweet, but was becoming overweight and showing signs of depression.

The Blue Grass Boys left for a cross-country trip on November 22, 1963.[101] (Bill Keith first learned of the Kennedy assassination that day during a phone conversation with Earl Scruggs.) In Florida, one of their shows was canceled by the promoter in the wake of the national mourning over events in Dallas. They turned around and drove up to New York City to play Town Hall. Despite this unsettling beginning, there was a sense that things were getting better. It was the band's first trip on a "new" tour bus, a well-worn 1947 Flxible.

But in New York there was a scattering of boos among self-righteous folkies when Melissa sang her country numbers.[102] Then the band went to Wheeling, West Virginia, to play on the WWVA *Jamboree*. Melissa began to come apart. She marked all over Bessie Lee's sable coat with lipstick and ruined it, her antagonism to her mother's rival resurfacing. On the *Jamboree*, she came out to sing the sentimental waltz "Dreaming of a Little Cabin." She started the song, then burst into tears.

Bill put Melissa on the bus, but she went into hysterics and ran into the street. After Melissa was calmed and shepherded back into the vehicle, the sad little caravan headed west, destination Los Angeles and a return engagement at the Ash Grove.

Ralph Rinzler was traveling along in his Chevy Nova station wagon. Bill was riding with him. Ralph took the moment of privacy to tactfully tell Bill that Melissa was not in good health and needed a doctor's care.

"You ain't tellin' me my daughter's crazy!" Monroe shot back.[103] He instructed Rinzler to stop the car, got out, and stomped onto the bus.

Ralph had taken a grave risk by demanding that Birch be replaced as manager of the Brown County Jamboree. Now he had almost totally transgressed by being so frank about Melissa's condition. Monroe had cut off others for much less. Somehow, their friendship survived even this.

The situation with Melissa stabilized, and the return engagement at the Ash Grove was a success. When the act scheduled for the following week canceled, the Blue Grass Boys were invited to stay over. Monroe accepted.

But Bill Keith gave his notice. Traveling wasn't getting any easier, despite the bus. The money wasn't good. No recording sessions were planned. Melissa seemed to be a part of the show for the foreseeable future, and he was worried that her condition might worsen.

Another factor proved to be the deciding one: Monroe's profile had risen to the point where he had been invited to appear on the popular ABC television network show *Hootenanny*. But its producers had banned Pete Seeger from the program because of his association with left-wing politics. Prominent folk singers, among them Joan Baez, Judy Collins, and Ian and Sylvia, had signed a petition stating they would not appear on the show until Seeger had been invited. Keith realized that he most likely wouldn't be playing the five-string if it hadn't been for Pete Seeger. He decided to leave the Blue Grass Boys before their *Hootenanny* taping.

Keith agreed to train a replacement banjo player, a talented local musician. Keith coached him on kickoffs and tempos, and the young guy played the second week at the Ash Grove as a Blue Grass Boy. It was Ry Cooder, the future studio musician and solo artist, guest player with the Rolling Stones, and producer-star of the first digitally recorded pop music album.[104]

Rinzler was also withdrawing from day-to-day involvement with Monroe, having moved back to New York in the fall of 1963.[105] He continued as Bill's overall manager until well into 1965 but arranged for Ken Marvin, a respected Nashville promoter and former member of the Lonzo & Oscar country comedy team, to take over as Bill's booking agent.

There had been no open break. Rinzler was simply having a difficult time keeping up with his New York commitments and Greenbriar Boys gigs while living in Nashville. He had been named to the board of directors of the Newport Folk Festival. And he had lost money as Monroe's manager, although money had scarcely been his object.

Ralph Rinzler had been a man with a mission, and he had been victorious. Bill Monroe and Doc Watson were developing national reputations, and even if Monroe's fortunes remained pitifully below those of Flatt and Scruggs, he was on the way back up. And thanks to Rinzler, Bill Monroe had been firmly crowned with the regal title "the Father of Bluegrass."

In 1964, Melissa returned to touring with her father. Bessie Lee was in no mood to be generous about Melissa's occasionally erratic behavior. Such were Bessie's frustrations that she poured out her heart — and some serious suspicions — in a letter to her friend and ally Ralph Rinzler.

On February 14, while the Blue Grass Boys were on a package show with Johnny Cash and his future wife June Carter, Bessie wrote to Ralph on the stationery of the Pantlind Hotel in Grand Rapids, Michigan. Her clear and beautiful handwriting was in poignant contrast to her confused and tortured feelings.

It was Valentine's Day, she noted, but not for her.[106] Bill wasn't even introducing her onstage anymore, a stark contrast to years past. To make matters worse, Bill had decided this was to be her last road trip with the band. Bessie had no idea what the future held, where she would go or what she would do. A job, she wrote, would probably be a necessity because "my life's earnings are invested in his property." She berated herself for having been a fool for so long.

Bessie fretted about whether Ralph, Del McCoury, and others would get monies owed them. But her greatest concerns focused on Bill and Melissa. She alleged that "it was obvious that it was more than a father & daughter relationship" and that the tour was abuzz with gossip about this. The situation, Bessie claimed, had alienated several of Bill's peers, not only Johnny Cash but also Tex Ritter, the singing cowboy star and then-president of the Country Music Association. The situation was so bad, she worried, that soon Bill might not be able to hire any musicians through the local union or even get bookings.

"He is ruining himself and hasn't enough sense to realize it," Bessie wrote, adding of Melissa: "She's has [sic] really showed herself on this tour." If Rinzler replied to this letter, no copy has been found, although he and Bessie did stay in touch.

How to evaluate all this? It is indeed likely that Bessie Lee's earnings were invested in Bill's property. She probably helped him pay for the second farm on which they started living in 1954 and perhaps also for the Bean Blossom park, although her name is not on these deeds.

But what of Bessie's hints of incest between Monroe and his daughter? Several important factors argue that there was nothing improper about Bill and Melissa's relationship.

It is highly significant that these suggestions were unknown before the author's discovery of Bessie's letter in Ralph Rinzler's files. Such a story would have become quickly established in the gossip-prone world of country music had it been true (especially if such prominent performers as June Carter and Johnny Cash actually believed it). Yet the story was never repeated, casting immediate doubt on it. Nor did Monroe ever have problems getting bookings or hiring sidemen because of Melissa, as Bessie predicted.

In later years, Johnny and June Carter Cash gave Bessie a job as a secretary at their House of Cash music business in Goodlettsville, Tennessee.[107] But the Cashes also remained friends with Bill, who was invited over to Johnny's house for jam sessions ("guitar pulls," as Cash called them).[108]

Mr. and Mrs. Cash did not respond to interview requests and the other principals to this episode are dead. But Del McCoury was on the tour, having left the Blue Grass Boys on or about February 7, only one week before Bessie wrote to Rinzler.[109]

McCoury confirms that shortly after he left the band Bessie Lee also stopped touring with Monroe. But Del expresses genuine surprise at Bessie's allegations. He discounts the idea of a romantic relation between father and daughter.

> I never got that at all. I knew that Bessie didn't like Melissa very much. It could have been her way of getting back at both of them. She was jealous of Melissa. Bill would buy those kids things, he would buy Melissa and James all kinds of things he wouldn't buy for Bessie — clothes and expensive coats. It seems that when I was working with him, he never bought her things. I think she was angry at those kids.[110]

McCoury adds that Monroe was noticeably reconnecting with his children, making up for the times when the road and his love affairs had caused him to neglect his family. James was being taken along on more tours and being groomed for the bass player's role.

As has been noted earlier, Monroe's almost compulsive womanizing was restricted by certain moral boundaries: He never made advances toward the wives or girlfriends of his sidemen, for example. Bessie Lee's suggestions of incest between Bill and Melissa can be rejected.

However, the letter reveals the depth of Bessie's frustration and pain. In 1964, Bill did ask her to quit the road and keep house for the two of them at Bill's farm.[111] Bessie must have realized that after years of being the road girlfriend, she would now be a de facto housewife while another woman would be taking her place. Her fears were justified. Her letter to Ralph Rinzler documents the beginning of the process by which Bill Monroe inexorably cut this devoted woman out of his life. And like the demise of Bill's marriage to Carolyn, the process would be painfully prolonged.

Bill Keith had now been gone many months. But "Brad" had opened the door for other talented northerners to be hired as Blue Grass Boys. More followed. One was a friend of Bill Keith's, banjo player Steve Arkin of New York City.

Arkin played for Monroe one summer when he was a nineteen-year-old college student. But not during just any summer: This was the summer of 1964, "Freedom Summer," the height of the battle against segregation, the season of civil rights workers coming down from the North. Northerners were easy to spot, and many southerners bitterly resented their presence. In fact, civil rights workers Chaney, Goodman, and Schwerner were murdered on June 21, 1964, while Arkin was on tour with Monroe.

Monroe evinced high respect for Arkin's musicianship, holding him to be a better backup banjo player than Bill Keith. "He could beat Brad all over playing a back-up," Monroe declared.[112] "Now there ain't no way around it. . . . He could put stuff in it and make it sell. . . . But he couldn't carry a melody like Brad could do it."

Unfortunately, Arkin seems to have flunked some Monroevian character test. Perhaps it was Steve's lukewarm reaction to a tune Monroe composed for him to play on the banjo, an instrumental that Monroe declared would make the young Manhattanite famous.[113] When Monroe would ask for a banjo number to be played, Steve would never select this new original. Soon, Monroe was playing head games with Arkin. Specifically, he never paid Steve, which added to the New Yorker's stresses.

There was a lot of tension in the air, and I was a northerner traveling through the South. I hardly ever went into a general store to get a sandwich or a Coke when someone didn't question me about my motives for coming down there.

Bill is legendary for his parsimony. It's probably his Scots-Irish heritage. He wasn't overly forthcoming with compensation for band members, notwithstanding his great musical leadership. At one point, I had to ask him for money for breakfast. "How much do you reckon you'll need, Steve?" And I said, "Well, how's about two and a half bucks, Bill?" He'd say, "That's too much, you can get a good breakfast for a dollar seventy-five."

Finally, I kinda screwed up the courage to ask if maybe he couldn't pay me like the other guys in the band, like a weekly salary. Actually, I'm not sure the other guys were getting one either. Bill said, "You know, you Jewish people are all alike, you're all after the almighty dollar."

So finally I called the musicians' union in Nashville of which I was a member and asked what they recommended. The guy on the other end of the line said, "You tell MUN-ro that he'll give you ev'ry cent that's comin' to you or he'll never play the Opry again." Here I am, a nineteen-year-old kid, and I'm trying to visualize precisely how I would walk up to Bill Monroe and phrase that.

So I abandoned that, and then I thought, Well, maybe I'll ask my parents to wire me some money. So I walked over to the Gulf station — we were in Lavonia, Georgia, and the only pay phone was in this Gulf station in the middle of town — and there was a group of locals in their overalls sucking on reeds. I said, "Excuse me," to get inside the station to get to the phone. They sort of parted like the Red Sea, and I went inside and said, "I'd like to make a collect call to New York City."

I felt the pressure of their eyes on my back, and then I noticed they had formed a phalanx around me. So when my mother answered the phone, I just said, "Hi, Mom, I want you to know I'm having a great time down here picking the five-string with Bill Monroe and the Blue Grass Boys!"

I couldn't tell her the whole story or ask her to wire me money or anything. So I said goodbye and hung up the phone.

Then one big guy walks up to me and says, "You're a Yankee fellar, aren't cha?" And I said, "Yeah." And he says, "You sure you're not down here to interfere with our way of life?" And I said, "No, no, no, no. I'm down here playing with Bill Monroe and the Blue Grass Boys." And he said, "Well, you said you could pick a five. Is that true?" I said, "Yeah."

He said, "No Yankee can pick a five. And I didn't hear nothin' about Bill bein' in town. So let's go down and see where he's at."

So I walk across town and this whole entourage is following me. Bill is leaning against the bus with his hat pulled down, filing his nails. Now, remember, Bill is ticked off at me. He sees me with these guys following me. He gets this little twinkle in his eye. He pulls his hat back down and continues filing. I walk up and say, "Hey, Bill!"

And he says nothing.

Then the biggest of these big guys kind of elbows me aside and walks up and says, "Hey, Bill, we didn't know you was in town, but we found this Yankee down at the gas station, and he's tryin' to tell us he can pick a five-string. That can't be true!"

Monroe just keeps filing his nails. And he doesn't say anything for a long time. Then he tilts his hat back, and looks up, and he just says, "I believe he can."[114]

The story is quintessential Monroe: the sideman being tested (and apparently flunking the character test even if Arkin passed the musical challenges with flying colors); Bill's quick read of a situation; and his wry sense of humor, expressed through his exquisite (if, for Arkin, excruciating) sense of timing.

But what of the anti-Semitic remark about Jews being "after the almighty dollar"? Was that also quintessential Bill Monroe?

The evidence is that it was not. If Monroe had truly harbored prejudice against Jews, he would not have hired Arkin in the first place. As Monroe's career revived, he was not desperate for musicians and there were plenty of non-Jewish banjo players willing to step onto the bus. Monroe trusted Ralph Rinzler as he did few other people, and he must have been aware of Rinzler's Jewish background. He also worked successfully with producer Harry Silverstein.

Southerners were flattered by northerners who became sincerely involved in their music, their reactions no different from that of black blues masters upon first hearing white guitarists like Mike Bloomfield and Eric Clapton. When a talented Yankee picker also turned out to be

Jewish, their surprise and pleasure was even greater. In 1959, the Green-briar Boys won first prize in the old-time band division of the famous Union Grove Fiddlers Convention in North Carolina; in 1961, the New York Ramblers, featuring mandolinist and Rinzler protégé David Gris-man, won in the bluegrass band category. These bands were predomi-nately Jewish. It would have been easy for the judges to give the top prizes to local groups, but they didn't. They welcomed quality musicians without prejudice.

Gene Lowinger had been the New York Ramblers' fiddler. Having substituted at the last minute at a Monroe show in the New York area, in June 1965 he went to Nashville to take up Monroe's offer of a job. Mon-roe referred to him affectionately as "our Jewish cowboy." When Monroe used that line at the Newport Folk Festival — which of course had many Jews in its audience — Gene finally asked Bill to stop. Bill did.

Lowinger was as curious about the veteran southern musicians as they were about him. He treasured moments spent with Opry performers Sam and Kirk McGee, real farmers who came to the Ryman literally with dirt under their fingernails and played old-time music.

One night, the McGees had a backstage visitor, a friend from a neigh-boring farm. "Why don't you go get your fiddle and play with us?" one of the brothers asked Gene, then leaned over to the neighbor and exclaimed, "Wait'll you hear this Jew boy play the fiddle!"[115]

Says Lowinger:

There was really nothing malicious about it at all. It was just so strange to these people to conceive of not only someone from the North but a Jewish person who didn't have horns or gold in his teeth, you know, to be playing this music.

It was just so incongruous to [Bill] that this whole audience for his music existed outside the South, that people like me would care about it. It just fascinated him.[116]

CHAPTER 7

HIS BEST DAYS
ON EARTH
(1965 TO 1983)

The beginning and end of every artistic activity is the re-creation of the world around me through the world inside of me. — Johann Wolfgang von Goethe

Carlton Haney, all 5 foot 5 inches and 200 pounds of him, was rotund with enthusiasm, rolling with ideas.

"It's gonna be a wonderful thing!" he declared.[1] "It's gonna be a bluegrass FESTIVAL!"

It was early 1965, and Haney was in a dressing room at the Opry, laying out his vision for an impassive Bill Monroe. A thirty-seven-year-old former battery factory worker from North Carolina, Carlton had become a hustling agent-impresario extraordinaire.[2] His clients had included Don Reno and Red Smiley, Conway Twitty, Loretta Lynn, Merle Haggard, and Monroe himself. While booking Bill in the mid-1950s, Carlton had also briefly dated his daughter Melissa.

Now Carlton wanted to promote an all-bluegrass show. Haney and other promoters had already presented one-day events, but Carlton had in mind a whole weekend of the music.

And there was more. A true visionary, Haney's grand scheme was to build up to a dramatic Sunday finale in which the story of Bill Monroe's music would be told onstage. How? By reassembling memorable editions of the Blue Grass Boys using Monroe alumni now playing in the other bands.

"Ah'm gonna tell the bluegrass STOW-ree!" Carlton exulted.[3]

The tradition of weekend-long fiddlers' conventions went back nearly a century and a half in the South, but they were not Haney's model. His use of the word "festival" — now ubiquitous in describing bluegrass events — was something brand-new in this context and directly reflective of his true inspiration, the Newport Folk Festival.

Carlton had been shown around Newport by Ralph Rinzler and was fascinated by its format of main-stage shows and small workshop programs.[4] The folk revival, which had adopted bluegrass after it was orphaned by the twin storms of rock 'n' roll and the modern Nashville sound, was now mentoring its great leap to independence, the bluegrass festival movement.

The concept of building a show around Blue Grass Boys reunions was no mere stunt. Carlton believed in it with evangelical zeal.

His enlightenment had come backstage at the Opry one night in November 1957.[5] Monroe was jamming with an elite cadre of former sidemen. At one point, Don Reno tried to kick off the lively love song "Live and Let Live," but Bill kept stopping to retune his mandolin, a silent signal of dissatisfaction. Finally he said, "Let me start it."

When he did, the hair stood up on Haney's arms. Reno had of course played the introduction perfectly, but there was something about Monroe's rhythm that utterly electrified the jam session. Opry performers began crowding into the dressing room and around the doorway.

Seeing these onlookers drawn by the magic of Monroe, Haney thought: If I could get all the musicians that worked with him, and put them on a stage somewhere, people would pay to hear it.[6]

*   *   *

When it came time for the show on Labor Day weekend of 1965, Haney had to wire money so Bill could get his bus fixed and travel. When he arrived, Carlton informed him that he had booked motel rooms for the band at $3.50 a day each.

"What's the fifty cents for?" Bill asked.[7]

"Well, that's what it costs," Carlton said.

"Well, I'm gettin' rooms for three dollars," Bill said.

"Well, that's how much they cost," Carlton said.

"Well, I'll pay for it," said Bill. "But next year, I'm not gonna stay there!"

Carlton's decision to hold the festival in Fincastle, Virginia, near his Roanoke base of operations, was a miscalculation. He got local publicity, but he was more than 230 miles away from the bluegrass hotbed of Washington and farther yet from Philadelphia, New York, and Boston, cities full of bluegrass-loving folkies.

Still, Haney got an announcement in *Sing Out!* and many northern devotees joined longtime southern fans of the music at his show. Young pickers who would soon form the next generation of bluegrass stars made the trip. The setting was not an upscale city park à la Newport nor even a rustic but established country music venue like New River Ranch. It was an ad hoc setup at Cantrell's Horse Farm — essentially a cow pasture with some picnic tables, outhouses, and a very small temporary stage. The whole experience was not much above a camping trip, with Carlton as scoutmaster. You had to be a true believer, almost a cultist, to come to something like this.

Ralph Rinzler, who had collected detailed information about Monroe's bands for his unrealized discography, wrote the narration for the finale,[8] which Haney grandiloquently titled "The Story of Blue Grass Music, with Music and Narration by the Artists Who Recorded and Performed the Songs for the Last Quarter Century." Since it was not known until the last minute who would be performing, Rinzler stood behind the stage and wrote on the fly, handing up pages to emcee Carlton.

There was a sense of solidarity at Fincastle, a shared identity and commitment, the wonderful feeling of being able to look around and think: Here are all these other people who love this music just like me.[9]

Unfortunately, there were only about five hundred people looking around that first year, and it took Haney a while to pay off all the bands.[10] But it was a landmark: Monroe and Scruggs had made bluegrass a distinctive sound; fans and disk jockeys had named it as a genre; Rinzler had given it a history; and now Carlton Haney had turned it into a movement.

Monroe's band that summer was one of his hottest in years. With the exception of son James on bass, they were all non-southerners: Gene Lowinger of New York on fiddle, Lamar Grier of Maryland on banjo, and a twenty-two-year-old from Massachusetts who would prove to be one of Monroe's greatest singing partners: Peter Rowan.

Rowan was born in 1942 in Wayland, Massachusetts, real Henry David Thoreau territory.[11] Peter grew into a musical free spirit, picking to the beat of different strummers. He performed for a while in a high school rock band but soon was captivated by the country music being played on radio and in bars around Boston for transplanted southerners, and by the folk music springing up in Harvard Square. Through Don Stover, a West Virginia expatriate and former Blue Grass Boy who had coached Bill Keith, he got turned on to Bill Monroe.

In the fall of 1964, Rowan learned through Keith and Rinzler that Monroe needed a guitarist-singer for a tour of New England and Canada. "You know," Keith said, "a lot of people have just been just filling in with Bill. I've got a feeling you could do more."[12]

Rowan did. Monroe invited him down to Nashville. It was one of Bill's typically vague invitations — "If you come to Nashville, I can help you"[13] — but Peter responded. In November, after a few weeks of hanging around, he got a job in the Blue Grass Boys.

He got more than he bargained for: Rinzler, still Bill's overall manager but busy with other projects, delegated Peter to be Monroe's booking agent. He was soon going head-to-head with gruff promoters who packed Saturday night specials in their socks and claimed that they hadn't made enough money to pay the band. Rowan would report back to Bill then return, saying, "Mr. Monroe says you have to pay him." The promoters would pay up every time.

Monroe coached Peter on his singing.[14] Rowan had a ringing and sincere voice, equal parts maturity and innocence. Their duets were exciting. Peter was awed by Bill as a poet and energized by his creativity. Standing next to him onstage was like standing next to a fire, a burning bush that was not consumed. Soon the flames engulfed him.

Equally on fire for the music of Bill Monroe was Richard Greene, a Los Angeles native who would become one of the truly legendary bluegrass fiddlers.[15]

Born in 1942, Greene took violin lessons as a child, then got turned on to old-time music and bluegrass while a student at Berkeley. One day at the Ash Grove, he saw Scotty Stoneman playing fiddle for an enthralled crowd. Stoneman's raucous, adventurous, but thoroughly virtuoso playing had made him a cult figure in bluegrass. Stoneman became Greene's idol; Scotty, in turn, exposed Richard to the recordings of his hero, Chubby Wise, the greatest of which were made with someone named Bill Monroe.

Exposed to the primal bluegrass, Richard Greene started telling anyone who would listen, "I want to play with Bill Monroe. That's the whole focus of my life."

His networking worked. In early 1966, Greene got a last-minute call from Ralph Rinzler to join Monroe in Montreal and subsequently landed a full-time job with the Blue Grass Boys. Highly influenced by Stoneman's improvisational pyrotechnics, Richard made "Orange Blossom Special" very much his own. When Monroe unleashed him on that fiddle tour de force for the first time on the Opry, he knew what the effect would be. As the avalanche of cheers crested, Monroe was already strumming rhythm, lifting Green into an encore.[16]

In years past, Bill had kept in mind a reservoir of potential sidemen throughout the South to call upon. Now a national talent pool was starting to flow toward him. He was very fortunate it happened when it did.

All-bluegrass shows were proliferating, and Monroe, after all, was the music's leading figure. The "1st International Folk-Bluegrass Festival," held on July 10, 1966, at Lake Whipporwill Park near Warrenton, Virginia, advertised "In Person — Everybody."[17] And that was the case. Promoter Stu Brooks even managed to get Bill Monroe and Flatt and Scruggs on the same program, the first time for a decade and a half that they had shared a stage outside the Ryman Auditorium. In a compromise worthy of a Middle Eastern peace settlement, Monroe and Flatt and Scruggs shared top billing, with Lester and Earl getting the prestige of closing the afternoon and Bill, as the last act in the evening, closing out the festival.

A new publication called *Bluegrass Unlimited* was promoted that day. Started by Washington-area enthusiasts as a mimeographed newsletter, it would play a crucial role in the propagation of Monroe's music. As *Bluegrass Unlimited* grew into a real magazine, its calendar listings, record reviews, and general articles all fulfilled a growing need — information for the burgeoning audience of bluegrass fans.

Carlton Haney reprised his Roanoke festival on Labor Day weekend 1966 and began to expand his yearly festival offerings into a true circuit. Monroe began to feature more bluegrass at his own Brown County Jamboree in Bean Blossom, Indiana.

The Stanley Brothers appeared at Bean Blossom on October 16, 1966.[18] The audience that day had no idea they were witnessing the Stanleys' last full-length concert appearance.

Carter was seriously ill, his poor health worsened by the effects of long-term drinking.[19] He was hospitalized the following month with internal bleeding and died on December 1.[20] He was only forty-one years old.

Bill had never approved of Carter's drinking, feeling it prevented him from getting "the good part out of music."[21] Despite this and his anger twenty years earlier when the Stanleys had copied him, Bill had come to love Carter and Ralph. He interrupted a tour in the Deep South, flew north, and finished the journey by car to the top of the Virginia mountain where Carter was being laid to rest. He sang an a cappella rendition of "Swing Low, Sweet Chariot," then touched the coffin with his fingertips and said, "We'll meet again."[22] Bill later confided to a friend that getting through the song without breaking down was one of the most difficult things he ever had to do.[23]

Meanwhile, Bill's collection of energetic twenty-year-olds was forming into one of the finest editions ever of the Blue Grass Boys, a throwback to the Jimmy Martin days, full of enthusiastic young talents seemingly oblivious to the hardships and lack of money. They were awestruck but fierce, worshiping Bill but also challenging him. Says Richard Greene:

> We rehearsed, we practiced, we played those instruments for Monroe. If he didn't like something, boy, we'd want to change it. [The veteran] musicians didn't have that attitude of cooperation. They had to go along with that old man. . . . Monroe would lose interest in giving instructions to those guys. They weren't eager, bright-eyed sponges soaking up every tiny comment and nuance that guy made or played. That's how we were. Even James caught the bug.[24]

The classically trained Greene began to comprehend Monroe's almost mystical opinions on fiddling. For example, Bill spoke reverentially about "the ancient tones."[25] Often playing for dances unaccompanied, the old fiddlers had to get the most out of their instruments, so they learned to play a loud, lower note (usually a root note, like an A in the key of A), then quickly fiddle melody notes while the first was still vibrating. To Bill, this layering of vibrations created not only a traditional sound but an "ancient" one.

Greene was also fascinated by the way Monroe would simplify fiddle tunes.[26] Texas- and contest-style fiddlers would heavily ornament tunes like "Gray Eagle" or "Soldier's Joy" and call for extra guitar chords behind them, creating jazzlike effects. But Monroe would deconstruct such tunes to their very essences and insist that his sidemen play only the most basic chords in accompaniment.

To Monroe, therefore, the notes that a bluegrass musician chose to play at any given moment — and how these notes were attacked, held, and shaped — were of supreme importance. Hence his deceptively simple praise of someone who "played a good note" or "put a good note in there."

Peter Rowan realized that he and the other talented neophytes were reinforcing bluegrass as a style.

> You had people listening to Bill, loving his music and then playing with him, and bringing back to the music what they liked about it. . . . I

think Bill would pick up on what people liked about his music and feed it back in, and say, "This is the way my music goes."[27]

But, as had happened so many times before, Bill's chaotic love life and his prickly ego threatened the glad camaraderie and smooth operation of the band.

Bessie's fears about being replaced had been quite justified. Bill's new flame was Virginia Stauffer.[28] Pretty and dark-haired, she was nicknamed "Gypsy." Their relationship had begun as far back as the mid-1960s. (This is probably the reason that Bessie wrote so poignantly to Ralph Rinzler from Grand Rapids in 1964 that "I don't even get my name called on the stage anymore." Stauffer, a Michigan native, was probably in the audiences during that tour.)

Like Bessie, Stauffer was a substantial, attractive lady who liked to dress and make herself up glamorously (even braving the rank toilet of the band bus to do so.)[29] Their relationship was not as tempestuous as the affair with Bessie. Bill seemed just to need someone to talk to and relax with on the road. Virginia was also a talented songwriter, contributing high-impact numbers to his repertoire: "With Body and Soul," "I Live in the Past," and "The Road of Life." Bill would introduce these songs onstage by saying they were written by "an old gypsy woman" or "an old lady from Michigan," affectionate references to Virginia. Bill returned the compliment, writing the instrumental "Virginia Darlin'" in her honor.[30]

Bessie knew something was going on. She finally browbeat Peter Rowan into giving her the basics. Soon thereafter, backstage at the Opry, Monroe walked up very close to Peter and said, "Some old lady's been talking."[31]

It was not a comfortable situation for the young guitarist. Soon, things got a lot less comfortable.

A trip to England in the summer of 1966 — Bill's first overseas jaunt — was both successful and surreal. The band played everything from house concerts packed with attentive folkies to collegiate parties crammed with indifferent revelers to an acclaimed concert at Albert Hall. The Blue Grass Boys explored psychedelic-era London.[32] (James Monroe didn't quite know what to make of the whole scene nor of

Greene and Rowan's enthusiasm for it.) A man from India came up to Monroe after a show and said there were sounds in Bill's music that reminded him of home.

American folk singer Tom Paxton was on the British charts with "The Last Thing on My Mind."[33] Bill announced that he was going to record the song once they got back. Although Monroe didn't explain his reasons, Paxton's composition obviously touched him. With its confession of mistreatment and its plea for a loved one's return, "The Last Thing on My Mind" was a kinder, gentler "Can't You Hear Me Callin'."

But Richard Greene was not sure that Bill should do this kind of material. He shared his reservations with Peter Rowan, who in turn asked Bill if it might damage his image as a traditional artist.

Monroe immediately put up an icy wall of silence. James was shocked. "You just never tell Daddy what to do!" he admonished Rowan. The next day, Peter tried to ameliorate the situation. He told Bill that "The Last Thing on My Mind" might be a good number to record.

"You have put me off it, Pete," Bill said. "You have ruined it for me. You have ruined it."

This seemingly trivial incident erased much of the legacy of this outstanding edition of the Blue Grass Boys. In the studio, Peter Rowan was pointedly relegated to baritone singer in trios where James sang lead. Only one of the powerful Monroe/Rowan vocal collaborations from their concert repertoire was ever captured on record: "Midnight on the Stormy Deep," a lofty effort that ranks among the great Monroe duets.

Greene, not in the doghouse, was rewarded with featured fiddling on several rousing instrumentals, notably "Turkey in the Straw" and "Dusty Miller." The band's recording of "Blue Night" was kicked off by a Richard Greene fiddle solo that was wild, fierce, yet beautifully controlled. Monroe, always at his best when challenged, replied with vocals and a mandolin break that were as defiant as any musical statements he ever made.

The Blue Grass Boys didn't have time to do anything mechanical. They had to learn the songs and record them, knowing every moment that Bill Monroe recorded would be historical. There was an edge, a rightmindedness, a readiness, and it kept Bill from approaching the sessions merely as a short-term earning opportunity.[34]

The money was certainly needed. The Blue Grass Special was an old bus dubbed by the band "The Blue Grass Breakdown," and with good reason. On one occasion, Rowan and Greene were forced to hitchhike nearly forty miles to borrow a car from a friend of Bill's so they could continue a tour. (The vehicle they returned in was an Edsel.)

In an odd way, the bus aided the creative process. Once stranded, they would have nothing to do while awaiting aid but write songs. The wistful instrumental "Crossing the Cumberlands" came during a breakdown in those mountains.[35] Monroe developed the melody, the band suggested the chords.

On another occasion, the bus broke down overlooking a valley on a windy day. Bill turned to Peter and said, "Now I want you to remember this."[36] Then he sang:

> The wind is blowing 'cross the mountains
> And down o'er the valley way below . . .

Rowan, a lover of Lord Byron and the romantic poets, sang right back:

> It sweeps the grave of my darling.
> When I die, that's where I want to go . . .

An anthem of immortal love, "The Walls of Time" was born. Yet perhaps because of Bill's lingering pique, it was not recorded until after Rowan left the band. (Even then, Peter had to keep reminding Bill that he deserved co-writing credit.)[37]

Despite Bill's resurgent reputation, gigs were scarce. Rowan was a novice at booking, and the festival movement had yet to hit full stride. Bill's oak-tough playing and ax-edged singing and his regal persona had earned him adulation among hardcore bluegrassers and the folk crowd, but general audiences found it somewhat inaccessible, especially compared to the Osborne Brothers' mellifluous harmonies or the listener-friendly Flatt and Scruggs show. The Blue Grass Boys' main staple became the WSM *Friday Night Frolic* radio show (paying $17.50 per man) and the Saturday night Opry ($27.50 each).[38]

And so things came apart. Richard Greene left in early 1967, Rowan shortly thereafter, followed by Grier in the summer.

Bill was still able to attract top young talent. And soon an old hand began to sculpt a smooth face on the craggy granite of Bill's music. Kenny Baker had returned.

Monroe had begun teaching Richard Greene the fiddle tunes played by his uncle Pen. Now Monroe began brushing up on them in earnest, sometimes late at night up in the front of the bus,[39] ostensibly to keep the driver awake, but also with a definite goal in mind: an entire "Uncle Pen" album. And Baker became his fiddler of choice for it.

Baker drew the Blue Grass Boys into an increasingly sophisticated sound. He was an impeccable player but without the impassioned slicings of a Red Taylor or even a Richard Greene. With Baker back on the fiddle, the emphasis was on smoothness. Even Monroe was forsaking the gymnastic flights of his earlier career in favor of more evenly textured playing.

One thing had not changed, and that was Bill's almost compulsive need for the attentions of women. Even in his mid-fifties, Monroe remained a powerful, romantic, and highly attractive figure. Women were as drawn to him as he was to them. But in truth, his flings could take on an air of almost comic pathos.

Peggy Ann's Truck Stop in Rockwood, Tennessee, was a favorite place to get hamburgers and coffee when heading out on tour from Nashville, and for Bill to make calls. One night, a band member was surprised to overhear Bill in the midst of telephone negotiations, but not for a concert appearance.

"You be there tomorrow," Bill was saying.[40] "No, you take the day off. . . . I'll pay you a day's wages. . . . No, that's too much! . . . I can't pay you that much, you don't make that much money, now come on! . . . Well, I'll buy your gas, I'll pay for your gas and your food. . . . Now, you be there. . . ."

Then — clearly at the insistence of the person on the other end of the line — the dialogue turned to visualizations of certain highly personal activities. Monroe was of course not doing anything improper in public, just standing there quietly talking on the pay phone. But soon he was frantically waving dollar bills, trying to get change so the conversation could be completed.

The woman at the cash register already had a roll of dimes in hand. She'd seen and heard this all before.

These out-of-town liaisons provided thrills and eased the road's loneliness. But Bill needed real emotional connections. Despite being involved with both Bessie and Virginia, he began a third serious affair.

Hazel Boone Smith of North Carolina was a divorced mother of two boys and very much Bill's type: attractive, robust, intelligent, creative, and strong-willed.[41] Carlton Haney had introduced them at a festival. A romance blossomed, and Bill convinced Hazel to move to Nashville. There she worked for various music groups as an office manager and publicist, eventually becoming a reporter for country music publications. (She is credited with coining the phrase "Outlaw Music" to describe the sound of graying country music rebels Willie Nelson, Jessi Colter, Tompall Glaser, and Waylon Jennings.)

As promiscuous as Bill was, he had a truly nurturing side with women. Concerned about good manners, he taught an embarrassed and tearful Hazel how to handle a knife and fork properly in a restaurant. ("Now shut up that cryin'. Loretta [Lynn] didn't know how to eat when she came to town either!") He bought lotion for her work-chapped hands. When she became seriously ill with a fever, he drove over with a station wagon full of groceries, cooked for her, bathed her heated face, and forced her to eat something to keep up her strength. And he told her how beautiful she was, a heartfelt compliment that Hazel — who had always been unfavorably compared to her pretty mother — had seldom been given.

Their relationship was volatile, a potent source of inspiration for them both. During one argument, Hazel told Bill pointedly, "Oh, walk softly, 'cause you're walking on my heart!" The remark sank deep.[42] Bill created a melody and chorus; singer-guitarist Jake Landers wrote some verses and shared composer credit for "Walk Softly on My Heart." (Meanwhile, the affair provided material for Smith's own excellent songwriting, including "Love Ain't the Question, Love Ain't the Answer" and "Lord, It Sure Rains Hard in Tennessee," recorded by other country artists.)

Why did Bill need to have so many women? Hazel confronted him and found out.

It was this, and it was so simple. Everybody left him. His parents, Uncle Pen, his brothers and sisters going up to Hammond. Or when he thought something would work out, somebody else would leave him. If he went to go home, he was always afraid that he would come back and no one would be there. So he had to have more than one person so he wouldn't be left alone.[43]

Soon, more people were going to leave him. Gigs for 1969 were slow to come in, and by Thanksgiving 1968 then-singer/guitarist Roland White felt it was time to quit. He contemplated moving his family back to California, but then had an idea. Since Roland was also a skilled mandolinist, and knowing that Flatt and Scruggs harbored no ill will toward the Blue Grass Boys, he discreetly asked Lester Flatt if he and Earl would consider using the instrument again. (For several years, the Foggy Mountain Boys had contained an extra rhythm guitar instead of a mandolin.)

"Well, you know how it is between me and Bill," Lester replied.[44] "I don't like to hire a man right out from under him. He wouldn't like that."

Roland said he understood but intended to leave Monroe anyway.

Then Lester said, "Well, there's going to be some changes made after the first of the year. I'll keep it in mind."

Roland attached no special significance to Lester's comment. When he gave notice, Bill begged him to stay at least through the end of February because of an upcoming European tour. (This was one of the major frustrations of being a Blue Grass Boy: Bill often neglected to give out the touring schedule, and Roland had no idea the trip was in the offing.) When the Blue Grass Boys returned from overseas, Roland telephoned his wife.

"Lester Flatt called!" she said excitedly.

"What's going on?" Roland asked.

"Oh, you haven't heard! Lester Flatt and Earl Scruggs have broken up! He's looking for musicians."

Behind-the-scenes tensions had finished the fabled act. Producer Bob Johnston had gotten the duo to record material by Bob Dylan and other folk-rockers.[45] Earl seemed fine with it, but a weary exasperation had begun seeping into Lester's voice. He hated the stuff. It sold well, but Flatt was painfully aware of how it alienated their longtime grassroots fans. And two of Earl's talented sons had begun playing on their albums: With Louise still managing the band, it now seemed to Lester more of a Scruggs operation than a Flatt and Scruggs partnership.[46]

Lester and Earl made their final public appearance together on February 22, 1969, on the Grand Ole Opry.[47] Flatt explained to the Foggy Mountain Boys that he was officially leaving, but they would be welcome to come work for him. They did to a man. Martha White continued to sponsor Flatt and his new outfit, christened the Nashville Grass.

Earl and his sons formed the Earl Scruggs Revue. Although basically an acoustic group, its drums and electric bass riled bluegrass hardliners. Yet founding the Revue had been the ultimate act of traditionalism, rooted in Earl's happy childhood memories of family music making.

At the last moment, on March 6, 1969, Earl and Louise Scruggs had formed a business entity called "Blue Grass Music, Inc."[48] and tried to lay claim to the name "Foggy Mountain Boys." (Flatt, of course, responded with a lawsuit.) If Bill Monroe knew of the controversy, the irony was certainly not lost on him: after years of distancing themselves from the term, the Scruggs camp had formed a corporation using the name "Blue Grass."

Bill had been grooming his son for the lead singer's job. Now with Roland White's departure, it was time for James to step up to the microphone.[49] For years, the younger Monroe had stayed out of the spotlight. He hung sheetrock. He worked at a sausage company and then a machine company. His entry into the music business was helping at his father's office doing bookings. Then in 1964, James had replaced Bessie Lee Mauldin as bass player in the Blue Grass Boys. Needing a player during a tour through Georgia, Bill had thrust the unwieldy instrument upon his boy and said, "Just get up on stage and hold it and play rhythm." James did and saved the day.

Tall and well-built, James favored his mother with his dark hair and eyes. But he had much of his father's lonesome individualism and determination to prove himself. James had a sense of humor about his on-the-job training: "I learned in some of the finest places you could learn," he told the *Tennessean*.[50] "Carnegie Hall, the Newport Folk Festival, Albert Hall in London. . . ." But all the time, James felt the weight of the audiences' expectations.[51] He was, after all, Bill Monroe's son.

Elsewhere in the Monroe family, things were not well. Bill's brother Charlie had been enjoying supper one evening at the home of some Rosine friends, Loretta and Stanley Allen and their son Wendell, a sometime musician and avid local historian. Charlie was saying goodbye to Wendell at the gate when he became uncharacteristically somber.

"Wendell," Charlie said, "do you know where a man could get two hundred dollars?"[52]

Wendell didn't have that kind of money. He was heartbroken, realizing how badly off Charlie must be.

Charlie was badly off indeed. He had retired from music in the late 1950s and tried running a coal mining business, using the huge reserves still under the Monroe property on Jerusalem Ridge. Capital investment and plunging prices for high-sulfur coal had caused the enterprise to fail. In 1964, Charlie had been forced to sell the family land.

Charlie's wife, Betty, then developed cancer. She died on New Year's Day 1967. Charlie spent all his money for her medical care, even selling his expensive Martin D-45 guitar.

In 1968, Bill had gone to Owen Bradley and pitched a concept: a Bill and Charlie Monroe album.[53] In the early 1950s, Bill had gotten Charlie a contract with Decca, for whom his older brother recorded eight sides, including the popular "I'm Old Kentucky Bound," "Find 'Em, Fool 'Em, Leave 'Em Alone," and "That's What I Like About You." Bill's concept was not a Monroe Brothers duet album but a mix of already available separate tracks by the Blue Grass Boys and the Kentucky Pardners.

"I want to help Charlie," Bill said, and Owen agreed as a favor. The album, *Bill Monroe and Charlie Monroe*, was released in February 1969. The cover featured a new photo of the brothers together, instruments in hand, big smiles on their faces.

This joyous rapport was short-lived. Not long thereafter, Charlie married Myrtha Gammon, a spunky lady from the Nashville area who was devoted to him. Mert, as she was called, had once worked at the Ryman ticket window. She and Bill had dated.[54]

"Brothers is not supposed to mess with the other brother's leavings!" Bill fumed to Hazel Smith. He genuinely felt that Charlie's marriage had been a violation of boundaries. Before this, Bill would call Charlie and visit him, bringing huge bags of dogfood for his foxhounds. After the marriage to Mert, no more calls, no more visits, no more Bill.[55]

The only people able to get the Monroe boys together were the folkies who had befriended them earlier in the decade — Ralph Rinzler, Mike Seeger, and Alice Gerrard. Rinzler was now at the Smithsonian, and the annual Smithsonian Festival of American Folklife held each Fourth of July weekend on the Capitol Mall was his brainchild. Kentucky was the featured state in 1969, so Ralph wanted a reunion of the original Monroe Brothers, Birch, Charlie, and Bill. It was a success and to outward appearances all was fine.[56] Alice, Mike, and Ralph sat happily on the stage as the brothers played the old songs, including "My Lord's Gonna Lead Me Out," learned at a Rosine singing school.

If Bill appeared at all distant that day it was not because of unease with Charlie's marriage or lingering bitterness about childhood injustices. Too much water had gone under the professional bridge. Bill was his own artist, and he was uncomfortable playing with his brothers in public. As he later told Rinzler:

> Birch and Charlie's ideas about music is different from mine. I have never bothered them about how they believe in music. The music they would like, I can't stand it. I don't like it at all. I don't like fiddle music the way they would play it or guitar the way they would play it. They play with just a running time. There's no beat to it. I play my music with a beat you can hear.[57]

That music and the man who made it were honored in October 1969 during Bill's thirtieth anniversary with the Opry. WSM presented him with a plaque that noted that he had "set the standard for all Bluegrass Music."[58] A year later, in October 1970, Bill achieved the industry's highest honor when he was inducted into the Country Music Hall of Fame.

Decca wisely used the occasion to release an album called *Bill Monroe's Country Music Hall of Fame.* He also received a special *Billboard* magazine pioneer award at this time.[59]

Despite such accolades and his loyal attempt to help Charlie, Bill had major financial problems. Federal tax lien records show that from 1965 through 1970, Monroe failed to file personal or 941 (employee withholding) taxes.[60] (These taxes were paid in full in 1970 and 1971, and the liens removed.)

The booming festival movement was about to change all this for the better. Events began sprouting up like their bluegrass namesake, and musicians actually started making money. Big-name artists began promoting their own shows.

Carolyn Brown Monroe had reentered Bill's life as a booking agent. The neglected wife who had once stabbed Bill during an argument and abetted Melissa's beating of Bessie Lee was now proactive in getting work for her former husband. She would call the network of country and bluegrass promoters, asking, "Do you have anything for Bill?" If anyone came through with a booking, she never failed to say a thank you.[61]

Monroe's relation with Carlton Haney ended at about this time during a dispute about the appearance fees Carlton was offering Bill.[62] But ever afterward, when Haney read about a particular year — someone's birthday, a record release, a historic event, anything — he automatically compared it to 1965, the year of his first festival. For Haney, 1965 became the benchmark of his entire existence.[63]

In September 1970, another benchmark, another ending: Bill moved out of the farm on Allen Road and left Bessie alone.[64] The Carolina Songbird was now caged with the responsibility of the property's upkeep. She was not in good health; her diabetes and heart problems were becoming more serious by the year. Bill moved in with Virginia Stauffer in a trailer park she was managing on a strip highway on Nashville's south side.[65]

Bill and Virginia lived comfortably in a cottage apartment on the grounds. It was home to him. She threw birthday parties for him, including a big bash on his sixtieth.[66] He adopted a stray dog. He loved a comfortable old recliner in the living room and often fell asleep in it.

One winter's night, Bill awoke to find the thermometer outside dip-
ping down below zero, the cold invading the little cottage.[67] He got out a
mandolin and found it was slightly out of tune from the change in tem-
perature. On a whim, sitting there in the recliner, he decided to create a
new mandolin tuning. He had used retunings before (most notably on the
instrumental "Get Up John") but this time he decided to also compose
something based on the tuning. He came up with an almost incomprehen-
sible C-sharp minor tuning and then started playing with it. Moment by
moment in the chilly space, a melody emerged. It warmed into an entire
composition, almost a mini-concerto. Bill was thrilled. It was quite unlike
anything he'd written before. It was very good, and he knew it.

Bill held this one back an especially long time before recording it —
nearly a decade. But that is a short time, after all, for a masterpiece.

Bill was beginning to compose more and more tunes, but with Kenny
Baker back in the band the Uncle Pen album was a personal priority. Bill
had retained in memory about thirty of Pen's favorites, and he instructed
Baker closely in them, trying to keep all of Pen's notes "the way he played
them."[68] Eleven made it to the album. "Jenny Lynn," Bill's favorite, of
course opened the proceedings.[69] With a perfect blend of tone, noting,
and expression, Kenny Baker raised Pen Vandiver's repertoire of dance
tunes to high art.[70]

The LP, *Bill Monroe's Uncle Pen*, wasn't Bill's only tribute to his mentor. On Sunday, September 16, 1973, in the Rosine cemetery, a large
crowd of relatives and guests looked on as Bill unveiled a headstone to
Pendleton Vandiver and a smaller stone for his son, Cecil.[71] Bill finally
had the ceremony he had been denied more than forty years earlier for
want of a phone call from home.

But Charlie (who was notable by his absence during the dedication)
and many longtime Rosine residents believed that the headstones Bill
had afforded were in the wrong place: Pen and Cecil, they recalled, had
been buried about 100 feet to the north of the new monument.[72] Still,
there was happiness that a beloved local figure had been honored at last.

Bill took a large supply of the Uncle Pen albums to his June 1972 bluegrass festival in Bean Blossom. They quickly sold out. The festivals were
having that kind of benefit. They created a specific market in which

bands could earn badly needed money through direct-to-audience record and souvenir sales. Instrument vendors, bluegrass magazines, and independent record companies began renting table space at the shows. And musicians now had steady work from spring through autumn. In addition to Haney and Monroe, other promoters and stars began producing their own events, creating a true circuit. The shows also reinforced the music's sense of community. In parking lot and campground jam sessions, pickers learned new songs and techniques. Just about everyone made new friends. These colorful events also attracted the news media and curious first-timers, raising the music's profile. By 1973, there were nearly seventy such events, the next year more than one hundred.[73] (Today, there are some five hundred bluegrass festivals worldwide.)[74]

The Brown County Jamboree had long been a nexus for the growing bluegrass network. Fans traveled hundreds of miles to hear Bill play some of his best concerts in the informal setting of the low-roofed barn, which was decorated with farm tools, filled with a hodgepodge of old theater seats and folding chairs, and heated in cold weather by wood stoves. Aficionados taped the performances; copies were swapped throughout the bluegrass underground. In 1964, a banjo-picking member of the California-based Black Mountain Boys named Jerry Garcia journeyed here with a friend, planning to audition for Monroe. Intimidated by the mere sight of the formidable Kentuckian, Garcia went back home without even speaking to Bill.[75] He subsequently joined a folk-rock band that became the Grateful Dead. Garcia's tolerance of Dead fans taping his live shows was a direct outgrowth of his experiences at the Brown County Jamboree and other bluegrass venues.[76]

Bill had been finally persuaded in 1967 to stage his first all-bluegrass outdoor event at Bean Blossom.[77] At its peak, Monroe's festival was a ten-day affair, the biggest and most successful of its kind. A sea of cars, campers, vans, and buses flooded the parking lot. Tents mushroomed in the fields and woods. The scent of suntan oil rose during the hot days, wood fire smells in the chilly nights. There was music everywhere, on the main stage and in jam sessions. Everyone mingled: Yankees and Rebs, the hippie-haired and the crew-cutted, folkie fans and life-long Opry listeners, white collar and blue collar and people wearing no shirts. Americans met fans from overseas. (Monroe booked the Bluegrass 45, a crackerjack

Japanese ensemble, for his 1971 event; they were the hit of the show.) No one was a stranger.

The main attraction was Bill Monroe himself, treated by visitors with a mixture of familiarity and awe. Bill was in his glory at Bean Blossom, pressing the Blue Grass Boys into service each year to fix up the facilities, then donning bib overalls and work gloves to outlabor them all; greeting old friends and new fans; autographing albums; posing for pictures; jamming in the old barn (and sometimes playing booming backup guitar to groups of fiddlers); never hurrying yet seeming to be everywhere at once.

At the main stage area, shaded by trees in a far corner of the grounds, Monroe delighted in having a dozen of the music's greatest fiddlers join him, romping through traditional favorites like "Gray Eagle." At the end, Bill would invite the audience to sing along on "Swing Low, Sweet Chariot." He would extend his hands, then pull them back, as if embracing everyone in sight. And he would say, "I call you all my children."[78]

With the Flatt and Scruggs partnership dissolved, Bill quickly reached out to Earl. The Earl Scruggs Revue appeared at the 1970 Bean Blossom festival, although Earl and Bill did not perform together. (However, they appeared together that year in the public television documentary *Earl Scruggs — Family and Friends*, playing a medley of Monroe's songs.) Fans wondered: Could there ever be peace between Bill and Lester?

In January 1971, Lance LeRoy, Lester's agent, was standing by the Opry water cooler when James Monroe walked up. James had maintained cordial relations with Lester and Earl, often speaking to them backstage despite his father's directives, a thoughtful and even courageous gesture that they deeply appreciated. Now James spoke apologetically to Lance about the continuing strained relations with Flatt ("You know how Daddy is . . ."), then said, "Daddy is interested in having Lester on his festival at Bean Blossom this year."[79]

Lance was caught by surprise but believed there wouldn't be any problem. "Well, I'd like to play Bean Blossom if we get our price," Flatt told him. "Just as long as people don't expect us to sing together. I'll just work with my own band."

What happened at the festival should not have come as a surprise to anyone, including Lester. Flatt's group, the Nashville Grass, was in the warmup room. Lester was facing a wall, tuning his guitar. Someone came in and greeted Roland White and the other band members. Then Lester felt a gentle tap on his shoulder.

He turned around. It was Bill Monroe, his hand extended.

"Welcome to Bean Blossom," Bill said.

Lester shook his hand and thanked him. The small talk that followed loomed large. It was their first conversation since Bill had snubbed Lester backstage at the Ryman in the early 1950s. Lester had simply wanted Bill to speak first. Now he had.

Then Monroe asked, "Lester, will you come out and sing one with me?"

"Sure, Bill," Lester replied.

Bill Monroe & His Blue Grass Boys played the festival's final set on Sunday to almost unbearable anticipation. Finally Monroe said, "Now I'd like to bring out a friend of mine that worked with me in the forties."

The crowd had exploded to its feet by the time Lester Flatt appeared in the stage doorway. Bill and Lester publicly shook hands as a roar filled the Indiana woods. Bill had a smile on his face and a twinkle in his eyes, as if to say: I'll bet you all never thought I'd do it.[80]

They sang the old favorites, the crowd cheering each one. That evening, as the Nashville Grass drove out of the festival grounds, Flatt seemed pleased but sad. He turned to Roland White.

"You know," Lester said, "it could have been like that years ago."[81]

Bill Monroe was a bitter feuder, but once he buried the hatchet it stayed buried. He and Flatt toured together with their bands and appeared at each other's festivals. "Bill was wonderful to work with," says Lance LeRoy. "He was always cooperative."

Lester Flatt was a professional to the end. Plagued by health problems in his final years, he continued to perform, taking to a stool onstage but still "laid back and pickin'" as he liked to say. When he had surgeries, Monroe and Scruggs visited him in the hospital. All three were friends again by the time Lester died of a cerebral hemorrhage on May 11, 1979.[82]

As the seventies progressed, James Monroe sought to establish his identity. In 1971, he started his own band, the Midnight Ramblers.[83] He proved to have an ear for strong material, drawing on the darkly brilliant writing of Nashville-based songwriter Damon Black for "Tall Pines," "Sweet Mary and the Miles in Between," and "I Haven't Seen Mary in Years."

James received positive reviews, but the bluegrass world at large never seemed to warm to him. A 1970 *Bluegrass Unlimited* piece about a church benefit played by the Blue Grass Boys reported that "James Monroe looked a little uncomfortable, but was in good voice."[84]

In a 1972 *Atlantic* magazine article about Bean Blossom, Robert Cantwell deemed the Midnight Ramblers a "most interesting and appropriately named group," adding that "James Monroe has a corpselike pallor and shadowy eyes; his music has the eerie loveliness of an Easter basket or a funeral wreath . . . and in many respects he himself seems a dream, a ghost. Incidentally, he is Bill Monroe's son."[85]

Some fans demonstrated their loyalty to his father in the most insensitive way.[86] James would often be greeted by an audience member who complimented him on his performance but quickly added that as good as James was, he would never be as great as his dad.

"It's hard for any boy to come up under his father," Bill told the *Tennessean* in 1972. "But I've tried every way to help him, and I'd a lot rather help him than myself."[87]

That statement would prove even truer as time went on.

The bluegrass festival movement began attracting notice in Nashville. On Wednesday, October 13, 1971, at the beginning of the annual country music disk jockeys' convention, the first "Early Bird Bluegrass Concert" was held at the Ryman. Monroe headed up a Who's Who of the music: Lester Flatt, Mac Wiseman, Ralph Stanley, Don Reno, Red Smiley, Bill Harrell, Jimmy Martin, Jim and Jesse McReynolds, the Country Gentlemen, Carl Story, the Goins Brothers, and James Monroe. The show was an acknowledgment that bluegrass had come to national prominence.

(In private, Monroe's attitude toward the country music industry was humorously jaded. At one disk jockey convention, he anonymously wrote on a sheet of paper "You're all crazy as hell" and slipped it under the door of the Decca suite.)[88]

Bill's leadership role as the nurturing father of bluegrass was evident in his support of female musicians. He had encouraged country-cowboy singer Rose Maddox to record bluegrass and even appeared (anonymous by name but not by his unmistakable playing) on her 1962 *Rose Maddox Sings Bluegrass*. In the late 1970s the Wildwood Girls would be regularly featured at the Bean Blossom festivals, with Monroe taking a generous paternal interest in their education as music professionals.[89] Now he was encouraging Hazel Dickens and Alice Gerrard, who were performing together. His strong opinions about their male backup musicians surprised Hazel.

> We didn't have enough self-esteem to ask them to play it where we wanted to sing it. We'd say, "Oh sure, if you can't play in B-flat we'll go to A or G or whatever you need."
> Bill said, "No, you shouldn't do that. You make them play in whatever key you sing best. If they can't play in that key, get rid of them, get some other musicians." He was the first guy who ever said that to us.[90]

Bill advised Hazel and Alice on vocal arrangements and gave them a song of his to record, "The One I Loved Is Gone." To increase their self-confidence, and because he simply enjoyed singing with them, he made a point of getting Hazel and Alice up to perform with him at the all-day, all-night picking parties and feasts being held each year around Bill's birthday by fiddler Tex Logan (then a researcher at Bell Labs in New Jersey) and his wife, Peggy.

Despite his many love affairs, Monroe did not look on women as mere sex objects. If they worked hard at music, he respected this. And he had empathy for anyone who had struggled — as he had — against disparaging attitudes.

The now-legendary bashes at the Logan home were good for Bill, too. They expanded his world (here he met everyone from garage mechanics to corporate executives) and gave him a sense that he was widely loved.[91]

In truth, all the Monroes were loved. In the spring of 1972, Jimmy Martin had befriended Charlie and Mert, then living in Springfield, Tennessee.[92] To say the Monroes were in a state of genteel poverty would be generous. Their house was only slightly better than a shack. Charlie was stone broke. He had worked in an Otis elevator factory and as a cook in a Howard Johnson's restaurant. Now he was reduced to picking up bottles by the roadside for the deposit money.

During one visit Jimmy brought a mandolin and, after some coaxing, got Charlie to fetch his guitar and sing two old favorites, "Down in the Willow Garden" and "Who's Calling You Sweetheart Tonight?" He still had the voice and the great performing presence.

Martin said that Carlton Haney would certainly book Charlie on his bluegrass festivals. "Take a bunch of your records and a bunch of pictures to sell," Jimmy said. "I'll have my group play behind you. You can get on some show dates with me and even ride on my bus."

Charlie was incredulous. Only vaguely aware of the festival movement, he was sure he was a has-been. He finally agreed, but insisted that if he didn't go over with the crowds he wouldn't expect to be paid.

Of course, he received a hero's welcome at Haney's shows. Jimmy Martin took great satisfaction in watching Charlie sell out of albums and photographs. But to Charles Pendleton Monroe, more precious than the money filling his once-empty pockets was the outpouring of love from his fans. As he told interviewer Douglas Green:

> They come up and shake your hand, and they put their arm around you, and they tell you how they've missed you, and you can tell by the look on their face that they're telling straight facts. I'm glad. I'm really glad.[93]

With bluegrass record sales leaping by the thousands thanks to such artist-to-fan transactions at the festivals, Bill's label now began to take him more seriously. MCA, which had acquired and succeeded Decca, did an all-star two-record set recorded live at Bill's 1973 festival. *Bean Blossom* was the most successful album of Bill's career: Released in January 1974, it spent fourteen weeks on the country charts, breaking into the top 20 and reaching number 17.

However, its jacket was proof that Decca/MCA still wasn't quite sure how to promote Monroe. The art department, upon being told this was a music festival album, created a quasi-Woodstock cover edged with flowers and forest creatures: butterflies, birds, even a little frog.

Upon receiving his first copy, Monroe put on his eyeglasses and carefully appraised it. Then he looked up and tendered his pronouncement.

"I don't believe I care for the frog," he said.[94]

*   *   *

Bill could not — or would not — take part in one of the biggest nights in Grand Ole Opry history.

On Saturday, March 16, 1974, the Opry moved to Opryland U.S.A., a $46 million, 358-acre theme park about nine miles northeast of the downtown.[95] The new Opry house had state-of-the-art production facilities, a 110-by-68-foot stage, a dozen dressing rooms, kitchenette and lounge, 4,400 seats, unlimited parking, and, best of all, air conditioning. (A public outcry saved the Ryman from the wrecking crew. It was restored for use as a concert hall.)

Richard Nixon appeared that night at the first show held in the new facility. Roy Acuff, the chief executive of Opry personalities, showed the nation's chief executive some of his famous yo-yo tricks — surely a welcome break for the beleaguered president at the height of the Watergate scandal.

Although now one of the Opry's senior members, Monroe did not attend, instead playing an out-of-town gig. As he explained to his friend Willie Nelson, "You know, Willie, I'm a Democrat. And besides that, I don't have no yo-yo."[96]

That year also saw a milestone in the scholarly acceptance of Bill Monroe as a major American artist. The Country Music Foundation Press published *Bill Monroe and His Blue Grass Boys: An Illustrated Discography* by Neil Rosenberg. The former banjo-picking manager of the Brown County Jamboree was now an assistant professor in the department of folklore at the Memorial University of Newfoundland. His detailed information about Bill's recording sessions and releases was a true validation of Monroe's work.

Yet Bill was miffed about the book. He began asking mutual friends how much money Neil had made on it.[97] In fact, Neil had earned nothing on this scholarly work.

Ordinarily blasé about money, Monroe took a crass mercenary attitude toward this labor of love because he simply hated the thought of anyone making money on his name, even if it benefited him in the long run. When *Country Music* planned a major cover story on Bill for its May 1976 issue, Carolyn Monroe complained to Hazel Smith, who was now writing for the publication.

"They're just trying to sell magazines and use his name!" Carolyn said.[98]

Hazel had to explain that the article would be the equivalent of tens of thousands of dollars in promotion. Bill cooperated.

This focus on money was paradoxical, because to bluegrass purists Monroe was an artistically untainted David resisting the commercial Goliath of Nashville. If Ralph Rinzler had been a prophet crying in the wilderness, his sermons about Bill's folk roots had been seized upon in unintended ways by a growing hardcore of bluegrass "traditionalists," classicists who embraced an increasingly fundamentalist orthodoxy. To them, Monroe was greater even than a biblical hero: He was a veritable Jehovah.

One *Bluegrass Unlimited* reader made a significant choice of words when, in a letter in the July 1970 issue, he protested nontraditional instruments: "The great Bill Monroe is our father of bluegrass and when we use or mix electric or drums with bluegrass, we are sinning against him and all he stands for."[99] The deification of Bill Monroe was well under way.

Yet Monroe laudably clung to the old ways on esthetic grounds. Studio engineers, in their continuing quest for cleaner recordings, were taking advantage of the new multitrack technology by miking musicians individually, separating them with sound-absorbent barriers, then giving them headphones to help hear their fellows. Monroe insisted that his band not be given headphones or separated.[100] His approach yielded a more unified, live-in-the-studio sound.

Bill was still juggling his relationships, but more and more he seemed to yearn for deeper spiritual connections. One rainy day, he was with Hazel Smith. She complained about the weather. Bill took her outside and made her tilt her head up and look.

"God made this rain," he said.[101] "Do you see any two drops alike? You'll never see anything on this earth more beautiful than this."

Driving on I-65 near Nashville, Bill proposed to her.[102] Hazel started laughing. She knew he couldn't be a husband. It wasn't just that he was promiscuous: She knew that now, with his resurgent fame, he was married to the world. She laughed all the way home while Bill fumed.

Meanwhile, Bessie Lee Mauldin, who had been left nearly destitute, decided that she deserved as much as any spouse. On April 15, 1975, she filed in Chancery Court for Davidson County for divorce from Bill Monroe, presenting herself as Bill's common-law wife.[103]

Bessie asserted that at the time of Bill's divorce from Carolyn in August 1960, she had not been told that Bill was enjoined from marrying her. Bill's avoidance of the topic had finally come back to haunt him. So did their behaving like man and wife: According to Bessie's petition, she and Bill had traveled together in "Alabama, Georgia and South Carolina, which states recognize common law marriage, and in each of those states, Defendant and Complainant registered as man and wife. Moreover, Defendant introduced the complainant as his wife, provided for her as he would a wife, and, in fact, advised her that they were man and wife, having consummated their marriage in the states hereinabove mentioned."[104]

Bessie alleged that she "purchased automobiles for the Defendant, made loans to the Defendant, and completed other transactions with the Defendant, all with promises of payment which never came." These allegations were consistent with her claims to Ralph Rinzler that her money had been tied up with Bill's. If true, they certainly explain how Bill survived the hungry 1950s.

Bessie received a settlement from Bill of $75,000.[105] In return, she waived all further claim on Bill's property or the name Monroe.

While Bessie was bringing some closure to her life, Charlie was facing his final crisis. He had suffered a heart attack soon after his rediscovery by the bluegrass festival circuit but had recovered and returned to performing. Bill had never visited him in the hospital and only called when Charlie was asleep, which Charlie and Myrtha interpreted as a hurtful snub.[106] What they didn't realize was that Bill just couldn't bring himself to speak with Mert again, so he phoned at a time when, he hoped, she had left Charlie's room for the night.[107]

Charlie played and recorded, earning a modest living and enjoying the adulation of his faithful fans. But he developed cancer. At the end he was a gaunt man, although he retained his great grin and love of performing. He played a final show in his hometown of Rosine, then just a week later, on September 27, 1975, died at the Camp Springs music park in Reidsville, North Carolina, where he had been living in a little home provided him by Carlton Haney.[108]

His funeral was held in the Methodist church in Rosine. Bill attended, propped up by Hazel Smith. He wept, torn between genuine grief at the loss of his brother and lingering hurt at Charlie's relationship with Mert.[109]

A massive thunder and lightning storm swept through the July 1976 Berkshire Mountain Bluegrass Festival in Hillsdale, New York. It was nothing compared to the tempest that entered Julia LaBella's heart that weekend.

Julia was a young woman from Texas who was living in Massachusetts and starting to get into bluegrass.[110] A friend said she'd have a good time at the festival. There she met Bill Monroe. The following December, she set out in a snowstorm and drove all the way from New England to Nashville just to be with him. She was twenty-one, he was sixty-five.

The age difference made their relationship especially difficult for some members of Bill's family to accept. But this new romance was a new beginning for Bill.

One of the first things the lovers did that spring was to go out to Bill's farm and start renovating its dilapidated two-story cabin.[111]

Bill's farm was a few minutes from Interstate 65 and only about thirty minutes to the new Opry house. But to enter the gate at the end of Allen Drive was to travel back nearly seventy years in time.

Its 288 acres contained huckleberry and gum trees, blackberry bushes, and gardens and pastures.[112] There were numerous outbuildings — two stock barns, sheds, workshops, a large dog pen, chicken roosts — but the main cabin was the center of Bill's universe. It was now totally rebuilt into an enlarged two-story, tin-roofed structure on its original nineteenth-century stone foundation. Its rustic yet comfortable interior featured exposed log walls, tongue-and-groove ceilings, and a cut stone fireplace. Outside, a wraparound porch with chairs and a high-backed church pew was just the place for visiting and music making.

Bill kept horses, dogs, chickens, cats, and cattle. At the top of the property were hollows turning off to the right and left from the main pasture.

Bill could throw his powerful voice up the center and have it reverberate into each hollow. The cattle would come to his call, just like pets.[113]

He loved his bull Bobo. He could even ride on this gentle beast.[114] But Bobo was kept on the farm too long, and Bill's cattle started becoming inbred. Hazel Smith's sons Billy and Terry, as well as others who worked at the farm, finally convinced Bill to acquire a new breeder. The bull that arrived was no Bobo.[115]

Bill went into the new bull's enclosure carrying a bale of hay. He turned his back on the animal. Suddenly, it lashed out with its hind feet and knocked him facedown. Bill slowly got up, plastered with mud and dung, only a small clean spot allowing him to see through his thick eyeglasses. Billy Smith fought to stifle his laughter. An older farmhand didn't even try, openly guffawing at his muck-covered boss.

Showing absolutely no emotion, Bill waited until the general mirth subsided. Then he turned and kicked the bull in its hindquarters, so hard that the massive beast's back feet seemed to come off the ground.

The farmhands gasped, expecting the bull to gore Bill. Instead, the animal looked around with what can only be described as genuine amazement. Monroe carefully cleaned off his glasses and then strode out of the pen.

After three or four days of touring, Bill loved to get back to farmwork for its mental relaxation ("It gets me away from a lot of noise and nerve-wrackin' people")[116] and physical invigoration. He had a formula for a perfect Saturday:[117] He liked to arise early and eat a hearty breakfast. He would then go out and work on the farm. He would come in for lunch and then take an hour's nap. He would then get up and work until dusk, come in for a bath, relaxation, and dinner. Then he'd go play the Opry and afterward get in a car and drive all night to his next series of bookings.

Although Bill may not have realized it, this was also the perfect formula for building great strength, almost like the training schedule of an Olympic athlete — an initial fueling; a morning training session; recovery in the form of food and sleep; then afternoon exercise and more food and rest; finally, diverting leisure activities to end the day. No wonder that, until very late in life, Bill retained his legendary strength and was, as he put it, a "stout fellow."

Bill was an old-fashioned man of the earth who plowed with mule teams, using tractors only if there was an especially large job to do. He trimmed the manes and tails of his horses in exactly the same way it was done on his father's farm.[118] He loved to stretch and repair fence lines. He hauled timber out of his hills to use for fence posts and other repairs and liked everything made out of sawmill lumber, just as it had been on his father's farm.

Bill cherished the property. It was his strength and refuge and more: It was the reinvention of his Jerusalem Ridge childhood with only the happy times remaining.[119]

In addition to new girlfriend Julia, Bill had also acquired a new singer-guitarist: Wayne Lewis, a native of the coal country of eastern Kentucky who had grown up listening to Monroe on the *Opry* on a battery radio. Wayne was hired Christmas 1975 at a show in Ohio.[120] He would have an eleven-year tenure, the longest of any Monroe lead vocalist.

Bill Monroe was fit, happy, and revitalized. He had a new love and, with Baker and Lewis, the core of a polished, reliable band. He was venerated throughout the folk and country music worlds, the grand old lion of bluegrass proudly leading the pride. But now some young tigers were nipping at his heels.

They called their music "newgrass." Considering the energy and sheer attitude of bluegrass, and its eclectic roots, it was only a matter of time before hot young pickers would be pushing the envelope, melding bluegrass with pop, jazz, and swing, and basically rocking out with acoustic instruments.

Prominent among these adventurous youngsters — indeed, helping to name the style — was the New Grass Revival. Sam Bush of Bowling Green, Kentucky, the band's mandolin and fiddle player, had developed a brilliant if flashy technique, highlighted by blazing ascending and descending scales. Bush hadn't started out to be a rebel. In fact, he says, "the most majestic thing I ever saw" was Bill Monroe onstage at the Ryman performing "You'll Find Her Name Written There."[121]

Bush began making the 200-mile trek to the Sunday shows at the Brown County Jamboree. One afternoon in 1967, he was jamming backstage with Blue Grass Boys Byron Berline and Roland White when Monroe wandered by.

"Son, I want you to stay with that fiddle," Monroe said.[122] "We don't have enough good young fiddlers coming up." Bush realized that if Monroe wanted him to stay out of the mandolin ranks, he must be doing something right.

Upon hearing one young mandolinist pick a wild break, Monroe commented caustically, "Boy, that ain't no part of nothin'."[123] Monroe and the bluegrass classicists started attacking newgrass on the same grounds that staid music critics deplored jazz — that it was allegedly an ego-driven excuse for improvisations in which musicians abandoned the melody at the earliest possible moment and made no further reference to it for the rest of the song.

Monroe also didn't like the newgrassers' long hair or the rumors that most were pot smokers. Not that he was hostile to the counterculture, per se: "The mountain people have been with me 30 years," he told *Newsweek* in 1970. "But my hippie fans know when the music is played right. And the college kids are my biggest audience."[124]

The intensely competitive Monroe was probably having ego problems with the newgrassers. The plain fact was that these twenty-somethings were more technically proficient than the sixty-something Bill, and their athletic playing was winning applause.

Meanwhile, David Grisman, a Ralph Rinzler protégé and Monroe devotee from New Jersey, was living in California and developing his own newgrassy sound, a blend of bluegrass, swing, and Jewish klezmer that he called "dawg music" (after the canine nickname bestowed on him by friend Jerry Garcia).

In 1974, the Great American Music Band featuring Grisman and fiddler Richard Greene opened for Monroe at the Palomino Club in Los Angeles. In attendance was one of Grisman's mandolin students — Bob Dylan.[125] Tagging along was Robbie Robertson, lead guitarist for The Band.

Dylan and Robertson were eager to meet Bill. (Dylan's interest in Monroe went beyond mere curiosity. "I'd still rather listen to Bill and Charlie Monroe than any current record," he later commented.[126] "That's what America's all about to me.") Grisman had promised to introduce them. But then, disaster: Richard Greene was firmly snubbed when he tried to greet his old boss. Grisman assumed that he too would be on the Monroevian blacklist for some unknown transgression. Unaware of all this, Dylan and Robertson kept nudging Grisman down the hall to Monroe's dressing room. Grisman walked his last mile to what promised to be the most humiliating experience of his life.

The trio walked up behind Monroe. Bill turned and looked at them. Then he cracked a big smile and extended his hand to David.

Infinitely relieved, Grisman made introductions. Monroe provided Dylan with a guitar, and in the dressing room they sang "I Saw the Light."

The New Grass Revival did not fare as well with Bill. In 1976, at a festival in Virginia, members Sam Bush and Courtney Johnson were chatting with Kenny Baker when Monroe walked up. As it turned out, the Blue Grass Boys didn't have a banjo player that day.

"Come on, Bill, we need a banjo player," said Baker.[127] "Let's get Courtney."

Monroe looked at the longhaired Johnson.

"No sir," Monroe said.

"Come on now, Bill," Kenny persisted. "We need a banjo picker. Let's get Courtney."

"No sir, I'll not have it."

Baker kept pushing the issue and pushing Bill's buttons, deadpan but getting a kick out of putting his employer on the spot.

Suddenly, Monroe turned to Johnson. "What is it you all call that music you do?" he asked.

Caught by surprise, Courtney managed to answer, "Eh . . . you mean newgrass?"

"Yes," said Monroe. "I hate that."

End of discussion. For one of the few times since 1941, the Blue Grass Boys went onstage as a banjoless foursome.

Sam and Courtney thought the incident was funny, even endearing. So they were saddened when others retold the story and simply reduced it to Monroe's final pronouncement on newgrass: "I hate that." Taken out of context, it made him seem nasty when he had been primarily trying to fend off the persistent Kenny Baker.

Today, Bush downplays any competitiveness on Monroe's part.

I can't really say there was any jealousy or anything like that. I just think around 1970 we looked like hippies and we definitely played differently. We weren't trying to change bluegrass. We were just playing the way we played. I know there was a concern among traditionalists that the music would change and there wouldn't be any Bill Monroe or Flatt and Scruggs–style bluegrass any more. But their music has stood the test of time; there's been a big resurgence in 1940s-style bluegrass.[128]

But the music could not go anywhere without proper promotion. Carolyn Monroe had done her best, and now she was ready to retire. In 1977, Buddy Lee Attractions, a major Nashville booking agency, received an unexpected overture from Bill.[129] Lee signed him on as a client and handed him over to Tony Conway.

Conway was young and a relative newcomer to the staff. But he was from Kentucky and he was familiar with bluegrass. He looked on this living legend of American music as his own special project. Shocked that Monroe had been getting only about $2,500 per date, Conway slowly raised Bill's fees. He booked Monroe aggressively on the college circuit and got him onto network television, being especially successful in pitching Bill to award shows and specials.

It proved easy for a savvy, well-established agency like Buddy Lee Attractions to promote Monroe. The festival movement had firmly established him as "the Father of Bluegrass." His records were now selling well. The 1977 album *Bill Monroe Sings Bluegrass Body and Soul* spent four weeks on the country charts, peaking at number 37.

Bill Monroe was back in the big time.

In July 1977, Butch Robins of Virginia returned for a second go at being Bill Monroe's banjo player.[130] He stayed through Labor Day 1981. In that time, their relationship was probably the most contentious Monroe ever had with a sideman, making his famous cold war with Earl Scruggs seem a mere snit by comparison.

Robins had played at the first multiday bluegrass festival at the Bean Blossom park, held June 24–25, 1967. Then only eighteen years old, Robins was hailed by *Bluegrass Unlimited* as "another Monroe miracle. He ranks among the best banjo players Bill has ever had. He's just good enough to make it hard to imagine any room for improvement."[131]

Yet Butch lasted only three weeks. Monroe expected him to live in Nashville on a hundred dollars a month. Then, Robins says, "I got my ass chewed out real good at rehearsal at the Opry house because I didn't know the baritone to 'Angel Band.'"[132] Not only is lower harmony to this number especially challenging, Monroe rarely performed the song. Angry and disillusioned, Robins had gone home.

Now he was back with a musical vengeance. On the opening nights of the Bean Blossom bluegrass festivals (events were being staged in both June and September), Monroe prided himself in engaging in extended onstage jams. He and Butch would trade off breaks, Robins echoing Monroe's themes, then going him one better.[133] Challenged, Monroe would respond with ever more inspired solos. It was like watching a rising boxer acting as sparring partner for a champion, the younger man almost proving too much for the champ to handle, then the older man coming back and getting his blows home.

Sometimes the old master didn't like this musical athlete's technique. A banjo solo for "John Henry" on a 1979 live Bean Blossom album kind of evaporated. The second half of a banjo break for "Come Hither to Go Yonder" on the 1981 *Master of Bluegrass* LP was plunged down in the mix, and the mandolin boosted with heavy reverb to cover the hole. The effect was ludicrous. Monroe hadn't liked Robins's solos on these numbers but wouldn't rerecord them.[134] Instead, he was perfectly willing to cut them out even if it meant spiting himself — just as he had defaced his mandolin by gouging out the "Gibson" inlay, just as he had neglected to record Peter Rowan's lead singing.

Robins resented the way Monroe could pick at people, hold grudges, and be more taskmaster than teacher.

> In his ignorance — and there's no sin in ignorance, it's just before you've been enlightened to the facts of what's going on — he developed some of the wonderfulest little games to play with people when it came to interpersonal relationships you've ever seen in your life.
>
> What did he ever teach anybody? He threw it out but he never had any intention of teaching anyone. How many of Monroe's alumni

succeeded in the music business because of the help that he gave them? . . . The first group that left him, he passed a petition around the Opry to keep them off of it.

He wasn't a teacher. He did what he did. If you caught a ride on that comet and picked up something while you were in there, fine. Otherwise, you're just a tool that he used. . . .

There's just another side to it. It's no more or less valuable, but for all the people who want to put him on a pedestal, there's another side.[135]

If it was a love-hate relationship, there was also profound love on Robins's part. He came to admire Monroe as a truly primal man, an instinctual being who felt and then acted, a child of nature who had developed his higher consciousness to amazing levels.

I wanted more than anything in the world to get him out on his porch [with recording equipment] and start him playing — play to the sound of the birds, play to the sound of the wind blowing. Because he could do that. He got to a place and proficiency where he could do that. . . .

This guy's a god to me. He is the ultimate channel for musical expression in the human species. He taps into something that's timeless.[136]

One night, about four in the morning, the two were awake on the bus. Robins was softly playing his banjo, Monroe was playing solitaire. Bill mentioned a song of his, and Butch asked how he had come to write it.

Monroe looked at Robins through his thick-lensed glasses.

"I never wrote a tune in my life," he said.[137]

"What do you mean by that?" asked Robins, surprised.

"Those tunes are all in the air," Monroe replied. "I just happened to be the first one to pick them out."

James Monroe continued in music. He and Bill had successfully collaborated on two well-received albums, *Father and Sons* (1973) and *Together Again* (1978). But he was looking for other ways to make his mark. In 1980, he opened James Monroe's Club at 1929 Division Street in

Nashville. The nightclub closed after only three weeks due to losses.[138] It would not be James's last foray into the hospitality business.

Of all the women in Bill Monroe's life, his friends said, she didn't seem his type. And they meant that as a compliment.

Della Scivers Streeter was pretty, intelligent, and strong, just like the other women who had meant the most to Bill. But she was also tall and slender, with the look of an executive secretary. That, in fact, was what she was.

The daughter of a man who had booked shows for Bill in Florida and Georgia in the 1950s, Della had known Bill since she was an eight-year-old.[139] By now married and divorced, Streeter had been working in Minneapolis as a secretary in the legal department of Control Data Corporation. In 1973, CDC assigned her the task of opening a Nashville office. She had been in touch with Bill sporadically over the years; now he had helped her find an apartment in a good neighborhood and a reliable car dealer. He had been gallant and protective. They frequently had dinner together, but the relationship had been strictly platonic.

By 1980, that was changing. They were falling in love. One night after dinner, Bill asked her to marry him.

> At that time, I'd been in Nashville long enough to know he had a bit of a reputation. So I said I couldn't do that. I told him I loved him, I knew I loved him, but I was afraid of the other women. Bill said, "Now, they don't mean a thing to me!" In his mind, they didn't. I think when he said they didn't mean a thing to him, he meant he didn't love them.[140]

Della knew about Julia LaBella. That relationship was having its highs and lows, but she wisely recognized it was far from over. So Bill's proposal was gently declined. For the time being.

Now that Bill's fortunes had so thoroughly revived, he experienced a creative renaissance. His current producer, Walter Haynes, was delighted that Monroe was again hitting the studio with a gung ho attitude and his material already arranged.[141] And he had lots of material, says Julia LaBella:

Music was in his head constantly. No matter if he was in the car, riding to go somewhere, or just sitting at home. Or on the bus — he wrote a *lot* of tunes on the road. He got a lot of ideas traveling. From the lay of the land, or he'd think back about old times. . . . And he could hear just how he wanted the fiddle to sound, to drag that bow out and make it go back to those days.[142]

During a tour of Britain with the Dillards, the travel bus was filled with musicians zonked by jet lag. All except one, as Rodney Dillard recalls:

I was trying to sleep but Monroe kept nudging me and saying, "Hey, Dillard, hey, Dillard, what do you think of this?" and he'd start singing me lines to a song he was writing. "Hey, Dillard, hey, Dillard, I got this song about someone down where you're from," and he'd sing me a line about some lady from Missouri. I realized, about the fourth time he did this, here's a man much older than me that had this youthful enthusiasm and sense of wonder and this whole energy about his music and what he did. He was like I was when I was twenty-four years old, excited about everything, excited about a line in a song.[143]

In 1980, Bill started a new project, an all-instrumental album. Because he could not write music and was uncomfortable using tape recorders, he had developed a unique notation system:[144] He would jot down impressions about a place or situation that could jog his memory and rekindle feelings, allowing him to re-create a musical impression.

By this point, every one of Bill's original compositions, even the instrumentals, had a story behind it. On tour in Virginia, the bus drove past a Catholic church called Our Lady of the Blue Ridge.[145] "'Lady of the Blue Ridge,'" Monroe mused, turning to his fiddler. "That's a good name for a fiddle tune, don't you think, Kenny?" And so it became.

One Christmas, Bill and Julia watched the classic 1951 movie version of Charles Dickens's *A Christmas Carol*.[146] Bill saw much of himself in Alastair Sim's marvelous portrayal of Scrooge: a balding man with trailing white hair, emotionally abandoned as a child, who has become lonesome and embittered, a miser of the spirit. Bill was moved to write "Old

Ebeneezer Scrooge," its three parts representing the spirits of Christmas past, present, and future.

Bill and Julia were having dinner with Ralph Rinzler and a friend around this time, and Rinzler — still hoping to write Monroe's biography — had a tape rolling for posterity. Bill talked about his childhood home, about the loss of his mother's lap, about farming, and, of course, about music. He was especially excited about a particular composition.

> Ralph, you heard that number I wrote that I never got a title for it? That I tuned different [for]? You ought to hear that, man. . . . That sound, it was bound to have been 100 years old or on back. It could tell two or three different stories. It could tell a story about a soldier going across, you know, and leaving his sweetheart. It could tell about a man way on up in years, his wife had died or he had had bad luck with his lady friends through the years. It could tell another kind of a story. But it's sad.[147]

It was the composition that he had devised that bitterly cold night at Virginia Stauffer's place. It would receive a title — "My Last Days on Earth" — because soon Bill Monroe felt certain that he was facing those days.

By 1980, Monroe was playing about two hundred dates a year and traveling tens of thousands of miles. It was a tough life for a man nearing his seventieth birthday. Bill remained stoic about his discomforts, as gritty as he'd been in childhood when he refused to complain about his dislocated hip or his appendicitis. Finally, in the last week of February 1980, after increasing pain and being unable to eat, he collapsed.[148]

The problem could no longer be ignored, and the diagnosis was grim. Bill Monroe had cancer of the colon.

He was admitted to Baptist Hospital for surgery. He thought he was going to die. Julia tried to comfort him. Bessie Lee called him at his room. Hazel Smith got a call from Bill in tears. Shortly after she arrived at the hospital, there was a gentle knock on the door and in walked Earl Scruggs.

Scruggs sat down. "I heard you been sick, Bill," he said.[149]

"Yes, cancer," Monroe said simply.

Earl opened his heart in that moment, thanking Bill for putting the banjo in bluegrass and probably saving him from life as a millworker. With Hazel's urging, both men confessed how much they had loved and respected each other, even during their bitter estrangement.

Hazel called John Hartford, the Missouri-born composer of "Gentle on My Mind," one of the most played and recorded songs in history, a true Monroe devotee and a lymphoma survivor. Hartford marched into Monroe's hospital room and bluntly told the patient that he could beat cancer, too.[150] It was the beginning of a true friendship between the men, of deep talks and not just superficial chats.

Bill had a large section of colon removed.[151] The surgery was successful. But he had mixes of his new album brought to the hospital. He seriously thought he might die in the middle of the project.[152]

And so "My Last Days on Earth" was finally named and recorded. Walter Haynes was intrigued by this ominous yet majestic creation.[153] There were no lyrics, so Walter asked Bill what he heard in it. A choir of angels, Bill said. A vocal chorale singing "ahh" tones paralleling the melody was scored and added. So was a violin and cello section. Finally, Bill, Walter, and Julia listened to effects records from the studio library and picked out bird and ocean sounds. The final harmonics Bill played on the mandolin very consciously represented a clock giving up its last chimes and then stopping, time running out.

It was the most unbluegrass recording of Bill Monroe's entire career. And it was one of his greatest.

After being discharged from the hospital, Bill stayed for about a week with James.[154] But his son was divorced and not equipped to care for his father. Longtime Monroe sideman Clarence "Tater" Tate was not playing in the Blue Grass Boys at the time, nevertheless he and his wife Lois moved Bill into their home, where he stayed for the next two months.

Characteristically, Bill went back on the road weeks before the doctors gave him permission. Determined to get his strength back, he was soon doing the physical labor that he relished. One day, Tater was amazed to see Bill carrying a tree trunk. It was narrow and trimmed of its branches but still more than fifty feet in length. Bill had hefted up one end and

Bessie Lee Mauldin, Bill, and Melissa Monroe, with Joe Stuart, Bill Keith, and Del McCoury at the Brown County Jamboree, 1963 *(Bill Bongiorno)*

Fiddler Richard Greene and guitarist-vocalist Peter Rowan, two of Bill's most talented and devoted sideman, in 1966 *(Edwin Huffman)*

Ralph Rinzler (with camera) documents activities at the landmark Fincastle, Virginia, bluegrass festival, September 1965 *(Tom Isenhour)*

Carlton Haney, mastermind of the bluegrass festival movement *(Edwin Huffman)*

James Monroe takes center stage under his daddy's appraising eye *(Ron Petronko)*

Bonded by music, their visual handicaps, and a common brilliance: Bill with Doc Watson at Bean Blossom, 1971 *(Ron Petronko)*

Kenny Baker fiddles for a festival crowd while Clyde Moody guests on guitar, circa 1971 *(Edwin Huffman)*

Hitting a trademark high note
(Ron Petronko)

Four decades after his death, Uncle Pen finally gets a headstone: Bill with James, Geanie (Mrs. Speed) Monroe, sister Bertha, and onlookers at the September 1973 dedication *(Carl Fleischhauer)*

After the restoration of his mandolin's headstock *(Dan Loftin*, The Tennessean*)*

The old lion and the young tigers: Monroe with David Grisman and Sam Bush. *(*Bluegrass Unlimited*)*

John Duffy opts to tenor Ralph Stanley without anyone's help *(Winnie Willard)*

The one-time exhibition square dance swings at the 1982 Kentucky Fried Chicken Bluegrass Festival *(Bluegrass Unlimited)*

President Ronald Reagan greets Monroe and (partially hidden) his agent Tony Conway.
(Bluegrass Unlimited)

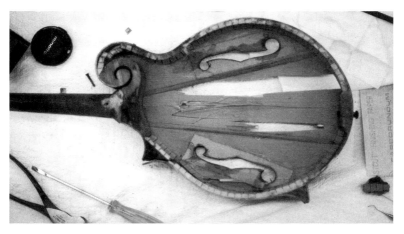

Interior view of the vandalized 1923 Gibson mandolin during its repair
(Bluegrass Unlimited)

On the Country Music Association 30th anniversary show with young Nashville stars and admirers (center, left to right) Emmylou Harris, Vince Gill, and Ricky Skaggs *(Alan L. Mayor)*

The little boy from Jerusalem Ridge makes good: awarded the National Medal of the Arts by President Bill Clinton, October 5, 1995 *(Associated Press)*

walked forward until it balanced on his shoulder. The boss, Tate figured, was well on the road to recovery.

Bill was also on the road to a spiritual reawakening.[155] Like his terrible 1953 car wreck, the cancer had been a wakeup call. Bill became friendlier, more approachable. He began attending church services Wednesdays and Sundays. He wanted to "get right," as southern Christians say, with his maker and his fellows.

He even got right with the Gibson Company.[156] After decades of declining quality in their acoustic instruments, Gibson was reinstating the techniques of Lloyd Loar and other master craftsmen. Through George Chestnut, a Nashville instrument repairman, and Billy Grammar, an Opry member, Bill received an overture: Gibson wanted to restore the battered headstock of his famous F-5, free of charge. It was given a new mother-of-pearl "Gibson" to replace the logo gouged out by Bill's pocket knife. Gibson also presented Bill with a rattlesnake rattle found inside the sound chamber: Bill had slipped one into his instrument, just like Uncle Pen.

And there is no question that Bill Monroe wanted to get right with James, the son he had neglected during the boy's youth.

James had big plans outside music. The Monroes had begun putting their money into attractions that would trade on the Monroe name. In the spring of 1981, Bill and James opened the Monroe Manor Steakhouse and Lounge at 4011 Dickerson Road. Plans were laid for an exhibit at the club.[157] The restaurant soon closed — Dickerson Road, far from Nashville's downtown, was hardly a dining destination — but the idea of a Bill Monroe museum survived. It would soon be resurrected on a grand scale.

Bill had every reason to want to reconnect with his family. Early in 1982, he lost the last of his brothers.[158] Birch, in failing health, had returned from Indiana to stay with a friend in Horton, near Jerusalem Ridge. On May 15, he suffered a heart attack and died in the Owensboro hospital. Now, of J.B. and Malissa's children only Bill and Bertha remained. Birch joined the others in their line in the Rosine cemetery. A sentiment carved on his headstone was fitting: "Fiddler, Friend to All."

Bill soon had another health siege.[159] In July, he toured New England and Canada. The band and the bus crossed by ferry from Maine to Nova

Scotia. During the night, Bill admitted to Julia that he was not feeling well.

The next morning, a horrible sound came from the back of the bus, the screams of a human being in utter agony. It was Bill. He had developed a urinary tract blockage and tried to grit it out. Now his bladder had burst.

He was rushed to a hospital where his bladder was repaired in emergency surgery. Then he was taken to a larger facility in Halifax. As fate would have it, the festival he was supposed to play was being held right across the street.

Explanations were made to the audience, and the Blue Grass Boys appeared as a foursome. The promoter visited Bill in the hospital and found him worried about disappointing his fans. Not about to discourage such spirit in his advertised headliner, the promoter asked Julia to help get Bill dressed. Shocked and furious, she refused.

Meanwhile, Tony Conway had called the Grand Ole Opry to ask if its corporate Learjet could be chartered to bring Bill home. The plane was immediately provided without charge. Buddy Lee Attractions personnel soon arrived but were greeted by an empty hospital room. Bill had managed to dress and get himself transported across the street. He played a complete set sitting in a wheelchair. He finally returned to Nashville on a stretcher. Conway was exasperated, but he realized that, for Bill, not to be able to play for his fans was worse than any mere pain.

September 13, 1982, was the final night of the Kentucky Fried Chicken Bluegrass Festival in Louisville. It was also Bill's seventy-first birthday, and he decided to give a present to his longhaired musical rivals.[160] Newgrass mandolinists Sam Bush, David Grisman, and Mike Marshall had been playing together at the show, and Claire Kenner Lampkin, a KFC event coordinator, was sent over to them as an emissary: Bill Monroe wanted the young men to join him for a number. Hearing this, they took to the stage as excited as kids who get to play catch with their favorite baseball star. Monroe acknowledged that it was "a healing thing" and "a special moment."

Shortly afterward, Sam Bush was diagnosed with testicular cancer.[161] Two major operations followed, both successful, but leaving him in a hospital bed, tubes down his throat, his medical bills mounting.

The telephone rang. His wife took the call and then said, "Well, thank you, Mr. Monroe, I'll tell him." Hearing this, Sam gestured frantically for the receiver. Bill said that he had survived cancer and that he wanted Sam to get well too. He promised to participate in any benefit concerts and made good on his vow.

But there was one person with whom Bill could not maintain such happy connections. In the late fall, Julia LaBella left him. Bill was more vital and virile than many men half his age, but the generation gap between them had finally grown too wide. She ran off to Texas with a musician close to her own age and they married.[162] But like Bessie Lee, like Carolyn, like Jimmy Martin, and like Butch Robins, her loyalty and love would one day bring her back.

Bessie Lee Mauldin had been living in an apartment in Hendersonville and working at House of Cash, Johnny and June Carter Cash's office, as a secretary and receptionist. By 1982, she was in poor health, overweight, and an insulin-dependent diabetic with heart problems. That autumn, she had a diabetic episode and passed out at home.[163] Fortunately, a friend discovered her and called an ambulance. After her hospitalization, she returned home to Norwood, North Carolina, where her sisters cared for her.

Della Streeter adored Bessie. When she was a child and her father had booked Bill, the glamorous bass player had seemed like a movie star to her. They had become reacquainted in Nashville, and now Della stayed in touch by phone.

During one conversation, Bessie said, "I loved him."[164]

"Who, Bessie?" Della asked, knowing full well who she meant.

Bessie would not speak his name. She only repeated, "I loved him."

Soon afterward, on the evening of February 8, 1983, the Norwood rescue squad responded to a report of a woman having a heart attack.[165] Charles Harris, an assistant police chief and an amateur musician, was the first to arrive. The victim was Bessie Lee. Even as CPR and oxygen were administered, Harris hoped against hope that she would recover and perform at a little country music jamboree he ran in town. They had often spoken about it.

Bessie was declared dead at Stanley Memorial Hospital in Albemarle. The cause was acute myocardial infarction due to diabetes. She was sixty-three years old.[166]

Bill was rehearsing at his home with John Hartford for his next project, the all-star album *Bill Monroe and Friends*, when he was called to the phone.[167] He returned and said, "Bessie Lee passed away." Then he was silent.

She had loved him indeed. She had been his companion, the mother of one of his children, and something even greater — his muse. She made music with him and helped save that music when she became the ally of Ralph Rinzler.

Bill did not attend her funeral.[168] He probably knew he would not receive much of a welcome if he did.

Bessie Lee Mauldin was buried next to her father in the Norwood town cemetery. It was a depressingly cold and overcast day. Then, just as the casket was being lowered and final farewells were being said, the sun broke through and smiled down on the Carolina Songbird.[169]

CHAPTER 8

BLUE MOON OF
KENTUCKY SETTING

(1983 TO 1996)

I am wealthy in my friends. — Shakespeare, *Timon of Athens*

A joke was going around Nashville about a musician who died and went to heaven. During a tour of paradise, he and St. Peter were passed by an imperious silver-haired figure, dressed impeccably in a white suit and Stetson and carrying a mandolin.

"Who was that?" exclaimed the new arrival.

"Oh, that's God," replied St. Peter impatiently. "He thinks he's Bill Monroe."

This affectionate gag wasn't only inspired by the ego and bearing of its subject. Bill had become more than an elder statesman of country music, more than a living legend: He was now a musical divinity. Producer Walter Haynes had been so inundated with requests for appearances on *Bill*

Monroe and Friends that it could have been a 2-LP set.[1] The lucky few to make the cut included Johnny Cash, the Oak Ridge Boys, Willie Nelson, and Barbara Mandrell. The project was a commercial success (released in March 1984, the album spent six weeks on the country charts, peaking at a respectable number 61), although it was not distinguished artistically: All these stars were unique stylists in their own rights, so it was difficult for most of them to blend with Bill. John Hartford, with his deep appreciation of the music of Monroe and Scruggs, came closest on his original "Old Riverman."

A large poster board was signed by each artist, then framed and given to Bill as a surprise present. When it came Waylon Jennings's turn, he thought back to those precious Texas childhood evenings spent listening on the radio to his father's favorite Opry star, and wrote: "If only my Daddy could see me now."[2]

The seventy-two-year-old Kentuckian contemplated retirement but took inspiration from logs of locust wood he had cut on his farm for fence posts. The wood seemed dry and dead, but green branches had sprung from it. "Isn't that something?" Monroe marveled.[3] "It's a good, strong wood that gets harder and better the older it gets."

Many around Nashville would agree, and not just the old guard. Monroe was a hero to the hottest new stars in town, the "New Traditionalists" who were returning country music to its classic sensibilities.

Ricky Skaggs and Keith Whitley had started their professional careers as Ralph Stanley protégés who also loved Monroe. As a teenage member of the Nashville Grass, Marty Stuart had practically grown up in Lester Flatt's bus and spent long hours with Monroe when Lester and Bill toured together. Vince Gill had played in bluegrass bands before achieving mainstream country success. Emmylou Harris had been turned on to the harmonies of the Louvin Brothers by her mentor, country rocker Gram Parsons, and from there came to love bluegrass. All of them, as Emmylou put it, had "been to bluegrass school, which is Monroe school,"[4] and they lauded Monroe as an inspiration.

Other young country superstars were well aware of Monroe's importance to overall American popular music. "Put Bill Monroe singing 'Rocky Road Blues,'" said Dwight Yoakam, "and I'll show you where rock 'n' roll got fifty percent of its cool."[5] Such high-profile veneration was impossible to ignore. And behind the scenes, within the Music Row Studios where million-selling country records were being produced, the Monroe legacy was exercising additional influence: Not only were stars like Skaggs and Stuart his direct devotees, many active Nashville session musicians — particularly fiddlers — had come up playing Bill's music and were adding a bluegrass flavor to their work on major hits.[6]

Of course, Bill Monroe's reputation had grown far beyond Nashville. After hundreds of appreciative newspaper and magazine articles, and the imprimaturs of folklorist-intellectuals, bluegrass was finally recognized as a legitimate American art form and Monroe as a true innovator. He had received a National Heritage Fellowship award in 1982.[7] On May 17, 1983, accompanied by his agent Tony Conway, he returned to Washington to attend a special arts and humanities luncheon hosted by President and Mrs. Ronald Reagan.[8]

Tony often had to remind Bill about little details and now a reminder was crucial: They absolutely would not be admitted to the White House without their invitations. Tony mentioned it again just before they left for the airport. Sure enough, Bill's was still in his briefcase on his tour bus. A driver rushed the case over to the Buddy Lee Attractions offices just in time for Conway and Monroe to catch their plane.

At Nashville Airport, Bill was recognized by a young security woman who chatted breezily with him while the briefcase slid through the X-ray scanner. In Washington they were met by an official limousine, then checked through the gates at the White House. Bill was notorious for throwing letters (sometimes opened, sometimes not) and other items into his valise. Now he fished around in the mess and produced the invitation.

Tony and Bill were then shown to a waiting room where they encountered another luncheon guest — Frank Sinatra. Sinatra shook hands with Monroe and told him how much he'd admired Bill's music. These were not hollow platitudes: He specifically mentioned listening to *The Grand Ole Opry* in the 1940s and enjoying the singing of Monroe, Acuff, and other stars.

"Now, what did you say your name was?" Bill asked.[9]

"I'm Frank Sinatra."

"And what is it that you do?"

"I'm a singer."

"I believe I've heard of you," said Bill, deadpan.

"Well, I hope so," Sinatra replied with considerable grace.

After the luncheon, Conway and Monroe headed back to Nashville so Bill could play the Friday Night Opry. As they passed through Washington airport security, there was a sudden commotion. Conway looked around on the X-ray screen, and his stomach churned.

On the screen was the sharp, nasty silhouette of a .357 magnum handgun.

Airport security opened Bill's valise and found the weapon tied up in a velvet presentation bag. It was fully loaded, six rounds in the cylinder. The identifying numbers on the barrel had been filed off.

Conway and Monroe were summarily surrounded, put up against the nearest wall, and searched. The story Monroe told was absolutely true: Yes, it was his briefcase and his pistol; the weapon had been a gift from a fan who was worried about him traveling with large sums of cash; Bill had forgotten the gun was in there; he had only been carrying the briefcase because his luncheon invitation had been in it.

Bill and Tony were locked in a downstairs holding cell. When the unhappy duo explained why they'd been in Washington, Secret Service agents showed up. As the situation tumbled from bad to worse, Bill kept asking, "Do you think you could let us go now? I have to play the Opry."[10]

Conway managed to keep this embarrassing incident out of the newspapers but was unable to keep his client from having to pay a $15,000 fine. Senate minority leader Robert Byrd of West Virginia (a friend of Bill's and an accomplished amateur fiddler) tried unsuccessfully to have the case dismissed. All things considered, Bill was lucky. He could have been imprisoned.

In many ways, the trip to Washington sums up Bill Monroe's life and career in the mid-eighties. He was known to people as humble as the Nashville airport employee and as prominent as Frank Sinatra and the president of the United States. Playing for his fans (especially at his beloved Opry) was his greatest priority. He was sharp about music and people but almost somnambulant about business and paperwork.

And as his tremendous physical strength slowly declined, he increasingly relied on psychological gambits to retain a sense of power and control in his interactions. Pretending not to know people was becoming a favorite and rather rude trick.[11] Bill would also literally get people off balance by shaking hands and then yanking them a half step forward.[12] (He usually reserved this gag for people he knew well.) But throughout his life, Monroe moved people around with a kind of mental judo.

Monroe returned to his Opry dressing room one night to find someone playing his mandolin. "Let me show you something," he said to the interloper, who immediately handed him the instrument. Bill took it, put it in its case, and quietly walked out of the room.[13] On another occasion, two brothers, a guitarist and a banjo picker, came backstage and asked Bill if they could play a number with him. They were talented but highly competitive, joshing about how the other one couldn't keep up. The boys kicked off a song. Soon, the tempo kept going in and out of sync. The brothers left the dressing room, humiliated and tossing accusations at each other. The culprit, of course, had been the mischievous Monroe, subtly shifting the placement of his mandolin chops to foul up their timing.[14]

Bill's rhythm tricks were a favorite method of testing the tenacity of prospective Blue Grass Boys. Bill Keith once watched a singer-guitarist audition. The music kept slowing up. After the dejected fellow left, Monroe remarked, "You see? I could push him right down."[15]

Monroe admitted that his favorite leadership method was to lead people around.

Through my life, there's been very few that's argued with me . . . it's just because, in talking with them, I stayed ahead of them, or just kept them under control, you know, the way I thought it should be to get along. There's no trouble to handle people, you know, to do that, if you know what you're doing and stay ahead of them. And it ain't wrong. It's in order to keep them on the right track.[16]

It was another of his many paradoxes that the mischievous and even manipulative Monroe was also a genuinely spiritual person. At the time, he was attending the church of preacher Jimmy Snow, son of Opry star Hank Snow.[17] (Over the years, Bill also went to churches attended by friends and fellow Opry members Skeeter Davis, Ricky Skaggs, and the White family.)[18] One day, Snow asked if Bill would like to accompany him on a visit to the Holy Lands. It turned into a mini-tour, with the Blue Grass Boys booked for concerts at the Sea of Galilee, in Jerusalem, and in Tel Aviv. Monroe's excitement grew as the trip approached. "We are going to where Jesus walked, where Jesus lived, where Jesus was born and where he died," he told his banjo player Blake Williams and Blake's wife, Melinda. "I can't believe that I'm actually going to be there."[19]

Despite his age, the stress of travel, and the heat, Monroe was indefatigable. In every narrow street and ancient bazaar, at every turn on the modern roads, he was curious and amazed. From Bethlehem to Masada to the Dead Sea, he led the bus in singing gospel songs. His concerts were triumphs. Performing at the Sea of Galilee, a huge full moon shining behind him, he launched into "Blue Moon of Kentucky" and the crowd came to its feet. He encored seven times that night. Bill had been pleasantly surprised that Jewish Americans like Gene Lowinger, Steve Arkin, and David Grisman had become his devotees; now he was happy, indeed profoundly moved, that Israelis loved and understood his music.

But even these emotions were secondary to his feelings upon climbing the Mount of Olives and looking down upon Jerusalem as Jesus had done. Melinda Williams overheard Bill musing to himself.

We are all here for a reason. We all have a purpose in our lives. Mine, I know, is music. And maybe I can spread God's message through my music. I've come full circle.[20]

What precisely did Bill mean by coming "full circle"? What feelings from childhood days on Jerusalem Ridge might have been stirred on a hill overlooking its namesake, the holy city? Melinda didn't know, but she saw tears streaming down Bill's face. A day or two later, Jimmy Snow baptized him anew in the Jordan River. He emerged, drenched from head to foot, singing "I Saw the Light."

Back home, not all was holiness and uplifting spirituality. The fan who had sent the .357 magnum was not being entirely melodramatic in his concerns. Bill was becoming increasingly vulnerable to theft.[21]

Tony Conway ensured that Bill was playing for guarantees, not percentages, then slowly increased his fees from a surprisingly low $2,500 to $3,500, then gradually up to $7,500. (In his final years, Bill earned $10,000 per show. Even then, Conway felt that this living legend was underpaid.) For years, Bill had contractually required he be paid in cash, and the Blue Grass Boys had gotten used to having tens of thousands of dollars on the bus.

Tony became convinced that Bill was losing large sums through theft. He had no idea who was responsible. Too many people were coming on and off the bus as it traveled all over the country, and given Bill's notoriously loose treatment of money, he had no hope that temptation could be removed. So in the mid-1980s, Tony changed the contracts and had Bill paid by certified check.

The Father of Bluegrass was becoming a grandsire to people like Conway, who was now acting more like an overall manager than a booking agent.

> I felt like he was a national treasure. I just knew that somebody needed to take care of him. During the time that I was really involved in his career, I knew that there was nobody, even the people he had hired, who would pay attention to much details for him. I just felt like I had to do it. He became almost a grandfather figure to me.[22]

Conway was pleased with Monroe's overall health, but Bill, after all, was approaching his mid-seventies. He had a heavy summer schedule and invariably insisted on playing despite heat or thunderstorms. So Tony began to add contract riders mandating that Bill would be provided with an air-conditioned dressing room, that his record sales/autograph table at festivals would be set up in the shade and ice water provided for him, that all festival stages would have a roof against sun and rain, that the sound systems would be grounded for safety.

None of this made Conway popular. Some promoters approached Bill in private, saying, "I wish we didn't have to deal with Tony. I wish we could just deal with you."

Monroe refused to circumvent his agent. "He's a good man," said Bill. "He's from Kentucky, you know."[23]

Bill relied heavily on his secretary, Betty McInturff, with whom he had a happy working relationship. (Betty was yet another of the women who proved indispensable in organizing Bill's professional life.)[24] But Bill left overall business operations to his son, James, who began looking for ways to use the growing recognition of the Monroe name to better advantage.[25] Bill's personal and financial support of James's projects was seen by many observers as reflecting a wish to help his son make a mark in life and to make up for the years Bill had neglected his family. In a 1983 *Louisville Times* profile aptly titled "The Real, Actual, Down-home Bill Monroe," writer Ronni Lundy reported that Bill had "little contact with his daughter, Melissa; and his relationship with his son, bluegrass and country performer James, has been marbled with the stress that comes when a powerful father dominates the field of endeavor pursued with far less success by his child."[26]

In October 1983, Bill and James formed a corporation to start a bluegrass museum and hall of fame. The concept was that the hall would induct one or two new members every year. "I think the bluegrass people, the entertainers, need that," Bill told *Bluegrass Unlimited*.[27] "It would give them something to work for." The Monroes bought four acres of land at 2620 Music Valley Drive, and through extensive renovations and additions converted an existing building into the museum. But the site was exactly a mile and a half from Opryland, past unimproved fields and a campgrounds, far from the busy motels and restaurants catering to the tourists.

The Bill Monroe Bluegrass Hall of Fame and Museum celebrated its grand opening on June 4, 1984.[28] Visitors entered to find a souvenir store and record shop, and a lobby dominated by a portrait of Bill Monroe with his famous F-5. The museum's display cases were filled with memorabilia: Birch Monroe's fiddle; a mandolin built for Bill by prominent luthier Randy Wood; a copy of the first Monroe Brothers record, "What Would You Give in Exchange for Your Soul"; a special presentation baseball bat made by the Hillerich & Bradsby Company and stamped as the "Genuine Bill Monroe Louisville Slugger." There were clothes worn by Bill, photographs, letters, posters, and awards.[29]

In short, it was a memento-crammed home den on a massive scale, precious to family and friends, perhaps, but only of passing interest to the general public. This is what the Monroes had set up at a huge cost on a little-traveled section of road beyond Opryland.

Friends tried to support the venture. Blue Grass Boys old and new appeared at special events, especially on Bill's birthday. One day, Opry star Skeeter Davis visited the museum with a group of friends. She found Bill alone and sad.

> Really all that was wrong, it was the wrong location. People would go down [just] so far and turn back, thinking "I don't see it." That's what they'd tell me. Once the streetlights ran out, people didn't think there was anything else further down that road. I think Bill took it personally.[30]

The enterprise began to bleed money. Soon, 1984 became a year of even greater losses.

Carolyn Minnie Brown Monroe died on July 31.[31] She was interred in the Monroe family plot in the Spring Hill Cemetery just north of the city of Nashville. The granite memorial stone marking the plot was inscribed with verses written by James and with heritage symbols, a Scottish clan Munro crest and a feather-and-arrowhead design referring to Carolyn's Native American roots.

Kenny Baker, who played on and off with Monroe for nearly a quarter of a century, felt so deeply about his tenure with the master of bluegrass that he often stated, "When Bill quits, I'll quit, too."[32] It didn't turn out that way.

In the autumn, just as the band was leaving for a prolonged tour, Kenny's brother was hospitalized. Baker desperately wanted a tour schedule so that his family could find him if the situation worsened.[33] Had he approached Bill's secretary or Tony Conway, he certainly would have gotten one. Instead, he did what he had done for years. He asked Bill. And Bill did what he had done for years about providing schedules to his musicians. Nothing.

Now with his brother seriously ill, Baker's frustration was boiling into real anger. Finally, at a show on October 12, in Jemison, Alabama, an audience member kept calling for "Jerusalem Ridge." This musical impression of foxhunting in Bill's childhood was proving one of his most popular newer instrumentals. But the fan was loud and had obviously been drinking. Bill apparently didn't realize this or was delighted by a hearty request for one of his favorite tunes.

"Kenny, get that 'Jerusalem Ridge,'" Monroe instructed.

"Get it yourself, old man," he retorted, then walked off the stage. Kenny Baker never again played as a member of the Blue Grass Boys. Monroe was stunned. Once more, his great fear of desertion by a loved one had been made terribly real. And once more, Bill had brought it on himself.

Monroe played on regardless. He contributed a mandolin part to Ricky Skaggs's version of "Wheel Hoss" for his admirer's Columbia/Epic album *Country Boy*. In February 1985, the track won a Grammy for Country Instrumental of the Year. (A version of "Uncle Pen" from the album *Don't Cheat in Our Home Town* had hit number 1 on the country charts the previous October.) There was not yet a separate bluegrass category, and Bill had never won a Grammy, so Ricky presented his award to Monroe at the Bluegrass Hall of Fame and Museum. Bill held it aloft with pride.[34]

Skaggs and Columbia had decided to do a music video for the album's title track.[35] Director Walter Miller had a concept: A southerner turned New York executive has a stern Dutch uncle–type relative who chews him out for going urban. Miller asked if Skaggs had any ideas for casting the latter part.

"You've just described Bill Monroe," Ricky answered.

Miller was intrigued, but asked, "Can he act?"

"Well, he can do the chewing out part real good," Skaggs said with a laugh. "And he's got great facial expressions."

A plot was cooked up in which a character named Uncle Pen (Monroe), wearing his cowboy hat and carrying a travel bag, is ushered into the Manhattan office of the executive (Skaggs). He looks around the sumptuous suite and declares, "I heard it was bad, boy, but I never thought you'd sink to this."

"Well," Ricky meekly responds, "this is pretty good."

"You're getting way above your raisin' is what's happenin'," Pen insists.

Grabbing a guitar (every midtown office should have one), Skaggs musically defends himself: "I'm just a country boy / Country boy at heart!" Uncle and nephew trek across Times Square (encountering then-mayor Ed Koch in a cameo as a cabbie), then descend into a subway populated with break dancers, members of Skaggs's band, and young Broadway hoofers. Pen one-ups the break dancers with the old Kentucky backstep and then happily hits them up for busking change. As the duo strolls off into the metropolis, Pen admits that Ricky is still a country boy.

Monroe later guested in other music videos, including a cameo for Run C&W, a bluegrass/soul music satire act, and as one of the celebrity suitors knocking at the dressing room door of Loretta Lynn, Dolly Parton, and Tammy Wynette in "Silver Threads and Golden Needles." But never did he have a role as lengthy or as truly funny as this.

Tony Conway had explained that the shoot would be a simple thing, a one-hour matter, and assured Bill he'd be there. But a last-moment commitment forced Tony to send another Buddy Lee agent in his place, and Monroe was needed for more than fifteen hours of location shooting. The director wanted him look like a real down-homer, so the costumer presented some old clothes obtained at a Salvation Army store.

"I can't believe they'd want a man to wear something like this on a television show," groused Bill, who had resisted hillbilly garb his entire career.

"Bill, this is not a television show, it's a video," Ricky explained, "and you're an actor today."

"I don't care," Bill replied. "That ain't no part of nothin', a man dressin' up like that. That looks sorry, right there."

When Bill got home, Tony Conway was temporarily relegated to the Monroe doghouse. But when the finished video started airing on the Nashville Network, Bill was delighted. He started asking everyone he met, "Did you see my video on TV?"

Several players filled in at fiddle in the wake of Baker's loss. One was Glen Duncan of Indiana, whose life had been changed one afternoon at the Brown County Jamboree hearing Monroe with Kenny Baker play "Uncle Pen." Now he was in Nashville, making a name for himself as an Opry sideman and session player. One night, Glen got a call from an acquaintance, singer Kathy Chiavola. After some small talk, she asked if Glen would still be interested in playing fiddle for Monroe.

"I sure would," said Glen.[36] "What do I have to do to get in touch with him?"

"Well," said Kathy, "he's standing right here."

Gone was the supremely confident talent solicitor of the 1940s who personally called prospective sidemen. The kinder and gentler Bill was using mutual friends as buffers against rejection.

There was a pro forma audition at Monroe's office. ("Now don't you think he'll look powerful in a hat?" Bill asked Betty McInturff approvingly.) Meanwhile, Glen asked Betty what the job paid. Bill didn't actually know.

Glen was now ready to play the Opry as a member of the Blue Grass Boys. Bill asked him, "What do you want to fiddle for the folks tonight?"[37]

"'Wheel Hoss,'" replied Duncan without hesitation. It was a hot number, and of course it had just been a hit for Ricky Skaggs.

Pumped by the adrenaline of the situation, Glen tore off at a furious pace. Kenny Baker was a smooth fiddler with consummate tone, but he was not generally a fast one. Monroe and the other Blue Grass Boys were caught by surprise, like defensive linemen flatfootedly watching an opposing back make an unexpected break for the goal line.

When his mandolin solo came around, Bill took off in pursuit. Suddenly, near the end, the pick slipped out of his fingers.

The errant plectrum flew end-over-end, looking like a bad pass being examined on slow-motion replay. It landed out of bounds near the footlights. Bill refused to concede the game. He strummed the lower strings with his thumb and then filled the final measure by rapping his knuckles one-two-three-four beats against the mandolin's body. Unable to chop rhythm when Glen Duncan returned for his final fiddle solo, Monroe shifted his mandolin under his arm and danced the Kentucky backstep while the audience cheered. Was there no end to this man?

Monroe used his next LP, *Bill Monroe and Stars of the Bluegrass Hall of Fame*, to promote the museum enterprise. Among the stars was John Duffey, a former member of the Country Gentlemen who co-founded the Seldom Scene, an inventive and highly popular Washington-area band. Duffey appeared on "Remember the Cross," a potent gospel number that he often performed in concert as a guest with the Blue Grass Boys.

Duffey was a hot mandolin player and, the son of an opera singer, a piercingly powerful high harmonizer. He was also a character, a big man with a flattop haircut and a flamboyant attitude. He liked to drink Scotch and smoke cigarettes, and he did both right in front of the abstentious Monroe. He loved to tell Bill (the more onlookers around, the better) that he was getting old and couldn't cut it anymore.[38] During an all-star finale at one show, John jumped in, put his hand over Bill's mouth, and sang the high part himself. In short, he was a larger-than-life, mandolin-picking, tenor-singing, huge-egoed alpha male in a world that already had one. Monroe had Duffey down in his book for a day of reckoning.

It came at a festival where the Blue Grass Boys and the Seldom Scene were both appearing. Bill slipped into the backstage area and hid around a corner. When Duffey came offstage, Monroe jumped him.

But instead of pummeling him, Bill grabbed the hefty Duffey in a bear hug and heaved him clear off the ground, shaking him and cheerfully yelling, "Hello, John! Hello, John!"

"Arrgh!" cried Duffey in mock terror. "Somebody get this madman off me!"[39] Monroe had comically made his point about who was still top dog, and Duffey had good-naturedly accepted it. As odd as it seemed, the two men really liked each other.

*   *   *

On April 1, 1985, Bill returned to his farm and announced that he was getting married.[40] He imparted this information with classic Monroe deadpan, and it was April Fool's Day, so some farmworkers assumed that he was kidding.

But he wasn't. His new wife was to be Della Streeter. Bill had proposed again. Della had accepted on condition that Bill prove his commitment by initiating his fidelity a year before their marriage. To the best of her knowledge, he had been a man of his word.

They were married on April 24. Bill was seventy-three, she was forty-three. They were very happy. Della understood him. She gave up her job because Bill in his old-fashioned way didn't want her to work.[41] Della may have been a corporate type, but she was down to earth. Bill was surprised and pleased when she donned a pair of blue jeans and, unbidden, went right to work in the barn.[42] Backstage at the Opry, Minnie Pearl and other stars welcomed her warmly. Friends were happy that Bill had managed to attract such a classy lady so late in his life.[43]

For Della, as it had been for the other women in Bill's life, it was about love, not fame or fortune. Two days before the wedding, the couple signed a prenuptial agreement.[44] Della waived rights to Bill's property in the event of a divorce. Appended to the agreement was a November 30, 1984, financial statement submitted by Bill to the Bloomington National Bank of Bloomington, Indiana. The agreement and the financial statement were filed with the Sumner County clerk, becoming public record.

Bill Monroe's net worth was given at $1,209,207.53. His greatest assets were a total of $1,275,000 in real estate (his farm, the Bean Blossom park, the Dickerson Road office of Monroe Enterprises, the museum, and the festival field near Beaver Dam, Kentucky). The remaining $265,000 of assets included musical instruments, jewelry, household furnishings, vehicles, and livestock. He had total liabilities of $364,576.63, about half of that in mortgages and the other half in bank loans.

Bill's income for 1983, the most recent available year, was just $97,237.78. His income from royalties was given as only $12,500 and "generally exceeding $10,000.00 per year." The figures are surprisingly low. Even if Monroe did not earn the staggering royalties enjoyed by writers and performers of Top 40 country hits, the earning potential of his musical catalog was surely much greater. His records were selling well, and his songs were widely recorded by bluegrass bands.

Bill's real estate generated no income. He held no stocks or bonds. He had only $11,284.16 in cash.

After exactly a half century as a professional entertainer — fifty years after he left the Sinclair refinery in 1934 to play music full time — this was all Bill Monroe had retained.

Within a few years, events would show just how financially vulnerable he had become. But now he was learning how personally vulnerable he was.

In September, the band returned from a tour.[45] It was late at night. Glen Duncan looked at Bill's Cadillac and thought something seemed wrong with it. Then he realized: It had been vandalized, spray-painted with threatening phrases directed at Bill.

A reign of terror had begun. The bus was broken into several times. The band would find the door pried open and would have to call the police before they could set foot in it again. One night, a death threat was phoned into the Grand Ole Opry. Opry officials said a woman had called and took her seriously enough to contact the Nashville Metro police. After Bill's show, they escorted him to the Sumner County line, where Sumner County sheriff's men were waiting. They took Bill the rest of the way to his farm, searching the premises thoroughly before leaving. For a while, Bill did his Opry shows with extra security standing in the wings.

The stress took a toll that, in its own way, was worse than that of the 1953 car accident. Even a three-day tour would descend into misery. Bill was typically fine the first day, then not too good the second, and very shaky by the third, singing and even playing badly. To his poor diet (he was unable to give up the fried chicken and potatoes of his youth) and the stresses of travel was now added awful anxiety.[46] The thrill of performing and the adulation of his fans lifted him: Onstage and at the autograph table he was energetic and seemingly healthy. But back on the bus, he could go from chipper to drained in just an hour.[47]

If the stress caused by his anonymous enemy weren't bad enough, the Monroes' business ventures were in serious financial trouble. In retrospect, the signs were clear. For one thing, Bill was drumming up work beyond what Buddy Lee Attractions was booking for him.

One evening in 1985, backstage at the Opry, Bill asked Charlie Louvin if he could find some gigs for him in Charlie's native Alabama.[48] Charlie said he'd try, but privately had no intention of doing so. On Mother's Day weekend 1983, Charlie had launched his own festival, spending some $30,000 for major site improvements and advertising. Top bluegrass bands had volunteered to play for free that first year to get Charlie started. Monroe had made the same promise but never showed up, playing the Friday Night Opry instead. With Bill a no-show, some fans accused Charlie of false advertising.

Afterward, Bill claimed he wasn't sure what night Charlie wanted him there. Louvin believed the real reason was that he had declined Bill's offer to join the venture as a partner, and that had offended Bill. Furious, Charlie called Bill a lying son of a bitch to his face. Bill weakly retorted that maybe bands would show up if Charlie paid them.

So when Bill again brought up the subject of getting gigs in Alabama, Charlie said, "Yeah, they're real interested in having a show, but when I tell them that Bill Monroe is who I'm booking, they kind of back down because they're afraid you won't show."[49]

Knowing full well that Charlie was lying — and why — Bill left the dressing room without another word. Louvin, a religious man, now regrets that he gave into the temptation to get even.

Another sign of the Monroes' cash problems came on October 16 at the organizational meeting of a new trade group, the International Bluegrass Music Association. Bill and James attended the morning session. (Although the first meeting was held in Nashville, the IBMA soon made its headquarters in Owensboro, Kentucky.) Bill paid for everyone's lunch and then disappeared. The message, some participants felt, was that Monroe would not involve himself in the IBMA yet would not actively oppose it.[50] But during the opening session, James unexpectedly offered to sell the contents of their museum to the new association. It was explained that any such acquisitions would be far in the future, and the matter was not pursued.[51]

Meanwhile, the secret crime wave against Bill was turning even uglier. In October, there was a holdup at the secluded Bluegrass Hall of Fame and Museum. A cashier was struck and the day's receipts taken. No arrests were made in the case.[52]

Then, around 12:45 P.M. on November 13, 1985, Monroe, Della, and the farmhands followed their usual routine of driving off to lunch.[53] Della was going shopping, so she and Bill took separate cars.

Della was the first to return; she unlocked the front door and started to climb the stairs to the second floor. Looking back into the living room, she noticed something.

Bill's famous 1923 Lloyd Loar Gibson F-5 mandolin and another Loar were lying in front of the fireplace.

They had been smashed in.

She ran to the phone and called the office. Unable to bear to tell Bill in those first moments, she spoke with James. She told him what had happened and asked him to come home with his dad. James instructed her to call the police immediately. Then Bill left the office and went home alone to face the disaster.[54]

Bill and the police arrived at about the same time. Someone had forced a second-story door that was accessible by an outside stairway, then made his or her way downstairs. A fireplace poker had been thrust point down into the helpless instruments. Holes were pierced in portraits of Bill and Birch Monroe that hung over the fireplace. A framed sketch of the farm was also smashed. Nothing had been stolen. It was more than vandalism. It had been a virtual act of rape.

Monroe was tearful, devastated. The two mandolins were packed up and taken to the new Gibson factory in Nashville, along with a paper bag full of pieces of broken wood. The latter action was well-intentioned and nearly disastrous: Gibson craftsman Charles Derrington was presented not only with the wrecks of the instruments but about 150 mixed slivers of wood. There was no immediate way of telling which piece had come from which mandolin.

The instruments were in a ghastly state.[55] Bill's primary mandolin had been heavily damaged, with two openings in the top about the width of butter knives. But Derrington saw cause for hope. Almost miraculously, the poker had missed the primary Loar's inner braces and tone bar (the wooden support that is tuned during the instrument's construction by shaving it into the proper size and shape). It was as if a human being had been stabbed in the throat but the vocal cords uninjured. It might be possible to restore the famous instrument with most of its legendary timbre intact. (The secondary Loar had suffered less top breakage but its tone bar had been broken, making its damage ultimately worse.)

The mixed splinters of wood were a severe problem, but the two instruments had different finishes, so by painstakingly examining each piece under a magnifying lens, Derrington could sort them out. He also had experience with an acoustically transparent epoxy that would transmit vibrations as if the energy were moving through undisturbed wood fibers. For the next three months, Charles Derrington worked forty-hour weeks doing nothing but repairing Bill's primary mandolin.

Monroe had to leave town on a northeastern tour, so Gibson loaned him the best F-5 they had in house. It provided the one moment of levity on this post-apocalyptic trip.

Bill arrived at his first show to find there was no pick with the mandolin. Picks were not a detail to which he ever paid much attention, and he was not carrying a spare. Fiddler Glen Duncan eventually produced a pick he had gotten as a promotional item at a trade show. It was a big, garish, Day Glo–hued thing intended for heavy metal guitarists. But it was stiff enough for Monroe's purposes.

The band stopped in New York City, where Monroe gave a mandolin seminar to a group of raptly attentive Monroephiles. The inevitable questions followed.

"What kind of strings do you use?"

"Gibson bronze are the best."

"What kind of pick do you use?"

Without blinking, Bill held out the Day Glo monstrosity. "I use this kind right here."

The devotees murmured in awe.[56]

Back in Nashville, sometime between December 8 and December 13, a safe said to contain $10,000 in cash and some rings was stolen from Monroe's parked touring bus. It was found, empty, in a creek.[57] There was no telling whether the thefts were connected to the vandalism

and threats. Bill Monroe, who had once been so self-reliant and pugna-
cious that he had accompanied DeFord Bailey through the toughest
neighborhoods, now at age seventy-four contemplated hiring a bodyguard.[58]

The crimes eventually ceased, and on February 25, 1986, the restored
mandolin was presented to Bill in a little ceremony at the Gibson facilities.[59] Monroe strummed a first chord and the instrument reverberated. It
would require some playing back in, but its fabled tone had survived. Bill
beamed and embraced the Loar as if it were a child brought back from a
seemingly fatal illness.

There was much speculation as to who had tried to destroy the instruments. One aspect of the crime was much commented on — the use of a
fireplace poker in a downward thrusting motion. Some persons believed
that a man would grab the mandolin by its neck like a tennis racket and
smash it against a doorway, or stomp on it heel first. To them, the poker
indicated that the vandal was a woman, perhaps a spurned lover. An
anonymous writer in the January 1986 issue of *Country Music* noted that
the perpetrator seemed to have an insider's knowledge of Bill's home and
his habit of leaving the farm at lunchtime. Bill, James, and Della felt that
a farmworker who had been dismissed may have been responsible.[60] But
no arrests were ever made.

Although Charles Derrington had almost miraculously raised the mandolin from the dead, it existed below its true potential. Like many virtu-
osos, Bill was woefully ignorant of the mechanics of his instrument or
how to set it up for optimal sound.[61]

As often happens after decades of string tension, the mandolin's neck
was slowly raising up, causing the action (the distance between the
strings and the fingerboard) to get higher and higher. Bill had always
favored a high action because it prevented the strings from buzz-
ing against the frets when he strummed forcefully. But now even Bill's
strong hands had difficulty playing with nuance. A skilled craftsman could have reset the neck and made the mandolin easier to play, but
Bill refused, erroneously fearing that it would change the instrument's
tone.

The high action, Bill's fascination with tone, and his aging motor skills combined to influence his final mandolin style. Bill took his mid-1960s melodic deconstructions to the ultimate: He was now playing spare lines, broadbrushing the main themes, yet his playing remained engaging because of his unique right hand rhythm. Talented Monroe mandolin disciple Mike Compton compared him to the painter Cézanne, skillfully shading and coloring so that his simple lines took on impressionistic depth and complexity. Still, Bill remained a fierce player on the instrument. "I whip it like I'd whip a mule," he told Compton.[62]

Of all his years, 1986 was truly a landmark. His mandolin, truly a part of himself, had been saved. A half century earlier, in 1936, he had made his first recordings with the Monroe Brothers; forty years earlier had seen his historic first recordings with Flatt and Scruggs; thirty-five years ago he had begun recording for Decca; twenty years before he had started his summer bluegrass festival at Bean Blossom (and exactly ten years later he had added the autumn festival). And 1986 would see his seventy-fifth birthday.

In the spring of this auspicious year, Bill and James moved the two-and-a-half-year-old Bill Monroe Bluegrass Hall of Fame and Museum to Music Village U.S.A., an entertainment complex in Hendersonville that attracted tour buses.

"We're expecting to draw a whole new crowd of people up here," James told the *Nashville Banner*.[63] "We're around country music now."

But rather than cut their losses, the Monroes retained the museum site. In the summer of 1987, after $800,000 of additions and renovations, they reopened the building as a nightclub called Monroe's Bluegrass Country.[64] The menu featured hefty beef, fish, and chicken entrees. Live bands provided the rhythms for a 1,200-square-foot dance floor ("the biggest in Nashville,"[65] according to club promotional material). It had two lounges, private dining rooms, video games, a souvenir shop, and even a shoe shine parlor. Open seven days a week from 4:00 P.M. to 2:30 A.M., Monroe's Bluegrass Country was evidently intended for late-night revelers. But its location far from the rebounding Nashville downtown made it inaccessible to the crucial walk-in trade.

If James and Bill did not know when to discontinue inadvisable invest-ments, Bill certainly did not know when to change inadvisable behaviors. Or how.

On March 12, 1987, there was a filing for divorce in the marriage of Bill and Della Streeter Monroe on the basis of "irreconcilable differences."[66] At issue, not surprisingly, were allegations that Bill had committed adul-tery, and Della's lawyer was ready to pin him down. During the pre-trial interrogatories, Bill was asked about specific women and dates. A repre-sentative of a Nashville motel was subpoenaed to bring guest records. One set of questions suggested that Bill's advancing age had not dimmed his love of spicy telephone conversations: He was asked if a specific woman had made calls "during which were discussed your past sexual activity together and plans for future sexual activity?"

Perhaps in a reference to the Little Georgia Rose, Monroe was also queried about other dependents besides his wife and children, and, if they existed, how much he was spending to support them. (Because the case was settled out of court, the answers were not submitted into evi-dence and are not in the public record.)

On November 21, 1988, a final decree of divorce was granted. From wedding ceremony to divorce filing, Bill's final marriage lasted less than two years.

Della Streeter had honestly believed that Bill would be faithful to her.

Oh, yes. He promised me he would. Had it been Bill, he would have been. But Bill Monroe couldn't. Bill Monroe was the man on stage, the music man. But Bill — just Bill — was my husband.

The Bill Monroe on stage was the man with the big ego. I think it fed his ego to have a lot of different women. Maybe he was searching for the right feeling, the right one. And of course, unlike most other men, he had access to the multitudes.

The Bill at home was an attentive, loving husband. He liked to talk about a lot of different things. He enjoyed picnics. If he was going to be out working in the garden or with the livestock most of the morning,

I'd make a picnic lunch and take it out with a blanket. And we'd sit out and find a nice place in the pasture and eat lunch.

We'd sit out on the bench in the backyard and listen for his fox-hounds at night when he'd turn them out. I'd take hot chocolate out, and we'd drink it and listen to his dogs.[67]

Della and Bill became cordial again, occasionally speaking on the phone. Della told him, "I'm only sorry we got married because it ruined a beautiful friendship."

Bill chuckled in agreement.[68]

Emory Gordy Jr., a musician/songwriter who had become a sought-after A&R man for MCA, produced Bill's next LP, *Southern Flavor*. The title track was one of Bill's strongest instrumentals in years, in some ways familiar with its modal chord shifts but also tantalizingly fresh, a jam session picker's dream. In 1988, the album won the first Grammy in the newly created bluegrass category.[69]

As successful as *Southern Flavor* was, it was a poignant watershed. Bill's voice was losing intonation, going flat when reaching for trademark high notes on favorites like "Mule Skinner Blues." Although the problem was not constant, it was becoming more frequent. So as much as Bill disliked overdubbing and using headphones, he had agreed to sing additional vocal takes on open tracks of the master tape. During mixdown, Gordy switched from track to track, selecting the best lines and assembling them into relatively flawless vocals.[70]

The June 1988 Bean Blossom bluegrass festival opened under a cloud: The Brown County Jamboree was for sale. The *Indianapolis News* reported that the seventy-six-year-old Monroe was giving up his nearly two-hundred-shows-per-year touring schedule to devote more time to his Nashville business interests. "He's been on the road for 53 years, and his doctor wants him to come off it," James Monroe told the *Brown County Democrat*.[71] James added that they'd had a hard time finding a replacement for Birch Monroe as the park's manager. "There was nobody up there to run it, and it kind of fell apart," he said.

"I don't want to just quit," Bill told a reporter.[72] "I've got too many fans and friends all over the world. They're on my side. It would be a sad thing not to see them any more." There were no buyers, and in January 1989, the property was taken off the market. Bill continued his grinding touring schedule.

Bill soon received more unhappy ink.[73] On May 1, 1989 — in the most bizarre incident of his event-filled life — he was arrested, charged with assault, and released on $500 bond.

A fifty-one-year-old dog trainer from Birmingham, Alabama, told Sumner County authorities that she was having a relationship with Monroe and had gone to his farm. According to her complaint, Monroe "became angry, hit her in the face with a Bible, knocked her down, kicked her in the face." The woman later told the *Nashville Banner* that she had been using the Good Book as something of a lie detector to test Monroe's fidelity: "I said, 'Swear on it to me that you have not been running around, because that way you'll tell me for real.' He said, 'I'm not going to do it' and — swack — right in the mouth." She added, "It was a big ol' Bible."

Tony Conway and Bill's attorney insisted that the woman was a stalker who had been calling Bill as many as twenty times a day, that she had created a disturbance at the farm and refused to leave. It was Monroe, they said, who had first called the police, a claim confirmed by Sumner County authorities.

It is likely that Bill, feeling assaulted himself, grabbed the book and swatted the woman indignantly. But he certainly did not use the Bible to administer a beating. On the day before a court hearing, Sumner County Sheriff Richard Sutton confiscated a loaded .25 caliber semi-automatic pistol from the complainant's pickup truck. Assistant District Attorney Dee Gay told the judge that he had "serious problems with the credibility and mental condition of the witness." The charges were dismissed, and Monroe was exonerated.

Bill's national profile continued to rise, but in more pleasant ways. When *Rolling Stone* did a pictorial of modern pop stars and their musical heroes for its September 21, 1989, issue, former bluegrass musician Chris Hillman of the Byrds rock band proudly posed next to Monroe, both holding their Gibson F-5 mandolins. "If he hadn't influenced my life so much," said Hillman, "I might have gone through another year of college or gone to Vietnam."[74] And on Saturday, October 28, Monroe took the stage of the Grand Ole Opry to celebrate a half century on the show. The event was broadcast live on the Nashville Network, the country music cable channel on whose programs Bill was also becoming a popular guest.

But just the week before this happy anniversary, Bill had spent two days in the Hendersonville Hospital for tests and to have his heart medication changed.[75] The superhuman who had refused to take painkillers after his 1953 car accident was becoming almost like anyone his age.

Bill cared a lot for the music and cared little for the expected behavior of a star. He happily played for free with pickup groups of musicians of varying quality at various local venues.[76] The excellent young Nashville bluegrass outfit, the Sidemen, appeared Tuesday nights at the Station Inn in Nashville, and Bill often showed up to play with them. The Belle Cove, a nightclub at a marina on a Hendersonville lake, was a Wednesday-night Monroe hangout in the later years. The Long Hollow Jamboree, a truly rustic country music showplace only a few miles from Bill's Sumner County farm, was a favorite place to jam on Thursday nights. They even fed Bill supper.

If he was in town on weekends, he would attend jam session parties. (Onlookers at one such event were treated to the precious sight of some young rock musicians jamming with an old man on their reggae version of "Blue Moon of Kentucky," quite unaware that the old man — Monroe — was its composer.[77]) Friends were worried that Bill was not getting any rest, but his need to make music was insatiable.[78] "Is there any music anywhere tonight?" he'd ask.[79]

Sometimes Bill was joined at the Belle Cove by a female vocalist — his daughter Melissa. The finality of the divorce between her parents had been difficult for her, and the tours with her father in 1963 and 1964 rare ventures into the outside world. After her mother died, she became even more withdrawn. When Bill brought her to dinner or to sing with him at the Belle Cove, she brightened up, and her fine, strong voice was in evidence. But her performances of her popular composition "Is the Blue Moon Still Shining?" took on an extra pathos because it was clear that her own life had little radiance. Melissa was a dark-eyed, lovely, pleasant young lady but noticeably fragile, not in good health.[80] Her father was very protective of her.

Melissa's health declined. She ate poorly, gained a great deal of weight, and developed diabetes.[81] On September 27, 1990, she was admitted to Hendersonville Hospital with heart and kidney problems. She was soon moved to the Hillhaven Nursing Home in Hendersonville, where she died on December 3 at age fifty-four.[82]

As nervous as Bill had once been about television, he was never averse to making short films. He had appeared in half-hour country music television shows filmed in the mid-1950s by Al Gannaway and even in a real curiosity, the 1966 B-movie *Second Fiddle to a Steel Guitar,* as one of the Opry acts inserted between the antics of comedians Leo Gorcey, Huntz Hall, and Arnold Stang.

Now New York–based filmmaker Rachel Liebling was putting together a documentary, *High Lonesome: The Story of Bluegrass.* Released in 1991, it was a loving assemblage of performance segments, interviews, archival photographs, and old film clips that not only told the music's story but perceptively captured the world from which it had come. Monroe was of course the central figure, framing the film with sequences shot on Jerusalem Ridge during what proved to be his final visit to his childhood home.

Ralph Rinzler, who had been promoted to Smithsonian assistant secretary for public service, championed Liebling's efforts during the excruciating search for funding.[83] And in 1993 he actively facilitated an instructional video on Monroe-style mandolin featuring the master himself. Bill performed well, but simply could not dissect his playing any more than a champion sprinter can run in slow motion. So Homespun Video owner/producer Happy Traum created a companion tape with Sam Bush teaching Monroe's techniques. Sam spent a full six months studying the Monroe footage before shooting his own. Bill's one-time newgrass nemesis was again struck by the beauty of Monroe's playing, what Bill chose to leave out as well as what he chose to include.[84]

The Homespun videos and the Liebling documentary had poignant meaning for Rinzler. He knew they would be among his final opportunities to establish Bill Monroe's place in American music history.

Because Ralph Rinzler was a dying man.

Bill had completed the gospel album *Cryin' Holy Unto the Lord* in 1990. Vic Gabany, an Owen Bradley protégé and Opry engineer, soon began recording the Blue Grass Boys on speculation. Gabany had been given to understand that — unbeknownst to bluegrass fans and even to Bill himself — MCA had quietly dropped Monroe, although the label remained open to future projects.[85] Bill's records were extraordinarily inexpensive to produce, but now they were only modest money makers in the exploding multibillion-dollar world of country music.[86]

MCA spokespersons insist that Bill remained with the label until his death,[87] and indeed Bill's final guest appearances on friends' records list him as appearing "courtesy of MCA." However, Vic Gabany was now personally bankrolling Bill's recordings, and with the exception of a 1994 four-CD retrospective set, MCA Records released no further recordings of Monroe during his lifetime. It was certainly a tribute to Monroe that he had stayed with MCA so long. Most of his country and bluegrass peers from the Decca days — Ernest Tubb, Kitty Wells, the Osborne Brothers, and Jimmy Martin, all name artists with loyal followings — had been let go in the 1970s.

Gabany did three studio sessions with Monroe, in November 1994 and January and May 1995, as well as recording at Bean Blossom in 1994 and 1995. The final edition of the Blue Grass Boys was proving to be a strong mix of young and veteran players: Tom Ewing, an Ohioan who had replaced Wayne Lewis, was a solid vocalist-guitarist and writer. (He helped Bill complete "The Days Gone By" for the *Southern Flavor* album, the last unrecorded original vocal that Monroe put on disk.[88]) Ewing and banjo picker Dana Cupp Jr. provided not only strong rhythm support for Bill but knew to prompt him onstage if he forgot a lyric. Robert Bowlin and Tater Tate were twin fiddling. And bass player Ernie Sykes had become the last Blue Grass Boy ever hired.[89] The group was energetic and cohesive; its members were dedicated to staying with Bill until the end.

Knowing the inconsistencies of Monroe's voice, Gabany planned to do an all-instrumental album giving emphasis to his deep selection of unrecorded original tunes. Gabany was sensitive to Monroe as an artist and a man. For the artist, Gabany selected a studio with an analog recording system, which brought a warmer sound to acoustic instruments than modern digital equipment. And for the aging gentleman, Gabany found ways to get Monroe to accept a seat, tune his mandolin, or end a session without hurting his pride.[90]

Gabany was amazed by Bill's method of writing instrumentals:

There was a story behind every one. For example "Northern White Clouds": On the bus coming back from a trip up north, he looked out the window and saw some of the prettiest white clouds he'd ever seen against a pure blue sky. The way he described it was so vivid. He would write down notes that reminded him of the experience. From these notes would come certain sounds that he would relate to a particular title. It was very strange and wonderful.[91]

Gabany also knew how to get the best performances out of Bill.

Anytime you could bring in a pretty girl or a famous musician, either of those would get Bill going every time. Then he was pushed to give that kind of "See? There!" performance. Bill played best when he was pushed.[92]

If Bill's loyal fans had no idea of the uncertainties of his recording career, they similarly never grasped the significance of the 1992 closing of the Bluegrass Hall of Fame and Museum at Music Village U.S.A. It was relocated to a new white colonnaded building erected on the Brown County Jamboree property. Uncle Pen's cabin — or at least a restoration thereof — was part of the exhibit.[93]

Doug Hutchens was a former bass-playing sideman with whom Bill was surprisingly candid. Hutchens had been instrumental in arranging birthday tributes each September and in tracking down all the bona fide Blue Grass Boys to give them commemorative belt buckles. But what had really won Bill's respect was Doug's unstinting work ethic during setup weeks at Bean Blossom. So when Doug visited one day and found Bill rocking back and forth on his heels, he felt he could ask what was wrong.

"I'm in torment," Bill admitted.[94]

Bill was feeling his years. He couldn't put in the hard work at the farm and couldn't find reliable help to do the chores as he liked them done. He made sure that his garden was always planted, but became unable to harvest it.[95]

Age was making Bill if anything more beautiful. His eyes seemed a paler blue, his skin had a translucency, his bearing was even more regal. (Singer Emmylou Harris watched one night as Monroe entered a Kennedy Center banquet, and the other guests — rich and famous persons not easily impressed — gazed at him admiringly.)[96] But now the years of touring and the recent heavy stresses were conspiring to rob Bill of health. In August 1991, he had undergone double bypass heart surgery. (Just two weeks later, the stubborn Monroe insisted on making an appearance on the stage of the Opry.) In March 1994, he fell outside his cabin and broke his hip.[97] Surgery was successful, and he recovered with surprising speed.

At such times of crisis, he always had his farm to come back to. It remained his refuge, his strength.

Then, on Saturday, April 23, 1994, he lost it.

The newspaper advertisement was for the "absolute auction" of "244 Scenic Rolling Acres Rustic Two Story Log Home Plus 3 Bedroom 2 Bath 2 Story Home."[98] So that prospective bidders would not miss the property's significance, a boxed subheadline declared it was "The Legendary Bill Monroe Farm, Father of Bluegrass Music."

The various enterprises set up by James and Bill had lost large amounts of money. There were bank loans due and other expenses to be covered. Bill had resisted Tony Conway's urging that he hire a financial adviser.[99] Often suspicious of outsiders when it came to money matters, Bill couldn't believe that a financial professional would keep his business confidential. Now Conway found himself sitting on the cabin porch with the Monroes and Bob Whittaker, president and general manager of the Grand Ole Opry, feeling as if he were attending a wake.

First, most of the farm's movables were auctioned. Bill liked big vehicles. A big collection was driven off. Bill had cherished running fence lines on his property. His posthole digger was sold. He loved horsepower of the old-fashioned variety. Four quarter horses, a horse-drawn rake, a wagon, plows, a harness, and a blacksmith forge were all taken away. Even the farm's dinner bell went on the block. Bill stood by, braced by a walker and his last reserves of resolve, and watched it happen.

Next came the land itself. James had wisely arranged that as a condition of any sale Bill would be allowed to use the log house and approximately fourteen acres around it for the rest of his life.[100] Tony Conway hoped that he could buy the entire property and sell it back to the Monroes when their financial situation improved.[101] With his wife's agreement, he was attending the auction with a letter of credit from their bank.

Conway found himself bidding against a stranger, a man in his late twenties or early thirties dressed in camouflage pants, T-shirt, and a baseball cap, leaning up against a fence. It quickly became obvious that those combat fatigues had deep pockets. Conway reached the limit of his credit and dropped out. Auctioneer Feller Brown brought down his gavel at $375,000 and gave the stranger the nod. Conway was angry and upset, feeling he had failed Bill.

Then Bob Whittaker walked up and gave the man a happy hug. This good old boy was in fact an attorney representing Gaylord Entertainment, present owners of the Grand Ole Opry. "We weren't going to let anything happen to Mr. Monroe," said a smiling Whittaker.[102] Conway was unhappy at first about not being forewarned about the Opry's parallel plans to keep the property from developers, but realized that Gaylord had played its cards so close that not even Bill or James knew what was going on.

Gaylord immediately rehabilitated the log house, which had been allowed to become seriously dilapidated.[103] The company had no plans for the property; it just wanted to make Bill comfortable. It was a Nashville-style gesture that would be unknown in New York or Hollywood.

In a huge irony, Monroe received $10 cash in hand for the sale — the same amount he had tendered forty years earlier when he bought the place and began making payments on it. Most of the $375,000 went to settle the remaining $314,894 of a $350,000 loan made to Bill on March 26, 1987, by the Bank of Goodlettsville.[104]

Monroe did not publicly lay the blame on anyone, but he was obviously saddened not to hold clear title to the world he had created for himself at the end of Allen Road.

"It's a shame," he said afterward. "You hate to lose anything like that."[105]

Predictably, the sale shocked the bluegrass world. So much so, that James was moved to take out a full-page advertorial in the September 1994 issue of *Bluegrass Unlimited*.[106]

Entitled "May the Circle Be Unbroken" and subtitled "The Truth About Bill and James Monroe," the ad stated that a "vicious rumor was spreading among bluegrass promoters as well as fans, a rumor that James Monroe caused his father, the legendary Bill Monroe, to go so deeply into debt that the elder Monroe had lost his farm. For James Monroe, a bluegrass performer who had recently announced he was back on the road for full-time bookings, the effect was devastating."

James stressed that Bill did not lose the farm. It was sold. He further noted that "Bill Monroe was the sole owner of the land" and the sale "was Bill Monroe's decision." James said that when Bill was advised by his CPA to sell the property, James insisted on the proviso that Bill retain his house and some acreage as a lifetime estate.

James gave this account of the situation: The debt on Bill's farm was a loan that had consolidated six previous notes ("all of which bore the signature Bill Monroe"), this consolidation having decreased the existing debt service by $20,000. But due to Bill's advanced age, the loan was short term with a call.

"When it was decided to move the museum to Music Village, adjacent to Twitty City," the advertorial stated, "another equal partnership was formed to build a dinner theater, known as Monroe's Bluegrass Country, at the original building site. Eventually, this property was successfully sold for $650,000."

The advertorial concluded: "These are the facts. It is the hope of the Monroe family that setting the record straight will bring to a halt all rumors and bring our family back together, stronger than ever."

Cash flow had been a nagging problem for the Monroes' various businesses. On January 14, 1982, a tax lien was filed against James W. Monroe doing business as Monroe Manor Steak House and Lounge, 4011 Dickerson Road.[107] Another lien was filed on October 9, 1984, against Monroe and Associates Inc.[108] On February 25, 1987, Third Century, Inc. obtained a summary judgment against the Monroes and the Bill Monroe Bluegrass Hall of Fame for $29,949.02 in back payments plus $7,487.25 in legal expenses for a total of $37,436.27.[109] The liens and the judgment were eventually satisfied and released.[110]

The Monroes had borrowed large sums and taken out mortgages on the site of their office and a tract near Beaver Dam, Kentucky, on which they held festivals.[111] There were many rumors as to where Bill's money had gone over the years. Bill and James were certainly working together, but James had the concepts. (His *Bluegrass Unlimited* advertorial clearly stated that the Hall of Fame and Museum "was designed and built by James as a tribute to his father and other bluegrass greats.") The concepts were good ones, just as J. B. Monroe's general store in Horton and Charlie's coal mining business had been good concepts. Yet other factors had intervened. In Bill and James's case, although some celebrities have opened successful restaurants and museums, such ventures usually have the odds stacked against them.

As popular as Bill Monroe was, his name alone was not enough to draw the crowds. To assume heavy debts was highly risky, like a gambler betting a deed that the next turn of the cards will bring the big win.

Bill was little concerned with money.[112] He could be stingy when he didn't have it. But when he was flush, he could be extraordinarily generous. This came out during the many benefits he played: After one such fund-raiser for a Huntington, West Virginia, children's shelter, Tony Conway watched in amazement as Bill took a big chunk from a stack of money he had been paid and handed it right back to the organizers without even counting it.[113]

*   *   *

The willingness of Bill's associates to save his farm was an outward manifestation of how beloved Monroe was. This good feeling had been a two-
way street. Nashville was friendlier to Bill Monroe because Bill Monroe
had become friendlier to Nashville.

Della Streeter had noticed the process over the years:

I think a big factor was that in the mid-1970s, Bill opened up. He had
always been very closed, very private, not exceptionally friendly, almost
abrupt with people. [Now] he would take time to talk with people. He
would be more personal with his peers.[114]

Opry star Bill Anderson believes that the acceptance of Bill's music
had much to do with that.

My most fond memory of Bill is seeing him mellow in later years. He
had not been a friendly person. I think he had a certain amount of bitterness in him for a while. Maybe he knew he was playing this great
music, and why can't the world accept it and understand it.

When his acceptance came in later years, he warmed up so much as
a human being. It was the most wonderful metamorphosis. I'd seen
days when he would pass me backstage at the Ryman or out here [at
the new Opryhouse] even, and I'd say, "Hello, Mr. Monroe," and he
wouldn't ever speak. He'd just grunt, and that would be about it. But
then towards the end we got to the point where we'd cut up in the
halls, and it was just so much fun. And I think it was all due to the
acceptance of his music.[115]

One of those who cared was Julia LaBella. In May 1994, she came
back to Bill.[116] Not as a lover, but as a friend. After a dozen years, an
almost spiritual connection remained between them, just as it had with
so many of Bill's old lovers. Bill knew that Julia had been back in
Nashville for the past two years and was a WSM disk jockey. A woman
who had been living with him had left. He knew he could not live alone
but he was not ready to be put in a nursing home.

And so Julia came back. But Bill would not be spared the loss of other
dear friends.

*   *   *

On July 2, 1994, the Festival of American Folklife was in colorful blossom on the Capitol Mall when a colossal thunderclap punctuated the afternoon and rains swept the area.[117] In one performance tent, a Caribbean musician told the jittery audience that in his country, such a heavenly display signified that a great man had died.

Indeed, a great man had died. Ralph Rinzler had passed away at his Washington home at almost the precise moment that the thunder spoke.

Rinzler died of AIDS.[118] His illness had reinforced his resolve to complete important projects, especially those involving Bill Monroe.[119] Ralph had always been frustrated by how much of Monroe's greatest music had never gotten on disk, especially his duets with Doc Watson. So he had pored through his voluminous collection of concert recordings and solicited tapes from other collectors, listening to hundreds of hours of material. The result was two CDs subtitled "Off the Record": *Bill Monroe & His Blue Grass Boys: Live Recordings 1956–1969* and *Bill Monroe and Doc Watson: Live Duet Recordings 1963–1980*. Ralph Rinzler ended his life still championing the music of these men.

Monroe called Ralph about a month before he died, Doc Watson within just a few days. Ralph was moved to tears. Although he did not explain the nature of his malady, he let them know that he was dying.[120]

"Well, old friend," Doc had said, "if I don't see you anymore here, I'll see you over there."[121]

When Bill and Doc learned of the AIDS, neither passed judgment on Rinzler. Monroe appeared at a memorial service held at the Festival of American Folklife on July 7 and asked Mike Seeger to accompany him on guitar.[122] Still having trouble with his hip, Bill mounted the stage carefully, then performed "Wayfaring Stranger." Seeger realized that by including him — the friend who had been at Rinzler's side during his first involvement with Bill — Monroe was making a quiet, almost poetic statement.

Drifting away from his four-decade-long association with Decca/MCA, Bill now guested on his friends' recordings. He was far from becoming a musical charity case, however. Sessions recorded in late 1994 and released in 1995 proved to be his most meaningful in years, both musically and personally.

Former Blue Grass Boy fiddler Byron Berline got Monroe and Earl Scruggs to join him for a rousing version of "Sally Goodin'." It was Bill and Earl's first studio session together in forty-seven years and earned a Grammy nomination. With Bill on mandolin, Gary Brewer recorded "The Ozark Rag" and "The Old Kentucky Blues," two numbers that Bill had especially written for guitar.

Bill performed several originals, including the previously unrecorded "My Father's Footsteps," on Butch Robins's *Grounded, Centered and Focused*. The results were quite good, but age had not diminished Monroe's propensity for paining Robins, for whom the sessions were like having root canal work.[123]

Butch had a more pleasant experience overdubbing banjo on a lovely duet of "Stay Away from Me" that Kathy Chiavola recorded with Bill at his cabin. Bill's instrumental broadbrushing of the melody left spaces for Robins to add answer-back phrases on the banjo. Robins had sparred with Monroe at Bean Blossom jam sessions; now he was supporting him.

The recording had special meaning for Chiavola, too. Shortly after the arioso-voiced midwesterner had gotten involved in the Nashville music scene, Bill had offered her a job in his band but with romantic strings attached.[124] ("It gets awful lonesome on the road," Bill pleaded sadly.) Kathy declined both the job and the romance. Bill had reacted so petulantly to the rejection that she had finally gone to Bill's office to suggest they pray to heal their friendship. They did, and from that moment Monroe became a supportive platonic friend. Chiavola had discovered what Della Streeter had also learned: coexisting with the narcissistic Bill Monroe was just plain Bill, a mature and thoughtful gentleman.

Like all his relationships, Bill's interactions with other musicians remained puzzlingly contradictory. He genuinely rejoiced in making music with his friends, yet it was often a one-way street. His highest compliment was to offer an unrecorded composition ("This would be a good one for you to do"), but he showed no interest in receiving material from other composers. This frustrated admirers like David Grisman who wanted to collaborate with Bill or have him perform some of their work.[125]

And, paradoxically, Bill threw walls around his most revolutionary music. For years, he had claimed that he could have created other musics besides bluegrass. When a *Bluegrass Unlimited* writer and future Monroe biographer asked what these musics would sound like, Monroe looked uncharacteristically embarrassed, then smiled and said, "I wouldn't want to mention them."[126] Perhaps they would have involved horns: Monroe wrote a tune called "Tromboline" to be performed with trombone and mandolin, but never recorded it.[127]

One night backstage at the Opry, Monroe was jamming with banjo master and former Blue Grass Boy Sonny Osborne on some new, uniquely flavored Monroe tunes, old-timey but progressive and thoroughly compelling.[128] George Gruhn, a prominent Nashville-based instrument maker and a great fan of Bill's, was enthralled.

"Bill, that's some of the best music I've ever heard from you," Gruhn said. "You should record it."

"It wouldn't sell," Monroe replied.

"Bill, I think it would."

"It wouldn't sell," Monroe insisted.

George was unwilling to accept this answer. Finally, Monroe said, "I owe my fans bluegrass music, and this isn't bluegrass music."

Gruhn had the distinct impression that Bill was actually afraid his fans would love it. If so, this new sound might vie with bluegrass and everything else he had done for the past half century, forcing the supremely competitive Monroe to contend with an invincible musical rival — himself.

Age had not curbed Bill's feistiness nor his sharp tongue. Ricky Skaggs borrowed Bill's mandolin to use onstage one night and played hot licks up the neck in third positions where Monroe rarely ventured. Skaggs then handed the mandolin back.

"Did you find any place where it didn't sound good?" Monroe inquired acidly.[129]

Monroe's utterances became legendary. Bill, Tater Tate, and Wayne Lewis were walking down a street in Tokyo during a tour of the Far East. Unintelligible conversations in Japanese buzzed around them. Monroe, who detested foul language, remarked approvingly, "You know, boys, what I like about walkin' around the streets over here, you don't hear nobody cussin' and carryin' on all the time."[130]

And then there was the time the Blue Grass Boys did an early morning television show in New York City. A breakfast spread was provided. Monroe chomped into a bagel, then warned fiddler Billy Joe Foster, "Billy Joe, stay away from them donuts. They is the toughest things I've ever seen, and they ain't a bit sweet."[131]

The wonderful thing was, he seemed dead serious. But you could never quite be sure.[132]

As the years weighed on Bill, he mended fences with Charlie Louvin[133] and others he had had breaks with, just as he had made up with Lester and Earl. Now his thoughts were of Kenny Baker. Bill missed his favorite fiddler but was still angered by his departure. Julia LaBella tried to get him to appreciate Baker's side of things.

"Well, it shouldn't have happened like that," Bill said.[134] "It hurt me. We were together so long, it just shouldn't have happened like that."

But Bill wanted to make things right. As was now his practice, he reached out to Baker through intermediaries, making contact but insulating himself against rejection. He ended up shyly calling Baker, and a visit to the farm was arranged.

A reunion took place in Bill's barn, in a little workshop area where Bill puttered and repaired things. They sat and talked about the finer points of raising chickens and about old times.

That June, at Bean Blossom, it was Vic Gabany's turn to play emissary. He sounded out Kenny about guesting with the Blue Grass Boys. "If that's what the old man wants," Baker replied, "that's what I want."[135]

Monroe casually commented about "an old man backstage that plays the fiddle," and then Baker — like Lester Flatt fourteen years earlier — appeared to an emotional audience response.

"Kenny, it's good to have you out here," Monroe said.

"Bill, I've been waiting for this since 1985," said Baker.

And they again made music together.

Shortly after the reunion with Baker, Monroe saw bluegrass festival impresario Carlton Haney at a show.

"How long's it been since I spoke to you?" Bill asked.[136]

"Twenty-five years next week," Carlton answered, his mind, as ever, a steel trap for places and dates.

"Well, it's time to get that over with, isn't it?" Bill asked.

Carlton had remarried and sired a daughter late in life. Bill gave her a quarter, a custom born of his fond childhood memory of the coins his father gave him during Saturday visits to Rosine. Haney decided to put it aside so this special remembrance wouldn't get mixed up with any other money.

Carlton looked at the date on it. Chills ran through him, and tears filled his eyes.

It had been minted in 1965, the year of Haney's first bluegrass festival. The sacred benchmark of his life.

Monroe was proud to have performed for four consecutive presidents: Jimmy Carter, Ronald Reagan, George Bush, and Bill Clinton. On October 5, 1995, he again visited the White House.[137] On this occasion, he was among the honorees presented by President Clinton with the National Medal of the Arts.

It was the highest honor his country could bestow upon him as a musician, yet it was almost anticlimactic compared to what had happened two weeks earlier.

Bill had visited Rosine on September 21. It was no longer the bustling would-be city of Henry D. McHenry's vision, but for those who remained, there still lived community spirit and music. The old blacksmith shop was now housing the Ole Barn Jamboree. Organizers Hoyt and Eleanor Bratcher had a special event planned for that afternoon, the unveiling of a bronze plaque bearing Bill's likeness to be installed in the barn. The U.S. Navy bluegrass band Country Current performed. Bill was surprisingly shy about playing himself, but a guest saw that his mandolin was brought in from the car. Bill joined the Country Current onstage, performing "Blue Moon of Kentucky" and "Uncle Pen" and dancing a little. It was the last time he would ever entertain in his hometown.

After a meal, Monroe was driven up to Owensboro to attend his first convention of the International Bluegrass Music Association, another fence mended. In the trade show hall, he signed autographs at the Gibson booth sitting next to his friend Earl Scruggs. That evening at the IBMA awards show, when Del McCoury's son Ronnie won for mandolin player of the year, he went right down into the audience and presented his trophy to Bill.

Monroe remained accessible in public, but the tour bus became his refuge, an air-conditioned fortress where he could nap and regroup. When Monroe alighted from this wheeled redoubt, it was an event in itself. He would often find a crowd standing in a hot sun or pouring rain, waiting just to see him. Monroe would take in the sea of eager faces, then smile and sing the first line of his famous composition "Blue moon of Kentucky."[138]

". . . keep on shining!" the crowds would sing back, not missing a beat. And then they would cheer.

"You've got to get me more work," Monroe kept telling Tony Conway.[139] Tony insisted that Bill slow down. After talking to band members and Bill's doctors, Conway gradually began to pull him off the road, finally getting him down to about six appearances a month.

> The one thing I knew about Bill Monroe was that — more than any other entertainer — the one thing in the entire world that brought him out of his sickness or pains or sadness was being onstage. He could be asleep or in terrible pain or barely able to walk. But you let that spotlight hit him and he'd go as far as it was possible for any human being to go. For sixty minutes he could sing and dance and smile and communicate with an audience. . . .
>
> I've seen entertainers go out when they weren't feeling well, go out there and be a professional and get through a show. But I've never seen an entertainer pull up that energy like Bill Monroe.[140]

Julia LaBella says that the cutback in Bill's touring should have come sooner.

If you think about it, he'd been on the road since the 1930s. He was worn out. He was tired. . . .

It was hard for me to see him keep pushing himself. A lot of folks will tell you he loved to get out there and he loved the road. In some ways, he did. But he didn't want to do it at that pace at that stage in his life.[141]

Some nights at the Opry, Bill looked like he might collapse. Once he was taken to the backstage medical room, then rushed to the hospital to receive a massive transfusion.[142] He had been taking too much of his blood-thinning medication and had been bleeding internally.

In late 1995, Skeeter Davis flew into Nashville after a tour of Asia, then hurried to appear on that evening's Opry show. In the performers' area, she came upon an awful scene, Bill Monroe being wheeled out on a stretcher. He had collapsed backstage. Monroe seemed to recognize her as they passed. He weakly raised his hand. Davis turned and caught it and rushed along with him.

I don't know what's happening right now, she silently prayed, but God come into this situation and bring him back. Bring him back and let us be on the stage together next week.[143]

Her prayers, and those of the audience, were answered. The next week, Monroe was again hosting his portion of the Opry with Skeeter Davis as a guest. Afterward, he insisted on buying dinner for Skeeter and her band.

Could he keep bouncing back? The February 1996 issue of *Bluegrass Unlimited* carried an article "With Body and Soul — Notes from Wintergrass '95," which portrayed Monroe as appearing ill and almost senile at a festival in Tacoma, Washington. Writer Daniel Gore was praising the elderly musician for carrying on regardless, his spirit indomitable. But the Blue Grass Boys, Tony Conway, and others protested what they felt was an insensitive depiction of an eighty-four-year-old who was simply exhausted after a two-thousand-mile plane flight.[144] The article sparked the biggest controversy in the magazine's history.

Vic Gabany still had faith that Bill was a viable, even vital artist. He made plans to record a second "Bill Monroe and Friends" album. There were stars enough eager to do it. One was George Jones: The most admired vocalist in country music ranked Bill, Roy Acuff, and Hank Williams as his three idols.

"When you're ready to do it," Jones told Gabany, "just give me two weeks notice and I'll be ready."[145] Vic planned to start work in the spring of 1996.

Meanwhile, keeping Bill's life together had become extraordinarily problematic for Julia LaBella. While playing at the Long Hollow Jamboree or the Belle Cove, Bill would issue friendly invitations to have fans visit him, then be plagued by hangers-on and wannabes demanding Opry passes or tickets to stardom. He was no longer the strong, stern man who could repel undesirables with a stony stare. He was old, ill, vulnerable. Julia and Lincoln Hastings (a Lakota Indian from the Southwest who had been hired to act as Bill's driver and general assistant) would fend off such people.

Once Julia allowed herself the luxury of visiting her mother in Texas. She returned to discover that Bill had befriended a couple with children, hard-luck cases who were now in residence at the farm. She finally got them to leave.

Unlike Lincoln, Julia was not being paid by the Monroe office. She was helping Bill for free, working long evenings as a waitress to support herself. Her relations with James and other Monroe family members were strained to the breaking point. She was accused of either not giving Bill his medications or of overmedicating him. (LaBella says she brought in a home health care nurse to help sort out all of Bill's prescriptions.) When some valuable instruments went missing, her detractors wondered what she knew about them. But Bill had been blithely handing around mandolins for years. (He once told Ralph Rinzler that he owned seven or eight besides his trusty 1923 Gibson but they were "all loaned out.")[146] In an attempt to find them, Julia had Bill's Opry locker opened (he had long since lost the key), and she reported the losses to the police and major instrument dealers.

Julia was weary of the second-guessing, the no-win situations. And as strong as she was, she couldn't bear to see Bill failing. After nearly two years of this, she was at a breaking point, emotionally and physically. In February, she left Bill in Lincoln's care, drove away from the farm, and got on with her life.[147]

* * *

On February 21, 1996, Bill was helped into the Tracking Station Recording Studio in Nashville to play with Billy and Terry Smith.[148] Hazel's sons had grown into accomplished musicians, and their latest CD was a tribute to the man who had been their musical mentor and surrogate father. Bill harmonized adequately on "Walk Softly on This Heart of Mine," the number inspired years earlier by their mother's pointed admonition to Bill during an argument. His lead on "Blue Moon of Kentucky" was leaf shaky, yet the sincerity with which he sang remained tree-trunk sturdy. Out of respect for the man as he was, Billy and Terry decided not to use digital tricks to sweeten up the tracks.[149]

Afterward, Bill, Hazel, and the boys went out to eat. Bill was in high spirits and polished off a huge dessert.[150]

As the merry demi-family celebrated, no one knew that two landmarks had been reached: Almost precisely sixty years earlier, on February 17, 1936, as a member of the Monroe Brothers, Bill had made his first recordings. And now, in the company of the Smith brothers, he had made his last.

Bill played the Friday Night Opry on March 15.[151] He hosted two consecutive fifteen-minute segments, bringing on guests Skeeter Davis, Bill Carlisle, and Del Reeves. In addition to the opening and closing theme of "Watermelon on the Vine," Monroe performed "Down Yonder," a rollicking instrumental that he rarely presented, and "Stay Away from Me." The final vocal he sang was a duet with Tom Ewing on "True Life Blues," a 1940s classic by Blue Grass Boy Pete Pyle in which an unhappy marriage is observed from a neglected wife's point of view.

As was typical now, he ended by playfully fishing for reassurance: "Do you want us to come back and play for you again?" As always happened, the audience warmly confirmed that it did. Bill felt very tired as he left the stage, but was confident that he could return for the Saturday Opry.

The next day he was disoriented. Lincoln rushed him to Baptist Hospital in Nashville. The doctors at first suspected renewed complications from medication or even circulatory problems. The final diagnosis was grimmer — Bill had had a stroke. Further examination led them to believe that he had suffered an earlier stroke in February.[152]

Della Streeter visited him in the hospital. He called her his "sweet blue-eyed darling" and assured her he was not in pain.[153]

Many others came. Skeeter Davis was battling cancer and undergoing debilitating chemotherapy treatments, so a friend, Linda Palmer, visited in her stead. During Palmer's visit, Bill began to weep. He turned his face to the wall to hide his tears. "I didn't know until I was sick that people cared for me as much as they do," he said.[154]

Tony Conway had the famous Lloyd Loar F-5 mandolin for safekeeping. Now he visited Bill in the hospital, put it into his hands, and gave him a pick. Monroe regarded the instrument slowly and strummed it lightly. Suddenly, he kicked into a rousing instrumental that Tony had never heard, evidently a new composition. Then he sang "Blue Moon of Kentucky."

Maybe there was hope after all. Conway brought over a new Gibson F-5L mandolin that the company had given Bill as part of an endorsement deal. He encouraged the hospital personnel to let Bill play it as therapy. When Conway returned with bluegrasser-turned-country star Marty Stuart, Bill was unresponsive. "I know why you can't play that mandolin," Marty said brightly.[155] "You don't have your hat on."

Stuart found Bill's Stetson and carefully placed it on the aged, balding dome. Sure enough, Monroe came to life. He tore into "Wheel Hoss," and Stuart was soon playing a spirited duet with his idol. Then Bill tipped his hat and took a little bow. Just like he'd do onstage.

But Bill's condition deteriorated.[156] As it did, he was moved to Tennessee Christian Medical Center in Madison, to the Northcrest Medical Center in Springfield, and finally to the Beverley Health Care Center, also in Springfield, about twenty-five miles north of Nashville.

"We should all be friends," he had often said in his final years, and now his friends rallied around. Marty Stuart brought Johnny Cash, and the three held hands and prayed. Johnny said, "God, thank you for Bill Monroe."[157] Del McCoury and his sons, Kathy Chiavola and Ginger Boatwright, and many others sang and played for him. He would open his eyes and whisper, "That's fine, that's powerful."[158]

Butch Robins visited. He helped feed his old adversary, comb his hair, and with Lincoln's help gently put him back in bed. Ricky Skaggs comforted Bill. Hazel Smith sang "Jesus Loves Me" to him, and Bill laid his hands flat together, his fingertips touching under his chin, the way he always prayed.[159] "Now when you see that light that's pulling you in," she implored him, "don't you fight it."

Roland White, realizing how weak Bill was becoming, would ask questions that could be answered with a nod or simple facial expression.

"This is a new place," Roland said during one visit.[160]

That elicited a small smile from Monroe.

"Looks nice."

Another small smile.

"Got some pretty nurses here."

Big smile.

Tater and Lois Tate visited. Lois finally got Bill to understand who they were. He looked up and said, "You're still with me."[161]

Mac Wiseman and Opry singer Johnny Russell were saddened by what they found. Monroe seemed shrunken, unconscious. The nurses urged Wiseman to stimulate Bill's mind by talking to him. Mac asked, "Bill, do you know who this is?"

Monroe stirred slightly, then his lips silently formed the name "Mac Wiseman."[162] The genial voice that had attracted Monroe's attention over WCYB nearly a half century earlier attracted it one last time.

Billy and Terry Smith looked upon this once-powerful man with grief and frustration. "You're Bill Monroe!"[163] Billy commanded, cajoled, pleaded. "You're strong. I want you to get up out of this bed!"

For a moment, Bill's entire body seemed to pump up, his chest again assuming a barrel shape. The moment passed. Bill slowly relaxed and sank back within himself.

Jimmy Martin was at Bean Blossom for the September festival. James Monroe asked if he'd like to visit Bill in the nursing home.[164]

"Do you reckon he'd want me to, James?" said Martin, still stung by Bill's slights over the years.

"Now don't talk like that," said the younger Monroe. "You know good and well he'd like to see you. I'll set up a time and come and get you. I'd like to just see you shake his hand and tell him who you are and see if he'd know your voice. He doesn't know me now."

The opportunity never came. At 1:20 P.M. on Monday, September 9, 1996, at the Northcrest Medical Center, the great heart stopped.[165] The headline of the *New York Times* obituary, "Bill Monroe Dies," seemed like an oxymoron. It was all the more surprising because surely his iron willpower would have driven him to appear at his eighty-fifth birthday, a mere four days away, just a brief jump on the great tour of life.

He had been six almost totally different people: the cross-eyed, lonely child; the strong young man; the confident, occasionally arrogant star; the embittered and withdrawn has-been; the triumphant senior statesman of bluegrass; the beloved living legend of country.

He had not made the specific impacts of a Louis Armstrong, a George Gershwin, a Hank Williams, or an Elvis Presley, but he deserved to be ranked with any of them. In a multifaceted, trend-setting career, he had truly become the most broadly talented and broadly influential figure in American popular music history. He had been much more than the Father of Bluegrass: He had been an uncle to country music, a first cousin to the folk revival, and a grandfather to rock 'n' roll.[166]

He had been a forward-looking innovator, in truth a rebel, who had broken the rules and created an entirely new paradigm. Yet most of his music had been inspired by bygone places and events. He had been full of the blues but not depressed. Unhurried, he had a ferocious work ethic. He wanted to be the focus of attention, yet enjoyed sharing the spotlight. He had been cantankerous and eager to mend fences, a tyrannical taskmaster and a kindly instructor, a hurtful trickster and a Christian gentleman. He often seemed inaccessible, yet he inspired lifelong devotion. Compulsive in love, he retained certain strict moral boundaries. He made such an impression that people never forgot what he said to them; yet at times even his closest friends couldn't tell if he was serious or joking. He had felt himself to be an outsider, yet he had been at the center of so many people's universe. Fans had never met anyone remotely like him, yet they totally resonated with his music.

He was every inch a man. And yet, in both his hurts and his enthusiasms, he had never ceased being a little boy.

He had been all that talent and all those massive contradictions. He had been Bill Monroe.

*   *   *

What could have been going on in that inscrutable mind as consciousness ebbed away? Actually, we may have good reason to know.

During one of singer-songwriter John Hartford's visits to Bill in the hospital, the elderly musician had beckoned him close.

"This would be a good one for you, John," Monroe murmured. Then his lips moved and a melody issued forth.

"He was pitching me a song that he'd been writing lying there in bed," Hartford marvels.[167] "Right to the end, he was working."

✴ EPILOGUE ✴

Bill's viewing was held at the Madison Funeral Home. James and his son James II ("Jimbo") received condolences from Johnny Cash, Carl Smith, Jimmy Martin, Kitty Wells and her husband Johnny Wright, and many others.[1] The famous and the obscure, colleagues and neighbors and fans; all came to pay their respects. Earl and Louise Scruggs solemnly viewed Bill. Then they joined a group that had coalesced on one side, including musicians Ralph Stanley, Sonny Osborne, Larry Stephenson, and Glen Duncan as well as *Bluegrass Unlimited* general manager Pete Kuykendall.

Suddenly, Osborne hushed the conversations and pointed to the ceiling. "Listen to this," he said.

WSM was being piped into the funeral home. The station had been playing nothing but Monroe since Bill's passing. Now deejay and Opry announcer Eddie Stubbs was introducing "Heavy Traffic Ahead," the first song cut at the first recording session of the classic 1946–1948 Blue Grass Boys.

There stood Earl Scruggs, the last survivor from that session, and a collection of people whose lives had been forever changed by this music. The tinny speakers mounted in the ceiling of the funeral home gave the effect of a Grand Ole Opry broadcast coming over a little home radio on an evening long past. It was so eerie, and it was so right.

As Bill's music was drifting over the hushed gathering in Madison, other performers were canceling shows and hurrying back to Nashville for a service to be held at the Ryman Auditorium. Some arrived only just in time.

When the Ryman's doors were opened at 8:30 A.M. on September 11, people were already standing in line to be assured of a seat.[2] CDs of classic 1950s Monroe recordings played as mourners filed past an open silver-blue casket surrounded by floral arrangements. Bill's hat and glasses lay nearby. A studio portrait by photographer Jim McGuire, showing Monroe tenderly embracing his mandolin, stood at the head of the coffin.

Seated in the front row were James, Jimbo, and Bill's sister Bertha, the beloved "Berthie" who had played with him when their other siblings would not. Now a frail eighty-eight-year-old woman, supported by her niece Rosetta Monroe Kiper, Speed's daughter, the last of Malissa and James Buchanan Monroe's children wept for brother Willie. Peers, many dear friends (including Virginia Stauffer, Hazel Smith, Julia LaBella, and Della Streeter), fans, and the news media looked on.

Bill's recording of "My Last Days on Earth" was played to open the service. He had wanted "Wayfaring Stranger" sung at his funeral, just as he had performed it for Ralph Rinzler, his brother Speed, and so many others. Emmylou Harris did the honors, beautifully, backed by Ricky Skaggs, Marty Stuart, Vince Gill, and fiddler Stuart Duncan and bassist Roy Huskey Jr. Also performing were Ralph Stanley, Alison Krauss, and Patty Loveless.

Although exhausted by an all-night trip, Connie Smith took the stage and delivered a rendition of "How Great Thou Art" that was nothing less than a masterpiece, a sweet spot in spiritual time that stunned the assemblage and forced them to give out with thunderous applause, breaking the sorrowful silence. The Nashville Pipes marched in playing "Amazing Grace," bagpipes for this scion of Scotland.

It was so lovely and so solemn. Too solemn. Backstage, on the spur of the moment, Marty Stuart suggested they pick "Raw Hide."[3] Emmylou Harris smiled and said, "Do it." Ricky Skaggs grinned and said, "Well, why not?"

The musicians came out and tore into Bill's tour de force. The crowd went happily crazy. But it was also the moment when the most stoic attendees finally lost composure and cried.[4] The pride and the power, the attitude and the arrogance, the sheer vitality that had been Bill Monroe — all were invoked by that masterpiece.

"Take it, Bill!" Skaggs exclaimed as the top of the music came around a last time. The audience laughed appreciatively. It was as if really he could.

As the mourners had passed Bill's open casket, someone placed a quarter in the coffin in tribute to all the quarters Bill had given children over the years. By the time the service began, the back of the casket was lined with the coins. James Monroe asked the pastor to distribute them among children at the funeral and the rest to be used for charity. They became the last quarters given out by his father.[5]

Still, Bill didn't go to his grave without a remembrance of his custom. Skeeter Davis went up to say goodbye just before the lid was closed and slipped one last quarter into Mr. Bill's shirt pocket.[6] He was buried with it.

If the Ryman service had been mostly about the younger Nashville performers, the burial in Rosine the next day was about the old-timers and neighbors. What was so noticeable was the sadness and the expanding silence that enveloped the Rosine Methodist Church.[7] It was just like the aftermath of Malissa Vandiver Monroe's funeral, when little Bill had experienced his home as "silent and so sad."

More than a thousand people attended the final rites. James had a sound system set up to allow the huge overflow to hear what was taking place inside the church. Ricky Skaggs opened the service with an a cappella rendition of "Amazing Grace." From the back, a woman with a lovely, strong voice joined in. Most of the congregation did, too.

Ricky thanked James for sharing his father with the world. Alma Randolph, a black resident of Ohio County, sang the Reverend Thomas Dorsey classic "Take My Hand Precious Lord." African-American music accompanied Bill in death as it had in life, another circle closed.

Del McCoury, Wayne Lewis, Bobby Osborne, and other musicians performed or offered a few words. James Monroe spoke about his father and thanked the performers, "some of the best in the country," for coming to honor his daddy. Just before the coffin lid was closed, Lewis slipped a flatpick into Bill's hand.[8] Then William Smith Monroe was carried to the little lonesome graveyard to join his kin.

Bill's lonesomeness had been reinforced by his very longevity, surviving while so many others had passed on. Not only his brothers Charlie and Birch, and the rest of his immediate family except Bertha. Not only Carolyn and Melissa. Not only Elvis Presley. Not only Bessie Lee Mauldin and his rival Nelson Gann. Not only Ralph Rinzler. Not only Carter Stanley, Edd Mayfield, and Lester Flatt, but most of the earliest Blue Grass Boys: Cleo Davis (who had died in 1986); Art Wooten (1986); Tommy Magness (1971); Clyde Moody (1989); Stringbean (1973); Howdy Forrester (1987); Chubby Wise (1996); Don Reno (1984); Rudy Lyle (1985); Red Taylor (1987); Joe Stuart (1987); and far too many others. And he had outlived many of his major Opry peers: Not only Hank Williams, but Uncle Dave Macon (1952), Ira Louvin (1965), DeFord Bailey (1982), Ernest Tubb (1984), Roy Acuff (1992), and Minnie Pearl (1996).

He had attended most of their funerals. Now it was time for his. The heavens clouded then gave way to a sunny autumn afternoon. Ricky Skaggs and Ralph Stanley sang a cappella at the graveside. Ralph gave a poignant rendition of "Swing Low, Sweet Chariot," then placed his hand on the casket and said, "We'll meet again" — exactly as Bill had done at Carter's burial.

Bill's last will and testament, which he had signed July 17, 1991, named James as his personal representative and sole heir.[9] Article Five read: "If it shall be proved in any Court of law with appropriate jurisdiction that I have any children other than my son James William Monroe, then I direct that any such child shall inherit the sum of one dollar as that child's share of my estate." Even if this unusual clause was not a tacit admission of the existence of the Little Georgia Rose, it certainly protected the estate against claims by any illegitimate children that Bill might have fathered.

*   *   *

Lincoln Hastings died about two months after Bill.[10] He had been Bill's utterly devoted servant, waiting on him hand and foot, watching him with deepening concern as he weakened, and finally whisking him off to the hospital during the final crisis. All this Lincoln had done while dying of liver cancer.

On April 1, 1997, Bertha passed away. Her funeral and headstone cost about $5,000, a fortune to niece Rosetta Kiper with whom she had been living. James paid for it.[11]

James acted with additional sensitivity in the weeks and months following his daddy's death. He distributed items to Bill's friends. A necktie here, a sign or poster there. The small items meant so much.[12]

The monument over Bill's grave was dedicated on April 25, 1997.[13] Its twenty-foot-high obelisk was carved from a single twenty-ton block of granite, white like Bill's hat. An all-star benefit concert at the Ryman had helped pay for the $80,000 marker.[14] Etched on it was an image of Bill with his dog Stormy that had been used on the cover of the album *Bluegrass '87*. Covering Bill's grave was a horizontal stone slab inscribed with the story of Bill's life as written by James. The inscription concluded: "Walk softly around this grave for my father Bill Monroe rests here as the blue moon of Kentucky shines on."

Bill had said this about his childhood:

> For many years, I had nobody to play with or nobody to work under. You just had to kindly grow up. Just like a little dog outside, tryin' to make his own way, trying to make out the best way he can.[15]

During Bertha's funeral, from out of nowhere, a little dark-haired puppy came walking across the cemetery. It ambled slowly but in a definite direction — toward Bill's grave.

Then, in front of everyone, the tiny animal, all big eyes and soft fur and innocence, lay down and curled up on the last resting place of the lonesome little boy from Jerusalem Ridge.[16]

✶ NOTES ✶

To differentiate between oral and published sources (since some interviewees have also written cited books or articles), interview sources are given by name only and published sources by years (or, in the case of multipart articles, by months and years). Multiple interviews or multiple publications within a year are differentiated by the appellations [B], [C], etc. (See Bibliography for complete information.)

All interviews were conducted by the author unless otherwise noted. Interviews with Bill Monroe by Ralph Rinzler are given as "Monroe via Rinzler" followed by the tape's Smithsonian Folklife file number. (See Bibliography for information, as known, on these interviews.)

Monroe Brothers recording session information comes from McKuen 1967 and Rust 1970. Data on Blue Grass Boys sessions from 1940 to 1974 from Rosenberg 1974; 1974–1985 from American Federation of Musicians of the United States and Canada, Local Union 257, session sheets for Decca Records ("Bill Monroe 1970s" file), archives of Country Music Foundation, Nashville, Tennessee; and 1985–1996 from the database "Bill Monroe Recordings, Complete Chronology 1981–1996" compiled by Neil V. Rosenberg (Rosenberg February 19, 1999). These will not be individually cited except in the case of annotations from these sources.

Information on *Billboard* chart positions of recordings by Monroe and other artists is primarily from Whitburn 1996 or Whitburn 1997 and in general will not be individually cited.

Abbreviations:

BUF: *Bluegrass Unlimited* magazine files, Warrenton, Virginia

CMFA: Country Music Foundation archives, Nashville, Tennessee

SFA: Archives of the Smithsonian Institution Center for Folklife Programs and Cultural Studies, Washington, DC

TSA: Tennessee State Archives, Nashville, Tennessee

CHAPTER ONE: BLUE MOON OF KENTUCKY RISING
(THE BEGINNINGS TO 1929)

Principal information about Ohio County, Rosine, and the Monroe family was obtained during the preparation of R. D. Smith 1996 and R.D. Smith 1997. Additional information was gathered during subsequent visits to Ohio County in 1997 and 1998; from personal communications by regional historians Wendell Allen, Jerry Long, and Harry D. Tinsley; and from J. Monroe October 1971 and D. Green January 1973.

1. R. Schumer.

2. H. Smith.

3. Rooney 1971, pp. 80–81; Rinzler 1975.

4. Monroe via Rinzler FP-1993-CT-0520.

5. J. Penny.

6. Throughout the book, "old-time" music is taken to be rural southern music that has close connections to British Isles traditions, is performed primarily with stringed instruments, and became established prior to the recording and radio eras. Of course, much old-time music carried over into the mass media age, but this broad definition helps differentiate old-time music from later forms, such as bluegrass and country.

7. Battle, et al., 1885.

8. Copy in J. B. Monroe papers, private collection.

9. Rinzler 1975.

10. Ohio County, Kentucky, Circuit Court Records, Equity File 3966, Case 2503 (Ohio County Library, Hartford, KY, Microfilm Box 37).

11. U.S. census of 1900, Rosine Precinct, Ohio County, Kentucky.

12. Bartley, et al.

13. Ohio County Deed Book 27, p. 252. Although a deed search has proven inconclusive, it is likely that this parcel was part of John Monroe's original Ohio County holdings.

14. Rinzler 1963.

15. Specific information from James Buchanan Monroe's ledger books encompassing the years 1904–1908 (marked "1904/1905/1906") and 1910–1923 (both SFA); and the years 1899, 1908, 1911–1912, 1914, and 1916 (private collection).

16. Bill later created a scorching variation on the traditional fiddle tune "Katy Hill" and named it "Tall Timber" in honor of the old, valuable wood (Rinzler 1965).

17. For Vandiver family history, see Lindeman 1975 and L. C. Anderson (undated).

18. The *Hartford Herald* of August 3, 1892, noted that the couple was "united in the holy bonds of matrimony at the bride's home near Horton yesterday."

19. Foster 1969/70.

20. Ohio County deeds, passim, with indicating marks in place of signatures for Malissa Monroe and Pen Vandiver; also, Malissa's listing in the 1900 census gives "no" for reads, "no" for writes, and "yes" for speaks English. This may explain the many spelling variations on Malissa's name in official records: She pronounced it to census takers and clerks, who spelled it as best they could. The author has opted for the spelling used by her family in the *Hartford Herald* wedding announcement and on her headstone.

21. Bill revealed this to band member Glen Duncan.

22. F. J. Harvey.

23. Rinzler 1975.

24. Kiper, May 14, 1997. The story of Buck swimming the Green River is well known to his and Malissa's descendants.

25. Birth years for the Monroes from their headstones in the Rosine cemetery and other standard genealogical sources. Census records show that the year 1890 carved on Harry's headstone is incorrect and should be 1893.

26. Kiper, May 14, 1997.

27. Bill Monroe biography sheet, Buddy Lee Attractions, Nashville.

28. J. B. Monroe 1911 record book, private collection.

29. D. Green January 1973.

30. G. Ruby. Goldie Ruby's mother was the visitor.

31. J. B. Monroe 1911 record book, private collection.

32. Liner notes to album *Bill Monroe: The Father of Bluegrass,* RCA Camden CAL 719.

33. R. Schumer.

34. H. Smith.

35. Foster 1969/70; Monroe via Rinzler FP-1993-CT-0520.

36. D. Green January 1973.

37. Foster 1969/70; Monroe via Rinzler FP-1993-CT-0520.

38. H. Smith.

39. Sulloway 1996, passim.

40. Monroe via Rinzler FP-1993-CT-0250. Bill recalled the midwife's name as Mandy Stuart (handwritten note, collection of John Hartford).

41. B. and P. Logan.

42. J. Monroe October 1971.

43. L. and S. Allen.

44. R. D. Smith 1997.

45. Kiper/Kurtz.

46. H. Smith.

47. J. Monroe October 1971.

48. Bill spoke to Doc Watson about childhood episodes of abuse, but Watson declines to discuss them. The specific episodes involving a sibling's alcohol use were told by Monroe to band member Butch Robins.

49. Battle, et al., 1885. However, the Vandivers had a reputation for rowdiness, and perhaps there was more alcohol use on that side of the family.

50. For example, J. B. recorded purchasing whiskey for $1.75 from Riley Hunt on September 9, 1911 (record book, private collection).

51. Wolmuth 1986.

52. H. Smith.

53. Information on Pen Vandiver from W. Allen 1974; S. Crowder June 1993; Foster 1969/70; D. Green January 1973; and Ohio County marriage and realty records.

54. For example, page 177 of the J. B. Monroe ledger book marked "1904–1906" (SFA) lists payments to Pen Vandiver in 1907. Pen worked in his brother-in-law's top wage bracket, a dollar a day.

55. Monroe via Rinzler FP-1993-CT-0262.

56. McNulty 1992.

57. Wolfe 1975.

58. Reminiscences by the Monroe brothers of Uncle Pen and the Vandiver family are found on the final track of *Bill Monroe & His Blue Grass Boys: Live Recordings 1956–1969*, Smithsonian/Folkways SF CD 40063.

59. Monroe via Rinzler FP-1993-CT-0262.

60. Foster 1969/70.

61. Rinzler 1975.

62. Monroe via Rinzler FP-1993-CT-0262.

63. Green January 1973.

64. J. Monroe November 1971.

65. Lawrence 1987.

66. J. Monroe November 1971.

67. Kentucky Vital Records, death certificate; Kiper/Kurtz.

68. Tinsley; Monroe via Rinzler FP-1994-CT-0520.

69. The author has reached this conclusion through interviews with Hayward F. Spinks (current owner of the old Monroe property) and Ohio County historian Harry D. Tinsley plus an examination of J. B. Monroe's ledger book for this period.

70. Kiper/Kurtz.

71. Streeter.

72. This was another childhood memory Bill shared with fiddler Glen Duncan.

73. H. Smith.

74. J. Monroe October 1971.

75. Robins Hubert Stringfield: Rinzler 1975.

76. Bill Monroe, personal communication to the author, 1970.

77. Hurst 1972. Later, while working in Chicago, Bill bought a mandolin for forty dollars (Rooney 1971, p. 26). This was a sizable investment in an instrument in those days, so perhaps it was the Gibson F-7 that he used in the Monroe Brothers, purchased used.

78. Rinzler 1975.

79. See Marini 1989, passim.

80. Wolfe 1975.

81. Rinzler 1975.

82. J. Monroe October 1971.

83. J. Monroe October 1971; Hume 1976. For more on hill foxhunting, see Mitchell 1973.

84. Rooney 1971, p. 56.

85. Green January 1973; Charlie Monroe, personal communication, 1972; L. and S. Allen.

86. H. Smith 1997; Monroe via Rinzler FP-1993-CT-0262.

87. Lawrence 1980; McNulty Crowder 1993; and Lightfoot 1980.

88. Lawrence 1980.

89. Allen 1974; Ruby; and Hines.

90. Rooney 1971, p. 24.

91. Rooney 1971, p. 23.

92. Rooney 1971, p. 24.

93. Taylor.

94. W. Allen [B].

95. Green January 1973; Tribe 1975.

96. Green January 1973.

97. McCoury.

98. Respiratory ailments plagued the Monroes. Maude was hospitalized for a time at the Hazelwood tuberculosis sanatorium in Louisville (August 16, 1919, entry, J. B. Monroe ledger book, SFA; Kiper [B]), and Birch nearly died of pneumonia when he was a teenager (Monroe via Rinzler FP-1993-CT-0250).

99. J. Monroe November 1971.

100. J. Monroe November 1971.

101. Monroe via Rinzler FP-1993-CT-0250.

102. Ruby.

103. McNulty Crowder 1993.

104. J. Monroe October 1971. Even J. B. Monroe had not been immune to his brother-in-law's wheelings and dealings, as witness a July 8, 1923, ledger book notation: "Pen Vandiver in Hors Trade 25.00" (SFA).

105. J. Monroe November 1971.

106. Foster 1969/70; Bill Monroe, liner notes to the album *Bill Monroe's Uncle Pen* Decca DL 75348; Hume 1976; H. Smith.

107. Foster 1969/70.

108. Wolfe 1975; Ruby.

109. H. Smith.

110. Abramson 1980.

111. Monroe via Rinzler FP-1993-CT-0250.

CHAPTER TWO: THE BIG CITY, THE BIG COUNTRY (1929 TO 1938)

Primary information about the Monroes in the Chicago area and the subsequent Monroe Brothers act comes from D. Green February 1973; Monroe via Rinzler FP-RINZ-RR-0006; Rinzler 1975; Hurst 1977; J. Monroe November 1971; Wolfe 1975; Wolfe 1996[B]; and Wolfe 1998. These sources occasionally give different details but are in general agreement as to events and chronology.

1. W. Davison.

2. Garkovich 1989, p. 104.

3. Garkovich 1989, pp. 105–106.

4. Monroe in the documentary *High Lonesome: The Story of Bluegrass Music*, Shanachie 604.

5. Green February 1973.

6. Davison.

7. Hurst 1977; Davison.

8. H. Smith.

9. R. Schumer.

10. Krishef 1978, p. 8.

11. H. Smith.

12. H. Smith.

13. G. Monroe/Allen; "Pneumonie fever" also claimed Pen's son Cecil when he was only a teenager (McNulty 1992).

14. Foster 1969/70.

15. Lawrence 1980. Despite heart disease being the likely cause of death, some of Shultz's friends insisted on a scenario like that attached to legendary blues man Robert Johnson — that Arnold had been poisoned by jealous rivals.

16. D. Green February 1973.

17. Tribe 1975.

18. Corbin 1970; Hurst 1984. Another source (Case 1945) gives the Hammond station as WIND.

19. D. Green February 1973.

20. Monroe via Rinzler FP-RINZ-0006.

21. Bruce 1979B.

22. Photocopy of cast photo, BUF.

23. Bill said that on his mandolin break for "Sinner You Better Get Ready" he was specifically "trying to copy colored folks" (Monroe via Rinzler FP-RINZ-RR-0006). In particular, the bluesy minor third to major third slide became a hallmark of Monroe's style.

24. Monroe via Rinzler FP-1993-CT-0262.

25. In fact, it forced him to develop his quick, accurate falsetto style. "That's the truth," Bill later told interviewer Ralph Rinzler (Monroe via Rinzler FP-RINZ-RR-0004).

26. B. Price [B].

27. Davidson Co. No. 34918; grave marker, Monroe family plot, Spring Hill Cemetery, Nashville.

28. J. Monroe November 1971.

29. *Bluegrass Star* magazine, November 1971, p. 7, photo "Carolyn, Bill and Melissa, 1937."

30. LeRoy.

31. Kuykendall.

32. H. Smith.

33. D. Green February 1973.

34. Rosenberg 1985, p. 31; Scruggs 1974.

35. D. Green February 1973.

36. Lester Flatt via Marty Stuart in the documentary *Bill Monroe — The Father of Bluegrass*, Original Cinema OC-10013.

37. Bill Monroe via Skaggs in *Bill Monroe — The Father of Bluegrass*, Original Cinema OC-10013.

38. D. Green February 1973.

39. D. Green February 1973.

40. Rosenberg 1985, p. 31.

41. J. Monroe November 1971.

42. Official and family records confirm that Carolyn was pregnant with Melissa prior to her marriage with Bill. Melissa Kathleen Monroe's birthdate is given on her birth certificate as September 17, 1936 (North Carolina State Board of Health, Bureau of Vital Statistics, Mecklenburg County, Certificate No. 1419; Melissa was registered as a nonresident birth at Presbyterian Hospital in Charlotte, her parents residing at 312 Butler Avenue in Greenville, South Carolina). This date is also given on her funeral service program (Madison Funeral Home Chapel, December 5, 1990, BUF) and her obituary in *Bluegrass Unlimited* (January 1991, p. 14). A September 14, 1936, birthdate was listed by her brother James for her death certificate (Tennessee Department of Health, Verification of Death Facts), but the three-day difference is

not significant given the agreement on year. Bill and Carolyn's wedding date of October 18, 1936, is recorded both on their marriage license (Spartanburg County, South Carolina, Marriage License Book T, p. 591) and in Carolyn's divorce petition (*Monroe vs. Monroe*, Davidson County, Tennessee, No. 34918).

43. Hartford [C]; H. Smith; Forrester; Kuykendall.

44. Rosine, Kentucky, cemetery headstone; Wendell Allen [E].

45. Garkovitch 1989, p. 107.

46. D. Green February 1973; Rinzler 1975.

47. D. Green February 1973.

48. McKuen 1967.

49. Rust 1970.

50. *Bluegrass Unlimited*, March 1982, p. 7.

51. J. Monroe November 1971; Scott.

52. Monroe via Rinzler FP-1993-CT-0262.

53. D. Green February 1973.

54. Scott.

55. Scott.

56. D. Green February 1973.

57. Scott.

58. Scott.

59. Rosenberg 1985, p. 35.

60. D. Green March 1973.

61. Charlie Monroe, personal communication, 1972; Bill also specifically denied the rumors that they had broken up over a woman (Nash 1988, pp. 350–351).

62. Rooney 1971, p. 32.

63. Nash 1988, p. 350.

64. D. Green February 1973.

CHAPTER THREE: HIS OWN MAN (1938 TO 1945)

Primary information about the hiring of Cleo Davis and the formation of the Blue Grass Boys comes from Erbsen February and March 1982. Additional information about Bill's first bands via Rooney 1971, J. Monroe December 1971, and Rinzler 1975.

1. Scott.

2. Scott.

3. J. Monroe December 1971.

4. J. Monroe December 1971.

5. Burrison 1977, passim. Monroe was a great admirer of the Skillet Lickers and McMichen. Their uses of multiple fiddles played in harmony obviously influenced his further development of this sound.

6. Krishef 1978, p. 8.

7. Erbsen February 1982.

8. Erbsen February 1982; J. Monroe December 1971.

9. Erbsen March 1982.

10. Erbsen March 1982.

11. Erbsen March 1982; J. Monroe December 1971.

12. Monroe, personal communication, 1970. Bill also commented that it "gave me confidence that I could handle a solo number" (Monroe via Rinzler FP-RINZ-RR-0004).

13. Wolfe 1975.

14. Hume 1976.

15. These then-unusual keys also demanded increased virtuosity from musicians, especially fiddlers, helping to raise standards of technique in country music.

16. Seckler. For a history of WSM and the Opry, see Krishef 1978, p. 6, and Hagen 1989, p. 5. Additional information from Stubbs and Stubbs [C/D].

17. Hagen 1989, pp. 8–9. There had been earlier presentations of old-time music on WSM, but Thompson's appearance led to its regular presentation and the subsequent *Opry* show.

18. Hagen 1989, pp. 24–25.

19. Seckler.

20. Erbsen March 1982.

21. Hagen 1989, p. 51.

22. Nash 1988, p. 334.

23. Hay 1945, p. 52.

24. Erbsen April 1982. Here the recollections of Cleo Davis and Bill Monroe differ. Monroe later spoke of encoring on "Mule Skinner," but Davis recalled that it was the overall performance that prompted an encore, for which the band dipped into its repertoire for another uptempo number.

25. Seckler.

26. Scott.

27. Williams via Stubbs.

28. Seckler.

29. Hartford [C].

30. Ellis.

31. LeRoy.

32. Erbsen March 1982.

33. Stubbs [C].

34. This collection of Monroe's personality and physical traits is gleaned from interviews, published sources, and the author's own recollections.

35. Nash 1988, p. 353.

36. J. Monroe December 1971.

37. Erbsen March 1982.

38. North Carolina State Board of Health, birth certificate; *Mauldin Monroe vs. Monroe* 1975, Davidson Co. No. A-5787. Information about the Mauldin family from E. and H. Mauldin; L. Mauldin; S. and V. Mauldin.

39. L. Mauldin.

40. Forrester; Kuykendall; Streeter.

41. *Mauldin Monroe vs. Monroe* 1975, Davidson Co. No. A-5787.

42. L. Mauldin; *Mauldin Monroe vs. Monroe* 1975, Davidson Co. No. A-5787.

43. *Monroe vs. Monroe* 1959, Davidson Co. No. 34918; *Mauldin Monroe vs. Monroe* 1975, Davidson Co. A-5787.

44. Hartford [C]; Forrester.

45. Hartford [C].

46. Forrester.

47. *Monroe vs. Monroe* 1959, Davidson Co. No. 34918.

48. Hurst 1975, p. 94 and p. 341; Krishef 1978, pp. 48–49.

49. Ryman Auditorium program displays.

50. Rooney 1971, p. 36; James Monroe December 1971.

51. Shumate.

52. Shumate.

53. Rooney 1971, p. 36.

54. Rhodes 1978.

55. Shumate.

56. Shumate.

57. J. Monroe December 1971; Wiseman.

58. Hartford [C].

59. Rinzler 1969.

60. Scott; additional remembrances of the tent show from Kiper [B].

61. Robins; R. Greene.

62. The Bailey story is given in Rooney 1971, pp. 36–37.

63. Wolfe 1982.

64. Monroe picture file, SFA.

65. Information on the five-string banjo's history from Tony Trischka (personal communications) and B. Keith.

66. Wolfe 1982.

67. Forrester.

68. Rinzler 1975.

69. Sally Ann Forrester sang high harmony on "Nobody Loves Me" and "Come Back to Me in My Dreams," two bouncy but wistful trios waxed by Monroe on February 13, 1945. "Put Me in Your Pocket," a wartime song about a soldier carrying his

sweetheart's picture, became her most requested number on the Opry, although it was never recorded (Forrester).

70. Forrester.

71. Forrester.

72. Davidson County, Tennessee, Deed Book 1258, p. 168.

73. Hay 1945, p. 52.

74. There is an ongoing debate as to when Monroe actually acquired his now-famous mandolin. Bill himself recalled different years during different interviews. The auditory evidence leaves little question, however, that it is the mandolin he played on his first Columbia session on February 13, 1945. The author takes the view of vintage instrument expert Tony Williamson on the October 1943 time period.

75. From Lloyd Loar mandolin database compiled by Tom Isenhour.

76. *Country Music*, January 1986, p. 19; Williamson. In interviews, Bill variously recalled the price as $125 and $150.

77. History of the mandolin and other fretted instruments in American folk/country music via Gruhn, Isenhour, and Williamson.

78. Wolfe 1975.

79. Rosenberg 1974 errs in giving the setting as Castle Studios in Nashville. Later research by Eddie Stubbs has revealed the Chicago locale.

80. Rooney 1971, p. 36.

81. Wiseman.

82. The song was not an original, however, having been brought into the band's repertoire by Dave "Stringbean" Akeman (Monroe via Rinzler FP-RINZ-7RR-0002).

83. Data on Nelson Gann and his family from State of Tennessee Bureau of Vital Statistics, birth certificate of Nelson Campbell Gann; U.S. Census, for Lebanon, Tennessee, 1920; Smith County, Tennessee, Cemeteries, Volume 1, p. 68 (Microfilm Roll A-6155, TSA); and Nashville city directories, TSA.

84. Even Bessie's sisters Stella and Virginia are unsure.

85. S. and V. Mauldin.

86. Rosenberg; S. and V. Mauldin.

87. Horstman 1986, p. 151.

88. Rao 1999.

89. Shumate.

90. Shumate.

91. Biographical information on Lester Flatt from Rhodes 1979; Lambert/Seckler 1982, passim; and Gladys Flatt.

92. G. Flatt.

93. Rhodes 1979.

94. H. Smith; Haney.

95. Rhodes 1979.

96. Biographical information on Don Reno from Wernick 1967, and D. and R. Reno.

97. Shumate.

CHAPTER FOUR: BLUEGRASS (1945 TO 1953)

1. Rhodes 1979.

2. Scruggs via D. Green 1974; Shumate.

3. Rhodes 1979.

4. Scruggs via D. Green 1974.

5. Scruggs via D. Green 1974.

6. Biographical material on Scruggs, including his early music experiences, from Scruggs via D. Green 1974; Rosenberg 1991; and Rosenberg 1998[A].

7. Scruggs via D. Green 1974.

8. French 1967.

9. Tape of Opry broadcast circa 1946.

10. Tape of Opry broadcast circa 1946.

11. Rhodes 1979.

12. Bush.

13. Scruggs via D. Green 1974.

14. Hartford [D]; Kuykendall.

15. Kuykendall, personal communication, February 1999. Watts would later become a member of Hank Williams's Drifting Cowboys.

16. Eddie Stubbs [C].

17. The commonalities have long been noted by master bluegrass vocalists. As Peter Rowan has put it, "To me, bluegrass singing is like fiddle playing . . . short bursts of a few notes and then a long held out thing" (Wernick 1976, p. 16).

18. G. Duncan.

19. A typographic error in Rosenberg 1974 has rendered the earlier date as October 2.

20. A Rosine sharecropper family used to sing it, including some extra verses Bill did not perform (Monroe via Rinzler FP-RINZ-RR-0006).

21. O'Brien.

22. Biographical information from John Wright 1993; Reid 1998; and Ralph Stanley.

23. Stubbs [D].

24. Stanley.

25. Garkovich 1989, p. 97. For an analysis of bluegrass as a reinvention of old-time string band music for transplanted southerners, see Cantwell 1984, passim.

26. Live tape of Opry program circa 1946.

27. Rinzler 1975.

28. Stubbs.

29. Gabany.

30. Helm/Davis 1993.

31. Watson.

32. Stubbs [D].

33. Grand Ole Opry member and former disk jockey Charlie Walker remembers "Footprints in the Snow" being a particularly popular record in his native Texas.

34. Rosenberg 1974, p. 42.

35. R. Kiper [C].

36. The story of the writing of "I Hear a Sweet Voice Calling" via Rosetta Monroe Kiper, who was there at the time.

37. Mrs. Kiper also remembers well the writing of "The Little Girl and the Dreadful Snake." Kiper [C].

38. For example, an analysis (Childrey 1990) of images and metaphors in Monroe's music considers his version of "Little Joe" but overlooks the wealth of songs about dying or injured children in Bill's repertoire. Another analysis (Ayers 1975) totally misses this genre of Monroe song. (Ayers even fails to recognize Monroe's "true songs" about love affairs as a true category, putting "Used to Be" under "Home, Past, Rural Oriented Titles" and completely omitting any discussion of "Can't You Hear Me Callin'," "On and On," "Letter from My Darling," et al.)

39. B. Robins.

40. H. Smith; Hartford [C].

41. These memories of the farm and Bill's tours from Kiper [B].

42. G. Flatt.

43. G. Flatt.

44. G. Flatt.

45. Keith.

46. Polk's Nashville City Directory, 1947 and 1948; Fite via Schott; and Schott.

47. Martin. When asked about the writing of "Along About Daybreak," Monroe once replied, "Well, there's a true story behind that song, but it don't need to be printed." (Humphrey 1992, p. 29) But Bill related it to Jimmy Martin and its importance is obvious: Not only is this powerful number likely the first autobiographical composition Monroe ever recorded, its construction — stark and bluesy, with heavy use of the pentatonic scale — strongly indicates that it was created independently of Bill's more mellifluous collaborations with Lester Flatt.

48. Kuykendall.

49. Lashlee.

50. Kuykendall.

51. G. Flatt.

52. French 1967; Rosenberg 1998A; and Stubbs [D].

53. G. Flatt.

54. G. Flatt.

55. Information on the history of the group from French 1967; Rhodes 1974; Rosenberg 1991; G. Flatt; and Rosenberg 1998[A].

56. And some of his material. At an October 20, 1950, session for Mercury Records, Flatt and Scruggs recorded "Pike County Breakdown," a supercharged instrumental reworking of the old folk song "Sweet Betsy from Pike" that Monroe had written under the pseudonym Rupert Jones but not yet recorded. It was released in May 1952 and Bill was quickly forced to cover his own composition at a July 26 Decca session.

57. Wiseman.

58. Haney.

59. The story of this incident and its aftermath via Mac Wiseman.

60. The formation of the Shenandoah Valley Trio and Bill's bus purchase also via Wiseman.

61. Wiseman.

62. Ewing.

63. Rinzler 1975; Wiseman. Columbia executive Art Satherley knew full well that he might lose Monroe if the Stanleys were signed (J. Wright 1993, p. 55).

64. Stubbs [D].

65. Rumble 1994, p. 54.

66. Wiseman.

67. Duncan.

68. Simpson County, Kentucky, Marriage Bond No. 446; *Gann vs. Gann*, Davidson Co. No. A-5787.

69. *Gann vs. Gann*, Davidson Co. No. A-5787.

70. Information for comparison of release dates of Monroe and Williams material from Rosenberg 1974, p. 42, and Escott 1994, pp. 286–289, respectively.

71. Information on Martin's youth and early career from Martin; Martin [B]; and Skinker 1998[C].

72. *Monroe vs. Monroe* 1959, Davidson Co. No. 34918.

73. Jimmy Martin clearly remembers Carolyn and Bill conversing civilly, and Bill handing Carolyn money for the children's support.

74. Martin [B]. There is little question as to her parentage. Della Streeter (Bill's second wife and also a friend of Bessie Lee's) was told by Bessie that the girl was her and Bill's child. The accounts of Martin and Streeter are confirmed by another person who knew Bessie and Bill but has requested anonymity. (This source relates that the child was not named Rose; the song is a variation on Bill's earlier "My Rose of Old Kentucky.") Bill told Della that it was Bessie's child, but he did not directly acknowl-

edge paternity (Streeter [B]). He maintained the same position when speaking to his close friend Hazel Smith about the subject (H. Smith). Rosetta Monroe Kiper, one of Bill's nieces, recalls that Bessie accompanied Bill on a visit to Rosine some time before 1940 and told some Monroe family members that she was pregnant with his child (R. Kiper [D]). This is consistent with Bill's statements to interviewer Ralph Rinzler (FP-RINZ-RR-0005) that the song was composed around 1949 when the girl was twelve or fourteen years old. Thus she could have been born between 1935 and 1937, bolstering speculation that Bill was already going with Bessie at the time he married Carolyn. Ervin Mauldin, a cousin of Bessie's, confirms that Bessie had a baby but does not know its gender nor what became of it (E. Mauldin, signed statement). Bessie's sisters say they are unaware that she had any children, but they also report that she was once out of touch with the family for a year or two (V. and S. Mauldin).

75. Rhodes 1989.

76. Scott.

77. Respecting the woman's apparent desire for anonymity, the author has not attempted to locate her. However, she did resurface late in Monroe's life. Bill told Della Streeter that sometime in the early 1980s, the Georgia Rose had visited him backstage at the Opry (Streeter [B]).

78. Martin [B]. Monroe admired Williams's material but not his phrasing, holding that Hank "drug it to death" in the singing (Monroe via Rinzler FP-RINZ-RR-0004).

79. Martin and Martin [B].

80. Rinzler 1966; H. Smith.

81. Martin and Martin [B].

82. Martin.

83. Martin [B].

84. Martin [B].

85. Martin.

86. Monroe via Rinzler FP-1993-CT-0262.

87. The stories of the creations of "Raw Hide" and "Uncle Pen" via Martin.

88. Rinzler 1965.

89. Hugh Ashley was a songwriter from Arkansas and "Ira Wright" was a pseudonym for Eli Oberstein, the same man who had signed the Monroe Brothers to RCA Victor. Oberstein put out Ashley's song on one of his own labels in the 1940s. He took a share of the songwriting royalties (a standard practice then) and later played the song for Paul Cohen. Although Monroe rather defensively told Ashley that he had written "Uncle Pen" before "The Old Fiddler," Hugh's speculation that his song inspired Bill seems quite justified (Rosenberg/Wolfe 1989, p. 17).

90. Nashville *Tennessean*, April 15 and May 5, 1951.

91. Horstman 1986, p. 188.

92. Complicating the evaluation of "Kentucky Waltz" is an assertion by former Monroe lead singer Clyde Moody ("The Hillbilly Waltz King") that he had written the song. See Moody's comments in Stubbs 1992.

93. Melaragni 1979.

94. Monroe's irritation by claims that the five-string had made bluegrass wasn't wholly prompted by his one-time feud with Scruggs: Bill's music had been built around the fiddle, and he was proud of keeping old fiddle tunes alive within country music (Monroe via Rinzler FP-1993-CT-0262). Therefore he became angered when the fiddle's role was downplayed by banjo-oriented commentators. (See L. M. Smith 1965 and 1967.)

95. The parallels between Monroe and auteur film director John Ford underscore the point. Both had talented protégés (Earl Scruggs for Monroe and John Wayne for Ford) whom they raised from obscurity and who, in turn, helped establish their mentors' fame. And just as Ford was once critically pigeonholed as a mere director of westerns, causing his overall influence on the cinema to go unrecognized, the "Father of Bluegrass" label has obscured Monroe's broad impact on American popular music.

96. Martin.

97. And sometimes less. For example, an October 30, 1952, appearance at the Sandy Theater in Crossville, Alabama, yielded an after-tax net of $126.14 of which the band received 50 percent, a pitiful $63.07 (financial record, collection of Mike Dunn).

98. Martin.

99. Martin. Monroe later tried to put a positive spin on the Blue Grass Boys' high turnover in the 1950s and '60s, insisting: "I would have never wanted to keep the same group twenty-five years. Bluegrass would never have advanced at all" (Monroe via Rinzler, FP-RINZ-RR-0005).

100. Bradley.

101. Stubbs [D].

102. Bradley.

103. Bradley.

104. Bradley.

105. Information on Melissa Monroe's recording career from the CMFA.

106. Martin.

107. Martin; H. Smith.

108. *Gann vs. Gann*, Davidson Co. No. 21303.

109. *Mauldin-Monroe vs. Monroe* 1975, Davidson Co. No. A-5787.

110. Information on Nelson Gann's latter years from Polk City directories of Nashville, 1947 through 1975 (TSA); Fite via Schott; and Social Security death records.

111. *Country Song Roundup*, February 1952.

112. The story of the gouging of the "Gibson" inlay from Fowler 1979 and Monroe via Rinzler FP-1993-CT-0262.

113. Stanley.

114. Biographical information on Edd Mayfield from Hutchens 1983 and Curtis.

115. Monroe recounted this incident to his friend Hazel Smith.

116. Skinker 1998[B]; Brown County, Indiana, Deed Book 69, p. 456, and Book 107, pp. 131–133; and Rosenberg. Birch was given employment as the park's manager, and putting the deeds in his name certainly protected Bill's property in the event of a divorce from Carolyn.

117. Bessie Lee told Mr. and Mrs. Buck White about the final moments before the crash (B. White). Additional information from a newspaper item reproduced in Rosenberg/Wolfe 1989, p. 28.

CHAPTER FIVE: IMPACTS: ROCK 'N' ROLL, FLATT AND SCRUGGS, FOLK MUSIC (1953 TO 1961)

1. Nash 1988, p. 353; J. Martin.

2. Rosenberg/Wolfe 1989, p. 28.

3. Rosenberg.

4. J. Martin. Monroe later recalled walking into the emergency room under his own power (Nash 1988, p. 353). But so horrible were Bill's injuries that Martin is skeptical of this recollection.

5. J. Monroe December 1971.

6. Bradley.

7. J. Monroe December 1971.

8. *Bluegrass Unlimited*, March 1983, p. 11.

9. Bradley.

10. Information on Martha White and its sponsorship of the Flatt and Scruggs band from Williams's nephew, Wynn Williams.

11. C. Smith.

12. Lester Flatt told the story of this encounter to Lance LeRoy, Flatt's agent in his latter years. The anecdote also underscores how poor Monroe's vision was, since Lester first attributed Bill's behavior to his bad eye.

13. Martin.

14. Wiseman.

15. Sumner County Deed Book 156, pp. 35–38.

16. J. Monroe December 1971.

17. B. Price [B].

18. L. Mauldin; V. and S. Mauldin.

19. H. Smith [B]; J. Martin [B].

20. J. Martin [B].

21. *Elvis Presley — The Sun Sessions* CD, RCA Victor 6414-2-R.

22. Cited in Perkins/McGee 1996, p. 78. Elvis was widely identified as a country singer at this stage of his career. In 1954, a booking agent wrote in response to an inquiry by Scotty Moore, Presley's guitarist: "I don't have anything at present where I could place your artist. There are few outlets for hillbilly entertainers around Chicago" (cited in Kuntz 1999).

23. Guralnick 1994, pp. 128–129.

24. Martin.

25. Morrison 1996, p. 59.

26. Stanley.

27. DeCurtis 1996.

28. Recollections of Monroe's influence on Perkins and Presley music from Perkins/McGee 1996, pp. 11–26.

29. Rumble 1994, p. 60.

30. Perkins/McGee 1996, pp. 219–220.

31. Perkins/McGee 1996, pp. 215–216.

32. Cash/Carr 1997, p. 289.

33. Cash/Carr 1997, p. 110.

34. Curtis. Holly's early bands contained two other Monroe fans, Sonny Curtis and Waylon Jennings.

35. Hicks [B].

36. Stubbs 1998.

37. J. Martin.

38. Rosenberg May 1984.

39. Rosenberg January 1985.

40. The Foggy Mountain Boys now had the stable — and phenomenal — lineup of former Charlie Monroe sideman John "Curly" Seckler on mandolin, singing superb tenor to Lester's leads; fiddler Paul Warren, equally adept at playing scorching hoedowns or lilting ballads; lovable bassist/comedian "Cousin Jake" Tullock; and Burkett "Uncle Josh" Graves, who renewed the Hawaiian-style resonator guitar's popularity in country music and made it the perfect acoustic alternative to the electric pedal steel guitar.

41. LeRoy.

42. LeRoy.

43. LeRoy.

44. LeRoy.

45. Seckler.

46. Keith; G. Flatt; LeRoy.

47. LeRoy.

48. W. Williams.

49. Seckler.

50. T. Ellis; C. Smith.

51. J. Martin [B].

52. LeRoy.

53. Rosenberg.

54. LaBella.

55. H. Smith.

56. D. and R. Reno, with other recollections of Bessie via Ellis, Rosenberg, and Streeter.

57. S. and V. Mauldin; R. Mauldin. Bessie's statements to her family are highly credible. Had she been lying about her songwriting, she surely would have laid claim to Monroe numbers more famous than "Cheyenne" or "Voice from On High."

58. Martin; McCoury.

59. Seckler.

60. Stubbs [C].

61. Wiseman.

62. G. Duncan; Stubbs [D]. As noted, Monroe did not originate or even pioneer the use of harmony fiddles. He owed a particular debt to the prior recordings of string band leaders Gid Tanner and Clayton McMichen and western swing giant Bob Wills.

63. H. Smith.

64. Kershaw.

65. C. Smith. Smith feels that Monroe is equally its composer, since Charlie was playing the bluegrass music that Bill had created and taught him.

66. Nashville *Tennessean*, September 27, 1958. The loss of the Cadillac and the forced use of Bessie's station wagon must have particularly galled Bill, who favored fine touring cars (Wesbrooks/McLean/Grafton, p. 132; Price [B]).

67. The last days of Mayfield from Hutchens 1983; Monroe via Rinzler FP-RINZ-RR-0005.

68. H. Smith.

69. Pete Seeger 1961, p. 32.

70. Lomax 1959.

71. Rosenberg 1974, p. 3.

72. Tate.

73. Cooke.

74. Hartford [C].

75. Rosenberg 1985, p. 151.

76. Rosenberg 1985, p. 151.

77. *Monroe vs. Monroe* 1959, Davidson Co. No. 34918. The information and quotes that follow are from the case file.

78. *Mauldin Monroe vs. Monroe* 1975, Davidson Co. No. A-5787.

79. Information about Don Owens and the first one-day, all-bluegrass show from Stubbs 1998.

80. Rosenberg 1985, pp. 135–136.

81. Rosenberg 1985, p. 178.

82. Cited in Rosenberg 1985, p. 181.

83. Recorded on July 6, 1951, and credited to Audrey Butler, this became Bill and Carter's most popular vocal collaboration. Monroe later stated that it was written by Betty Blazer, one of several professional wrestlers who made Nashville's Tulane Hotel their headquarters (Monroe via Rinzler FP-RINZ-7RR-0002). If so, perhaps "Betty Blazer" was Ms. Butler's ring nom-de-plume!

84. The Monroe-Stanley exchange was captured by several persons who taped the show. It is cited in Rosenberg 1985, p. 179.

85. Rosenberg 1985, p. 180.

86. Rosenberg 1985, pp. 180–181.

87. Stubbs 1998.

88. The Hatch Show Print advertising poster order records (CMFA) confirm the recollections of sidemen that Monroe was actually quite busy during this period. But he was earning scant money because of declining crowds and percentage-only payments.

89. Tate.

90. Ellis.

91. McPeake.

92. Ellis.

93. Bradley; McPeake.

94. Ellis.

95. Ellis.

96. Ellis.

97. Ellis.

98. McPeake; Ellis.

99. Rosenberg 1991, p. 7.

100. B. Anderson.

101. Rumble 1994, p. 54.

CHAPTER SIX: RENAISSANCE: FOLKIES AND YANKEES (1962 TO 1965)

1. Rumble 1994, p. 62.

2. Perkins/McGee 1996, p. 286.

3. B. Anderson.

4. Ellis.

5. Ellis.

6. For more on its origins, see Rosenberg 1985, pp. 5, 11–13, 88–90, 111–116.

7. Louise Scruggs, Madison, Tennessee, letter to Dave Magram, January 8, 1963.

8. Louise Scruggs, Madison, Tennessee, letter to Dave Magram, March 2, 1964.

9. The story of Ralph Rinzler's first encounters with Monroe from Rooney 1971, pp. 77–80; Rinzler 1975; Rinzler 1993; M. Seeger; R. Stanley; and H. Dickens.

10. Seeger 1997.

11. Rooney 1971, p. 79.

12. Biographical and personal information on Rinzler from SFA, passim; Swarthmore 1970; R. D. Smith 1979; Harrington 1994; K. Rinzler; and Werman.

13. Werman.

14. Goldsmith 1998, p. 262.

15. Watson.

16. R. D. Smith 1979.

17. Biographical information via M. Seeger.

18. Biographical information via H. Dickens.

19. H. Dickens.

20. This and the anecdote about the microphones via Mike Seeger.

21. Rooney 1971, p. 77.

22. Smith 1979.

23. Rinzler 1963.

24. Rinzler later shared these thoughts with Monroe during a taped interview (Monroe via Rinzler FP-1993-CT-0262).

25. H. Dickens.

26. Rooney 1971, p. 79; Rinzler 1975, p. 204.

27. Seeger.

28. Rinzler datebooks, SFA, May 4, 1962, notation.

29. The story of the meeting between Monroe, Rinzler, Seeger, Mauldin, and the Stanleys primarily from Mike Seeger but confirmed by Ralph Stanley.

30. M. Seeger.

31. Rosenberg 1985, p. 180.

32. M. Seeger.

33. Rinzler 1993, p. 5.

34. Rinzler 1993, p. 6.

35. Rooney 1971, p. 79.

36. Rinzler 1993, p. 6.

37. Rinzler 1963.

38. Gentry 1961, p. 273.

39. By the late 1950s, Monroe had taken over emcee duties in concert, partly because his shyness had abated but probably out of necessity, since the lead

singer/guitarist position had become a revolving door. However, his stage patter had been limited to quick perfunctory comments. ("Thank you thank you and now I'm gonna sing a couple of solo numbers, the first one's called 'My Little Georgia Rose.'") Although Rinzler may not have specifically directed Bill to talk about Pen or Arnold, Ralph showed him that audiences were interested in his roots.

40. Rinzler datebooks, SFA.

41. Logan.

42. Gerrard.

43. McCoury.

44. Dickens.

45. McCoury.

46. Rinzler 1993, p. 6.

47. Rinzler 1993, p. 6; Seeger.

48. Monroe via Rinzler FP-1993-CT-0262. Seeger was also a good friend to Earl Scruggs. The feuding parties never forced mutual friends to take sides.

49. Rinzler shared these impressions with Monroe during the same taped interview (Monroe via Rinzler FP-1993-CT-0262).

50. Information on his background and early music career from B. Keith.

51. One writer has claimed that Baker had to convince a "dubious" Monroe to hire Keith. But Keith's recollection suggests that Monroe made his mind up very quickly.

52. Monroe's prediction and Del's private reaction via McCoury.

53. Keith.

54. McCoury. Even Bessie Lee had the same impression.

55. Keith.

56. Von Schmidt/Rooney 1994, p. 158.

57. McCoury.

58. Keith.

59. Biographical information on Kenny Baker from Rooney 1971, pp. 68–69; J. Monroe January 1972; and Skinker 1998.

60. Dillards/M. Jayne.

61. Dillards/Webb.

62. Keith.

63. H. Smith.

64. Dillards/Jayne.

65. Watson.

66. Rinzler 1993, p. 7.

67. Rosenberg 1998[B].

68. Watson.

69. He later diplomatically shared his regrets about the Keith situation with Mon-

roe during a 1966 taped interview. Bill didn't explain why he hadn't continued to record Brad Keith (Monroe and Greene via Rinzler FP-RINZ-7RR-0004).

70. Shelton 1963[B].

71. Gerrard; for more about the uneasiness some southern string band musicians had with the folk revival, see Cantwell 1996, pp. 298–303.

72. Dillards/Jayne.

73. Rosenberg.

74. Rosenberg.

75. Bill Turbeville, Rock Hill, South Carolina, letter to Ott Devine of WSM, June 17, 1963, Rinzler papers, SFA.

76. John McKenzie, Gloucestershire, England, letter to Bill Monroe, May 24, 1963, Rinzler papers, SFA.

77. Irv Dinkin, New York, N.Y., letter to Ralph Rinzler, June 11, 1963, Rinzler papers, SFA.

78. Rosenberg 1991, p. 3.

79. Schmidt/Rooney 1994, pp. 157–158.

80. Harry Cooke, Lancaster, Pennsylvania, letter to Ralph Rinzler, June 10, 1963, Rinzler papers, SFA. Joe A. Bryan, Boaz, Alabama, letter to Bill Monroe, June 27, 1963, Rinzler papers, SFA.

81. Rosenberg.

82. Rosenberg. Birch Monroe was widely loved, but these impressions are universally shared by friends and acquaintances.

83. The confrontation was witnessed by Jim Rooney, who later rode back to Nashville with Keith and Monroe. Von Schmidt/Rooney 1994, pp. 159 and 162.

84. Rosenberg.

85. Rosenberg.

86. Rosenberg.

87. Rinzler 1975, pp. 205 and 219. In 1982, Ralph entered into a tentative agreement with the University of Illinois Press. But other projects, his later responsibilities as head of the Smithsonian Institution Center for Folklife Programs, and a final illness prevented Rinzler from doing any writing on the book (McCulloh).

88. Monroe via Rinzler FP-RINZ-RR-0005.

89. In the liner notes to the 1966 Columbia *The Versatile Flatt and Scruggs*, Nat Hentoff wrote that "it is a mistake to categorize Flatt and Scruggs as only a 'bluegrass' combo although they are certainly masters of that bristling idiom." The term was soon dropped entirely from the duo's albums.

90. Bradley.

91. Neil Rosenberg, Bloomington, Indiana, letter to Ralph Rinzler, June 8, 1963, Rinzler papers, SFA.

92. Keith.

93. The story of Bill and Bessie's surprise visit to the "Bluegrass Rest Home" from Von Schmidt/Rooney 1994, p. 157, and Bill Keith.

94. The story of the visit to Rosine from Rooney 1971, p. 80; Rinzler 1993, pp. 20–22; and Blue Grass Boys/McCoury.

95. Rinzler 1993, p. 20.

96. Rinzler 1993, p. 21.

97. Reflecting on the visit to Rosine, Del McCoury agrees with this interpretation.

98. 1963 datebook, Rinzler papers, SFA.

99. McCoury.

100. This compilation of Monroe road stories from Rooney 1971, pp. 85–87; Rinzler 1993, pp. 21–22; Keith 1997; Blue Grass Boys/Keith and McCoury October 1997; and McCoury.

101. Keith.

102. Al Steiner, personal communication, 1995.

103. Keith.

104. Keith.

105. Rosenberg 1985, p. 186.

106. Bessie Lee Mauldin, letter to Ralph Rinzler, February 14, 1964, Rinzler papers, SFA.

107. Streeter; Bessie's death certificate lists her occupation as "music secretary."

108. Cash/Carr 1997, p. 289.

109. The timing is clear in McCoury's mind because he was married shortly thereafter.

110. McCoury. Del has no ax to grind against Bessie, speaking well of her as a person and praising her bass playing as highly underrated.

111. *Mauldin Monroe vs. Monroe*, Davidson Co. No. A5787.

112. Rooney 1971, p. 92.

113. Arkin, personal communication, 1995.

114. Blue Grass Boys/Arkin.

115. Blue Grass Boys/Lowinger.

116. Blue Grass Boys/Lowinger.

CHAPTER SEVEN: HIS BEST DAYS ON EARTH (1965 TO 1983)

1. LeRoy. Lance LeRoy was in the dressing room when Haney pitched his festival concept to Monroe.

2. Biographical information about Carlton Haney from Haney; Bartenstein; and Bartenstein 1998.

3. LeRoy.

4. Rosenberg 1985, p. 204.

5. Haney.

6. Haney.

7. Haney.

8. Rinzler 1975.

9. This feeling is stressed by numerous attendees (Bush; Isenhour; Magram; and L. Martin).

10. Stanley.

11. Biographical and career information via Rowan and Rowan [B].

12. Rowan [B].

13. And it matched the vagaries of his financial situation. During better times, Monroe was more forthright about recruiting musicians.

14. In particular, Bill stressed that certain words should be emphasized and filled with meaning (Wernick 1976, p. 16).

15. Biographical information via R. Greene.

16. Bush.

17. Program, 1st International Folk-Bluegrass Festival, July 10, 1966, Lake Whipporwill Park, author's collection.

18. Carlson 1966; Stubbs [D].

19. Artis 1975, p. 38; Wright 1993, pp. 4 and 84–85.

20. *Bluegrass Unlimited*, December 1966 and January 1967. Carter's death was attributed to a liver ailment (Rosenberg 1985, p. 320).

21. Monroe via Rinzler FP-1993-CT-0262.

22. Stanley.

23. H. Smith.

24. R. Greene.

25. Greene and Monroe expounded on Bill's fiddle theories in a unique seminar-style private demonstration taped by Ralph Rinzler (Monroe and R. Greene via Rinzler FP-RINZ-RR-0004 and FP-RINZ-RR-0006).

26. R. Greene.

27. P. Rowan [B].

28. Stauffer; R. Greene; D. Green; and P. Rowan [B].

29. Rowan [B].

30. Rosenberg; R. White; V. Stauffer; P. Rowan [B].

31. Rowan [B].

32. Rowan [B].

33. The story of the fallout over this song via R. Greene and P. Rowan [B].

34. R. Greene.

35. R. Greene.

36. P. Rowan [B].

37. P. Rowan [B].

38. R. Greene.

39. R. White.

40. R. White.

41. Biographical information from H. Smith.

42. H. Smith.

43. H. Smith.

44. R. White.

45. Johnston had also produced Dylan for Columbia (Rosenberg 1991). See also Koon 1974 regarding the duo's divergence from bluegrass.

46. Artis 1975, p. 56; Lambert/Seckler 1982, pp. 52–54.

47. Lambert/Seckler 1982, p. 56. Several sources erroneously list their appearance on the Tennessee state float in Richard Nixon's inaugural parade as their last appearance together.

48. Lambert/Seckler 1982, pp. 55–56.

49. Biographical and career information on James Monroe from Kuykendall 1973.

50. Hurst 1972.

51. Kuykendall 1973.

52. Allen 1998. Additional information about Charlie's difficulties and the sale of the old Monroe land from Green March 1973; Ohio County Deed Book 164, pp. 75–78; and Spinks.

53. Bradley.

54. H. Smith; R. White.

55. H. Smith.

56. Gerrard. Rinzler, who was recovering from a broken leg, sat on the stage, put his leg up on a piano bench, and smiled happily.

57. Monroe via Rinzler FP-1993-CT-0262.

58. *Bluegrass Star,* December 1971.

59. *Billboard* 1970.

60. Sumner County, Tennessee, Lien Book 5, pp. 406 and 450; Book 6, p. 69; Book 7, pp. 26, 138, and 185; and Book 15, pp. 559 and 594.

61. B. Price.

62. Lundy 1983; Kuykendall. Haney's version is that he and Bill had accomplished all they could together and mutually decided to move on (Haney).

63. Haney.

64. *Mauldin Monroe vs. Monroe* 1975, Davidson Co. Chancery Court A-5787.

65. Stauffer.

66. Wiseman.

67. Monroe via Rinzler FP-1993-CT-0250; R. Smith 1985; Stauffer.

68. Hurst 1972; Monroe via Rinzler FP-1993-CT-0262.

69. "The White Folks Ain't Treating Me Right" was renamed "Poor White Folks" for the album. The "Lee Weddin Tune" was, as Bill understood it, not named after a marriage ceremony but a Kentucky fiddler named Lee Weddin (Monroe via Rinzler FP-1993-CT-0262).

70. In March 1976, he recorded *Kenny Baker Plays Bill Monroe* (County 761), a collection of Monroe tunes (many of which were certainly shaped by Baker himself). Kenny didn't even hire a mandolin player for the sessions, knowing full well that Bill would just show up (K. Baker, personal communication, 1976).

71. H. Smith 1973.

72. Bill Vernon, personal communication, 1995; F. J. Harvey.

73. Rinzler 1975.

74. *Bluegrass Unlimited*, January 1999.

75. King; Rumble 1994, p. 43.

76. Rosenberg 1985, p. 197.

77. Rosenberg.

78. Smith 1996.

79. The story of Lester and Bill's reconciliation via LeRoy.

80. Flickinger.

81. R. White.

82. G. Flatt; Seckler.

83. Rhodes 1978. In 1971, James also started *The Bluegrass Star*. Although informative and entertaining, the magazine attracted scant advertising and was eventually sold to *Bluegrass Unlimited*.

84. Koon 1970.

85. Cantwell 1972.

86. Hurst 1972.

87. Hurst 1972.

88. Monroe via Rinzler FP-RINZ-7RR-0002. In his liner notes for the Lonesome Pine Fiddlers album *Kentucky Bluegrass* (Starday/Nashville NLP 2020), Bill wrote that he liked to get together with this band to hunt, play music, and "perhaps make a little fun of the current crop of commercial singers who claim to be country performers."

89. Koskela.

90. H. Dickens.

91. H. Dickens; B. and P. Logan.

92. J. Martin 1997. Jimmy's recollections are confirmed by Gloria Belle Flickinger, then Martin's bass player, who went on the visit and later played for Charlie during his comeback.

93. Green March 1973.

94. J. Pruett.

95. Krishef 1978, pp. 62–63 and 68.

96. H. Smith.

97. Rosenberg; Rosenberg June 1, 1998.

98. H. Smith.

99. Elkins 1970.

100. Gabany.

101. H. Smith.

102. H. Smith.

103. Bessie Lee's complaints regarding her claimed common-law marriage to Bill are found in the case file for *Mauldin Monroe vs. Monroe* 1975, Davidson Co. No. A-5787.

104. However, in her filing Bessie did not include one additional claim she made to family members — that she and Bill had gone through a marriage ceremony in Mexico (E. Mauldin, signed statement).

105. H. Smith.

106. Charlie and Myrtha Monroe, personal communication, 1972.

107. H. Smith.

108. Associated Press in *Trenton Evening Times,* September 29, 1975; Haney.

109. H. Smith.

110. Biographical information via Julia LaBella.

111. LaBella.

112. Information about Bill's farm via Lundy 1983; Wolmuth 1986; Feller Brown 1994; LaBella; and B. Smith.

113. Monroe via Rinzler FP-1993-CT-0250.

114. Monroe via Rinzler FP-1993-CT-0250.

115. B. Smith.

116. Hurst 1977.

117. Rooney 1971, p. 85.

118. Lundy 1983.

119. Bill was well aware of this dynamic, once observing that working on the farm "brings you back to the way you was raised" (Wolmuth 1986).

120. Blue Grass Boys/Lewis.

121. Bush.

122. Bush.

123. Watson. Bill thus expressed severe displeasure on a variety of subjects. He would also grouse that an especially disappointing person or situation was "sorry" (as in "That's a sorry job you did fixin' that fence right there").

124. Saal 1970.

125. The story of the meeting of Monroe and Dylan via Grisman.

126. Cited in a 1994 MCA Records publicity release for *The Music of Bill Monroe 1936–1994.*

127. The story of Baker, Monroe, and the newgrassers via Bush.

128. Bush.

129. The signing of Monroe and information about Bill's latter career via Conway.

130. Robins.

131. Carlson 1967.

132. Robins.

133. Koskela.

134. Robins; Gabany.

135. Robins.

136. Robins.

137. Robins.

138. *B. H. Monroe vs. J. Monroe* 1968–1980, Davidson Co. No. 53319.

139. Biographical information from Streeter.

140. Streeter.

141. R. D. Smith 1985.

142. LaBella.

143. Dillards/R. Dillard.

144. Gabany.

145. LaBella.

146. LaBella.

147. Monroe via Rinzler FP-1993-CT-0250.

148. LaBella.

149. H. Smith.

150. Hartford [C].

151. LaBella.

152. Gabany.

153. The story of the recording of "My Last Days on Earth" from R. D. Smith 1985; LaBella; and Rosenberg 1998 [C].

154. Tate.

155. LaBella; B. White.

156. Hill 1982.

157. Hill 1981; menu, BUF.

158. *Bluegrass Unlimited,* June 1982, p. 4.

159. LaBella; Conway.

160. Lundy 1982; Bush; and Grisman.

161. Bush.

162. Lundy 1983; H. Smith; and LaBella.

163. E. Mauldin, signed statement; S. and V. Mauldin.

164. Streeter.

165. C. Harris.

166. North Carolina Department of Vital Records, death certificate.

167. Hartford [C].

168. S. and V. Mauldin. However, Bessie's sisters report that Nelson Gann wrote them offering his condolences.

169. S. and V. Mauldin.

CHAPTER EIGHT: BLUE MOON OF KENTUCKY SETTING (1983 TO 1996)

1. R. D. Smith 1985.

2. Gabany.

3. Lundy 1983.

4. E. Harris.

5. Cited in a 1994 MCA Record publicity release for *The Music of Bill Monroe 1993–1994.*

6. This insight from active Nashville session player and former Blue Grass Boy Glen Duncan. For more on Monroe's profound impact on American fiddling, see J. Wood 1997.

7. Monroe biography sheet, Buddy Lee Attractions.

8. Cumming. The story of Conway and Monroe's visit to the White House and its aftermath from T. Conway. Bill told the identical story to Hazel Smith.

9. Conway.

10. Conway.

11. Sometimes he even pulled this on close friends, which hurt their feelings (H. Smith [B]; T. Taylor).

12. M. Seeger; Gabany.

13. M. Seeger.

14. Rinzler 1975.

15. Keith.

16. Hume 1976.

17. M. Williams.

18. Davis; B. White; and Skaggs.

19. The story of Bill's visit to Israel via Nash 1998, pp. 339–340, and M. Williams. Also accompanying Bill on the trip was Didi Prestige, an aspiring singer and Monroe protégée who later changed her stage name to Diana Christian.

20. M. Williams.

21. Information on Bill's performance fees, contract riders, and problems with missing money via Conway.

22. Conway.

23. Conway.

24. McInturff. In another Monroe contradiction, although Bill was sloppy about most business details he was scrupulous about others. For example, he invariably called Mrs. McInturff at the Monroe Enterprises office precisely at 9 A.M. to check on his appointments and receive messages. She was the last of a line that had included Wilene Forrester, Gladys Flatt, and ex-wife Carolyn Brown Monroe, women he trusted implicitly with business matters and with whom he had platonic, thoroughly professional relationships. Clearly, his lifelong comfort with women extended beyond his love life.

25. Conway; McInturff; and Kuykendall.

26. Lundy 1983.

27. Menius 1984.

28. Invitation, BUF.

29. Descriptions of the museum and hall of fame from Hutchens 1984; Henson.

30. This observation and the quote that follows from S. Davis.

31. Information from Monroe family plot markers, Spring Hill Cemetery, Nashville.

32. Lundy 1983.

33. The exact date of Baker leaving the Blue Grass Boys via his biography on the 1999 International Bluegrass Music Association (IBMA) Hall of Honor ballot. Baker spoke of the circumstances of his departure during an oral history session videotaped at the 1995 IBMA "World of Bluegrass" convention in Owensboro, Kentucky. (During the taping, Kenny also stressed his tremendous respect for Monroe.) Additional details via Julia LaBella, with whom he subsequently discussed the breakup. Baker's dilemma was, unfortunately, not unique: Some Blue Grass Boys were forced to consult the *Bluegrass Unlimited* calendar listings to find out where they'd be next month (Stubbs [B]).

34. Skaggs.

35. The story of Bill's participation in the "Country Boy" video from Blue Grass Boys/Skaggs; Conway; and Skaggs.

36. G. Duncan.

37. The story of the raucous concert version of "Wheel Hoss" via G. Duncan.

38. Duncan; Streeter.

39. McIntyre.

40. Sexton.

41. Wolmuth 1986.

42. Streeter.

43. H. Smith; R. White.

44. Entered with financial statement appendage in Sumner County Deed Book 511, pp. 728–736.

45. The story of the vandalism and threats via Duncan and Streeter.

46. R. White. Roland White was especially worried about Bill's poor diet and declining health. He raised his concerns directly to Bill and James on more than one occasion.

47. Duncan.

48. Louvin.

49. Louvin.

50. Menius. Other IBMA organizers, however, believe that the Monroes remained suspicious of the organization until the last years of Bill's life.

51. Menius.

52. Sherborne 1985. This crime was apparently not linked to the threats and acts of vandalism directed at Bill, however.

53. The story of the break-in and smashing of the mandolins from Appleton 1995; *Country Music* 1986; and Streeter.

54. Streeter.

55. Goldsmith/Dearmore 1985; *Country Music* 1986; Goldsmith 1986; and Lanham 1986.

56. Duncan.

57. Appleton 1995.

58. Sherborne 1985.

59. Goldsmith 1986; Lanham 1986; and Streeter.

60. Streeter.

61. Gruhn.

62. Compton.

63. Canfield 1986.

64. McCampbell 1987.

65. Information on Monroe's Bluegrass Country from club promotional flier, BUF. The Monroes also planned at one time to build an amusement park near Beaver Dam, Kentucky, on land used for their Ohio County bluegrass festival. But the project was never begun, causing anger in some quarters back home (*Times-News*, October 17, 1991).

66. Information on the divorce proceedings via *Monroe vs. Monroe* 1987, Sumner County No. 4676–C.

67. Streeter.

68. Streeter.

69. Pareles 1996.

70. Gabany. Vic Gabany, who would later independently produce Monroe, helped engineer the *Southern Flavor* sessions.

71. *Brown County Democrat* 1988.

72. Carpenter 1989.

73. The story of the May 1989 assault charges against Monroe and his vindication from Appleton 1989; *Nashville Banner* 1989; Davis 1989; Goldsmith/Watson 1989.

74. *Rolling Stone* 1989, p. 69.

75. Orr 1989.

76. Bill's typical weekly jamming schedule at the end of his life via Baldassari; Duncan; and LaBella.

77. R. Howard.

78. Stubbs [D].

79. LaBella.

80. Duncan.

81. H. Smith; G. Flatt; M. Williams; and Duncan.

82. *Bluegrass Unlimited*, January 1991, p. 14; *Nashville Banner*, December 4, 1990; Tennessee Department of Health, Office of Vital Records, death certificate.

83. Correspondence, Rinzler files, SFA.

84. Bush.

85. Gabany. Vic Gabany, who personally funded several Monroe studio and in-concert recording sessions, is quite definite that Bill was no longer with the label. A source well acquainted with Monroe's recording career supports his assertion.

86. Not only are bluegrass records smaller sellers compared to hit country disks, bluegrass does not receive the airplay enjoyed by mainstream country.

87. Angie Jenkins Smith office, MCA Records, Nashville, Tennessee, personal communication, June 2, 1999.

88. Ewing.

89. Blue Grass Boys/Sykes.

90. Gabany.

91. Gabany.

92. Gabany.

93. *Brown County Democrat* 1992. Some Rosine residents maintain that the remaining structure on Tuttle Hill contained little, if any, of Pen's final dwelling when workers from Nashville arrived to cart it off (*Times-News*, October 31, 1991).

94. Hutchens [B].

95. Peter Rowan learned this while visiting Bill at his farm, and it provided the inspiration for his bittersweet composition "Let the Harvest Go to Seed" (Rowan).

96. E. Harris.

97. LaBella.

98. Feller Brown 1994.

99. Conway.

100. Sumner County Deed Book 426, pp. 348–351; Feller Brown 1994.

101. Conway.

102. Conway.

103. LaBella; Dunn.

104. Sumner County Deed Book 536, pp. 85–87; Sumner County Record Book 404, pp. 712–715.

105. DeParle.

106. J. Monroe 1994.

107. Davidson County Record Book 5842, p. 306.

108. Davidson County Record Book 6401, p. 281.

109. Davidson County Chancery Court No. 86-1411-I.

110. Davidson County Record Book 7605, p. 306.

111. Ohio County Mortgage Book 188, p. 704–706; Davidson County Deed Book 8889, pp. 439–442; Davidson County Deed Book 9281, pp. 698–701.

112. He was also well aware of how much money the enterprises were losing. During questioning by a lawyer trying to arrange support for Della Streeter, he was asked about the amount of his indebtedness. "It's a way on up there," Bill replied (Sumner County No. 4676–C).

113. Conway.

114. Streeter.

115. Anderson.

116. LaBella.

117. Jeff Place, SFA, personal communication, 1997.

118. Abrahams. Rinzler talked about his condition with Prof. Abrahams, who was a college classmate, and other close friends.

119. M. Seeger; Rosenberg; Abrahams.

120. Dickens; LaBella; Gerrard; and Watson.

121. Watson.

122. M. Seeger. The performance has been preserved on the videotape *Ralph Rinzler: A Celebration of Life*, Smithsonian Institution Center for Folklife Programs & Cultural Studies, 1995.

123. Robins.

124. Chiavola.

125. Grisman.

126. R. D. Smith 1985.

127. Tommy Goldsmith, personal communication, 1997. There are some tapes of the composition in private circulation, however.

128. Gruhn.

129. Blue Grass Boys/Skaggs.

130. Blue Grass Boys/Tate.

131. Blue Grass Boys/Skaggs.

132. And most Blue Grass Boys remain unsure to this day.

133. Louvin.

134. LaBella.

135. Gabany.

136. Haney.

137. R. D. Smith 1996.

138. R. D. Smith 1996.

139. Conway.

140. Conway.

141. LaBella.

142. Hutchens [B]; C. Smith.

143. S. Davis.

144. Letters, *Bluegrass Unlimited*, March 1996. Sandy Rothman, a California-based former Blue Grass Boy, also circulated "True Life News," a one-time newsletter criticizing the article and including additional letters of protest.

145. Gabany.

146. Monroe via Rinzler FP-1993-CT-0262.

147. LaBella.

148. CD booklet information, Billy and Terry Smith, *Bill Monroe Tribute* K-Tel 3642–2.

149. B. Smith.

150. B. Smith.

151. Information on Monroe's final Opry appearance via Stubbs [C].

152. Conway; LaBella; and Gabany.

153. Streeter.

154. S. Davis.

155. Conway; Stuart.

156. List of health care facilities via Stubbs [E].

157. Stuart.

158. Chiavola.

159. H. Smith.

160. R. White.

161. Blue Grass Boys/Tate.

162. Wiseman.

163. B. Smith.

164. J. Martin.

165. State of Tennessee, Office of Vital Records, death certificate. The cause of death was listed as probable myocardial infarction and atherosclerotic coronary artery disease.

166. Monroe's influence was formally recognized in May 1997 when he was posthumously elected to the Rock and Roll Hall of Fame in the roots artist category.

167. Hartford [C].

EPILOGUE

1. Stephenson; Stubbs [C].

2. Accounts of Monroe funeral services in Nashville and Rosine from Yeomans November 1996[A] and 1996[B]; Reuters 1996; E. Harris; Hutchens; Skaggs; Stuart; and Stubbs [C].

3. E. Harris; Skaggs; and Stuart.

4. R. Howard.

5. Blue Grass Boys/Lewis; Duncan.

6. S. Davis.

7. Streeter.

8. Blue Grass Boys/Lewis.

9. Sumner County Will Book, pp. 633–639.

10. Dunn.

11. Kiper [C].

12. Conway; LeRoy; and Stubbs [C].

13. Vied 1997.

14. At the April 17, 1997, event, Ricky Skaggs performed "Uncle Pen" on Bill's famous mandolin, which James Monroe had displayed at the Ryman for the occasion (Yeomans). Shortly thereafter, Skaggs purchased a Gibson F-5 also signed by Lloyd Loar on July 9, 1923. A comparison of the wood grains of mandolins approved on that date indicates they were literally made from the same tree (Isenhour).

15. Monroe via Rinzler FP-1993-CT-0520.

16. Kiper [D]; photo of puppy on grave with information on reverse, BUF.

⋆ BIBLIOGRAPHY ⋆

INTERVIEWS AND UNPUBLISHED CORRESPONDENCE

All interviews by the author unless otherwise noted.

Abrahams, Roger, telephone interview, December 17, 1999.

Allen, Loretta and Stanley, in-person interview, September 25, 1997.

Allen, Wendell, "Data on Arnold Shultz," letter to Ralph Rinzler, November 6, 1974, Rinzler files, SFA.

——— [B], in-person interview, September 25, 1996.

——— [C], in-person interview, May 12–13, 1997.

——— [D], in-person interview, October 20, 1997.

——— [E], in-person interview, June 27, 1998.

——— [F], telephone interview, April 27, 1999.

Anderson, Bill, in-person interview, April 10, 1999.

Arkin, Steve (see Blue Grass Boys, Fairfield, Connecticut, May 24, 1997).

Baldassari, Butch, in-person interview, August 19, 1997.

Bartenstein, Fred, telephone interview, April 23, 1997.

Bartley, Mrs. Carrel J., Elbert Leech, and Zelna Leech Shroader, in-person interview, October 20, 1997.

Belle, Gloria (see Gloria Belle Flickinger).

Blue Grass Boys reunion concert featuring segment "I Remember Bill Monroe," Fairfield University, Fairfield, Connecticut (Doug Tuchman, producer; with Steve Arkin, Bill Keith, Wayne Lewis, Gene Lowinger, Kevin Lynch, Ernie Sykes, Tater Tate), May 24, 1997.

Blue Grass Boys and friends concert "Remembering Bill Monroe," International Bluegrass Music Association convention, Louisville, KY (Ricky Skaggs, emcee, with Mike Compton, John Hartford, Bobby Hicks, Bill Keith, Del McCoury, Frank Wakefield), October 17, 1997.

Bradley, Owen, in-person interview, August 18, 1997.

Bush, Sam, telephone interviews, March 1–2, 1999.

Chiavola, Kathy, in-person interview, August 21, 1997.

Clements, Vassar, in-person interview, June 25, 1998.

Compton, Mike, in-person interview, May 18, 1997.

Conway, Tony, in-person interview, June 22, 1998.

Cooke, Jack, telephone interview, January 11, 1998.

Cumming, Greg (Reagan Presidential Library), telephone interview, May 25, 1999.

Curtis, Sony, telephone interview, April 10, 1998.

Davis, Skeeter, telephone interview, December 15, 1998.

Davison, Wilber, telephone interview, December 13, 1997.

Dickens, Hazel, in-person interview, October 15, 1997.

Dickens, James "Little Jimmy," telephone interview, July 13, 1998.

Dillard, Doug (see Dillards, The).

Dillard, Rodney (see Dillards, The).

Dillards, The (Rodney Dillard, Doug Dillard, Mitch Jayne, and Dean Webb), in-person
    interview, March 13, 1998.

Duncan, Glen, in-person interview, June 16, 1998.

Dunn, Mike, telephone interview, August 4, 1999.

Ellis, Paul Anthony "Tony," telephone interview, May 28, 1998.

Ewing, Tom, in-person interview, June 25, 1998.

Fite, T. G., via Fred Schott, telephone interview, April 7, 1999.

Flatt, Gladys (Mrs. Lester), telephone interview, August 3, 1998.

Flickinger, Gloria Belle, in-person interview, October 23, 1997.

Forrester, Robert, telephone interview, June 27, 1998.

Gabany, Vic, in-person interview, June 15, 1998.

Gerrard, Alice, telephone interview, May 28, 1998.

Green, Douglas B., in-person interview, June 23, 1998.

Greene, Richard, telephone interview, December 18, 1998.

Grisman, David, in-person interview, March 14, 1999.

Gruhn, George, in-person interview, June 17, 1998.

Haney, Carlton, telephone interview, June 9, 1997.

Harris, Charles, telephone interview, February 14, 1998.

Harris, Emmylou, telephone interview, April 25, 1999.

Hartford, John, telephone interviews, October 19, 1996.

———— [B], telephone interview, January 29, 1997.

———— [C], in-person interview, May 15, 1997.

———— [D], telephone interview, July 17, 1998.

Harvey, Francis Johnson, in-person interview, May 14, 1997.

Henson, Billy, in-person interview, August 20, 1997.

Hicks, Bobby, in-person interview, May 15, 1997.

———— [B], telephone interview, April 23, 1999.

Howard, Randy, in-person interview, October 17, 1997.

Hutchens, Doug, "The Last Trip Home," posting to bgrass-l@lsv.uky.edu, September 19, 1996.

———— [B], telephone interview, February 19, 1998.

Isenhour, Tom, in-person interviews, June 8–9, 1999.

Jayne, Mitch (see Dillards, The).

Keith, Bill (William Bradford), in-person interview, July 29, 1997 (see also Blue Grass Boys reunions, Fairfield, Connecticut, and Louisville, Kentucky).

Kershaw, Doug, in-person interview, June 18, 1998.

King, Jay, posting to www.healey.com.au/~mkear/monroe.htm September 1996.

Kiper, Rosetta Monroe, in-person interview, May 14, 1997.

———— [B], in-person interview, October 20, 1997.

———— [C], June 27, 1998.

———— [D], telephone interview, January 18, 1999.

———— and Bertha Monroe Kurtz, in-person interview, September 24, 1996.

Koskela, Kim, in-person interview, May 11, 1997.

Kurtz, Bertha Monroe (see Rosetta Monroe Kiper).

LaBella, Julia, in-person interview, May 20, 1997.

LeRoy, Lance, in-person interview, June 15, 1998.

Lewis, Wayne (see Blue Grass Boys, Fairfield, Connecticut).

Lindeman, Richard E., letter to Lola Cook Anderson re: Vandiver family history, September 7, 1975, Rinzler files, SFA.

Logan, Benjamin "Tex" and Peggy, in-person interview, December 6, 1997.

Long, Mike, in-person interview, October 23, 1997.

Louvin, Charlie, in-person interview, June 22, 1998.

Lowinger, Gene (see Blue Grass Boys, Fairfield, Connecticut).

Magram, David, telephone interview, August 30, 1998.

Martin, Jimmy, in-person interview, August 21, 1997.

———— [B], in-person interview, April 7, 1999.

Martin, Lou, telephone interview, March 1, 1999.

Mauldin, Ervin, signed statement, February 18, 1998, author's files.

———— and Hallie Mauldin, in-person interview, June 10, 1998.

Mauldin, Larry, in-person interview, June 10, 1998.

Mauldin, Stella and Virginia, in-person interview, June 10, 1998.

McCoury, Del, telephone interview, July 14, 1998.

McCullough, Judy, "Biography of Monroe," posting to bgrass-l@lsv.uky.edu, July 31, 1999.

McInturff, Betty, in-person interview, June 25, 1998.

McIntyre, Les, "Personal Thoughts on John Duffey," posting to bgrass-l@lsv.uky.edu, December 11, 1996.

McPeake, Curtis, telephone interview, February 4, 1998.

Menius, Art, in-person interview, October 15, 1998.

Monroe, Mrs. Geanie (widow of Bill Monroe's brother Speed), Rosine, Kentucky, via Wendell Allen, biographical sketch of Pen Vandiver (undated: circa mid-1970s), Rinzler files, SFA.

Monroe, James, telephone interview, October 21, 1996.

Monroe, James William (grandson of Bill Monroe's uncle, William M.), telephone interview, November 29, 1997.

Monroe, William Smith "Bill," in-person interview by Jack Brittane, place unknown, circa 1985.

—— by Orin Friesen, Wellington, Kansas, May 15, 1983.

—— in-person interview by Orin Friesen, 1986 (place and date unknown).

—— in-person interview by Jon Lawrence for KBRQ, Denver, at Telluride Bluegrass Festival, Telluride, CO, 1983 (date unknown).

—— telephone interview by Ralph Rinzler (Monroe probably speaking from his farm in Sumner County, Tennessee), Spring 1965 (Smithsonian Folklife collection FP-RINZ-7RR-0003).

—— in-person interview by Ralph Rinzler, Cambridge, MA, 2 A.M., February 6, 1966 (Smithsonian Folklife collection FP-RINZ-7RR-0002).

—— in-person interview by Ralph Rinzler, 1966 (place and date unknown) (Smithsonian Folklife collection FP-RINZ-7RR-0005).

—— in-person interview by Ralph Rinzler, Madison Square Garden, New York (date and year unknown), FP-1993–RR-0007, SFA.

—— in-person interview by Ralph Rinzler, place unknown, August 19, 1971, FP-1993-CT-0251, SFA.

—— in-person interview by Ralph Rinzler, place unknown, August 1971, FP-1993-CT-0262, SFA.

—— in-person interview by Ralph Rinzler, probably in Shoney's Restaurant, McGavock Pike, Nashville, Tennessee, circa 1979, FP-1994-CT-0520, SFA.

—— in-person interview by Richard D. Smith, Waterloo Village Bluegrass Festival, Stanhope, New Jersey, May 26, 1984.

—— in-person interviews by Pete Wernick, New York and Colorado, April 1966, October 1978, November 1978, November 1984.

—— and Richard Greene, in-person interview by Ralph Rinzler, place unknown, 1966, FP-RINZ-7RR-0004, SFA.

—— and Richard Greene, in-person interview by Ralph Rinzler, place unknown, 1966, FP-RINZ-7RR-0006, SFA.

O'Bryant, Alan, in-person interview, August 2, 1997.

Penny, Jim, Dundee, Scotland, letters to author, February 14 and February 15, 1999.

Pinson, Bob, in-person interview, August 21, 1997.

Price, Bill, telephone interview, February 13, 1998.

——— [B], in-person interviews, June 10–11, 1998.

Pugh, Ronnie, in-person interview, August 20, 1997.

Pruett, Jeanne, in-person interview, June 19, 1997.

Renfrew, Reba Murphy, telephone interview, June 27, 1998.

Reno, Dale and Ronnie, in-person interview, September 5, 1998.

Rinzler, Kate, telephone interview, January 10, 1997.

Robins, Butch, in-person interview, June 8, 1998.

Rogers, Mary Fanny, in-person interview, May 14, 1997.

Rosenberg, Neil V., in-person interview, February 24, 1998.

Rowan, Peter, in-person interview, December 5, 1997.

——— [B], telephone interview, May 17, 1999.

Ruby, Goldie Johnson, telephone interview, July 27, 1998.

Scott, Tommy, telephone interview, December 12, 1998.

Scruggs, Earl, unpublished in-person interview by Douglas B. Green for the Country Music Foundation oral history project, 1974.

Scruggs, Louise (Mrs. Earl), Madison, Tennessee, letter to David Magram, January 8, 1963, author's files.

——— Madison, Tennessee, letter to David Magram, March 2, 1964, author's files.

Seckler, John Ray "Curly," telephone interview, January 29, 1998.

Seeger, Mike, in-person interview, October 15, 1997.

Sexton, Cheryl, telephone interview, February 1, 1998.

Shott, Reverend Fred C., in-person interview, April 7, 1999.

Shumate, Jimmy, telephone interviews, December 20, 1997, and January 16, 1998.

Skaggs, Ricky, telephone interview, May 4, 1999.

Smith, Billy, in-person interview, June 24, 1998.

Smith, Charlie, telephone interview, April 20, 1999.

Smith, Hazel Boone, in-person interview, May 19, 1997.

——— [B], in-person interview, August 19, 1997.

Spinks, Hayward F., in-person interview, May 12, 1997.

Stafford, Tim, in-person interview, August 2, 1997.

Stanley, Ralph, telephone interview, January 7, 1998.

Stauffer, Virginia, telephone interview, July 20, 1998.

Stephenson, Larry, telephone interview, April 19, 1999.

Streeter, Della, in-person interview, April 9, 1999.

——— [B], telephone interview, July 29, 1999.

Stuart, Marty, telephone interview, April 22, 1999.

Stubbs, Eddie, in-person interview, Nashville, Tennessee, May 16, 1997.

——— [B], telephone interview, February 13, 1999.

——— [C], in-person interview, April 12, 1999.

———— [D], telephone interview, June 4, 1999.

———— [E], telephone interview, July 28, 1999.

Sykes, Ernie, telephone interview, April 6, 1999 (see also Blue Grass Boys reunion, Fairfield, Connecticut).

Tate, Clarence "Tater," in-person interview, May 18, 1997 (see also Blue Grass Boys reunion, Fairfield, Connecticut).

Taylor, Robert Arthur "Tut," telephone interview, February 4, 1998.

Tinsley, Harry D., in-person interviews, May 12, 1997, and October 20, 1997.

Wakefield, Frank (see Blue Grass Boys reunion, Louisville, Kentucky).

Watson, Arthel "Doc," telephone interview, June 3, 1998.

Webb, Dean (see Dillards, The).

Werman, Judy Rinzler, telephone interview, January 2, 1997.

White, Buck, in-person interview, June 25, 1998.

White, Roland, in-person interview, August 2, 1997.

Williams, Doc, telephone interview via Eddie Stubbs, April 24, 1999.

Williams, Melinda, in-person interview, June 12, 1998.

Williams, Wynn, telephone interview, December 28, 1998.

Williamson, Tony, in-person interview, October 16, 1997.

Wiseman, Malcolm "Mac," in-person interview, May 19, 1997.

Yeomans, MaryE, "The Songs of Bill Monroe at the Ryman," posting to bgrass-l@lsv. uky.edu, April 22, 1997.

Books, Articles, and Public Documents

Abramson, Rudy. "Monroe Tunes: Mid-America Picking Up on Bluegrass," *Los Angeles Times,* June 19, 1980.

Ahlgren, Calvin. "Bluegrass Documentary Hits All Right Notes," Datebook entertainment section, *San Francisco Chronicle,* December 5, 1993.

Anderson, Dan. "More than 5,000 graduate from UK," *Lexington Herald-Leader,* May 12, 1985.

Anderson, Lola Cook. *The Cook Family History,* private publication, Tucson, Arizona (undated).

Appleton, Charles. "Rings, cash stolen off Bill Monroe bus," *Nashville Banner,* December 17, 1985, p. 1.

Ayers, Tom. "'I Feel It Down Through Music': World View in the Titles of Bill Monroe's Recordings," *Journal of Country Music,* Fall 1975.

Bartenstein, Fred. "Carlton Haney," in *The Encyclopedia of Country Music,* New York: Oxford University Press, 1998.

Battle, J. H., W. H. Perrin, and G. C. Kniffin. "John H. Monroe," in *Kentucky: A History of the State,* Louisville: F. A. Battey Publishing Co., 1885.

Billboard. "Monroe & Carter to Country Hall of Fame," October 24, 1970.

————. "Beanblossom Bluegrass Fest draws 35,000," Amusement Business Section, July 14, 1973, p. 4.

Bolton, Bennett. "Brave last days of bluegrass king Bill Monroe," *National Enquirer,* July 23, 1996, p. 16.

Bragg, Rick. "A Balladeer of Bluegrass Is Now Gone Yet Lives On," *New York Times,* November 4, 1998, p. A14.

Brown County Democrat, "For sale: Home of the Bluegrass festival," March 30, 1988, p. 1.

————. "Country stars shine at the bluegrass festival," September 9, 1992, p. 13.

Bruce, Dix. "Bill Monroe: The Bossman of Bluegrass," *Frets,* May 1979.

————. "An Interview with Bill Monroe: 'Bluegrass — There's Not a Prettier Name in the World,'" *Frets,* May 1979[B].

Bumgardner, Ed. "That high-lonesome sound loses a voice," *Winston-Salem Journal,* September 13, 1998, p. D2.

Burrison, John A. "Fiddlers in the Alley; Atlanta as an Early Country Music Center," *The Atlanta Historical Bulletin,* Summer 1977.

Canfield, Clark. "Bluegrass legend Bill Monroe should have a moving year," *Nashville Banner,* May 9, 1986.

Cantwell, Robert. "Believing in Bluegrass," *The Atlantic,* March 1972.

————. *Bluegrass Breakdown: The Making of the Old Southern Sound,* Urbana: University of Illinois Press, 1984.

————. *When We Were Good — The Folk Revival,* Cambridge: Harvard University Press, 1996.

Carlson, Norman. "Brown County Jamboree," *Bluegrass Unlimited,* December 1966.

————. "Bluegrass Days at Bean Blossom," *Bluegrass Unlimited,* August 1967.

————. "Bill Monroe's Bluegrass Festival," *Bluegrass Unlimited,* August 1968.

Carpenter, Dan. "Bluegrass father hopes festival will play on," *Indianapolis Star,* June 18, 1988, p. 1.

————. "Bill Monroe will be back for annual wingding," *Indianapolis Star,* February 28, 1989.

Carr, Patrick. *The Illustrated History of Country Music,* New York: Dolphin, 1980.

Case, Floy. "Floy Case Reports" column, *The Mountain Broadcast and Prairie Recorder,* section one, December 1944.

————. "Floy Case Reports" column, *The Mountain Broadcast and Prairie Recorder,* September 1945.

Cash, Johnny, with Patrick Carr. *Cash: The Autobiography,* San Francisco: Harper, 1997.

Childry, Frank W. "Poetry from the Bluegrass: Image and Metaphor in Selected Lyrics from the Bill Monroe Repertoire," *Old Time Country,* Winter 1990.

Corbin, Everett. "'What Is More Country Than Bluegrass?' — Bill Monroe," *Music City News*, December 1970, p. 19.

Country Music, "It's a Crying Shame," January 1986, pp. 19–20.

Country Song Roundup, "Musical Monroes," February 1952, p. 15.

Cresson, W. P. "James Monroe's Ancestry," in *James Monroe*, Chapel Hill: University of North Carolina Press, 1946.

Crowder, Sara McNulty. "Pen Vandiver," *Bluegrass Unlimited*, June 1993 [see also Sara McNulty].

Davidson County, Tennessee, Chancery Court records. File No. A-5787, *Bessie Lee Mauldin Monroe vs. William Smith (Bill) Monroe*, 1975.

———. File No. 86–1411–I (Book 7192, pp. 455–456), *Third Century Inc. vs. William Smith Monroe and James Monroe d/b/a Bill Monroe Bluegrass Hall of Fame*, February 25, 1987.

———. File No. 86–1411–I (Book 7605, p. 306), *Third Century Inc. vs. William Smith Monroe and James Monroe d/b/a Bill Monroe Bluegrass Hall of Fame*, June 30, 1988.

Davidson County, Tennessee, Circuit Court records. Case No. 34918, *Carolyn Minnie Monroe vs. William S. Monroe*, 1959.

———. Case No. 46521, *Brenda Harris Monroe vs. James William Monroe*, 1965.

———. Case No. 53319, *Brenda Harris Monroe vs. James William Monroe*, 1968 to 1980.

Davidson County, Tennessee, Deeds. Book 1258, p. 168, Alexander and Pennie Schmittou to Bill and Carolyn Monroe, March 4, 1943.

———. Book 9254, pp. 511–514, James Monroe to Dyke Tatum (trustee), February 18, 1994.

———. Book 9641, p. 692, First Investment Corporation to James Monroe, March 30, 1995.

Davidson County, Tennessee, Record Books. Book 5842, p. 306, tax lien, James W. Monroe d/b/a Monroe Manor, January 14, 1982.

———. Book 6401, p. 281, tax lien, Monroe and Associates, October 9, 1984.

———. Book 6966, p. 218, affidavit of Melissa Monroe and James Monroe in the matter of the estate of Carolyn Minnie Brown Monroe, September 2, 1986.

———. Book 7589, p. 291, power of attorney assigned by Melissa K. Monroe to James W. Monroe, April 7, 1988.

Davis, Donna. "Monroe glad assault charge behind him," *Nashville Banner*, May 11, 1989, p. B1.

Dawidoff, Nicholas. *In the Country of Country*, New York: Pantheon Books/Random House, 1997.

———. "Bill Monroe: Good Sad," *New York Times Magazine*, December 29, 1996, p. 28.

DeCurtis, Anthony. "Bill Monroe: Father of Bluegrass Is Dead at 84," *Rolling Stone,* October 31, 1996, p. 20.

DeParle, Jason. "At Home with Bill Monroe — Lots to Sing, Little to Say," *New York Times,* June 9, 1994, C1.

Edwards, Joe. "'Sad Time': Bluegrass legend Bill Monroe dies at age 84," Associated Press item in *Charlotte Observer,* September 10, 1996, p. 4A.

Elkins, Paul L. "Electric is a Sin," letter, *Bluegrass Unlimited,* July 1970.

Erbsen, Wayne. "Cleo Davis: The Original Bluegrass Boy," *Bluegrass Unlimited,* February 1982.

———. "Cleo Davis: The Original Bluegrass Boy, Conclusion," *Bluegrass Unlimited,* March 1982.

Escot, Collin, with George Merritt and William MacEwen. *Hank Williams: The Biography,* Boston: Little, Brown and Company, 1994.

Feller Brown Realty and Auction. Advertisement for auction of Monroe farm, April 1994.

Foster, Alice (Alice Gerrard). "Growing Up in Rosine, Kentucky: An Interview with Bill Monroe," *Sing Out!* July–August 1969; reprinted in *Ohio County News,* Hartford, Kentucky, September 17, 1970.

Fowler, Ingrid. "The Master's Mandolin," *Frets,* May 1979.

French, Bob. "Interview with Lester Flatt and Earl Scruggs January 1967," *Bluegrass Unlimited,* July 1967.

Garkovich, Lorraine. *Population and Community in Rural America.* New York: Greenwood Press, 1989.

Geiger, Fred. "One Way of Looking at the First International Bluegrass Festival in Warrenton, Virginia," *Bluegrass Unlimited,* August 1966.

Gentry, Linnell. *A History and Encyclopedia of Country, Western, and Gospel Music,* Nashville: McQuiddy Press, 1961.

Gerrard, Alice (see Alice Foster).

Goldsmith, Peter D. *Making People's Music: Moe Asch and Folkways Records,* Washington: Smithsonian Institution Press, 1998.

Goldsmith, Tommy. "Bill Monroe's prized mandolin back in shape," *Tennessean,* February 27, 1986.

———, and Donna Dearmore. "Bill Monroe's trademark mandolin vandalized," *Nashville Tennessean,* November 15, 1985.

———, and John Watson. "Woman says Opry's Monroe kicked her, hit her with Bible," *Nashville Tennessean,* May 3, 1989.

———. "Fifty Years and Counting: Bill Monroe Drives On" in Kingsbury (ed.), *Country Reader,* Nashville: Country Music Foundation Press, 1996.

Green, Douglas B. "The Charlie Monroe Story, Part I: Boyhood in Kentucky," *Muleskinner News,* January 1973.

————. "The Charlie Monroe Story, Part II: The Monroe Brothers," *Muleskinner News,* February 1973.

————. "The Charlie Monroe Story, Part III: The Kentucky Partners," *Muleskinner News,* March 1973.

Guralnick, Peter. *Last Train to Memphis: The Rise of Elvis Presley,* Boston: Little, Brown and Company, 1994.

Hagen, Chet. *Grand Ole Opry,* New York: Owl Books/Henry Holt, 1989.

Harrington, Richard. "The Man Who Brought America to the Mall," *Washington Post,* July 4, 1994.

Hauslohner, Amy Worthington. "Bill Monroe: The Legend Continues," *Bluegrass Unlimited,* September 1991.

Hay, George D. *A Story of the Grand Ole Opry,* Nashville: Hay/WSM Radio, 1945.

Helm, Levon, with Stephen Davis. *This Wheel's on Fire,* New York: William Morrow & Co., 1993.

Hill, Laura Eipper. "Bill Monroe Opening 'Bluegrass' Steakhouse," *Nashville Tennessean,* April 17, 1981.

————. "Bill Monroe's Mandolin: The Ultimate Bluegrass Vintage Instrument," *Bluegrass Unlimited,* June 1982.

Hitchner, Earle. "Bill Monroe Remembered," *Wall Street Journal,* September 16, 1996, p. A16.

Homan, Becky. "Can bluegrass survive?" *Louisville Times,* Scene section, October 15, 1977.

Horstman, Dorothy. *Sing Your Heart Out, Country Boy,* Nashville: Country Music Foundation Press, revised edition, 1986.

Hume, Martha. "Daddy Bluegrass and His Blues," *Country Music,* May 1976.

Hurst, Jack. "Mellowing Father of Bluegrass," *The Tennessean,* June 25, 1972.

————. *Nashville's Grand Ole Opry,* New York: Harry N. Abrahms, 1975.

————. "Bill Monroe: From refined oil to slick music," *Chicago Tribune,* Tempo/Arts section, October 12, 1977.

————. "Bill Monroe sinks roots deeper into bluegrass turf," *Chicago Tribune,* Sunday Amusement section, September 6, 1981.

————. "Bill Monroe: Still the Pick of the Bluegrass Legends," *Chicago Tribune,* Tempo/Arts section, September 20, 1984.

Hutchens, Doug. "Edd Mayfield —The Mystery Man," *Bluegrass Unlimited,* August 1983.

————. "The Bill Monroe Museum and Bluegrass Hall of Fame: The Dream Comes True," *Bluegrass Unlimited,* October 1984.

Indianapolis News. "Bill Monroe is calling it quits in Hoosierland," June 17, 1988, p. A8.

Jones, Malcolm, Jr. "The Passing of a Patriarch; Bill Monroe's bluegrass aimed straight for the heart," *Newsweek,* September 23, 1996, p. 75.

Kingsbury, Paul (ed.). *The Country Reader*, Nashville: Country Music Foundation Press, 1996.

Koon, William Henry. "Gospel Bluegrass," *Bluegrass Unlimited*, August 1970.

———. "Newgrass, Oldgrass and Bluegrass," *JEMF Quarterly*, Spring 1974.

Krishef, Robert K. *The Grand Ole Opry*, Minneapolis: Lerner Publications, 1978.

Kuntz, Tom. "Word for Word — The Presley Papers," *New York Times*, Week in Review section, August 15, 1999, p. 7.

Kuykendall, Pete. "James Monroe," *Bluegrass Unlimited*, July 1973.

Lambert, Jake, with Curly Seckler. *The Good Things Out Weigh the Bad: A Biography of Lester Flatt*, Hendersonville, Tennessee: Jay-Lyn Publication, 1982.

Lanham, Charmine. "Bill Monroe's Mandolin Is Restored," *Bluegrass Unlimited*, April 1986.

Lawrence, Keith. "The Greatest? Guitar picker's life ended before promise realized," *Messenger-Inquirer*, Owensboro, Kentucky, March 2, 1980.

———. "Bill Monroe fathered his 'own' music," *Messenger-Inquirer*, Owensboro, Kentucky, September 27, 1987.

Lehmann-Haupt, Christopher. "Out of My Mind on Bluegrass," *New York Times Magazine*, September 13, 1970.

LeRoy, Lance. "Lester Flatt — His Boyhood and His Early Career," *Bluegrass Star*, February 1972.

———. "Lester Flatt — His Boyhood and His Early Career (Continued)," *Bluegrass Star*, March 1972.

———. "Lester Flatt — His Boyhood and His Early Career (Conclusion)," *Bluegrass Star*, April 1972.

———. "Master of Bluegrass Fiddle Soul . . . Chubby Wise," *Bluegrass Unlimited*, March 1996.

Lightfoot, William E. "Mose Rager," in *The Encyclopedia of Country Music*, New York: Oxford University Press, 1998.

Lomax, Alan. "Bluegrass Background: Folk Music with Overdrive," *Esquire*, October 1959.

Lundy, Ronni. "Not all high notes were from festival's music," *Louisville Times*, September 13, 1982.

———. "The real, actual, down-home Bill Monroe," *Louisville Times*, Scene section, September 10, 1983.

Malone, Bill C. *Country Music, U.S.A.*, Austin: University of Texas Press, 1985 (revised edition).

———. *Singing Cowboys and Musical Mountaineers: Southern Culture and the Roots of Country Music*, Athens: University of Georgia Press, 1993.

———, and Judith McCulloh (eds.). *Stars of Country Music: Uncle Dave Macon to Johnny Rodriquez*, Chicago: University of Illinois Press, 1975.

Marini, Stephen. Liner notes to *Sing and Joyful Be* by Norumbega Harmony, Ginnie Ely, North Reading, Massachusetts, 1989 (cassette — no catalog number).

Martin, John. "Legislator: Monroe funding in budget plan," *Owensboro Messsenger-Inquirer,* January 16, 1998.

McCampbell. "Blue Grass Country to open in mid-July," *Nashville Tennessean,* June 21, 1987.

McKuen, Brad. "Monroe Brothers Discography," *Bluegrass Unlimited,* December 1967.

McNulty, Sara. "Uncle Pen's Fiddle," *Bluegrass Unlimited,* July 1992.

Melaragni, Janet. "Ray Whitley: Rootin', Tootin', Singin' Star," *Pickin',* January 1979.

Menius, Arthur. "A Bluegrass Hall of Fame," *Bluegrass Unlimited,* February 1984, p. 10.

Monroe, Bill. Liner notes to *Bill Monroe's Uncle Pen,* MCA Records, DL7-5348.

Monroe, James. "Bill Monroe (From a Farm Boy to a Legend)," *The Bluegrass Star,* October 1971.

———. "Bill Monroe (From a Farm Boy to a Legend)" (continuation), *The Bluegrass Star,* November 1971.

———. "Bill Monroe (From a Farm Boy to a Legend)" (conclusion), *The Bluegrass Star,* December 1971.

———. Advertorial, *Bluegrass Unlimited,* September 1994.

Morrison, Craig. *Go Cat Go!: Rockabilly Music and Its Makers,* Urbana: University of Chicago Press, 1996.

Nash, Alanna. "Bill Monroe," in *Behind Closed Doors: Talking with the Legends of Country Music,* New York: Alfred A. Knopf, 1988.

Nashville Banner. "Bill Monroe arrested on assault charge," May 2, 1989.

———. "Daughter of Bill Monroe dead at 54," December 4, 1990.

———. "Town wants to keep old log cabin," October 29, 1991.

Nashville Tennessean. "Singer Asks Share of 'Kentucky Waltz,'" April 15, 1951.

———. "Monroe Says He Paid for 'Kentucky Waltz,'" May 5, 1951.

———. "Super-Depreciated Cadillac Brings Suit," September 27, 1958.

———. "Officials puzzled over missing contents of Bill Monroe's safe," January 16, 1986.

Oermann, Robert K. *America's Music: The Roots of Country,* Atlanta: Turner Publishing, 1996.

———, and Tommy Goldsmith. "High Lonesome Voice Stilled," *The Tennessean,* September 10, 1996.

Oliver, P. "Bill Monroe at the Albert Hall," *Jazz Monthly,* Vol. 12 (July 1966):20–21.

Orr, Jay. "Bill Monroe gets golden salute," *Nashville Banner,* October 26, 1989.

———, and Michael Gray. "Innovator and Mentor Monroe Lives on in Music," *Nashville Banner,* September 10, 1996.

Pareles, Jon. "Bill Monroe Dies at 84; Fused Musical Roots into Bluegrass," *New York Times,* September 10, 1996, p. D22.

———. "Hail! Hail! Rock-and-Roll," *New York Times*, May 6, 1997, C11.

Paxman, Art. "The Son of Bluegrass: James Monroe keeps dad's legacy alive," *Country Weekly*, March 24, 1998, p. 52.

Perkins, Carl, and David McGee. *Go, Cat, Go: The Life and Times of Carl Perkins*, New York: Hyperion, 1996.

Polk, R. L., & Co. *Polk's Nashville (Davidson County, Tenn) City Directory*, St. Louis, Missouri, various years 1939 through 1975.

Rao, Joe. "Sky Watch" column, *New York Times*, Sunday, March 28, 1999, Metro section, p. 29.

Rathe, Steve. "Bill Monroe," *Pickin'*, February 1974.

Reid, Gary B. "The Stanley Brothers," in *The Encyclopedia of Country Music*, New York: Oxford University Press, 1998.

Reuters News Service. "A Foot-Stomping Farewell to the King of Bluegrass," in *New York Times*, September 12, 1996, p. D19.

Rhodes, Don. "Lester Flatt," *Bluegrass Unlimited*, October 1974.

———. "Monroe, the father — Monroe, the son," *Bluegrass Unlimited*, February 1978.

———. "Lester Flatt: Talking with a Bluegrass Giant," *Pickin'*, February 1979.

———. "Bill Monroe: Still a star, still a good guy," *Augusta Chronicle*, November 19, 1989.

Rinzler, Ralph. "Bill Monroe — 'The Daddy of Blue Grass Music,'" *Sing Out!*, February–March 1963.

———. Liner notes (uncredited) to *Bluegrass Instrumentals*, Decca DL 74601, 1965.

———. Liner notes to *The High, Lonesome Sound of Bill Monroe and His Blue Grass Boys*, Decca DL 74780, 1966.

———. "Bill Monroe — Thirty Years," *Bluegrass Unlimited*, October 1969.

———. "Bill Monroe," in Bill C. Malone and Judith McCulloh (eds.), *Stars of Country Music: Uncle Dave Macon to Johnny Rodriquez*, Chicago: University of Illinois Press, 1975.

Rolling Stone. "Sweet Inspirations," September 21, 1989.

Rooney, Jim. *Bossmen: Bill Monroe & Muddy Waters*, New York: Dial, 1971.

Rosenberg, Neil V. "From Sound to Style: the Emergence of Bluegrass," *Journal of American Folklore*, April–June 1967, pp. 143–150.

———. "Reflections on Roanoke," *Bluegrass Unlimited*, January 1967.

———. *Bill Monroe and His Blue Grass Boys: An Illustrated Discography*, Nashville: Country Music Foundation Press, 1974.

———. "Thirty Years Ago This Month: May 1954," *Bluegrass Unlimited*, May 1984.

———. "Thirty Years Ago This Month: November 1954," *Bluegrass Unlimited*, November 1984.

———. *Bluegrass: A History*, Urbana: University of Illinois Press, 1985.

———. "Thirty Years Ago This Month: January 1955," *Bluegrass Unlimited*, January 1985.

———. "Thirty Years Ago This Month: June 1955," *Bluegrass Unlimited*, June 1985.

———. *Flatt and Scruggs 1948–1959*, booklet for compact disk set, Bear Family Records BCD-15472, Hambergen, Germany: Bear Family Records, 1991.

———. "Flatt and Scruggs and the Foggy Mountain Boys," in *The Encyclopedia of Country Music*, New York: Oxford University Press, 1998[A].

———. "Compiling the Bill Monroe Discography: Challenges and Issues," paper given at the Country Music Conference, Nashville, June 1, 1998[B].

———. "Bill Monroe Recordings, Complete Chronology: 1981–1996," personal compilation, August 26, 1998[C].

———, and Charles Wolfe. *Bill Monroe — Blue Grass 1950–1958*, booklet for compact disk set, Bear Family Records BCD-15423, Hambergen, Germany: Bear Family Records, 1989.

———, and Charles Wolfe. *Bill Monroe — Blue Grass 1959–1969*, booklet for compact disk set, Bear Family Records BCD-15529, Hambergen, Germany: Bear Family Records, 1991.

Rumble, John. "Cultural Dimensions of the Bluegrass Boom," *Journal of Country Music*, Fall 1975.

———. *The Music of Bill Monroe from 1936 to 1994*, booklet for compact disk set, MCA MCAD4-11048, Universal City, California; MCA Records, 1994.

———. "Bill Monroe," in *The Encyclopedia of Country Music*, New York: Oxford University Press, 1998.

Rust, Brian. *The Victor Master Book*, Volume 2 1925–1936, Stanhope, New Jersey: Walter C. Allen, second printing 1970.

Saal, Herbert. "Pickin' and Singin'," *Newsweek*, June 29, 1970, p. 85.

Seeger, Pete. *How to Play the 5-String Banjo*, Beacon, New York: published by the author, 1961 (3rd edition).

Shelton, Robert. "Folk Joins Jazz at Newport," *New York Times*, July 19, 1959, p. 7.

———. "Newport Folk-Music Festival Opens 3-Day Run Before 13,000," *New York Times*, July 27, 1963, p. 9.

———. "Folk-Music Fete Called a Success," *New York Times*, July 29, 1963, p. 15.

Sherborne, Robert. "Bill Monroe believes he may be in danger," *Nashville Tennessean*, December 1985.

Skaggs, Ricky. "Bill Monroe: Fire burned until the end," *Country Weekly*, October 8, 1996, p. 56.

Skinker, Chris. "Kenny Baker," in *The Encyclopedia of Country Music*, Oxford University Press, 1998.

———. "Bean Blossom," in *The Encyclopedia of Country Music*, Oxford University Press, 1998[B].

———. "Jimmy Martin" in *The Encyclopedia of Country Music*, Oxford University Press, 1998[C].

Smith, Hazel. "Monroe Homecoming," *Bluegrass Unlimited*, November 1973.

Smith, L. Mayne. "An Introduction to Bluegrass," *Journal of American Folklore*, July–September 1965.

———. "Additions and Corrections," *Bluegrass Unlimited*, January 1967.

Smith, Richard D. "Ralph Rinzler: Preserving American Folk Arts," *Pickin'*, November 1979.

———. "Bill Monroe: His Best Days on Earth," *Bluegrass Unlimited*, May 1985.

———. *Bluegrass: An Informal Guide*, Chicago: a cappella books/Chicago Review Press, 1995.

———. "William Smith Monroe: 1911–1996," *Bluegrass Unlimited*, October 1996.

———. "Returning to Rosine," *Bluegrass Unlimited*, December 1996.

———. "Monroes of Rosine, Kentucky — A Family History," *Bluegrass Unlimited*, January 1997.

———. "Bluegrass Music," in *The Encyclopedia of Country Music*, New York: Oxford University Press, 1998.

———. "Ralph Rinzler," in *The Encyclopedia of Country Music*, New York: Oxford University Press, 1998.

Spartanburg, County of, Probate Court, Spartanburg, South Carolina. Marriage certificate, William Monroe and Carolyn Brown, October 18, 1936, Marriage License Book T, p. 591.

Stewart, Peggy. "Family Gossip" column, *Rural Radio*, November 1938, p. 31.

———. "Family Gossip" column, *Rural Radio*, May 1939, p. 31.

Stubbs, Eddie. "Johnnie & Jack: The Recordings," in booklet to CD collection *Johnnie & Jack*, Bear Family Records BCD 1553, Hambergen, Germany: Bear Family Records, 1992.

———. "Don Owens — A Pioneering Figure in Bluegrass and Country Music," *Bluegrass Unlimited*, June 1998.

Sulloway, Frank J. *Born to Rebel: Birth Order, Family Dynamics and Creative Lives*, New York: Pantheon Books, 1996.

Sumner County, Tennessee, Civil Court Records. Case No. 4676-C. *William Monroe vs. Della Monroe*, 1987.

———. Deed Books, Book 156, pp. 35–38, Pasayan to Monroe, 1954.

———. Deed Books, Book 511, pp. 728–736. "Ante-Nuptial Contract, William Smith Monroe and Della Estelle Streeter," 1985.

———. Lien Books 5, 6, 7 and 15, William Smith Monroe and Bill Monroe & Blue Grass Boys listings, assessments 1969–1977.

———. Record Books, Book 404, pp. 712–715, Monroe to Bank of Goodlettsville, March 1, 1994, received March 4, 1994.

———. Book 426, pp. 348–351, Monroe to Opryland USA, Inc., May 20, 1996, received May 26, 1994.

———. Book 635, pp. 363–365, letter with attachment, Gaylord Entertainment Co. (Opryland) to Tax Assessors office, October 8, 1996, received October 11, 1996.

Swarthmore College Bulletin (writer uncredited). "Curator for the Common Man," May 1970.

Talvitie, William O., and Bruce Kaplan. "Bluegrass Music: Innovations in Context," *JEMF Quarterly*, Winter 1973.

Thompson, Catherine. "Charges against Monroe dropped," *Nashville Tennessean*, May 11, 1989.

Tichi, Cecelia (ed.). "Readin' Country Music: Steel Guitars, Opry Stars and Honky Tonk Bars," *The South Atlantic Quarterly*, 94:1 (special issue), Durham: Duke University Press, Winter 1995.

———. *High Lonesome: The American Culture of Country Music*, Chapel Hill: University of North Carolina Press, 1994.

Times-News (Hartford–Beaver Dam, Kentucky). "Ohio County gets another kick," October 17, 1991.

———. "The cabin's gone," October 31, 1991.

Tomlinson, Kenneth Y. "Winds of the Appalachians — Sometimes One Man Can Build a Tradition," *The American Enterprise*, March/April 1997.

Tosches, Nick. "Rockabilly!," pp. 217–237, in Patrick Carr, *The Illustrated History of Country Music*, New York: Dolphin, 1980.

Tribe, Ivan. "Charlie Monroe," *Bluegrass Unlimited*, October 1975.

———. "Charlie Monroe," in *The Encyclopedia of Country Music*, New York: Oxford University Press, 1998.

Vernon, Bill. "Last Respects to the Giant Charlie Monroe," *Pickin'*, January 1976.

Vied, Steve. "Monroe memorial dedicated," *Owensboro Messenger-Inquirer*, April 26, 1997, p. 1 of Region section.

Von Schmidt, Eric, and Jim Rooney. *Baby, Let Me Follow You Down: The illustrated story of the Cambridge folk years*, Amherst: University of Massachusetts Press, 1979 (second edition 1994).

Washburn, Jim, and Richard Johnston. *Martin Guitars: An Illustrated Celebration of America's Premier Guitarmaker*, Emmaus, Pennsylvania: Rodale Press, 1997.

Weintraub, Boris. "SRO for Mr. Bluegrass," *Washington Star-News*, November 12, 1973.

Welding, Pete. "Earl Scruggs and the Sound of Bluegrass," *Sing Out!* 12 (1962):4–7 n.2.

Wernick, Peter. "Interview with Don Reno," *Bluegrass Unlimited*, February 1967.

———. *Bluegrass Songbook*, New York: Oak Publications, 1976.

Wesbrooks, Willie Egbert "Cousin Wilbur," with Barbara M. McLean and Sandra S. Grafton. *Everybody's Cousin*, New York: Manor Books, 1979.

Whitburn, Joel. *The Billboard Book of Top 40 Country Hits*, New York: Billboard Books/Watson-Guptill, 1996.

———. *Joel Whitburn's Top Country Albums*, New York: Billboard Books, 1997.

White, Buck. "Closing Day at Brown County Jamboree," *Bluegrass Star,* December 1971.

White, Virgil D. *Genealogical Abstracts of Revolutionary War Pension Files, Volume II: F-M,* Waynesboro, Tennessee: National Historical Publishing Co., 1991.

Wilson, Joe. Review of "Bluegrass Breakdown: The Making of the Old Southern Sound," in Kingsbury (ed.), *The Country Reader,* Nashville: Country Music Foundation Press, 1996.

Wilson, John S. "Bluegrass Is Growing as Music for City Ears," *New York Times,* April 13, 1971.

Winfrey, Lee. "A Look at Monroe, Courtesy of PBS," *Philadelphia Inquirer,* July 12, 1974.

Wolfe, Charles. *The Devil's Box: Masters of Southern Fiddling,* Knoxville: University of Tennesee Press, 1972.

———. "Bluegrass Touches: An Interview with Bill Monroe," *Old Time Music,* London, England, Spring 1975.

———. *Tennessee Strings: The Story of Country Music in Tennessee,* Knoxville: University of Tennesee Press, 1977.

———. "'String,'" *Bluegrass Unlimited,* June 1982.

———. *Bill Monroe — Blue Grass 1970–1979,* booklet for compact disk set, Bear Family Records BCD-15529, Hambergen, Germany: Bear Family Records, 1991.

———. *Kentucky Country: Folk and Country Music of Kentucky,* Lexington: University Press of Kentucky, 1996 edition.

———. "The Monroe Brothers — Before Bluegrass," *Journal of the American Academy for the Preservation of Old-Time Country Music,* October 1996[B].

———. "Monroe Brothers," in *The Encyclopedia of Country Music,* New York: Oxford University Press, 1998.

Wolmuth, Roger. "Bill Monroe — The father of bluegrass music still calls his own tune," *People,* September 1, 1986.

Wood, Jim. "The Legacy of Bill Monroe," *Strings,* May/June 1997.

Wright, John. *Traveling the High Way Home — Ralph Stanley and the World of Traditional Bluegrass Music,* Urbana: University of llinois Press, 1993.

WSM, Inc. *Official WSM Grand Ole Opry History-Picture Book,* Vol. 2, No. 2, Nashville: WSM, 1961.

Yeomans, MaryE. "Monroe Memorial at the Ryman," letter, *Bluegrass Unlimited,* November 1996.

———. "Tears Fell on Rosine," letter, *Bluegrass Unlimited,* November 1996[B].

⋆ RECOMMENDED LISTENING ⋆

Bill Monroe's recording career spanned six decades, beginning with the first Monroe Brothers sides cut for RCA in 1936; resuming with the first Blue Grass Boys cuts for RCA (1940–1941); continuing with Columbia (1945–1949) and then Decca/MCA (1950–1990); then capped by final (and, to date, largely unreleased) sessions produced by Vic Gabany (1993–1995) and various guest appearances (1991–1995).

Monroe participated in some 220 formally recorded studio sessions and concerts, plus countless informally taped live shows. A forthcoming book-length annotated discography by country and bluegrass scholars Charles Wolfe, Middle Tennessee State University, and Neil V. Rosenberg, Memorial University of Newfoundland, will document this recorded output in detail. Rather than duplicate their efforts, the following is presented as a guide to listening. Emphasis has been given to important collections and to those currently available.

Music Recordings

The Essential Bill Monroe & The Monroe Brothers, RCA 07863–67450–2. If not essential certainly early, with all sixteen sides of the pre-banjo Blue Grass Boys, plus nine strong tracks by the duo of Charlie and Bill.

The Essential Bill Monroe and His Blue Grass Boys 1945–1949, Columbia/Legacy C2K 52478. A two-CD set encompassing the classic Columbia sessions with Flatt, Scruggs, Wise, and Wiseman. Features some alternative takes plus an informative booklet by Mark A. Humphrey.

In the Pines, County CCS-114–CD. Powerful 1950s Decca material, including the original version of "My Little Georgia Rose," the post-Elvis remake of "Blue Moon of Kentucky," and the haunting title trio.

Bill Monroe: Bluegrass 1950–1958, Bear Family BCD 15423.
Bill Monroe: Bluegrass 1959–1969, Bear Family BCD 15423.
Bill Monroe: Bluegrass 1970–1979, Bear Family BCD 15423.

These landmark four-CD sets contain Monroe's entire Decca/MCA output from the 1950 Martin/Lyle/Clements band to the 1979 Lewis/Robins/Baker group. Charles Wolfe, Neil Rosenberg, Eddie Stubbs, Richard Weize, and other experts have contributed historical and discographical information to the superbly illustrated booklets.

Bill Monroe, Country Music Hall of Fame Series, MCA MCAD 10082. Decca/MCA high points ranging from "New Mule Skinner Blues" of 1950 to "Southern Flavor" of 1988, selected by John Rumble and Chris Skinker. An excellent one-CD introduction to Monroe's music.

I Saw the Light, MCA-20760–CS. Classic 1958 gospel quartet album with spare, highly effective accompaniment by mandolin, guitar, and bass (and even organ).

Bill Monroe & His Blue Grass Boys: Live Recordings 1956–1969, Smithsonian/Folkways SF 40063. Riveting moments captured by Ralph Rinzler, Mike Seeger, and others at country music parks, theaters, and jams. Includes nearly ten minutes of the reunion of Birch, Charlie, and Bill at the 1969 Smithsonian Festival of American Folklife.

Bill Monroe and Doc Watson: Live Duet Recordings 1963–1980, Smithsonian/Folkways SF 40064. The companion CD to the live band collection showcases this formidable duo.

Kenny Baker Plays Bill Monroe, County CO-2708-CD. The master fiddler's 1976 tribute to his boss and collaborator, with Bill guesting on mandolin.

Bill Monroe & The [sic] Blue Grass Boys Live at the Opry, MCA MCAD 42286. Favorites by the band's latter-day lineup (featuring vocalist Tom Ewing), recorded in 1989 to honor Bill's fiftieth anniversary on the program. Opens with a rare 1948 radio transcription of "Mule Skinner Blues."

Bill Monroe Live from Mountain Stage, Blue Plate Music BPM-400. This May 1989 Public Radio International program captures a mix of old and new material.

Cryin' Holy Unto the Lord, MCA-10017–CD. Full band gospel music from 1990. Monroe's last work for MCA.

The Music of Bill Monroe from 1936 to 1994, MCA MCAD4 11048. This four-CD set with book by John W. Rumble is an excellent overview starting with the Monroe Brothers, continuing through the Blue Grass Boys' RCA, Columbia, and Decca/MCA periods, and ending with a track from the Gabany-produced sessions. The best overall Monroe sampler for the serious new listener.

Billy and Terry Smith, *Bill Monroe Tribute,* K-Tel 3642-2. His final studio recordings with other Monroe material performed by two of his musical stepsons.

Videos

High Lonesome — The Story of Bluegrass Music, Shanache 604. Combining archival and contemporary footage of Monroe and other performers, Rachel Leibling's award-winning 1991 documentary beautifully conveys a feeling for the people and places that gave birth to the music.

Bill Monroe — The Father of Bluegrass Music, Original Cinema OC-10013. An expanded version of the appreciative 1993 profile first broadcast on the Nashville Network.

The Mandolin of Bill Monroe, Homespun VD-MON-MN01 and VD-MON-MN02. Bill Monroe discusses his stylings on the first video; Sam Bush teaches them on the second.

☆ ACKNOWLEDGMENTS ☆

In this tomorrow world of the internet, e-mail, faxes, and beepers, it was delightful to find that the old ways survive.

Retired farmer Harry D. Tinsley is an expert on the history of Ohio County, Kentucky, home of the bluegrass music Monroes. But Mr. Tinsley does not have a telephone. So you write him by U.S. mail, suggesting a day and time to meet at the courthouse in Hartford (which Mr. Tinsley frequents, researching old documents for a newspaper column), wait a week or two, then call the county clerk's office where Harry has left you a message. This old-time system worked perfectly, and we spent many enjoyable hours searching primary records for the story of the Monroes.

Wendell Allen and his parents, Stanley and Loretta, of Rosine, Kentucky, kept farmers' ways because Wendell (another authority on Ohio County history) needed to arise early and commute to work in Owensboro. So that meant hearty country breakfasts of eggs, ham, grits, biscuits and gravy, orange juice, and coffee served at 4:30 A.M. The Allens provided a home away from home during my visits to Rosine and were marvelous sources of information about the Monroes and town history. (It saddens me deeply that both Wendell and his father passed away before the publication of this book.)

Many others helped reassure me that old-fashioned graciousness still lives. Please read about these wonderful people:

Historians: First and foremost, my warm thanks to Eddie Stubbs, fiddler, WSM radio show host, Grand Ole Opry announcer, and country music expert extraordinaire. He offered valuable insights and great encouragement throughout the project, and vetted the developing manuscript. Time and again, Eddie's personal recommendation facilitated access to major Opry stars. I can't begin to express my gratitude.

I also owe great debts to the authors whose earlier writings on bluegrass and Bill Monroe formed a foundation for my own work, notably Neil Rosenberg, Charles Wolfe, Jim Rooney, Bob Artis, Douglas B. Green, Lance LeRoy, John Rumble, Ivan Tribe, Robert Cantwell, and Mark Humphrey. Neil was additionally generous in sharing unpublished discographical information.

Among other writers, many thanks to Tom Ewing for providing little-known material on the Monroe Brothers; Wayne Erbsen for his invaluable articles on Cleo Davis and the first Blue Grass Boys; Sara Jane McNulty for researching Uncle Pen; Keith Lawrence on Arnold Shultz; Tommy Goldsmith on Bill's later career; and MaryE Yeomans and Doug Hutchens for their accounts of Bill Monroe's funeral services. Peter Wernick, Oren Friesen, Murphy Henry, Doug Hutchens, Jon Weisberger, and Art Menius provided recorded interviews, other useful material, or contacts, and Fred Bartenstein gave wise counsel at the outset.

In addition to Wendell Allen and Harry D. Tinsley, Rosetta Monroe Kiper, Eleanor and Hoyt Bratcher, Francis Johnson Harvey, the late Bertha Monroe Kurth, Goldie Johnson Ruby, Reba Murphy Renfrow, Mary Fanny Rogers, and Hayward Spinks provided me with firsthand information about the Monroes, as did Wilbur Davidson, who personally knew Bill and Charlie Monroe during their Sinclair refinery days.

Of course, special mention must be made of the late Ralph Rinzler, the first writer to thoroughly document Bill's roots and the greatest champion of his music. In addition to Ralph's published articles and liner notes, I benefited from a wealth of unpublished Monroe-related material found among his papers at the Center for Folklife Programs and Cultural Studies Archive, Smithsonian Institution. I have long admired Rinzler's work, and I hope he would have approved of my efforts. Grateful acknowledgment is made of the input of Mike Seeger, Alice Foster Gerrard, Hazel Dickens, and Neil Rosenberg, who were there when Rinzler sparked Bill's renaissance, and of the frankness of Roger Abrahams in discussing the final challenges that faced his good friend Ralph.

The Women: Bill Monroe revealed himself most genuinely to the women in his life. Yet the perceptive and articulate ladies who were so close to him have been a woefully ignored source of information on the man and the artist. I am profoundly grateful that Julia LaBella, Hazel Boone Smith, Virginia Stauffer, and Della Streeter agreed to speak with me for this project.

My thanks to friends of the late Carolyn Brown Monroe for their memories of Bill's devoted first wife, and to the relatives and friends of Bessie Lee Mauldin for bringing this vital but unjustly neglected personality to life for me. Let me make special mention of the absolutely invaluable assistance of Bill Price and Charles Harris, who knew Bessie and shared my commitment to finally establishing her deserved place in bluegrass history.

There were many other women who cared about and understood Bill even if they had no romantic involvement with him. My warm thanks to Kathy Chiavola, Hazel Dickens, Gladys Flatt, Alice Foster Gerrard, Emmylou Harris, Kim Koskela, Rosetta Monroe Kiper, Peggy Logan, Betty McInturff, and Melinda Williams. Unfortunately, Wilene "Sally Ann" Forrester was too ill to be interviewed and died while the book was in preparation, but her son Robert kindly retold her stories.

General Research: Voluminous thanks to Jeff Place and Stephanie Smith of the Center for Folklife Programs and Cultural Studies Archives, Smithsonian Institution, for making the seemingly endless process of excavating Ralph Rinzler material productive and even cheerful; Ronnie Pugh, John Rumble, Kent Henderson, and Laura Garrard at the Country Music Foundation for many kindnesses; Les Johnson, clerk of Ohio County, Kentucky, and his gracious staff; the knowledgeable Jerry Long of The Kentucky Room, Owensboro Public Library; Julia D. Rather and Ann Teasley Bomar of the Tennessee State Library and Archives for making a Yankee feel at home; Lori Ferris for locating a pivotal document in the records of Franklin County, Kentucky; Greg Cumming of the Reagan Presidential Library for a crucial date; Mike Dunn for providing fascinating Monroe historical material; Pete Kuykendall and the mellow staff of *Bluegrass Unlimited* magazine for letting me root through their files; and Nancy Cardwell of the International Bluegrass Music Association for providing innumerable connections.

Thanks also to the patient personnel of the United States Archives in Philadelphia; Tennessee State Department of Vital Records, Nashville; court and clerk's offices of Davidson and Sumner counties, Tennessee; North Carolina Department of Vital Records; Spartansburg, South Carolina, probate court; Princeton University Library; and the Mary Jacobs Memorial Library, Rocky Hill, New Jersey.

Fred W. Schott, Chief Chaplain of the Tennessee Highway Patrol, former T.H.P. officers A. M. Lashlee and T. G. Fite, Archie Hamm and Doug Woodlee of the Tennessee Bureau of Investigation, and William R. Gann and Gary R. Toms of the Gann Historical Society were all extremely cooperative during my investigation of the story of the late Nelson C. Gann.

Robert A. Schumer, M.D., Ph.D., assistant professor at Mt. Sinai School of Medicine in New York and a bluegrass fan, explained in detail the physiological and psychological implications of Bill's eye problems. George Gruhn, Tom Isenhour, and Tony Williamson were expert sources of information on bluegrass instruments. And thanks to Dale Monks for Mark Twain on the banjo.

Musicians and Peers: One estimate sets the number of bona fide Blue Grass Boys at 175, another at 302. Many are still living. It was just not feasible to interview them all, yet I will doubtless be criticized for omissions. ("You mean you didn't talk to . . . ?!") But I have tried to interview a cross section of important sidemen spanning major periods of Bill's career while also including a mix of guitarists, fiddlers, banjo pickers, and bass players.

My sincerest thanks to Jimmy Martin, the "King of Bluegrass" and the master singer-guitarist who helped Monroe fully define the "high, lonesome sound." Jimmy was consistently gentlemanly and candid during interviews. I wish to state that any information he has provided about Bill's private life was not volunteered but came in honest response to my direct questions. We have shared a wish to illuminate the true life of a man for whom we have the deepest respect.

Also gratefully acknowledged is the participation of these other Blue Grass Boys: Steve Arkin, Vassar Clements, Jack Cooke, Glen Duncan, Tony Ellis, Tom Ewing, Doug Green, Richard Greene, Bobby Hicks, Doug Hutchens, Bill Keith, Wayne Lewis, Tex Logan, Gene Lowinger, Del McCoury, Curtis McPeake, Alan O'Bryant, Bill Price, Butch Robins, Peter Rowan, Jimmy Shumate, Charlie Smith, Ernie Sykes, Tater Tate, Roland White, and Mac Wiseman. Thanks to Robert Forrester for memories of his parents "Howdy" and "Sally Ann" Forrester; to Dale and Ronnie Reno for conversing about their father Don; to Doug Hutchens and Sonny Curtis for information on Edd Mayfield; and, again, to the family and friends of Bessie Lee Mauldin. Special gratitude to three true American originals who knew Bill well and thought the world of him: Ralph Stanley and John Hartford, who were Blue Grass Boys for brief performances long ago, and Doc Watson, Bill's duet partner on memorable occasions.

Other musicians provided valued input: The Dillards (Rodney Dillard, Doug Dillard, Dean Webb, and Mitch Jayne), Gloria Belle Flickinger, Doug Kershaw, Kevin Lynch, Tommy Scott, Curly Seckler, Billy Smith, Roger Sprung, and Doc Williams. Thank you, Herb Pedersen, Todd Phillips, and Tony Trischka, for volunteering help and insights. My own impressions as a mandolinist of the evolution of Bill's style were supplemented by those of my betters on the instrument: Butch Baldassari, Sam Bush, Mike Compton, David Grisman, Lou Martin, and Barry Mitterhoff.

Many other colleagues of Monroe's were truly gracious, including Grand Ole Opry stars Bill Anderson, Skeeter Davis, Little Jimmy Dickens, Emmylou Harris, Charlie Louvin, Jeanne Pruitt, Ricky Skaggs, Marty Stuart, Charlie Walker, and Buck White. Among Bill's producers, I am so thankful to have interviewed Owen Bradley (and regret that this fine gentleman did not live to see my book completed), Walter Haynes (during an earlier magazine profile on Monroe), and the genial Vic Gabany. Tony Conway and Carlton Haney, who worked with Bill as booking agents during crucial stages of his career, were tremendously helpful. Lance LeRoy and Billy Henson, veterans of the Nashville country/bluegrass scene, offered valued insights and opened important doors for me, as did New York–based promoter Doug Tuchman.

Several key members of Bill Monroe's bands, including Kenny Baker, James Monroe, Sonny Osborne, and Earl Scruggs, did not respond to invitations to be interviewed. Their input was missed. James Monroe, Bill's son and heir, is preparing his own book on his daddy. It should be an extremely interesting addition to the growing body of work on this major American music figure when published.

Photographs: My thanks to all those credited with providing photographs, in particular to Mark Medley of the Country Music Foundation and to Pete Kuykendall and Linda Shaw of *Bluegrass Unlimited* magazine for assistance above and beyond.

On the Road: I am hugely indebted to my old friend Dan Calhoun and the good ol' boys at Calhoun's Garage, Skillman, New Jersey, for keeping my pickup truck rolling for more than two years and thousands of miles on this project without a breakdown. In addition to the aforementioned Allen family for putting me up in Rosine, thanks to Chris Stokes (and his property manager Micky Dobo) for providing use of "The Blue-grass Bunker," Chris's legendary basement apartment in Nashville, the absolutely per-fect base of operations during repeated trips to that city; and to Mr. and Mrs. Bill Price and Mr. and Mrs. Tom Isenhour for hospitality (and great music) during my visit to North Carolina.

A snappy salute to "Ranger Doug" Green for taking "Trooper Smith" to the Brent-wood YMCA weight training room as his guest and for being my partner during plain-clothes work on Murfreesboro Road. And much affection to Nancy for introducing my navigator to Pocohontas; to Lorayne for the travel tape; to Foli for reading the menu at the Log Cabin Restaurant with me; to Pam for outrunning the purple-sinister storm front; and to Linda for ensuring so perfectly that I would transcribe those final interview tapes.

I'm sincerely grateful to my main editor, Chip Rossetti, copy editor Mike Mattil, cover designer Amy Goldfarb, Heather Kilpatrick, esq., and Little, Brown and Co. vice president Michael Pietsch. I have been privileged to work with these true profession-als. My agent Chris Calhoun believed in me and this project every step of the way. And my mom, Mae W. Smith, and many other friends were always there with encour-agement.

Last but not least, my humblest thanks to Bill Monroe himself.

During his lifetime, I talked with him about the mandolin and also interviewed him for a *Bluegrass Unlimited* cover story. He always took me seriously and answered my questions courteously. I now know that he didn't treat everyone that way, espe-cially journalists, and that means the world to me.

And as I researched this book, it was the name of Bill Monroe more than anything else that opened doors. People loved and respected him, and they miss him, and they wanted to help tell his story.

Thank you, sir. It was powerful.

✴ INDEX ✴